Poe's *Pym*: Critical Explorations

Poe's *Pym*:

Critical Explorations

Edited by Richard Kopley

Duke University Press

Durham and London   1992

Library of Congress Cataloging-in-Publication Data

Poe's Pym : critical explorations / edited by Richard Kopley.
p. cm.
"Previously published material included in this volume"—T.p.
verso.
Includes bibliographical references and index.
ISBN 0-8223-1235-2 (cloth)—ISBN 0-8223-1246-8 (paper)
1. Poe, Edgar Allan, 1809–1849. Narrative of Arthur Gordon Pym.
I. Kopley, Richard.
PS2618.N33P64 1992
813'.3—dc20   92-2775
                                                          CIP

Previously published material included in this volume: *John Barth*:
"Still Farther South": Some Notes on Poe's *Pym*. Copyright © 1988
by John Barth. All rights reserved. This chapter previously appeared
in *Antaeus* (Autumn 1989), 7–18.
David H. Hirsch: "Postmodern" or Post-Auschwitz: The Case of Poe.
This chapter previously appeared in *The Deconstruction of Literature:
Criticism after Auschwitz* (Hanover, N.H.: University Press of New
England, 1991).
John T. Irwin: The Quincuncial Network in Poe's *Pym*. This chapter
previously appeared in *Arizona Quarterly*, vol. 44, no. 3 (1988),
1–14. Copyright © 1988 by Arizona Board of Regents.
G. R. Thompson: The Arabesque Design of *Arthur Gordon Pym*. This
chapter is a shortened version of *Romantic Arabesque, Contemporary
Theory, and Postmodernism,* which appeared in *ESQ: A Journal of the
American Renaissance*, vol. 35, nos. 3 and 4 (1989). By permission of
the editors of *ESQ* and of Washington State University Press.

Illustration on the title page and jacket from *Les aventures de
Gordon Pym,* illustrated by Lamotté (Paris: Librairie Arthème
Fayard, 1948), p. 117.

To the memory of Philip Young

Contents

Figuration

A Writer's View

A Bibliographer's View

Acknowledgments

I enjoyed considerable help in organizing the conference "*Arthur Gordon Pym* and Contemporary Criticism." I wish to thank the conference committee, composed of Poe scholars Richard P. Benton, Benjamin Franklin Fisher IV, James Gargano, and Kent P. Ljungquist; my Nantucket liaisons, Susan F. Beegel and Wesley N. Tiffney; and Penn State conference coordinator F. Wally Lester. The great—and gracious—assistance these people offered made my job much easier. I wish to thank, too, Nantucket historian Edouard Stackpole, who provided welcome encouragement early on.

I am grateful to Pennsylvania State University, DuBois Campus and Penn State, University Park, for sponsoring the conference. Vital funding was furnished by Michael H. Chaplin, former Associate Dean for Academic Affairs, Commonwealth Education System (CES); John W. Furlow, Jr., Director of Academic Affairs, Penn State, DuBois Campus; Theodore E. Kiffer, former Acting Dean, College of the Liberal Arts; Joseph W. Michels, former Associate Dean of Research and Graduate Studies; and Jacqueline L. Schoch, former Chief Executive Officer, Penn State, DuBois Campus. I am very appreciative of the substantial support provided by the Pacific National Bank of Nantucket and the additional generous support offered by the many Friends of the conference: the American Antiquarian Society, Concordia University, the DuBois Educational Foundation, Dr. and Mrs. Bruce V. English, Mr. and Mrs. Yuda Golahny, Mr. Jacob Goodwin, the Gordian Press, Inc., the Harbor House, Mrs. Irene Kopley, Mitchell's Book Corner, the Nantucket Field Station, the Nantucket Historical Association, the Nantucket Historical Trust, the 19th Century Shop, the Poe Foundation, the Edgar Allan Poe Society of Baltimore, *Poe Studies*, the Poe Studies Association, Drs. Fred and Suzanne Stutman, Dr. Steven Tuck, Viking Penguin, Inc., Worcester Polytechnic Institute, and Professor Philip Young. Without the aid of these institutions and individuals, there could have been no *Pym* Conference.

For their support and encouragement regarding the publication of this book, I am grateful to Margaret M. Cote, Associate Dean, College of the Liberal Arts, CES; John W. Furlow, Jr.; Donald T. Hartman, Chief Executive Officer, Penn State, DuBois Campus; Charles L. Hosler, former Senior Vice President for Research and Dean of the Graduate School; and David S. Palermo, Associate Dean of Research and Graduate Studies.

For his fine guidance regarding publication, I am grateful to Reynolds Smith, Senior Editor at Duke University Press. And, finally, for her abiding support, I am thankful to my wife Amy Golahny, Rembrandt scholar and honorary Poe person.

Conference Attendees

The following is an alphabetical list of those who attended the *Pym* Conference: John Barth (The Johns Hopkins University), Shelly Barth (St. Timothy's School), Susan F. Beegel (University of West Florida), Richard P. Benton (Trinity College), Mary K. Bercaw (Mystic Seaport Museum), Maureen Bollier (Williamsville, New York), Darla J. Bressler (Clarion University), Marie A. Campbell (Mount Saint Mary's College), Christopher B. Casey (Penn State, University Park), Curtis Dahl (Wheaton College), Elizabeth Dameron (Memphis, Tennessee), J. Lasley Dameron (Memphis State University), Robert M. Davis (Apro-Poe Productions), Joan Dayan (Queens College and CUNY Graduate Center), Susan R. Delaney (Penn State, DuBois), Richard G. Doenges (University of Bridgeport), William B. Drean (State College, Pennsylvania), Donald Dunlop (Iowa State University), M. H. Dunlop (Iowa State University), Amie M. Evans (State College, Pennsylvania), Grace Farrell (Butler University), Marjorie B. Feasler (Penn State, DuBois), Benjamin Franklin Fisher IV (University of Mississippi), James W. Gargano (Washington and Jefferson College), Mrs. James W. Gargano (Washington, Pennsylvania), Norman George (AproPoe Productions), Amy Golahny (Lycoming College), Louise A. Habicht (Southeastern Massachusetts University), Alexander Hammond (Washington State University), David H. Hirsch (Brown University), Melissa Hobbs (Penn State, DuBois), Kenneth A. Hovey (University of Texas at San Antonio), Dianne M. Hunter (Trinity College), John T. Irwin (The Johns Hopkins University), Shoko Itoh (Hiroshima University), Bill L. Jernigan (University of Florida), Jennifer S. Johnson (Mystic Seaport Museum), J. Richard Kelley (Port Jefferson, New York), Lorraine M. Kelley (Port Jefferson, New York), J. Gerald Kennedy (Louisiana State University), Sarah Liggett Kennedy (Louisiana State University), David A. Ketterer (Concordia University), Marion F. Koch (Brockway, Pennsylvania), Irene J. Kopley (New York, New York), Richard Kopley (Penn State, DuBois), William E. Lenz (Chatham College), F. Wally Lester (State College, Pennsylvania), Alexander S. Liddie (Trenton

State College), Patricia Liddie (Trenton State College), Kent P. Ljungquist (Worcester Polytechnic Institute), R. D. Madison (United States Naval Academy), Jane Mallison (Trinity School), Barbara J. Marshall (West Decatur, Pennsylvania), Joan Tyler Mead (Marshall University), Joseph J. Moldenhauer (University of Texas at Austin), David R. Noble (Ohio University, Belmont), Glen A. Omans (Temple University), Judy Osowski (Saint Cloud State University), Carol Peirce (University of Baltimore), Frank Pisano (West Virginia State College), Tracey L. Pollick (Bridgeville, Pennsylvania), Burton R. Pollin (CUNY), Alexander G. Rose III (University of Baltimore), John Carlos Rowe (University of California, Irvine), Colleen A. Shannon (Penn State, University Park), Georgia H. Shurr (University of Tennessee), William H. Shurr (University of Tennessee), Kenneth Silverman (New York University), Susan Smink (Cockeysville, Maryland), Edouard Stackpole (The Peter Foulger Museum), Werner H. Steger (University of Florida), Donald Tanasoca (North Haledon, New Jersey), Dwight Thomas (Savannah, Georgia), G. R. Thompson (Purdue University), Wesley N. Tiffney (Nantucket Field Station), Ichigoro Uchida (Kyoritsu College), Bruce I. Weiner (St. Lawrence University), Susan Welsh (Rutgers University), Elizabeth Wiley (Susquehanna University), Brien P. Williams (Brien P. Williams Company), Karen E. Wilson (Brockway, Pennsylvania), Paul A. Wilson (Brockway, Pennsylvania), Bill Wrenn (Wrenn Photocommunications), Donald Yannella (Barat College).

Note Regarding Frequently Cited Works

Throughout this book, the frequently cited scholarly editions of Poe's writings will be abbreviated as follows:

H   *The Complete Works of Edgar Allan Poe*, ed. James A. Harrison, 17 vols. (New York: Thomas Y. Crowell, 1902; rpt., New York: AMS Press, 1965, 1979).

M   *Collected Works of Edgar Allan Poe*, ed. Thomas Ollive Mabbott, 3 vols. (Cambridge, Mass.: Harvard University Press, 1969–1978).

P   *Collected Writings of Edgar Allan Poe*, ed. Burton R. Pollin, 4 vols. to date (Boston: Twayne Publishers, 1981; New York: Gordian Press, 1985–).

O   *The Letters of Edgar Allan Poe*, rev. ed., ed. John Ward Ostrom, 2 vols. (New York: Gordian Press, 1966).

Introduction

 In his "Exordium" of January 1842, Edgar Allan Poe observed, "The analysis of a book is a matter of time and of mental exertion. For many classes of composition there is required a deliberate perusal, with notes, and subsequent generalization" (H 11:3). While in 1957 Edward H. Davidson stated that Poe's *Narrative of Arthur Gordon Pym* (1838) had been "generally ignored or scanted by Poe scholars and critics,"[1] in the following years, much "time" and "mental exertion" were devoted to this work, and, in 1981, Frederick S. Frank acknowledged *Pym*'s having prompted frequent "deliberate perusal," terming the narrative "the most written-about of Poe's tales."[2] Frank identified nearly one hundred studies of Poe's longest fiction; so, too, did Douglas Robinson in 1982.[3] The increasing scholarly consideration of *Pym* and the approaching sesquicentennial of the book's first publication led, in the fall of 1983, to planning for the conference "*Arthur Gordon Pym* and Contemporary Criticism," the meeting from which this volume's papers are drawn.

The conference was held on 19–22 May 1988 on Nantucket Island, the setting of *Pym*'s earliest chapters. *Pym*'s final chapters were called to mind more dramatically by a preconference fire in an upper floor of the conference hotel and thick fog surrounding the island; fortunately, no one was hurt in the fire or deterred by the fog. And, happily, the link to the conclusion of *Pym* held up in a positive way as the conference did offer revelations.

Eighty-four scholars, students, and aficionados of Poe from the United States, Canada, and Japan attended the *Pym* Conference. The program featured six academic sessions complemented by the evening addresses of Guest of Honor John Barth and Keynote Speaker G. R. Thompson. Additionally, the Peter Foulger Museum provided a *Pym* exhibit, Mitchell's Book Corner furnished Poe and Barth displays, moviemaker Brien Williams and company showed a *Pym* film, and actor Norman George performed as Poe giving his final lecture. The four days on Nantucket were memorable for both cerebration and celebration, good scholarship and good fellowship. There was, in fact, a frequently stated wish for a follow-up, and, in lieu of a 1990 conference in honor of the sesquicentennial of "The Journal of Julius Rodman" (suggested by one participant), this book is offered.

Perhaps it would be fitting here to review briefly the plot of *Pym*. Young Arthur Gordon Pym of Nantucket suffers the destruction of his sailboat the *Ariel* and life-threatening injury because of the collision of his vessel with the ship the *Penguin*; nonetheless, possessed of romantic ideas about life at sea, he stows away on the ship the *Grampus*, bound for the South Seas, and experiences confinement, shipwreck, starvation, cannibalism, and the death of his closest friend. Rescued by the *Jane Guy*, he voyages to an island of deceitful murderous natives, survives their deadly landslide, witnesses their destruction of his ship and nearly all his shipmates, and, with his remaining comrade and a captured native, escapes in a canoe farther south, where he encounters a cataract, a chasm, and a mysterious enormous white "shrouded human figure" (*P* 1:206). Pym eventually returns to the United States, writes his narrative (with the assistance of one "Mr. Poe"), and dies shortly thereafter.

The dissensus regarding this fiction has been decided. While scholars generally agree that *Pym* is an important work, they have nonetheless cited diverse—sometimes divergent—bases for this view: the narrative's mythic resonance, its rich symbolism, its hidden irony, its sardonic humor, its generic hybridity, its aesthetic complexity, its seemingly contemporary ambiguity and self-reflexivity, and its critical place in Poe's oeuvre and in literary history. *Pym*'s Antarctic apparition—described as "a powerful vision," which is said to conclude "the finest passage in all his [Poe's] works"[4]—has elicited a particularly broad range of explication: it is death, a figure triumphing over death, knowledge, the limits of knowledge, goodness, perversity, the imagination, the narrative itself, the white at the bottom of the page, a Titan, a divinity, Christ, and Pym's unrecognized white shadow—a self-projection.[5] While we clearly cannot resolve here the nature of *Pym*'s strengths or the significance of its climactic image, we can resolve to engage fully the extraordinary critical pluralism evident concerning *Pym*, exemplified not only by the history of *Pym* criticism but also by both the *Pym* Conference and this volume.

In this volume's first section, "Literary Origins," Susan F. Beegel, Joan Tyler Mead, and J. Lasley Dameron propose that three of Herman

Melville's sources for the *Pym*-influenced *Moby-Dick*—Lay and Hussey's *Narrative*, Falconer's *Dictionary*, and Scoresby's *Journal*—served as sources for *Pym* as well. Bruce I. Weiner, Carol Peirce and Alexander G. Rose III, and Joseph J. Moldenhauer consider the influence of *Blackwood's Magazine*, Arthurian legends, and Carl Christian Rafn's *Antiquitates Americanae* on Poe's narrative. And, closing the section, Burton R. Pollin offers a chronological overview of Poe's myriad borrowings for *Pym*. In "Sociohistorical Contexts," Grace Farrell clarifies *Pym*'s relationship to Poe's mourning for his mother, and John Carlos Rowe elaborates the novel's relationship to American slavery. And in the following section, "Prefigurings," David H. Hirsch examines *Pym*'s anticipation of the dehumanization of man in the Holocaust.

"Figuration" then offers theoretical analyses of Poe's *Pym*, often indicating the self-reflexive quality of the narrative. Alexander Hammond discusses the figure of food as literary product, and J. Gerald Kennedy treats the figure of decomposition as suggestive of the limits of language. John T. Irwin reads the figure of the quincunx as an intimation of the structure of man's mind; G. R. Thompson regards this figure as representative of the Schlegelian *Roman*, characterized by the framed indeterminacy of the arabesque. In the penultimate section, "A Writer's View," John Barth evaluates *Pym*'s claim to verisimilitude, its debt to the wandering hero myth, and its identity as a novel. And in the volume's final section, "A Bibliographer's View," David Ketterer assesses *Pym* scholarship from 1980 through 1990 and casts an eye toward future developments.

The lively mix of methodologies in this collection and the variety evident within different approaches tend to suggest that *Pym* is still today what Douglas Robinson termed it ten years ago, "the interpreter's dream-text."[6] Assuredly, no book viewed as such for long could fail to generate eventually not only scholarly articles but scholarly books as well. Indeed, this collection, the first volume of criticism devoted to *Pym*, will soon be followed by J. Gerald Kennedy's volume in the Twayne Masterworks series, *"The Narrative of Arthur Gordon Pym": The Abyss of Interpretation*. And a suitable college text, an edition of *Pym* in the Norton Critical series, is being discussed. It is clear that, as Kennedy commented recently, "*Pym* has come into its own."

In Poe's story "The Landscape Garden" (and later in "The Domain of Arnheim"), artist-hero Mr. Ellison identifies as one of the four "elementary principles of Bliss" "an object of unceasing pursuit" (M 2:703–

4; see also 3:1268–69). *The Narrative of Arthur Gordon Pym* may be such an object. That the object never be fully attained is, of course, all-important, for, as Poe indicated through the heavenly spirit Agathos in the dialogue "The Power of Words," "to quench it [the thirst *to know*], would be to extinguish the soul's self" (M 3:1212). Yet that thirst may be allayed—gratifyingly so—as the following essays ably reveal.

Richard Kopley
State College, Pennsylvania
16 January 1992

Literary Origins

"Mutiny and Atrocious Butchery":

The *Globe* Mutiny as a Source for *Pym*

Susan F. Beegel

 "Mutiny and atrocious butchery," promises the title page of *The Narrative of Arthur Gordon Pym*, cataloguing the delectable horrors within, and the novel delivers an up-rising so gory that, like many another episode in Edgar Allan Poe's works, it easily seems the nightmarish fantasy of a diseased mind.[1] Perhaps that is why scholars have so long overlooked the many similarities between the fictional mutiny on Poe's Nantucket whaleship *Grampus* and a historic event that Alexander Starbuck has called "the most horrible mutiny that is recounted in the annals of the whale-fishery from any port or nation"—the mutiny on board the Nantucket whaleship *Globe*.[2] Yet if we explore the actual events of the *Globe* mutiny, Poe's probable knowledge of those events, and his indebtedness to them, we find that *Pym*'s "mutiny and atrocious butchery" owe more to reportorial accuracy than to a sanguinary imagination run amok, and we are reminded once again that until we know all of the sources for a given work of fiction, we cannot begin to appreciate the nature of its author's powers of invention.

Mutiny on the Whaleship *Globe*

A brief recounting of the facts of the *Globe* mutiny helps us to understand both the event's notoriety in nineteenth-century America and the ways in which Poe may have interacted with its history. On 15 December 1822, the Nantucket whaleship *Globe* set sail for the Pacific Ocean from Edgartown, on Martha's Vineyard.[3] Over one year later, as the vessel was cruising off Hawaii in January 1824, a psychotic boatsteerer named Samuel Comstock led four new hands, taken from Oahu's beaches, in the bloodiest and most famous mutiny ever to afflict Nantucket's whaling fleet.[4] Just before the midnight watch, Comstock led his conspirators into the *Globe*'s cabin and murdered Captain Thomas Worth, asleep in his hammock, with an axe blow that nearly split his head in two. At the same time, another conspirator, Silas Payne, entered first mate William Beetle's stateroom and hacked him to death with a boarding knife.

The second and third mates took alarm and barricaded themselves in another stateroom. Comstock wounded one of these men by firing a musket through the stateroom door and then had his fellow mutineers smash their way in. After a brief struggle, Comstock persuaded the wounded mate to give up the musket he had snatched and then treacherously shot him in the head. The other mate Comstock repeatedly bayoneted through the body. A fifth officer, Gilbert Smith, survived the mayhem by escaping to the forecastle, where he was sheltered by frightened crew members.

After the mutilated bodies of the dead and dying officers had been thrown overboard, Comstock began to suspect one of his men, a black steward named William Humphries, of conspiring against him. Humphries had been seen loading a pistol in the galley. Although he insisted that he wanted the pistol for defense against a countermutiny being plotted by Gilbert Smith, Humphries was found guilty of mutiny by Comstock and a "court" of his coconspirators. With unconscious irony, the mutineers hanged Humphries from the yardarm for his crime.

For the next several days, the *Globe* sailed nearly due west. According to historian Edouard Stackpole: "Comstock planned to reach some island, away from the usual cruisings of other whaleships, land and establish himself as the virtual king. He would then burn the ship, destroying the evidence of her identity and the mutiny. In his calculated, cruel plans, he no doubt had considered ways of killing most of the faithful men."[5] In a chain of small islands known to the natives as Mili and to English navigators as the Mulgraves, Comstock believed he had found a safe harbor for the fulfillment of his plans. Here he ordered the *Globe* anchored and the ship's supplies unloaded by intimidated crew members.

Comstock's reign as king of Mili was short-lived. The mutineers incensed the native population by using the men as pack animals and the women as concubines. Frightened by the growing numbers of angry natives around the whalemen's camp and believing that Comstock was conspiring with the islanders to kill the crew, mutineer Silas Payne shot Comstock in the back and beheaded him with an axe. Next, Gilbert Smith and five crew members who had been sent on board for supplies escaped Mili with the *Globe*, setting sail for Valparaiso on a dark night. Tragically, their flight marooned six loyal crew members on Mili with the three surviving mutineers, and the ship's departure triggered the native massacre Payne had feared. The population of Mili attacked the whalemen with spears and rocks, surrounding them and "mascerating [sic] their heads with large stones."[6]

Only two members of the *Globe*'s crew stranded on Mili were spared: William Lay of Saybrook, Connecticut, and Cyrus Hussey of Nantucket, both aged eighteen. Yet despite Gilbert Smith's prompt reporting of the *Globe* mutiny on his 7 June 1824 arrival in Valparaiso, Lay and Hussey were fated to remain on Mili for another seventeen months as slaves of the natives who had spared them. Sparse U.S. naval presence in the Pacific prevented the dispatch of a rescue mission until late in 1825, when an appeal by Nantucket merchants to the Secretary of the Navy prompted the sending of the schooner *Dolphin* to Mili to search for survivors and bring the mutineers to justice. In November 1825, a shore party commanded by Lieutenant Hiram Paulding finally located Lay and Hussey and took them from hostile natives. After a prolonged cruise with the *Dolphin*, the young men were returned home on board the frigate *United States*, reaching New York on 21 April 1827, five years after the ill-fated *Globe* had set sail from Edgartown.

Poe's Familiarity with the *Globe* Mutiny

Poe may have become familiar with the *Globe* mutiny because of its general notoriety, as a result of his friendship with maritime explorer Jeremiah N. Reynolds, or through an acquaintance with one or more published versions of the event. The *Globe* mutiny enjoyed wide fame in nineteenth-century America, and the story may have reached Poe as common knowledge. The petition of Nantucket whaleship owners to the Secretary of the Navy brought public recognition that the United States' naval presence in the Pacific was inadequate for the protection of American property and shipping interests. Coupled with the prestige conferred upon the navy by the *Dolphin*'s successful rescue mission, the *Globe* mutiny was directly responsible for an increase in the United States' Pacific fleet.[7] Two years after the rescue, Captain Catesby-Jones of the *Peacock* set a precedent for naval discipline of lawless whalemen when, on the island of Tahiti, he tried and ordered flogged six men accused of mutiny on the whaleship *Fortune*.[8] The *Globe* mutiny was also responsible for changes in whaleship routine. While prior to the incident, boatsteerers had been considered unofficial officers, after

Comstock's treachery, they were never again allowed to command the night watches on American whaleships.[9]

Nor was the *Globe*'s notoriety confined to naval and whaling circles. The fact that Samuel Comstock's skull and cutlass were disinterred and brought to New York for museum display in 1827 provides proof of the popular sensation created by the horrific events on board the *Globe*.[10] Whether or not Poe read either or both of the two *Globe* mutiny books published well before *Pym*'s appearance in 1838—William Lay and Cyrus Hussey's *A Narrative of the Mutiny on Board the Whaleship Globe of Nantucket* (1828) and Lieutenant Hiram Paulding's *Journal of a Cruise of the United States Schooner Dolphin . . . In Pursuit of the Mutineers of the Whaleship Globe* (1831)—their existence alone made the facts of the mutiny widely available to the general public. A third book, William Comstock's *The Life of Samuel Comstock, The Terrible Whaleman* (1840), was published two years after *Pym* and attests to the story's continuing fascination.

Poe may, then, have encountered common knowledge of the *Globe* mutiny in New York, Philadelphia, or any port city concerned with things maritime, but he is most likely to have done so in Boston, where he spent the spring of 1827 clerking in a waterfront warehouse and working as a market reporter for an obscure newspaper.[11] In April 1827, while Poe was thus ideally situated to hear gossip about the *Globe*, survivors William Lay and Cyrus Hussey were returned to New York aboard the frigate *United States*. At least four Boston newspapers carried news of the ship's arrival from the Pacific, and although none of them mentions the *Globe* mutiny directly, all report that Lieutenant Hiram Paulding of the *Dolphin* was among the returning officers on board the *United States*.[12] The *Dolphin*'s role in rescuing the *Globe*'s last two survivors was well-known in Boston—having been reported by the city's newspapers a few months earlier—and word of Paulding's return should have aroused the interest of the town where, three years earlier, Joseph Thomas, a member of the crew who had escaped with Gilbert Smith, had stood trial for mutiny in federal court.[13]

But Poe's friend Jeremiah N. Reynolds forms the strongest link between the *Globe* mutiny and *Pym*. In June of 1828, Reynolds was appointed a special envoy by the Department of the Navy and authorized to collect data about the South Seas from ship captains and owners. During the course of his investigations, Reynolds visited Nantucket. It's no exaggeration to say that every sentient adult on this small, isolated island of interrelated seafarers would have known the story of the Nantucket whaleship *Globe*, and Reynolds talked to "every individual navigator of those seas who could be found at home, with their log-books, and journals, and charts."[14] These individuals could easily have included relatives of the chief mutineer, Samuel Comstock, who was Nantucket born and bred, and relatives of the island's three victims and two survivors of the mutiny.[15] Reynolds is known to have met captains named Joy, Worth, Coffin, and Macy on his Nantucket visit.[16] Given the intermarriage common on and between Nantucket and Martha's Vineyard at this time, more likely than not these captains were relatives of the Joy who captained the *Lyra*, sailing in company with the *Globe* on the night of the mutiny; of the Worths and the Coffin who sailed to their deaths on board the *Globe*; and of the Coffin and Macy who became her subsequent owners.[17] In addition, Reynolds formed a valuable friendship with Samuel Haynes Jenks, editor of the Nantucket *Inquirer*, a newspaper which had given the *Globe* mutiny and its results considerable coverage since 1824.[18] According to Edouard Stackpole, a comparison of Jenks' editorials for the years 1821 through 1829 with Reynolds' reports suggests that Jenks gave Reynolds back issues of the newspaper, issues that contained articles about the *Globe* mutiny.[19]

Eighteen twenty-eight, the year that saw Reynolds' visit to Nantucket, also saw publication of William Lay and Cyrus Hussey's narrative of the *Globe* mutiny. The book's detailed description of the little-explored Mulgrave Islands, with its "observations on the manners and customs of the inhabitants" and "vocabulary of words and phrases used by the natives," would certainly have interested Reynolds (pp. 1, 105). If he did not borrow, purchase, or receive a copy of the Lay and Hussey narrative while on Nantucket, Reynolds would have had other opportunities to encounter the book in his 1828 travels to New London, where it was published in an edition of three thousand copies by printer William Bolles, and to Edgartown, where he may have met friends and relations of the Vineyard's eleven *Globe* victims and survivors.[20]

It is also possible that Reynolds was familiar with Lieutenant Hiram Paulding's 1831 *Journal of the U.S. Schooner Dolphin*. When the book was published, Reynolds was in Valparaiso, Chile, the port to which Gilbert Smith had sailed the stricken *Globe* and where the American consul had interrogated the escaped members of her crew.[21] The *Dolphin*'s story would also have been well known in Valparaiso, where the schooner remained for a time in 1828 when her officers, including Paulding, transferred to the homeward-bound *United States*.[22] If Reynolds did not encounter Paulding's book on land, he may have met it on board the U.S. Navy frigate *Potomac* when he sailed from Valparaiso as Commodore Downes' personal secretary in 1832.[23] Through his affiliation with the navy, Reynolds would have learned not only of the *Dolphin*'s dramatic rescue mission but also of the 1828 court-martial of her captain, "Mad Jack" Percival, for the licentious conduct of his men in Honolulu and their assault on disapproving missionaries. The *Dolphin*'s role in rescuing *Globe* mutiny survivors was brought out during the trial as evidence on Percival's behalf, and he was acquitted.[24] In view of the connections noted, as well as the *Journal*'s "particular description of a groupe of Islands never before explored, and forming perhaps, the latest inhabited portion of the globe," Reynolds may have had motive, as well as means and opportunity, for seeking out Paulding's volume.[25]

Poe not only read and used numerous works by Reynolds in constructing *The Narrative of Arthur Gordon Pym* but also seems to have enjoyed at least one meeting with the "Father of American Exploration" before completing his novel.[26] In a review of Reynolds' *Address on the Subject of a Surveying and Exploring Expedition to the Pacific Ocean and the South Seas*, Poe questions whether the explorer's critics have "ever seen him or conversed with him half an hour."[27] Poe's review contains other remarks implying his personal acquaintance with Reynolds, and perhaps not coincidentally this review appears in the same issue of the *Southern Literary Messenger* as the first installment of *Pym*.

It should be added that Thomas Willis White, owner of the *Southern Literary Messenger* while Poe was assistant and then editor (August 1835 to January 1837), knew Reynolds; White probably encouraged Poe's interest in Reynolds' work and may have introduced the two men.[28] Several scholars have speculated that in 1837 and 1838, when both Poe and Reynolds lived in New York, their friendship was extensive, while Burton Pollin postulates that during this period Poe may even have approached Reynolds for a position in his Antarctic expedition (*P* 1:18). Whatever the extent of the Poe-Reynolds friendship, the explorer almost certainly possessed detailed knowledge of the *Globe* mutiny garnered from his reading and travels, and his acquaintance with Poe is a plausible explanation of the similarities between *The Narrative of Arthur Gordon Pym* and the facts of the mutiny on board the whaleship *Globe*.

A final source for Poe's knowledge of the *Globe* mutiny may be one or both of the two books on the subject published before *Pym* was written. To date, no evidence exists to prove beyond a shadow of a doubt that Poe read either the Lay and Hussey narrative or the Paulding journal. However, while neither book was used as one of the "primary sources for verbatim copying or close paraphrase," both seem to have provided "hints or suggestions for details, situations, or episodes" (*P* 1:17). This lack of copying or paraphrase, accompanied by *Pym*'s apparent indebtedness to both the Lay and Hussey narrative and the Paulding journal, suggests that Poe may have written from memory of these texts or from memory of conversation about their contents rather than with the volumes open before him. This point, in turn, suggests that a friend briefly loaned the books to Poe or merely told him about them, and no friend was more likely to have done so than Jeremiah N. Reynolds.

Pym's Indebtedness to *Globe* Mutiny Narratives

The best argument in favor of Poe's knowledge of the *Globe* mutiny narratives, however, resides in a detailed exploration of *Pym*'s indebtedness to them. The novel shares the greatest number of similarities with the account of the *Globe* mutiny Reynolds is most likely to have read—William Lay and Cyrus Hussey's narrative. Poe seems to have borrowed many of his novel's plot elements from this version of the mutiny. Like *The Narrative of Arthur Gordon Pym*, the *Narrative of the Mutiny on Board the Whaleship Globe* may be described as "comprising the details of a mutiny and atrocious butchery" on board a Nantucket whaleship, "the massacre of her crew among a group of islands" in the Pacific, and the deliverance of her two remaining survivors by a schooner (*P* 1:53).

Although Lay and Hussey make it clear that "the ship *Globe* . . . belonged to the Island of Nantucket," they go on to state that "on the fifteenth day of December, we sailed from Edgartown, on a whaling voyage, to the Pacific Ocean" (p. 7). By 1822, when the *Globe* set sail, the shallow entrance to Nantucket harbor had filled with drifting sand, and large whaleships setting out heavy-laden with supplies for a five-year voyage could no longer negotiate the growing harbor bar. It became routine for many Nantucketers to anchor their ships in Edgartown harbor at the nearby island of Martha's Vineyard.[29] So familiar are Lay and Hussey with the necessity for this point of departure that they do not bother to explain that Edgartown is a Vineyard and not a Nantucket port.

Similarly, in recounting his family history, Pym tells us that his "father was a respectable trader in sea stores at Nantucket," while his "maternal grandfather . . . had speculated very successfully in the stocks of Edgarton New-Bank" (P 1:57). As Burton Pollin has remarked, "Poe gives no indication that the town [Edgarton] was not on Nantucket, but on nearby Martha's Vineyard, although he could scarcely be unaware of this fact" (P 1:217). The point may seem a small one, but perhaps Poe deliberately courted some confusion. It would give his narrative verisimilitude to imitate Lay and Hussey's casual treatment of Edgartown as a Nantucket port, and he could simultaneously undermine that verisimilitude with a joke to warn discerning readers that Pym's voyage commences from no harbor but the Edgartown of Poe's imagination.

However, the most striking similarities between *Pym* and the Lay and Hussey narrative are in the accounts of the mutiny itself. The *Globe* mutiny begins, as does the mutiny on board the *Grampus*, with an assault on the captain in his cabin. Comstock enters the *Globe*'s cabin "so silently as not to be perceived by the man at the helm, who was first apprised of his having begun the work of death by the sound of a heavy blow with an axe" (p. 13). Like the *Globe*'s helmsman, Augustus is unaware of any trouble on board the *Grampus* until he hears an "unusual bustle" proceeding from the cabin. There he finds his father unconscious and apparently dying from a head wound (P 1:85). Comstock has given his captain "a blow upon the head" "with an axe" (p. 13); Augustus' father, "lying along the steps of the companionway with his head down, and a deep wound in the forehead, from which the blood was flowing in a continued stream," has received similar treatment (P 1:85).

Pym, of course, is saved from the mutiny by Augustus' sanguinary message—" '*blood—your life depends upon lying close*' "—which warns him to remain secreted in the ship's hold (P 1:80). Gilbert Smith, the sole officer to survive the *Globe* mutiny, is also saved by a sanguinary message, albeit a message overheard rather than a note half-discerned. On hearing the noise in the cabin and going aft to investigate, Smith is astonished to behold "Comstock brandishing a boarding knife" and to hear him exclaim, " 'I am a bloody man! I have a bloody hand and *will* be avenged!' " (pp. 16–17). These sentences, the most dramatic in the Lay and Hussey narrative, could easily have inspired Poe's meditation on " *'blood'* . . . that word of all words—so rife at all times with mystery, and suffering, and terror" (*P* 1:80). Comstock's pronouncement leaves Smith "horror struck" (p. 17), just as Augustus' note fills Pym with "harrowing and yet undefinable horror" (*P* 1:80). Smith escapes forward, where members of the *Globe's* crew urge him to "secrete himself in the hold" (p. 17), advice which may have suggested Pym's unusual predicament as a stowaway trapped by a mutiny (p. 17).

Both the Lay and Hussey narrative and *The Narrative of Arthur Gordon Pym* contain scenes of "the most horrible butchery," as both the *Globe* and the *Grampus* mutineers indulge in the callous murder of men who beg for their lives. William Beetle, first mate of the *Globe*, pleads, " 'Oh! Payne! Oh! Comstock!' 'Don't kill me, don't.' 'Have I not always—' " until Comstock interrupts him with "a blow upon the head" with an axe (pp. 13–14). *Pym's* Englishman, who weeps "piteously" and entreats the mate "in the most humble manner to spare his life," receiving no reply save "a blow on the forehead with an axe," may owe something to the unfortunate Beetle (*P* 1:85–86).

Both mutinies, too, involve the cold-blooded murder of men who have surrendered on the understanding that their lives would be spared. In the Lay and Hussey narrative, a wounded officer named Lumbert surrenders to Comstock on obtaining such a promise, only to be bound, brought on deck, and heaved overboard: "But when, in the act of being thrown from the ship, he caught the plankshear and appealed to Comstock, reminding him of his promise to save him, but in vain; for the monster forced him from his hold and he fell into the sea" (p. 18). Like Comstock, the mate in *Pym* "induce[s] those below to yield" with "fair words" that prove his "diabolical villany [sic]," for upon their surrender, the seamen are "bound," "dragged to the gangway," and "forced over the side of the vessel by the other mutineers" after an axe blow from the cook (*P* 1:86).

The *Globe* mutiny results in two countermutinies: one of these is begun by the black steward, William Humphries, but it fails when he is discovered and hung for conspiring against chief mutineer Samuel Comstock; the second countermutiny is successful, ending in Comstock's murder by fellow conspirator Silas Payne. *Pym* also contains two countermutinies. After taking the *Grampus*, the mutineers have "frequent and violent quarrels" and divide into two parties, one headed by the mate, or chief mutineer, and the other headed by the black cook (*P* 1:102). The cook contemplates a countermutiny against the mate, but when one member of his gang is thrown overboard, a second accidentally drowned, and a third deliberately poisoned, he understandably abandons his plan. Dirk Peters then organizes a second, successful countermutiny against the mate, frightening him to death, and killing many of his followers.

An additional element these countermutinies have in common is the ironic reverence with which the murderers feel compelled to treat the corpses of their victims. In both the Lay and Hussey narrative and *Pym*, men are brutally murdered and their bodies flung overboard without compunction. But when, Macbeth-like, the mutineers of *Globe* and *Grampus* are "in blood / stepped in so far that, should [they] wade no more, / returning were as tedious as go o'er" (Shakespeare's *Macbeth*, 3.4.135–37), guilt begins to prey upon their imaginations. After shooting Comstock twice and beheading him with an axe, Payne then orders his victim, "as cruel, bloodthirsty, and vindictive a being as ever bore the shape of humanity," buried with full honors:

> All hands were now called to attend his burial, which was conducted in the same inconsistent manner which had marked the proceedings of the actors in this tragedy. While some were engaged in sewing the body in a piece of canvas, others were employed in digging a grave . . . which, by order of Payne, was made five feet deep. Every article attached to him, including his cutlass, was buried with him . . . and the ceremonies consisted in *reading a chapter of the bible over him and firing a musket!* (p. 28)

In *Pym*, the mate experiences a similar impulse toward the body of Hartman Rogers, a man he has poisoned:

> The body had been brought up from the cabin at noon to be thrown overboard, when the mate getting a glimpse of it . . . and being either touched with remorse for his crime or struck with terror at so horrible a sight, ordered the men to sew the body up in its hammock, and allow it the usual rites of sea-burial. (P 1:108)

The guilty conscience revealed by the mate at Rogers' burial culminates in *Pym*'s ghost episode, and the ghost episode may be indebted to Lieutenant Hiram Paulding's *Journal of a Cruise of the U.S. Schooner Dolphin*. Paulding recounts what William Lay and Cyrus Hussey told their rescuers about the haunted nights of the mutineers:

> After the death of the officers, Comstock made us all live in the cabin with him, where the mutineers used to sing, and carouse, and tell

over the story of the murder, and what they had dreamed. Payne and Oliver, who could scarcely ever sleep, spoke with horror of their dreams, and of the ghosts that appeared to them at night.[30]

In *Pym*, Peters visits the mutineers in the captain's cabin, where they have been drinking and "carousing," and inspires just such a conversation to set the stage for the appearance of Rogers' ghost:

> Presently he contrived to turn the conversation upon the bloody deeds of the mutiny, and, by degrees, led the men to talk of the thousand superstitions which are so universally current among seamen. (*P* 1:111)

In Paulding's journal, the ghost of the murdered Captain Worth actually comes to Comstock "with his wounded and bloody head, and show[s] him what he had done," just as Pym, attired as Rogers' ghost, appears to the mate with chalked and blood-splotched countenance.[31] But here the similarity between the two works ends, for while Poe's guilty mate drops "stone dead" from fright, the *Globe's* Comstock is unimpressed and simply orders the captain's ghost "to depart and never come again, or he would kill him a second time."[32]

Among the numerous source studies of *Pym*, only two trace the possible derivations of the novel's mutiny. D. M. McKeithan cites one mutiny from Archibald Duncan's *The Mariner's Chronicle*, whose only resemblance to the *Pym* incident is the mutineers' desire to practice piracy.[33] McKeithan also shows, through use of parallel passages, that Poe copied a speech given to Captain Bligh in *The Mariner's Chronicle* retelling of the mutiny on the *Bounty*. Yet the *Bounty* affair was bloodless, different from Poe's in every respect except the captain's speech on being set adrift and the men's interest in the voluptuous maidens of the South Seas.[34] Keith Huntress draws a parallel between the Gibbs-Wansley mutiny treated in R. Thomas' *Remarkable Events . . . and Remarkable Shipwrecks* and the *Pym* mutiny, identifying the Gibbs-Wansley mutiny as a source on the grounds that there are seven men in the brig *Vineyard's* crew and seven mutineers (out of a much larger crew) on the *Grampus*. One mutineer aboard the *Vineyard* was a black cook.[35] But black cooks were common throughout the American merchant and whaling fleets, and the presence of a black cook in both *Remarkable Events* and *Pym* is an unremarkable coincidence.

A novel in general, and *The Narrative of Arthur Gordon Pym* in particular, may draw on many sources for the events it depicts. Burton

Pollin chronicles nearly forty sources for the novel and asserts that more than one-fifth of *Pym*'s text is paraphrased from other works (P 1:17–28). While both *The Mariner's Chronicle* and *Remarkable Events . . . and Remarkable Shipwrecks* are proven sources for *Pym*, neither contributed so many elements to the story as did Lay and Hussey's *Narrative of the Mutiny on Board the Whaleship Globe*, and neither accounts for those events in *Pym* that seem most indebted to Lay and Hussey.

Poe's use of the Paulding journal as a source for the ghost episode is more problematic. Burton Pollin has uncovered at least three possible sources for the ghost episode, especially plausible as each involves the appearance of a mock ghost:

> The "masked ghost" episode may come from several sources: In 1900 Colonel T. H. Ellis, son of Allan's partner, recorded an episode involving Edgar, at about fifteen, as a sheeted ghost, trying to terrorize his father's guests of the Gentlemen's Whist Club. . . . In *The Mariner's Library* is the article "An Escape through the Cabin-Windows" . . . in which a mate, thrown overboard by two sailors, is rescued, hidden by the captain, and introduced at his normal station in port to the horror of the sailors who are suitably punished. The celebrated Amasa Delano, Melville's source for *Benito Cereno* in *Narrative of Voyages and Travels* . . . relates that . . . he and his mate showed a mop-constructed ghost through a cabin window to sailors talking about ghosts, who were "struck dumb, fixed immovable with terror." (P 1:259–260)

Since the *Globe* mutiny ghosts were thought to be real rather than faked, and since Poe's use of Paulding's journal is less likely than his use of the ghostless Lay and Hussey narrative, Pollin's research may mean that the similarity between the ghost episodes in *Pym* and Paulding is pure coincidence. Yet the appearance of a suitably "blood-boltered Banquo" to guilt-stricken mutineers in both works is certainly an unusual coincidence, and perhaps we can add a fourth item here to Professor Pollin's list of possible sources for the ghost.

Conclusion

The Nantucket whaleship *Globe* sailed into American literary history long ago with the 1851 publication of *Moby-Dick*. Both a " 'Narrative of the Globe Mutiny,' by Lay and Hussey, survivors. A.D. 1828" and a "Life of Samuel Comstock (the mutineer), by his brother, William Comstock. Another Version of the whale-ship Globe narrative" are mentioned in *Moby-Dick*'s "Extracts." [36] Indeed, Melville could not have escaped knowledge of the *Globe* mutiny, for the same frigate *United States* that returned whalemen Lay and Hussey home from their adventures in the Pacific later performed the same service for whaleman Herman Melville. [37] Charles Olson, by lyrical juxtaposition, suggests the *Globe*'s importance to Melville's "book of the law of the blood," and the towering figure of Captain Ahab, mutineer against God, owes not a little to Samuel Comstock, the "terrible whaleman." [38]

It is time now to extend our appreciation of the *Globe* mutiny's place in American literary history by recounting its contribution to Poe's *Pym*. The details of the mutiny, as Edouard Stackpole has observed, "bear a close resemblance to the old 'penny dreadfuls' that provided sensational reading for early 19th century readers. But, in this case, the facts were all too true, filled with a horror bordering on madness." [39] *Pym*, of course, bears a deliberate resemblance to the "old 'penny dreadfuls,'" as it satirizes and imitates the loosely factual mariners' chronicles so popular in Poe's day. But it has also borrowed some of its own "horror bordering on madness" from the true story of the *Globe*. To *The Narrative of Arthur Gordon Pym of Nantucket*, Poe's own "book of the law of the blood," the *Globe* mutiny has contributed "harrowing and yet indefinable horror," "mystery, and suffering, and terror," as well as one more instance of Jeremiah N. Reynolds' impact on the imagination of Edgar Allan Poe.

Poe's "Manual of 'Seamanship'"

Joan Tyler Mead

 The sources of all but two of Poe's digressions in *Pym* have been identified. As Professors D. M. McKeithan and R. L. Rhea have demonstrated, Poe copied almost directly from contemporary accounts of maritime adventures by Benjamin Morrell and Jeremiah N. Reynolds to construct the passages that describe the tortoise in chapter 12; the various islands visited by the *Jane Guy* in chapters 14 and 15; the south polar explorations up to early 1832 in chapter 16; and that curious marine animal the *beche de mer* in chapter 20.[1] No source for the first two digressions, both of which concern the management of a vessel at sea, has yet been suggested, although as long ago as 1895 George E. Woodberry theorized that Poe had used a "manual of 'Seamanship'" for the passages.[2]

The first of the unestablished digressions occurs in chapter 6, where there is a prosaic discussion about the proper stowage of a ship's cargo (*P* 1:97–99); and the second, in chapter 7, offers a description of the nautical maneuver known as "lying to," or holding a vessel so that the bow faces nearly into the wind (*P* 1:105–7).[3] Woodberry may have been correct, and a "manual of 'Seamanship'" may someday be unearthed which corresponds to the first digression, at least. However, a recent search among all guides to seamanship that could have been available to Poe has yielded these conclusions: Poe himself composed the digression on stowage; and he based the other passage, the one that discusses lying to, on material which he located in William Falconer's *A New Universal Dictionary of the Marine*, first published in London in 1769. This essay attempts to set forth the reasoning that lead to these conclusions—to identify, in other words, Poe's missing "manual of 'Seamanship.'"

The digression on stowage was probably written after Poe had changed his residence from Richmond to New York City.[4] He began working on *Pym* in 1836 while he was employed as editor and book reviewer of the *Southern Literary Messenger* in Richmond; because of serious disagreements with its publisher Thomas W. White, he resigned his duties in January 1837 and moved with his wife and mother-in-law to New York. Meanwhile, two early sections of *Pym* appeared in the *Messenger*. The first part, which was published in the January 1837 issue, ran to paragraph 4 of chapter 2; the longer second part, printed in the February issue, stopped at the end of paragraph 3, chapter 4. The passage on stowage occurs just two chapters after the end of the second installment. It may have been composed while Poe's urge to write a sales-worthy long work was still strong, and his zeal to do so may have resulted in his writing the entire digression himself.[5]

Evidence that indicates Poe's authorship of the digression is that it does not resemble any known possible source. By the 1830s there were numerous treatises on naval architecture, principles of navigation, and seamanship,[6] but none that discusses the principles governing the stowage of a vessel. Furthermore, the technique that Poe employed to impart an air of factual information to the digression is simply his use of appropriate-sounding terminology, such as "barrels," "hogsheads," "screwing cargo," "beam-ends," "shifting-boards," and "stanchions." These few terms could have been acquired by Poe from watching cargo being stowed in Boston or at Fort Moultrie or Fortress Monroe or in Richmond—all places where he had lived.

The entire passage, which emphasizes the dangers that are inherent in the stowage of any cargo, seems more imaginative than realistic. There is the statement that barrels which are screwed into a vessel's hold can be flattened by the pressure (only baled goods would be jack-screwed), as well as the improbable claim that a laden vessel could blow apart if tightly screwed cotton suddenly expanded.[7] Also, Poe's concepts of "shifting-boards" and "temporary stanchions" seem to be his own:

> When a partial cargo of any kind is taken on board, the whole, after being first stowed as compactly as may be, should be covered with a layer of stout shifting-boards, extending completely across the vessel. Upon these boards strong temporary stanchions should be erected, reaching to the timbers above, and thus securing everything in its place. (*P* 1:98)

According to *The Oxford Companion to Ships and the Sea*, shifting-boards are "longitudinal wooden bulkheads temporarily erected in the holds of ships" to restrict the shifting of a bulk cargo;[8] they are not laid atop the cargo, as Poe claims. Stanchions are permanent, not temporary, upright supports along the side of the vessel, to which the shifting-boards are lashed. The digression concludes with the example of the unfortunate schooner *Firefly* that "went down like a shot" when her cargo of corn shifted during a gale (*P* 1:99), although the description hardly provides time for her to fill with water.[9] The overall effect of the digression on stowage is metaphoric in that it presents an image of cargo which is not inert but dangerously volatile.

In contrast to his composing an original passage on stowage, Poe most likely turned to Falconer's *Dictionary* for the information that he used to write his digression on lying to. The enormous scope of the *Dictionary* is indicated by its subtitle, which promises "a copious explanation of the technical terms and phrases employed in the construction, equipment, furniture, machinery, movements, and military operations of a ship. Illustrated with a variety of original designs of shipping, in different situations; together with separate views of their masts, sails, yards, and rigging. To which is annexed, a translation of the French sea-phrases, collected from the works of Mess. Du Hamel, Aubin, Saverien, & c."[10] To write the *Dictionary*, William Falconer drew upon the knowledge he had gained firsthand from serving in the British merchant service and the Royal Navy. Besides being a professional seaman, he was also a poet, best known for the long poem *The Shipwreck*, first printed in 1762, which exhibits an interesting combination of neoclassical proprieties and firsthand nautical detail. (A contemporary considered the poem to be "the most important event in the literary life of Falconer.")[11] In his preface to the *Dictionary*, Falconer laments that other maritime dictionaries are "extremely imperfect," "very deficient in the most necessary articles," and "often vague, perplexed, and unintelligible." He acknowledges that he has used material from certain writers concerning the subjects of shipbuilding and artillery, but he adds that "whatever relates to the rigging, sails, machinery, and movements of a ship; or to the practice of naval war, is generally drawn from my own observations; unless where the author is quoted."[12] Ironically, Falconer died in 1769, the year the *Dictionary* first appeared. It became the most enduring of his nautical writings.

Falconer's *Dictionary* was republished several times between 1769 and the end of the century. An 1804 edition shows revisions by J. W. Norie, and in 1815 William Burney edited another version in which the work was "modernized and much enlarged." In his prefatory remarks, Burney states that the information which he added to Falconer's text encompassed "much general knowledge, drawn from various sources which are not always accessible to the generality of sea-faring men."[13] Burney's additions included an appendix, part of which he copied directly from Nathaniel Bowditch's *New American Practical Navigator.*[14] Subsequent editions of the Falconer-Burney text continued to be published at least through 1830.

This kind of text would have been a likely one for Poe to turn to in search of specific information about managing a vessel at sea. If he did consult the *Dictionary* for material about lying to, he probably did so not in Richmond, which he left in early 1837, but in New York. The Virginia State Library in Richmond did not acquire a copy of Falconer's *Dictionary* until 1953. However, the Mercantile Library in New York, which was established in 1820, owned a copy of the 1815 edition at least until 1866 (sometime after that date the book was either lost or stolen).[15] The 1815 edition is the one which Burney edited and enlarged and which includes the appendix. The copy of Falconer's *Dictionary* at the Mercantile Library may be the book that Poe read.

Despite the many publications on seamanship that were available in the late 1830s, only about eight of them have anything to say about the maneuver of lying to, and most of these sources devote just a few sentences to the subject.[16] Darcy Lever's *Sheet Anchor*, first published in London in 1808, treats the matter more fully than most of the others because Lever provides sequential instructions for maneuvering a three-masted ship in various procedures, from "Lying To under Different Sails" to "Waring" to "Scudding."[17] Lever's text, however, is a directive. Intended as instruction for junior members of the British Navy, it is phrased in a terse nautical vernacular, and because it is written in the imperative mood, the tone is crisp and commanding.

The information in Falconer's *Dictionary* is notable for several reasons. Like Lever's manual, the *Dictionary* offers a relatively extensive discussion of lying to, but Falconer provides a straightforward explanation rather than a series of commands. Any slight relationship between Lever's text and the digression concerns the subject matter alone, whereas the associations between Falconer's *Dictionary* and the digression involve nautical information, organization, and stylistic devices.

The *Dictionary*'s discussion of lying to occurs in three related entries, one under the heading "To lie to," and two others under "Lying-to." (The second of these occurs in the appendix, and is taken directly from Bowditch.) All three entries discuss the procedure in terms of favorable weather (emphasis is added):[18]

> Lying to:
> to retard a ship in her course, by arranging the sails in such a manner as to counteract each other with nearly an equal effort, and *render the ship almost stationary* ... usually ... by laying either her main-top-sail, or fore-top-sail *aback*. (p. 222)
>
> Lying-to is the act of *waiting for some other ship* ... or to avoid pursuing a dangerous course. (p. 250)
>
> Lying-to *in fair weather* is seldom practised but under three topsails. (p. 693)

The passage in Poe's *Pym* on lying to reads:

> *In moderate weather*, it is frequently done with a view of merely bringing the vessel to a stand-still, *to wait for another vessel*, or any similar object. ... the manoeuvre is usually accomplished by throwing round some portion of her sails so as to let the wind take them *aback*, when she *becomes stationary*.(*P* 1:105, emphasis added)

The correspondences are apparent. "In fair weather," says Falconer, lying to will "render the ship almost immoveable." Similarly, Poe declares that "in moderate weather" the maneuver will bring the vessel "to a stand-still." Both texts state that lying to is accomplished with the use of several sails and that there are several reasons for undertaking the procedure. Falconer uses the phrase "waiting for some other ship," while Poe's phrase is "to wait for another vessel." In addition, the words "stationary" and "aback" appear in both passages.

The single exception to the *Dictionary*'s condition of fair weather in the three entries occurs in the appendix, where the entry for "Lying-To" has a subsection titled "Lying-To in a Gale of Wind." Poe appears to echo the subsection in the first paragraph of the digression, when he declares, "But we are now speaking of lying to in a gale of wind" (*P* 1:105).

For the explanation of lying to in severe weather, the *Dictionary* has a separate four-paragraph entry titled "Trying." (According to a recent study, "trying" was an earlier term for lying to.) [19] In the *Dictionary*, therefore, the terms "lying to" and "trying" indicate different conditions of weather for the procedure that kept a vessel turned toward the direction of the wind. Falconer's discussion of trying was probably Poe's source for the remainder of the digression—that is, for most of its three paragraphs following the opening sentences. (Incidentally, Falconer himself wrote the information about trying which corresponds to the digression; the appendix to the *Dictionary* does not have an entry for this term.) Poe, of course, uses only the term "lying to"; possibly he did so to conceal the resemblance between most of the digression and the first three paragraphs of Falconer's explanation of "trying."

"In trying, *as well as in scudding*," says Falconer, "the sails are always reduced in proportion to the increase of the storm" (p. 584, emphasis added). This brief reference to scudding, as well as the association made between the two maneuvers of lying to and scudding, establish another relationship between the *Dictionary* and the digression. Poe states in *Pym* that he intends to discuss lying to in conditions of severe weather, but having said so, he does not do this. Instead, and still in the first paragraph of the digression, he turns to discuss a maneuver which is the opposite of lying to: now his subject is scudding, or putting the vessel before the wind so that she runs with it (P 1:105–6).

As noted above, Falconer briefly associates the two maneuvers. His reference to scudding makes his explanation different from those in other nautical guides, which do not draw such a comparison and indeed which do not even mention scudding within their explanations of lying to.[20] Poe's abrupt change in subject matter, from lying to (or trying) to scudding, is inconsistent with any other standard guide to seamanship of the period. Perhaps in Falconer's reference Poe recognized a means by which he could expand the digression and thereby enhance the impression of his own knowledge of ship handling, as well.

Furthermore, the *Dictionary*'s entry entitled "scud" and the entry in the appendix under "scudding" caution that scudding may endanger the ship's stern: "A sea striking the ship violently on the stern," Falconer warns, "may dash it inwards, by which she must inevitably founder" (p. 437). In the appendix, the entry (copied from Bowditch) advises that when a ship veers to scud, her sails "may be becalmed by the height of the waves breaking violently against the stern" (p. 698). Poe seems to echo the idea of such danger in his own sentence: "If a vessel be suffered to scud before the wind in a very heavy sea, much damage is usually done her by the shipping of water over her stern" (P 1:105–6).

In their second paragraphs, both the entry for "trying" and the digression name certain sails which are customarily used for lying to in severe weather. Falconer describes a sequence of different sails that can be employed, from the largest possible amount of canvas to the least. First he states that any one of the courses (the main sail, the foresail, or the mizen) may be used wholly or reduced by reefs. For the least possible amount of sail, he says, the "mizen-stay-sail" or the "main-stay-sail" would generally be used. Or, he adds, the ship might lie to "under bare poles" (p. 584). Poe describes a similar though less detailed arrangement of canvas, referring first to the use of a full foresail, and concluding that "the Grampus was generally laid to under a close-reefed foresail" (*P* 1:106). The specific sails that Poe names seem to have been his own arbitrarily named selections, because his list bears no resemblance to those recommended for lying to or trying in any nautical guide of the period.[21] Nevertheless, in the *Dictionary* and the digressive passage, the discussion of canvas moves from full to reefed, or shortened, sails. Unlike Falconer, Poe does not state that a vessel can lie to without any sail at all, but he does use this idea at the end of the digression.

It should be noted that Falconer describes the sails of a ship, that is, a vessel with three square-rigged masts: the foremast, the mainmast, and the mizenmast. Falconer's references to the sails of a ship establish another connection to Poe's digression, even though Poe's list of sails was probably fanciful. For Poe mentions "large square-rigged vessels," and he refers to "after-sails" (*P* 1:106), a term that Falconer defines elsewhere as "all those which are extended on the mizen-mast, and on the stays between the mizen and main-masts" (p. 6). The *Grampus,* of course, is a brig, a two-masted vessel without a mizenmast. Poe was basing his information on descriptions that refer to the canvas of a ship, as Falconer's do.

In their third paragraphs, the texts describe in some detail the vessel's situation when she lies to in a storm. The resemblance between Falconer's entry and Poe's digression is particularly strong here, in subject material and in corresponding language as well. Both paragraphs—the first by Falconer, the second by Poe—begin by stating why the positioning of the sail is critical to the vessel's stability.

> The intent of spreading *a sail* at this time is to keep the ship more steady, and by pressing her side down in the water, to prevent her from rolling violently; and also to turn her *bow* towards *the direction*

of the wind, so that *the shock of the waves* may fall more obliquely on her flank, than when she lies along the trough of the sea. (p. 584, emphasis added)

When a vessel is to be laid to, her head is brought up to the wind just so nearly as to fill *the sail* under which she lies, when hauled flat aft, that is, when brought diagonally across the vessel. This being done, the *bows* point within a few degrees of *the direction from which the wind issues,* and the windward bow of course receives *the shock of the waves.* (P 1:106, emphasis added)

Each of these paragraphs follows the previous discussion about using different types of sails in severe weather, but at this point both writers change to a single, collective reference: Falconer refers to "a sail," and Poe to "the sail." (Note that Poe makes the image of the angled sail more striking by saying that it is "brought diagonally across the vessel.") Falconer states that the sail will "turn [the vessel's] *bow* towards *the direction of the wind,*" and Poe declares that when the sail is set, "the *bows* point within a few degrees of *the direction from which the wind issues.*" Most important, there is Falconer's phrase, "the shock of the waves." Falconer uses the phrase as a subject: "*the shock of the waves* may fall more obliquely on her flank." Poe, who must have been impressed with the energy of the phrase, more effectively renders its forcefulness by employing it as an object that ends his own sentence emphatically: "the windward bow of course receives *the shock of the waves.*" Poe does not use the phrase anywhere else in his fiction, a fact which tends to support the idea that its appearance in the digression is a reflection of Falconer's text.[22]

In addition, the third paragraphs of both passages contain references to the vessel's helm. Falconer states that "while [the vessel] remains *in this situation,* the helm is fastened close to the lee-side" (pp. 584–85, emphasis added). Poe begins with similar wording: "*In this situation* a good vessel will ride out a very heavy gale of wind. . . . The helm is usually lashed down" (emphasis added). However, Poe expands upon the idea, stating that the vessel should not require "any further attention . . . on the part of the crew"; and he adds, "Indeed, the helm had far better be left loose than lashed very fast, for the rudder is apt to be torn off by heavy seas if there be no room for the helm to play" (P 1:106). Nautical authorities in the nineteenth century disagree as to whether or not the helm should be tied down while the vessel lies to,

27

but they all state that the presence of an alert helmsman is necessary. The idea of removing the element of human supervision must have been Poe's alone.[23]

In their third paragraphs, both texts mention the stabilizing effect of properly arranged sails and conclude with several sentences about the action of "falling off." Falconer explains that "as the ship is not then kept in equilibrium by the effort of her sails," the vessel moves "alternately to windward and to leeward," and "the contrary excess of the angle to leeward is termed her falling-off" (p. 585). He says, in other words, that while the appropriate amount and position of canvas, plus the rudder, will maintain the vessel's relative steadiness while lying to, some oscillation will occur, and falling off is part of that movement. Poe has similar ideas concerning the canvas and falling off, but with different intent. "If the violence of the wind, however, should tear the sail into pieces . . ." he says, "there is then imminent danger. The vessel falls off from the wind, and, coming broadside to the sea, is completely at its mercy." Then he echoes Falconer's earlier reference to lying to "under bare poles." "Some vessels," declares Poe, "will lie to under no sail whatever, but such are not to be trusted at sea" (*P* 1:106–7). It appears that Falconer's last paragraph of the entry on "trying" has provided subject matter and direction for the concluding paragraph of Poe's digression. But the passages end differently: Falconer finishes by describing a condition of relative stability, while Poe concludes abruptly with the suggestion of catastrophe.

Probably Poe used Falconer's *Dictionary* in this fashion: first, and logically, he read several entries that define the term "lying to." Then he pursued a reference to the word "trying," which explanation he followed for the most part throughout the digression. Also in the explanation of "trying" he found the mention of "scudding," and he incorporated that concept within the digression.

There are, of course, several notable differences between the two texts. The *Dictionary* explains the different effects of certain sails that can be set to execute and maintain the maneuver of lying to. Poe names several sails for the purpose, but his list appears to be an arbitrary one. The Falconer entry states that the ship's helm should be "fastened close to the lee-side," but Poe declares that "this is altogether unnecessary" (*P* 1:106), though a few sentences later he discusses the need for an alert helmsman if the vessel should have to be put around to scud. Falconer says that the movement of falling off is to be expected when a ship lies to, whereas Poe warns about falling off as a prelude to disaster. Poe's digression abbreviates, changes, and even contradicts some of the material in the *Dictionary*.

It is the sequence of information and the use of similar language that establish a striking resemblance between the two texts. Falconer's *Dictionary* and Poe's *Pym* contain, in order: an explanation of lying to in moderate weather; a description of lying to in foul weather, combined with a reference to the opposite maneuver of scudding; a list of various sails to be used for lying to; a description of the situation of a vessel which lies to, employing in that description the phrase "the shock of the waves"; a reference to the helm being lashed; and finally a discussion of the vessel falling off from the wind. Yet it must be noted that the descriptions of lying to and trying that are provided in Falconer's *Dictionary* create an image of relative equilibrium. When Poe wrote the digression on lying to, he adjusted the information that he found in the *Dictionary* so as to create a different effect, one that emphasizes the dangers inherent in the procedure.

There is an amusing addendum to the question of what Poe created and what he borrowed in the two digressions. Two sections from his digression on stowage—which he probably *did* write himself—appear to have been plagiarized in an authentic guide to seamanship, *Nautical Routine and Stowage, with Short Rules in Navigation*, by John McLeod Murphy and W. N. Jeffers, Jr. The book was published in 1849, the year of Poe's death, eleven years after the publication of *Pym*.[24] The section on stowage was written by Murphy, and his treatment of the subject appears to be knowledgeable, careful, and thorough.

Astonishingly, however, Murphy includes two large quotations from Poe's digression on stowage. One quotation makes up the last part of a note that Murphy attaches to directions for stowing grain and flour; the other comprises the entire note that follows his brief paragraph about stowing tobacco.[25] Each of these passages is surrounded by quotation marks. That the differences are few is evident below, where the passages from *Pym* are shown on the left, and Murphy's changes are shown on the right, in italics.

A lamentable instance of this heedlessness occurred to my knowledge in the case of Captain Joel Rice of the schooner Firefly, which sailed from Richmond, Virginia, to Madeira, with a cargo of corn,	*instance of heedlessness* *occurred in the case of Captain Joel Price,*

in the year 1825. The captain had
gone many voyages without serious accident, although he was in
the habit of paying no attention
whatever to his stowage, more
than to secure it in the ordinary
manner. He had never before sailed
with a cargo of grain, and on this
occasion had the corn thrown
on board loosely, when it did not
much more than half fill the vessel.
For the first portion of the voyage
he met with nothing more than
light breezes; but when within a   *breezes,*
day's sail of Madeira there came   *Madeira,*
on a strong gale from the N. N. E.   *from N. N. E.,*
which forced him to lie to. He
brought the schooner to the wind
under a double-reefed foresail
alone, when she rode as well as
any vessel could be expected to do,
and shipped not a drop of water.
Towards night the gale somewhat
abated, and she rolled with more
unsteadiness than before, but still
did very well, until a heavy lurch
threw her upon her beam-ends
to starboard. The corn was then
heard to shift bodily, the force of
the movement bursting open the
main hatchway. The vessel went
down like a shot. This happened
within hail of a small sloop from
Madeira, which picked up one of
the crew (the only person saved),   *crew, (the only person saved,*
and which rode out the gale in per-
fect security, as indeed a jollyboat   *as, indeed, a jolly-boat might*
might have done under proper   *have done, (p. 39)*
management. (P 1:99)

Thus, in a load of tobacco or flour,   *In a load of tobacco,*
the whole is screwed so tightly

into the hold of the vessel that the barrels or hogsheads upon discharging are found to be completely flattened, and take some time to regain their original shape. This screwing, however, is resorted to principally with a view of obtaining more room in the hold; for in a *full* load of any such commodities as flour or tobacco, there can be no danger of any shifting whatever, at least none from which inconvenience can result. There have been instances, indeed, where this method of screwing has resulted in the most lamentable consequences, arising from a cause altogether distinct from the danger attendant upon a shifting of cargo. A load of cotton, for example, tightly screwed while in certain conditions, has been known, through the expansion of its bulk, to rend a vessel asunder at sea. There can be no doubt, either, that the same result would ensue in the case of tobacco, while undergoing its usual course of fermentation, were it not for the interstices consequent upon the rotundity of the hogsheads. (P 1:97)	*such commodity as tobacco,* *tightly screwed,* *process of fermentation* —*Am. Pub.* (p. 40)

In general, Murphy uses more commas; he does not include references to flour that Poe includes in the passage on tobacco; and, of course, he omits certain transitional words that Poe used to move from Pym's narrative into the digression. There are two word changes: in Murphy, the name of the Firefly's captain is Price, not Rice, and toward the end of the passage about tobacco, he uses the phrase "process of fermentation" where Poe says "course of fermentation."

Murphy does not cite a source for the first quotation, but he attributes the second, cryptically and enigmatically, to "Am. Pub." Most likely he wanted the reader to assume that "Am. Pub." was the source for both quotations, which are located close to each other. We must conclude that he copied the passages from *Pym* since there seems to be no common source that Poe and Murphy used, and the two texts are nearly identical.[26] It may be that Murphy tried to conceal his use of Poe's novel, perhaps by reversing the order of the passages (in *Pym* the *Firefly* passage ends the digression), but more likely by attributing the paragraphs to the cryptic, ambiguous "Am. Pub." Murphy probably realized that *Pym* was fiction and suppressed its identification as his source so as not to undermine the validity of his own work. Of course, although this is unlikely, the enigmatic "Am. Pub." could represent a comical misunderstanding on Murphy's part. Did he actually think that *Pym* was a genuine travelogue?

To conclude: By means of the first two digressions, Poe developed a concept of perilous and uncertain balance. His digression on stowage offers an image of cargo that may shift or explode, and one chapter later the discussion of lying to, based on Falconer's *A New Universal Dictionary of the Marine*, emphasizes the risks that attend that procedure. Poe's "manual of 'Seamanship'" was in large part his own creation. Yet two wildly improbable portions of the first digression appeared some years later in a serious discussion of procedures for stowing a merchant vessel and thus became part of an actual "manual of 'Seamanship.'" Unlike the plagiarisms that Poe claimed and wrote about bitterly, this literary theft would surely have delighted him.

Pym's Polar Episode:

Conclusion or Beginning?

J. Lasley Dameron

 In all of the criticism and scholarship devoted to Edgar Allan Poe, there has been no more beguiling interpretative problem, it seems to me, than one to be found in his innovative and startling tale *The Narrative of Arthur Gordon Pym*. My primary objective here is to focus upon the puzzling conclusion of *Pym*, Poe's most successful prose romance of novel length. I argue that the concluding polar episode of this structurally episodic novel is open-ended and that Poe, whatever his ultimate intent, concluded his romance within the bounds of narrative realism. What appears to be an epiphany-like narrative climax, that is, "a shrouded human figure," can be interpreted on the natural, or literal, level as the culmination of a series of unusual, but not supernatural, visual experiences actually reported by those venturing into a polar region.

Vitally related to this objective is my exploration of the tantalizing possibility that Poe intended a sequel to *Pym* but did not, or was unable to, follow through. In the light of sources he very probably utilized, he had at hand abundant material to be used in a sequel which would continue to sustain an acceptable verisimilitude. Certainly his suspenseful "conclusion," if read in the light of, say, a serialized story to be concluded in subsequent episodes, reinforces my argument. From internal evidence it is clear that Poe originally never intended to do away with either Pym or his surviving character Dirk Peters. In view of Pym's capacity to survive so many perilous situations, his *post facto* demise by accident, as reported in the final unsigned "Note" of Poe's romance, obviously surprises the reader.

In composing *Pym*, Poe could hardly overlook the widespread practice among fictionists of composing narratives in serial or episodic form. During the 1820s and 1830s, scores of serialized sea stories appeared in the popular magazines of the day, and some of the more popular stories were offered to the public later as completed narratives. Thus, the initial three chapters of *Pym* were first published in two installments in the *Southern Literary Messenger* in January and February of 1837, eighteen months before Harper and Brothers published the romance in July 1838. If Poe's mind was geared to writing episodic or serialized pieces, one would be inclined to expect further examples of this pattern of thinking. And that is precisely what we find in the next travel piece Poe undertook after the publication of *Pym*. Immediately after the publication of *Pym*, Poe planned a twelve-part serialization of another travel account he was then producing entitled "The Journal of Julius Rodman," to be published from January through December 1840, in *Burton's Gentleman's Magazine*. Interestingly enough, he completed only six episodes of "Rodman," for reasons no one has been able to adduce.

But from the beginning it seems obvious that Poe planned *Pym* in a mode Joseph Ridgely has described as an "episodic sea adventure" (*P* 1:31). Having severed ties with the *Southern Literary Messenger* in early 1837, Poe was forced to look elsewhere for a publisher for *Pym*, whether the romance was serialized or not. And the fictional mode he had first adopted when he composed the two initial segments prohibited him from altering this episodic mode to another of the modes in which he was then composing, to wit, the short story mode. In a word, he was committed to "an episodic sea adventure." Thus, *Pym* and "Rodman" are examples demonstrating that Poe was devoting his creative efforts to the serial narrative form during the late 1830s, and that he was capable of keeping this mode of writing quite separate from the mode he was using in some of his best tales composed during the same period, "William Wilson" and "The Fall of the House of Usher."

And there is textual evidence to support the notion that Poe intended a sequel to *Pym*. The romance covers less than a year of the nine years Pym himself states as the projected time period of his adventures, beginning in June 1827, when he set sail as a stowaway on the *Grampus* (*P* 1:68–70, 122). In fact, Poe's title page cites "incredible adventures and discoveries still farther south" (*P* 1:53), experiences that obviously were not presented. If Poe's concluding chapter marks the discovery of a passageway running through the earth's center from pole to pole, as some critics have assumed,[1] then Poe abruptly ends his narrative at that point when Pym and Peters, as sole survivors, apparently, *first* enter this passageway running through the center of the earth. To leave his romance incomplete at this time, with his protagonists poised for further adventures, would seem to be a contradiction of the principle of verisimilitude.

I should like to proceed now to look at a particular and heretofore unexamined source for some of the bizarre effects described in Poe's conclusion to *Pym*, evidence offered in support of my contention that *Pym*'s final chapter cannot be considered supernatural when one considers some of the actualities of polar exploration. I will concentrate on the *Journal of a Voyage to the Northern Whale-Fishery; Including Researches and Discoveries on the Eastern Coast of West Greenland* by one William Scoresby, Jr. (1789–1857).[2] Scoresby's book was published in 1823, fifteen years before Poe's sea narrative appeared in 1838, and it is interesting, parenthetically, to point out that this very book was among those listed by Professor Sealts in his checklist of Herman Melville's reading prior to the publication of *Moby-Dick*.[3] Scoresby's journal, it should be noted, was one of a very few actual accounts of arctic exploration available to Poe just prior to the appearance of the initial three chapters of *Pym* in the *Southern Literary Messenger* in January and February of 1837. And when we compare passages from *Pym*'s closing paragraphs with passages in Scoresby's *Journal*, we see striking similarities in the descriptions of natural phenomena common to polar regions, descriptions that some Poe critics have regarded as hallucinatory or unreal. I argue that in relying upon Scoresby for some descriptive details, Poe achieved remarkably bizarre effects without compromising the careful verisimilitude which attends the novel almost from beginning to end.

Having indicated the general directions I plan to pursue in this study, let me say that I do not intend here to take issue with such distinguished critics as Alfred Kazin, who declares that *Pym* is not "'supernatural' until the very end";[4] and Harold Bloom, who finds the chasm Pym comes upon in the last few lines of the romance to be "the familiar Romantic Abyss, not a part of the natural world but belonging to eternity, before the creation."[5] My concern is not with these valuable symbolic interpretations of *Pym* but with the text itself and Poe's probable intentions in making that text. I hope to offer textual support to whatever wealth of meanings critics glean from the amazing metaphors and images in the romance.

I am suggesting that further digging into what we can show to be *Pym*'s most likely sources will reveal that Poe's final chapter is grounded in verisimilitude, a verisimilitude intended to achieve the effects of "novelty and wonder" (P 1:203)—to use Poe's exact words—and not necessarily the supernatural or even the preternatural. Professors Burton Pollin (*P* 1:215–363) and Richard Kopley, among others, have recently presented evidence that Poe stressed natural effects throughout *Pym*. Professor Kopley finds that Poe relied upon a brief essay attributed to J. N. Reynolds, a noted promoter of antarctic exploration, entitled "Leaves From an Unpublished Journal," printed in the *New-York Mirror* on 21 April 1838. Kopley proposes that *Pym*'s concluding polar episode foreshadows a sea rescue by a ship having a large wooden figure of a penguin as its bow.[6] In line with Kopley's approach, I base my argument on Poe's use of a readily available source, though not necessarily Kopley's particular one, but one which Poe referred to in his writings at least twice. In reviewing number 124 of the *Edinburgh Review*, Poe refers to Scoresby's journal in the December 1835 issue of the *Southern Literary Messenger* (*H* 8:87), and he makes mention of Scoresby once again in the January 1836 issue of the *Messenger* in his short review of Daniel Defoe's *Robinson Crusoe* (*H* 8:169). Scoresby's journal, a rather popular one, was published three times before *Pym* appeared in 1838 and was very likely discussed in a variety of popular serials Poe read. As noted earlier, Scoresby's book was in Melville's library.

Scoresby's *Journal*, one of the very few scientific accounts of polar travel published in Poe's lifetime, describes in elaborate detail the weather changes and the impact of the polar environment upon the senses. As to Scoresby's credentials as an impartial witness to what he saw, we can adduce the following. Scoresby devoted the early years of his adulthood to polar travel, later becoming an Anglican churchman; he is recognized for his contribution to the knowledge of terrestrial magnetism and made his last voyage to the Arctic in 1822, charting four hundred miles of the east coast of Greenland (*Britannica*, 1972). David Brewster, the *Edinburgh* reviewer and author of one essay on an arctic exploration published in the *Edinburgh* number Poe reviewed in the *Messenger*, judged Scoresby to be an "accomplished and excellent individual" whose services to science "have been rudely overlooked by the British government."[7]

Before proceeding with the evidence of Poe's use of Scoresby in his writings, I must present one more set of facts. If Poe knew Scoresby as well as I believe he did, it would seem plausible for us to find evidence of Scoresby in pieces other than *Pym*, especially pieces written prior to that important sea romance. And that is indeed what we do find, in Poe's "MS. Found in a Bottle," published in 1833 (*M* 2:130–46), five years before the publication of *Pym*. That Poe would find Scoresby's imagery useful in "MS." as he did in *Pym* is testimony to Poe's certainty that the natural and supernatural were not always mutually exclusive, for "MS." is a tale almost wholly supernatural in tone and content, as opposed to *Pym*, with its tone of verisimilitude. That Poe would find Scoresby's realistic, but extraordinary, account applicable to both the episodic tale and the short story should come as no surprise to those of us who know something of Poe's consummate craftsmanship.

Let us now look at the two stories and Scoresby's likely impact on both. The reader will remember that a Dutch ship is encountered in both Poe works; however, the vessel in "MS." is clearly the legendary *Flying Dutchman,* which, if sighted, portends immediate disaster to any ship within its vicinity. Dutch sailors in "MS." are the walking dead, and the narrator moves freely about the ghost ship without being noticed. By contrast, the Dutch brig in *Pym* carries a dead crew, and Pym and his fellow survivors of the *Grampus* watch helplessly as the strange ship drifts off with no prospect of their rescue. Poe's narrator in "MS.," upon finding himself aboard the *Flying Dutchman,* transcends reality as he hurries "onwards to some exciting knowledge . . . whose attainment is destruction" (M 2:145). He has "little time" to "ponder [his] destiny" as his vessel is helplessly led by a current perhaps toward the "southern pole itself" (M 2:145–46).

Unlike Pym, whose death by accident is reported in the unsigned note subsequent to *Pym*'s final chapter, the narrator in "MS." enters the supernal from which no return is possible, relating his fated doom in words that seem to echo passages from Coleridge's "Rime of the Ancient Mariner":

> In the meantime the wind is still in our poop, and, as we carry a crowd of canvass, the ship is at times lifted bodily from out the sea! Oh, horror upon horror!—the ice opens suddenly to the right, and to the left, and we are whirling dizzily, in immense concentric circles, round and round the borders of a gigantic amphitheatre, the summit of whose walls is lost in the darkness and the distance. . . . The circles rapidly grow small—we are plunging madly within the grasp of the whirlpool—and amid a roaring, and bellowing, and thundering of ocean and of tempest, the ship is quivering—oh God! and—going down! (M 2:145–46)

Here Poe's image of an Arctic sea surrounded by an "amphitheatre" of ice could have been drawn from Scoresby's *Journal*. Scoresby, in describing the atmospheric refractions he observed off the coast of Greenland, writes:

> While near objects, which are seen through a very rare portion of this vapor, are little or nothing elevated; bodies at the distance of the horizon, which are seen through a mass of it several miles in thickness, are elevated ten, fifteen, twenty, or even thirty minutes of altitude. . . . In most cases, the refracted portion of the distant ice is closely connected with the ice of the horizon, from whence it takes its rise; and when it assumes the columnar form, it presents *the appearance of a vast amphitheatre,* which is so disposed, that every observer, whatever may be his position, imagines himself to be in the centre of it. (pp. 168–69; emphasis added)

The concluding paragraphs of both *Pym* and "MS. Found in a Bottle" describe a headlong plowing of a ship through a bizarre sea toward what is described as a cataract. Upon escaping the cannibals of Tsalal, Pym and his companion Dirk Peters and their captive native Nu-Nu sail in a canoe southward on the Antarctic Ocean in hopes of "discovering other lands" and a milder climate (*P* 1:201–6). They first come upon a smooth sea with no ice in sight and then continue their journey for eight days, entering into a "region of novelty and wonder." They observe a light gray vapor on the southern horizon and sea water of a "milky consistency." A fine white powder falls from the sky, and the sea becomes increasingly agitated. The white ashy material continues to fall, before a "range of vapour" (described as like a "limitless cataract") comes into view. Darkness increases, "relieved only by the glare of the water thrown back from the white curtain (*P* 1:205). White birds scream "*Tekeli-li!*" and flee, and Nu-Nu suddenly dies. In the closing lines of his journal entry of 22 March, Pym tells of rushing into the embrace of a cataract and encountering at the opening of a chasm a "shrouded human figure," whose skin "was of the perfect whiteness of the snow" (*P* 1:206).

First, one very distinct similarity between Poe's *Pym* and Scoresby's *Journal* is the depiction of a first-person observer who witnesses unusual polar phenomena. Both works primarily explore the effects of visual experiences upon the human consciousness. Not to be found in Scoresby, however, is the image of a threatening cataract looming over the horizon of the sea, an image Pym mentions three times in the final entries of his journal.[8] But it is not altogether clear that a cataract actually exists in *Pym*, only the appearance of one, and since there is no description of a likely fatal plunge into a whirlpool as in "MS.," one is not surprised that Pym and Peters survive their polar adventure. Most important, some of the bizarre phenomena Pym describes as "apparent miracles" (P 1:172) upon entering the polar world could have been drawn from Scoresby's *Journal*. They include sea water having streaks of color, the appearance of a colored vapor on the horizon, an atmosphere impregnated with a white ashy powder, and the appearance of a huge white figure having human form.

The first of these four apparent miracles is the veined water found on the island Tsalal, obviously an unexplored area within the antarctic region. While moving about on the island, Too-wit, Pym's guide, along with other natives, stops to drink water of a "singular character," having "every possible shade of purple" and, at the same time, "when falling in a cascade, [having] the customary appearance of *limpidity*":

> Upon collecting a basinful, and allowing it to settle thoroughly, we perceived that the whole mass of liquid was made up of a number of distinct veins, each of a distinct hue; that these veins did not commingle; and that their cohesion was perfect in regard to their own particles among themselves, and imperfect in regard to neighbouring veins. Upon passing the blade of a knife athwart the veins, the water closed over it immediately, as with us, and also, in withdrawing it, all traces of the passage of the knife were instantly obliterated. If, however, the blade was passed down accurately between two veins, a perfect separation was effected, which the power of cohesion did not immediately rectify. (P 1:172)

Scoresby describes patches of color in waters off the Greenland coast as having

> several veins or patches of a remarkable brown-coloured, or sometimes yellowish-green coloured water, presenting a striking contrast to the blue sea around them. These patches ran in various directions, generally forming long streaks or veins, extending as far as the eye could discern the peculiar color. Their breadth was small, seldom exceeding forty or fifty yards, and sometimes much less considerable. (p. 351)

Scoresby reports that microscopic examination reveals the various colors of sea water to be the remains of some form of animalcules. As it is for the colored waters in *Pym*, cohesion is not generally possible for the contrasting hues forming each patch or streak. In a subsequent passage, Scoresby, like Pym, describes extraordinary characteristics of water streaked with veins of color:

> The surface of the sea to an extent of several leagues, was variegated by large patches, and extensive streaks of a yellowish-green color; having the appearance of an admixture with flowers of sulfur or mustard. Whenever the ship passed through any of this peculiar water, the patch or streak was divided, and did not again unite. . . . Suspecting it to be of an animal nature, a quantity of the yellow-green water was procured; and, on examination by the microscope, was found to contain animalcules in immense numbers. (pp. 353–54)

Next, Poe introduces Pym's concluding entries of his polar venture from 1 through 22 March by alluding to the Aurora Borealis, a spectacular phenomenon of the Arctic and no doubt familiar to his readers. He makes no reference to the Aurora Australis, or Southern Lights, which in Poe's day drew less attention than the Northern Lights. In his 1 March 1828 journal entry, Pym describes an unusual vapor, the second of the four extraordinary polar sights which may have been suggested by Scoresby:

> A high range of light gray vapour appeared constantly in the southern horizon, flaring up occasionally in lofty streaks, now darting from east to west, now from west to east, and again presenting a level and uniform summit—in short, having all the wild variations of the Aurora Borealis. The average height of this vapour, as apparent from our station, was about twenty-five degrees. (*P* 1:203)

In similar language, Scoresby records these impressions of the Aurora Borealis:

> The aurora first appeared in the north, and gradually extended in a luminous arch across the zenith, almost to the southern horizon. A dim sheet of light then suddenly appeared, and spread over the whole of the heavens to the eastward of the magnetic meridian. . . . The eastern aurorae were grey and obscure, and exhibited little motion; but the arch extending across the zenith, showed an uncommon playfulness of figure and variety of form. Sometimes it exhibited a luminous edge towards the west, in some places concentrated into a fervid brilliancy. The rays were a little oblique to the position of the arch; but generally parallel to each other, and commonly ran in the direction of the magnetic north and south. At one time they extended sideways against the wind; at another in the contrary direction. Now they shot forward numerous luminous pencils, then shrunk into obscurity, or dispersed

into the appearance of mere vapor. The colors were yellow-white and greyish-white. (p. 17)

Both Pym and Scoresby cite the appearance of gray vapor and relate this vapor to the actions of the Aurorae. In a later entry on 9 March, Pym reports the extended "range of vapour to the southward," assuming a "distinctness of form," and compares it "to nothing but a limitless cataract, rolling silently into the sea from some immense and far-distant rampart in the heaven." Like Scoresby, Pym, in an entry on 21 March, observes considerable motion within the vapor which at this point Pym identifies as a cataract containing "momentary rents, and . . . a chaos of flitting and indistinct images" (*P* 1:205).

The third of Pym's strange polar phenomena possibly drawn from Scoresby is a shower of a fine white-powdery substance falling from the sky. To Pym, the powder resembled ashes—"but [was] not such—" (*P* 1:205). On 9 and 21 March, the white ashy material continues to fall, Pym notes, and ultimately melts in the water. Scoresby reports that on one particular morning, all the rigging of his ship "was thickly covered with a double fringe of snowy crystals, consisting of the particles of fog that had been deposited during the night on the opposite sides of the ropes, as they were successively presented to the wind, on the ship being repeatedly tacked" (pp. 76–77). Later, Scoresby describes similar fringes of snowy crystals producing "shadows of snow, consisting of prisms or needles . . . mixed or alternated with the fog." Scoresby concludes that snowy crystals are "derived from a progressive and continued attraction of aqueous particles in the air, capable, under the influence of some law not yet explained, of producing an endless variety of regular figures" (p. 78).

The fourth of the apparent miracles perhaps indebted to Scoresby is Poe's "shrouded human figure"; the concluding enigmatic image of his narrative closely resembles Scoresby's description of a particular structure of drift ice he observed off the Greenland coast. The closing lines of Pym's final entry of 22 March are as follows:

> And now we rushed into the embraces of the cataract, where a chasm threw itself open to receive us. But there arose in our pathway a shrouded human figure, very far larger in its proportions than any dweller among men. And the hue of the skin of the figure was of the perfect whiteness of the snow. (*P* 1:206)

Scoresby writes of venturing in a rowboat among a field of ice floes:

In this investigation, I was much struck with the resemblance to works of art, of some of the numerous ponderous blocks of ice past which we rowed. One mass resembled a colossal human figure, reclining in the position of the Theseus of the Elgin Collection. The profile of the head was very striking; the eye, the forehead, and the mouth, surrounded by mustaches, were distinctly marked. Such resemblances in the forms assumed by the drift-ice and hummocks, which occur in an infinite diversity in the Arctic Seas, are not uncommon. In some instances, possibly, the aid of a fertile imagination may be requisite to put a shapeless lump of ice into form; but, in others, the resemblances are so striking and characteristic, that the eye of the most incurious can scarcely fail to be impressed by them. (p. 84)

Scoresby attributes the formation of ice figures resembling human and animal forms that occupy the "skirts of the main body" of the polar ice "to the detrition of the sea-water during high winds and considerable swells" (p. 85)—weather conditions, incidentally enough, that Pym records in the final entries of his narrative. Scoresby also points out that these figures are all the more startling because the "beautiful whiteness and reflection of light" often "conceal the defects of the surface, by preventing the inequalities from being detected by the eye" (p. 87).

To conclude, in light of Scoresby's *Journal of a Voyage to the Northern Whale Fishery*, one of *Pym*'s likely sources, *Pym*'s polar world of "novelty and wonder" largely becomes a series of plausible, if exotic, experiences. Poe reveals similarities with Scoresby in his treatment of the psychological effects of natural phenomena common to polar regions, first in "MS. Found in a Bottle" with its memorable amphitheater reference, and then in *Pym* with its descriptions of (1) sea water with veins of color, (2) a gray vapor on the horizon of the sea, (3) a shower of a white, ashy substance, and (4), most striking of all, the appearance of a huge snow-white figure.

And just as Coleridge had used a number of travel accounts in composing some of his most imaginative works, it is likely that Poe utilized other sources than Scoresby in writing the conclusion of *Pym*. Not only is there nothing in Scoresby's *Journal* to account for the image in *Pym* of the threatening cataract, there is nothing in Scoresby's work to account for Pym's encountering violent, agitated sea water apparently caused by the rise of the temperature beneath the sea.[9]

In using Scoresby's *Journal* as a primary source, Poe could convey at once the bizarre effect of "novelty and wonder" without violating the demands of verisimilitude. Hence, it is no surprise that Pym and Peters do survive and could, if Poe so chose, continue their adventures in another day, another episode. In doing so, Poe might even resurrect Pym or perhaps publish the so-called missing chapters alluded to in Poe's unsigned final note. Several options were open to him, and the final note is not necessarily the final word.

Novels, Tales, and Problems of Form in
The Narrative of Arthur Gordon Pym

Bruce I. Weiner

 On 2 July 1838, shortly before Poe's *The Narrative of Arthur Gordon Pym* was published, Cornelius Mathews wrote Evert Duyckinck to quarrel with him about the relative merits of novels and tales. The art of fiction, as far as Mathews was concerned, could thrive only in novels. He commented,

> Their preeminent merit lies in a well-fashioned, well-digested plot, and the most sagacious critics in speaking, particularly of Scott's novels, allude to them as works of art and give one of the series precedence over another by the degree of success with which the plot or *story* has been constructed—the harmony of one part with another—and the completeness and ingenuity with which the whole is wrought up. . . . Strike the best plots from the Waverley novels (whether good or bad) and Scott would have had no more readers than Hawthorne, nor have been a muse of higher order than the writer of 'Twice-Told Tales.'[1]

Mathews and Duyckinck were influential literary figures in New York, which was becoming America's literary capital and, largely through the efforts of Harper and Brothers, the center for publishing American fiction.[2] Poe gravitated to New York in February 1837 after being fired from his editorial position with the *Southern Literary Messenger*, hoping for literary employment with one of "The *Monthlies* of Gotham."[3] He had tried unsuccessfully in 1836 to interest Harper and Brothers in publishing a collection of his tales, and the firm provided some motivation for his undertaking *Pym* late in 1836, which he began to serialize in the *Messenger* just before he was dismissed. Declining to publish his tales, Harper and Brothers advised him in June 1836 that collections of previously published magazine tales and articles "are the most unsaleable of all literary performances" and that readers "in this country have a decided and strong preference for works (especially fiction) in which a single and connected story occupies the whole volume, or number of volumes, as the case may be."[4] The experience of Poe and Hawthorne seems to bear out the Harpers' reading of the marketplace, although it can be argued that the Harpers and other American publishers, impressed by Scott's success, were encouraging demand for two and three-volume novels, and that critical judgment in favor of the novel such as Mathews expresses developed in part for promotional purposes. Whatever the case may be, Mathews' comments and the circumstances of the literary economy in which Poe sought to complete his novel in 1837 provide a meaningful context for understanding problems of form in *Pym*.

Although Poe's employment with the *Messenger* began to establish his reputation as a magazinist, he was no doubt prompted by Harper and Brothers' rejection of his tales and the advice of others to attempt a novel. His editorial duties and financial circumstances, however, did not afford him leisure for extended composition. He began composing *Pym* for serialization in the *Messenger*, apparently without a clear conception of the whole, although probably aiming to produce a one- or two-volume novel. The serialization was aborted after two installments when Poe left the *Messenger*. The move to New York early in 1837 was not conducive to the development of a novelist. Without steady employment, Poe was even more hard-pressed to write for income, and the composition of *Pym* seems to have proceeded in stages under the influence of several sources, most notably, popular "mariners' chronicles" of disaster at sea, Benjamin Morrell's *Narrative of Four Voyages* (J. and J. Harper, 1832), J. N. Reynolds' *Address on the Subject of a Surveying and Exploring Expedition* (Harper and Brothers, 1836), and John L. Stephens' *Incidents of Travel in Egypt, Arabia Petraea and the Holy Land* (Harper and Brothers, 1837), the last two of which Poe reviewed in 1837.[5] None of these sources, however, controls Poe's composition of the novel, and thus the work has tended to resist generic classification.[6] The evidence suggests, moreover, that Poe composed carelessly with regard to matters of fact and style and did not think highly of his work (P 1:12–14). Despite the fact that the novel was written under some duress and evidently worked up from several sources without a controlling purpose or design, many modern readers find it structurally and thematically coherent.[7] The artistry of the novel, given the circumstances of its composition, is remarkable, but it does not meet the criteria Mathews and his contemporaries (including Poe) established for success or warrant modern readings which ignore the context of its composition. What formal and thematic coherence *Pym* has, I want to suggest, derives significantly from Poe's thinking about the novel and magazine tale in 1836 and 1837.

Poe was one of those sagacious critics who identified the art of fiction with well-plotted novels. As a young reviewer for the *Messenger* in 1835 and 1836, he expressed the prevailing view that novels were superior to tales as works of art and that their merit resided primarily in a well-managed plot. He indicated more respect for short fiction than did Mathews, praising, for example, Catharine Sedgwick's *Tales and Sketches*, Henry Chorley's *Conti, the Discarded: with other Tales and Sketches*, and Augustus Baldwin Longstreet's *Georgia Scenes*. However, none of Sedgwick's "sketches," Poe argued, "have the merit of an equal number of pages in that very fine novel," *The Linwoods* (H 8:162), and the merit of Chorley's title story is that it resembles in tone "that purest, and the most enthralling of fictions, the Bride of Lammermuir [*sic*] . . . the master novel of Scott" (H 8:233–34).[8] Moreover, as we have seen, Poe was being advised that collections of magazine tales and sketches were not marketable and that he should turn his talents to novel writing. Nevertheless, his tales and reviews in the *Messenger* were drawing mostly favorable attention, and periodical publishing seemed to offer opportunities for aspiring authors, especially impoverished ones.[9] Not surprisingly, he came to champion the magazine "article" and the muse of *Twice-Told Tales*, promoting in effect his own cause.

Poe's views of the relative merits of novel and tale were evolving as he began to write *Pym*. In reviewing Sedgwick, Chorley, and Longstreet in 1835 and 1836, he did not comment on the forms of tale and sketch as distinct from the novel. However, reviewing Dickens' *Watkins Tottle, and Other Sketches* in the *Messenger* for June 1836 (shortly after being informed by James Kirke Paulding of Harpers' reasons for rejecting his collection of tales), he took a critical turn in favor of the tale. Praising Dickens as "a far more pungent, more witty, and better disciplined writer of sly articles, than nine-tenths of the Magazine writers in Great Britain," Poe justified the art of the short story:

> We cannot bring ourselves to believe that less actual ability is required in the composition of a really good "brief article," than in a fashionable novel of the usual dimensions. The novel certainly requires what is denominated a sustained effort—but this is a matter of mere perseverance, and has but a collateral relation to talent. On the other hand—unity of effect, a quality not easily appreciated or indeed comprehended by an ordinary mind . . . is indispensable in the "brief article," and not so in the common novel. The latter, if admired at all, is admired for its detached passages, without reference to the work as a whole—or without reference to any general design—which, if it

even exist in some measure, will be found to have occupied but little of the writer's attention, and cannot, from the length of the narrative, be taken in at one view, by the reader.[10] (*H* 9:45–46)

Conflating the periodical essay and fictional tale, Poe's aesthetic of the magazine "article" attests to the persistent influence of Addison and Steele's *Spectator*. Given the contents of *Watkins Tottle*, however, it is clear that Poe meant to distinguish chiefly between the novel and short prose sketch and tale. Anticipating his review of *Twice-Told Tales* in 1842, he challenges the hegemony of the novel, appropriating its main formal feature, unity of design and effect, for the sketch and tale. Contrary to his assertion above, as Mathews' statement and Poe's own reviews suggest, novels *were* admired in his day for well-fashioned plots. As Nina Baym has recently shown, Poe's contemporaries defined the novel persistently in terms of formal unity of plot. The novel was expected to be realistic, confining itself largely, in the tradition of *Waverley*, to a treatment of observed reality and real people, but to be a novel, it had to be unified. This unity, reviewers argued, was to consist of a series of well-connected events, conducted toward a dénouement that dramatically revealed the design. The events themselves may be exciting, but without an artful development, reviewers maintained, they would fail to evoke the profounder "interest" readers feel in seeing the life of a protagonist complicated, cleared up, and explained. "Interest" and "dénouement," Baym observes, were the most important critical terms in discussions of the novel, relating form and function. Novels arouse interest, reviewers suggested, by appealing to the reader's desire for consummation, completeness, and explanation in life; the interest, therefore, is the product of development and dénouement, the formal, Aristotelian rather than representational aspect of the novel.[11]

The context of criticism illuminated in Baym's study makes Poe's definition of the short story seem less original than it is often supposed to be. In adapting the formal definition of the novel to the tale, however, Poe made an important modification. As applied to the novel by Poe and his contemporaries, unity of plot was a mimetic principle, requiring complication and artful working out of action at length. Tailoring the principle to fit the short tale, Poe made it expressive and lyrical. He demanded the same strict adaptation of parts to whole, but he conceived of the emotional effect of unity in the tale as narrower and more intense than in the novel. In doing so, Poe challenged the most popular notion about the novel—namely, that its appeal lay in in its power to arouse intense emotional interest. The emotional effect of unity in the novel, Poe argued in his reviews of *Watkins Tottle* and *Twice-Told Tales*, must be modified or diminished by pauses and interruptions in the reading. Not so in the brief tale, which, like the lyric poem, can be read in a single sitting, keeping the unity of effect intact.

In undertaking to write *Pym*, Poe was capitulating to the dominance of the novel in the literary marketplace, but at roughly the same time he was formulating a rationale for the short tale that counterfeits, to a degree, the literary and economic currency of the novel. What may have been the effect of this contradiction upon the composition of *Pym*? As his allegiance to periodical literature grew, Poe was perhaps inclined to parody the novel, especially popular novels of adventure, flouting their pretensions to verisimilitude and artistic unity. He may simply have been falling back on the strategy he had employed in his early tales, many of which seem intended to parody popular forms.[12] James Kirke Paulding had encouraged Poe's satiric bent in 1836 when, acting as Poe's agent with the Harpers, he conveyed their reasons for rejecting Poe's collection of tales. The Harpers claimed not only that the tales lacked "novelty" in being recently published, Paulding explained, but that they were too obscure for mass consumption: "[The Harpers] object that there is a degree of obscurity in their application, which will prevent ordinary readers from comprehending their drift, and consequently from enjoying the fine satire they convey." Paulding advised Poe to "apply his fine humour . . . to more familiar subjects of satire," praising his "quiz on [Nathaniel Parker] Willis" ("Lionizing") and "Burlesque of 'Blackwood['s]' [Magazine]" ("Loss of Breath") as "capital" examples which "were understood by all."[13] On the other hand, Poe's reviews in 1836 and 1837 of a new edition of Defoe's *Robinson Crusoe*, Washington Irving's *Astoria*, and J. N. Reynolds' *Address* to Congress concerning a United States exploring expedition in southern waters suggest a genuine interest in travel-adventure narrative and probably influenced his choice of subject for a novel (*P* 1:30–31).

Whether or not Poe intended to satirize popular travel narratives, he clearly violated his contemporaries' sense of the novel in writing *Pym*. Some reviewers praised the book for evoking a "deep," even "extraordinary, freezing interest," especially for those who "delight in the wonderful and horrible,"[14] but the majority found the plot too horrible and improbable, violating a *Robinson Crusoe*-like pretension to truth and the requirement of unity that sustains interest in a novel.

Although "written with considerable talent," opined a writer for the *New York Review*, "This work has . . . none of the agreeable interest of [*Robinson Crusoe* and *Sir Edward Seaward's Narrative*]. It is not destitute of interest for the imagination, but the interest is painful; there are too many atrocities, too many strange horrors, and finally, there is no conclusion to it; it breaks off suddenly in a mysterious way, which is not only destitute of all *vraisemblance,* but is purely perplexing and vexatious."[15] Poe's "Preface," written sometime after the *Messenger* installments, and his handling of some sources indicate an intention to mock travel-book conventions, but *Pym* is not a sustained parody or hoax. Pressed by circumstances and advice to produce a popular novel, Poe took up the task without the commitment and habit of composition of the practiced novelist or hack writer. The result was that he produced neither a carefully controlled fiction like *Robinson Crusoe*, which he greatly admired, nor a convincing hoax of "true-account" travel books like Jane Porter's *Sir Edward Seaward's Narrative*. Rather, his narrative is self-consciously ambivalent, at once emulating *Robinson Crusoe* and mocking travel-book conventions and clichés.[16] The form of *Pym*, it seems to me, owes less finally to Poe's self-conscious imitation of verisimilar travel narratives than to his developing concept of the short tale. *Pym* may be more disjointed than *Robinson Crusoe* or *Sir Edward Seaward's Narrative*, but its episodes exhibit individually a unity of design that Poe ascribed to the ideal magazine tale, especially those "tales of effect" in the early numbers of *Blackwood's Magazine*, which he praised in defense of his early stories and in reviewing *Twice-told Tales*.[17]

The *Blackwood's* tales of effect are magazine versions of the so-called explained mode of gothic fiction, which finds its fullest development in the novels of Ann Radcliffe. They detail sensations of a protagonist caught in a terrifying predicament, so terrifying as to produce a hallucinatory experience and finally a collapse into unconsciousness. Inevitably, however, after the intense dénouement, the protagonist regains his senses and explains his experience. Unlike the unified development of action, conflating fiction and real life, which reviewers in Poe's day associated with the novel, the action in the tale of effect is dual. The explanation functions as a counterplot, a second telling of the story that displaces the delusion or "fiction" of the protagonist's initial account with the "truth." The *Blackwood's* sensationalist is fascinated with terror and delusion, but the "effect" of his tale finally is to exorcise irrational states of mind and confirm the authority of reason and fact.[18]

We can see the pattern operating in the initial episode of *Pym*. Pym tells how his friend, Augustus Barnard, induced him to go sailing one stormy night after a party at Augustus' home. Augustus' cool and determined attitude and Pym's own wanderlust cause him to think his friend's "mad idea one of the most delightful and most reasonable things in the world" (*P* 1:58). Once at sea, however, Pym discovers that his friend's "assumed *nonchalance*" results from drunkenness. This is the first of many instances in the story when appearance does not coincide with reality, when deception masks the dangerous and irrational nature of seemingly delightful and reasonable things. What begins as a harmless prank ends up as a terrifying predicament. The inexperienced Pym is left to manage a small, unseaworthy boat in a raging storm. Overcome by the effects of liquor himself and the terror of his situation, he succumbs finally to "a loud and long scream or yell, as if from the throats of a thousand demons" and faints (*P* 1:60–61).

This, however, is only half of the story. Like his *Blackwood's* counterparts, Pym is rescued and restored to his senses so that he can tell his tale. He states, "I found myself, upon reviving, in the cabin of a large whaling-ship (the Penguin) bound to Nantucket.... The mystery of our being in existence was now soon explained" (*P* 1:61). The scream that had nearly frightened him to death was not a demon cry, as he had believed, but shouts of warning from the *Penguin*, which was bearing down upon the small boat. Establishing natural causes for the most delusive of Pym's sensations, the explanation counteracts the imaginative excess evoked by the predicament. The sober appearance of Pym and Augustus at breakfast the next morning may suggest a parody of *Blackwood's* thrillers, but protagonists in those tales rebound similarly from their experiences. Like many tales of effect, the first episode of *Pym* reads like a temperance tract, warning as much against unbridled imagination as against excessive drinking.

As David Ketterer has pointed out, the first episode anticipates a series of "pseudocrises" from which Pym is repeatedly rescued. Seeing the first episode as a microcosm of the whole, however, Ketterer interprets the whole as signifying a journey "through the mundane world of multiple deception toward an apocalyptic vision of arabesque reality."[19] Thus he joins other modern scholars who see in the repeated episodes of deception, delusion, and providential rescue a linear development and thematic coherence. According to Edward Davidson, the narrative may be read as "a symbolic parable of how the mind moves from an assumed coherence and reality of things to a recognition that everything, even the most logically substantial, is an illusion."[20] This is the "characteristic movement" in Poe's fiction, argues Patrick Quinn, from "the bare level of fact and routine human life to the level of dream and its haunting illusions."[21] The episodes of *Pym*, I would argue, taken individually and as a whole, are less oneiric and visionary than these readings suggest. In the *Blackwood's* thrillers, the pseudocrisis evokes visionary states of mind primarily to purge them in favor of common sense. The sensationalism in *Pym* is more subversive than that, but, as Paul John Eakin has noted, Poe exploits the *Blackwood's* scrape not only to transport his protagonists to the brink of consciousness and death, where they might catch a "glimpse of the spirit's outer world," but to return them so that they might communicate or "explain" their vision to the world. The characteristic movement in Poe's fiction, as Eakin contends, is not from reality to dream vision but there and back again. Thus Poe gives form to his ambivalence about the romantic quest for spiritual knowledge and the legitimacy of rational and visionary modes of understanding.[22]

The thematic implications of Poe's sensationalism are further illustrated in the second episode of *Pym*, which appeared nearly complete as a second installment in the *Messenger*, anticipating later renditions of the *Blackwood's* tale of effect, such as "The Pit and the Pendulum" (1842) and "The Premature Burial" (1844). Undaunted by their first escapade, Pym and Augustus concoct a scheme to get Pym aboard Mr. Barnard's brig, the *Grampus*, for a whaling voyage together. To avoid the opposition of his parents, Pym stows away in the hold of the ship in a large box that Augustus fits out with provisions for several days. Having practiced deception to get aboard the ship, however, Pym is no less deceived by his situation. Once again, what appears reasonable and delightful becomes terrifying. Attempting to retrieve a watch Augustus has left for him near the hatchway, Pym discovers that he is confined in a labyrinth of poorly stowed cargo. The disarray in the hold becomes the source and image of Pym's predicament, for he wakes up after his efforts to retrieve the watch "strangely confused in mind" (P 1:70). He must have been asleep for an unusually long time, for the watch has run down and much of his food and water has spoiled. Soon he is without light as well. Unable to tell time or to see, Pym loses hold of reason, giving way to "gloomy imaginings, in which the dreadful deaths of thirst, famine, suffocation, and premature interment" threaten him (P 1:75–76). Earlier he has dreamed of such tortures, waking at the moment of being attacked by a fierce lion, which turns out to be his dog, Tiger, caressing him. Although he is temporarily revived by Tiger's presence, his dream image of the lion's ghastly fangs is soon haunting him in fact as Tiger is driven by hunger and thirst to turn upon his master. Thus Pym's real predicament and his nightmares coalesce; asleep or awake, he is tormented by similar images and sensations. Moreover, in exerting his reason to discover a way to read a message Tiger is carrying, Pym undermines the integrity of rational thought:

> In vain I revolved in my brain a multitude of absurd expedients for procuring light—such expedients precisely as a man in the perturbed sleep occasioned by opium would be apt to fall upon for a similar purpose—each and all of which appear by turns to the dreamer the most reasonable and the most preposterous of conceptions, just as the reasoning or imaginative faculties flicker, alternately, one above the other. At last an idea occurred to me which seemed rational, and which gave me cause to wonder, very justly, that I had not entertained it before. (P 1:78)

The confusion of rational and imaginative faculties in this and other episodes seems to confirm visionary readings of the novel, yet we can still distinguish between the victim in the predicament, for whom reason is of no avail, and the narrator, who, rescued from this and subsequent scrapes, reflects rationally on the operation of his faculties in distress.

What seems rational to Pym at the time turns out to be rash and illogical. He uses some fragments of phosphorus to get a look at the piece of paper, but he fails to consider that the message might be on the other side. When he finds "nothing but a dreary and unsatisfactory blank," he tears up the note in a fit of disappointment (P 1:78–79). Gathering his wits once more, he collects fragments of the note and the phosphorous. This time, however, he glimpses only part of the message: "*blood—your life depends upon lying close.*" He forms "a thousand surmises" about the reasons why Augustus wants him to remain concealed but can "think of nothing affording a satisfactory solution of the mystery" (P 1:80). As several scholars have noted, Pym's predicament and the partially revealed note seem paradigmatic of the narrative itself, calling into question our ability to read reality through the senses or in language that presumably encodes it.[23] The pattern of the tale of effect still holds, however. There is a reprieve from every predicament, an explanation, if not always satisfactory, for nearly every mystery in the narrative. Augustus' message is explained when he finally shows up to rescue Pym. Poe writes, "He had brought with him a light in a dark lantern, and the grateful rays afforded me scarcely less comfort than the food and drink. But I was impatient to learn the cause of his protracted absence, and he proceeded to recount what had happened on board during my incarceration" (P 1:83). As always in the tale of effect, there are two simultaneous theaters of experience, one in the dark subterrane of imagination or dreams and the other in the surface world of reason and fact. Usually the explanation of the latter counteracts the experience of the former, purging the protagonist of his gloomy imaginings and restoring him to common sense. Augustus' tale is so grim, however—recounting a mutiny which has taken his father's life and divided the crew into warring factions—that matters of fact seem nightmarish, too. In this way, Poe complicates the *Blackwood's* formula, leaving in doubt the triumph of common sense.

The development of *Pym*, however, does not displace common sense ultimately with visions of an "arabesque" reality. Even in the longer stretches of the narrative, where Poe had ceased to compose for serialization, the pattern of the tale of effect prevails. Sensations in extremis and nightmarish visions continue to alternate with sober exposition. The second installment in the *Messenger* breaks off in chapter 4 before Augustus' account of the events that confine Pym in the hold is completed (in chapter 5). To offer further explanation of his predicament below deck, Pym expounds at the beginning of chapter 6 on proper stowage of cargo, although the passage is clearly digressive and transitional. We do not know whether, by January 1837, Poe had written more than appeared in the second installment, but he must have conceived the plot at least to the end of Augustus' explanation. The second stage of composition, whether it occurred before or after Poe's move to New York, began in effect with the initiation of another episode of sensations. In this stage, as Pollin and Ridgely show, Poe relied increasingly on incidents and language in popular chronicles of disaster at sea (P 1:19–20, 31–32). Rescued from the hold of the *Grampus*, Pym is victimized by the mutiny that confined him and by shipwreck. Although a longer episode than the previous one, comprising chapters 6 through 17, it still takes the form of a tale of effect. Reduced to madness and despair aboard the capsized *Grampus*, Pym and Dirk Peters, the only survivors of the ordeal, are picked up by the *Jane Guy* and soon restored to rational consciousness:

> In about a fortnight . . . both Peters and myself recovered entirely from the effects of our late privation and dreadful suffering, and we began to remember what had passed rather as a frightful dream from which we had been happily awakened, than as events which had taken place in sober and naked reality. I have since found that this species of partial oblivion is usually brought about by sudden transition, whether from joy to sorrow or from sorrow to joy—the degree of forgetfulness being proportioned to the degree of difference in the exchange. (*P* 1:148)

As in the *Blackwood's* tales of effect, pseudoscientific reflection neutralizes extraordinary sensations, consigning them to a doubtful realm of memory and dream and restoring the protagonist to a sober sense of reality. The sudden transition between irrational and rational states of consciousness shakes the authority of common sense but works finally to recommend it, if only because the alternative is so threatening. Poe seems to subscribe to a "negative Romanticism," voyaging out beyond the limits of reason only to recoil from dreamlike modes of experience and understanding, which in *Pym* produce no transcendental vision but rather a greater sense of confinement, uncertainty, and vulnerability.[24]

According to Ridgely, the appearance of the *Jane Guy* in chapter 13 marks a third stage of composition, in which Poe turns to a different source, Morrell's *Narrative of Four Voyages*, directing the narrative to capitalize on popular accounts of South Seas exploration (*P* 1:32–33). Although a shift is evident, it is consistent with the form of Poe's sensationalism. The several chapters that follow the advent of the *Jane Guy* (14 through 17) do not, as is usually the case in the tale of effect, explain away horrors experienced aboard the *Grampus*, but they do offset them with rational exposition. Reality becomes once again the commonsense world of observed phenomena as Pym mimics Morrell's accounts of previous voyages to the South Seas and of antarctic marine life. The apparent shift of purpose and tone here (and elsewhere in the narrative) that bothers many readers can be attributed to the logic of the tale of effect. The chapters that follow the *Grampus* episode are not merely, as Quinn suggests, more realistic ballast for Poe to cut loose in order to impel his narrative into a visionary realm but the usual antidote in tales of effect to suffering and delusion.[25]

Chapter 18 marks the beginning of the final episode in *Pym*. Another reversal of fortune occurs when the *Jane Guy* reaches the previously undiscovered island of Tsalal and is captured by treacherous natives. Because Poe's characterization of them is drawn from Morrell, Ridgely assigns the episode to the third stage of composition, although he admits it is "entirely self-contained" (P 1:33). Consistent with previous episodes, this one involves a series of terrifying predicaments—burial alive, starvation, a nearly fatal fall, and finally an encounter at the brink of a "limitless cataract" with a large "shrouded human figure," which, like previous demons, looms up before Pym. This last dénouement confirms for many readers the visionary design of the narrative, but it is not the end.[26] A "Note" is appended by the "editor" of Pym's text, accounting for the survival and inconclusiveness of the narrative and interpreting mysterious chasms that Pym discovered on Tsalal. The final explanations restore us once more to the known, "real world," although the imagined editor's conjecture about the hieroglyphic chasms, recalling Pym's misreading of Augustus' note, reflects ironically on the reliability of Pym's account. Ridgely attributes the chapter describing the chasms on Tsalal, apparently inserted late, and the editor's "Note" to a final stage of composition, in which Poe was influenced by Stephens' *Incidents of Travel in Egypt, Arabia Petraea and the Holy Land* and Alexander Keith's *Evidence of the Truth of the Christian Religion* (P 1:33–36), but, like the chapters that follow the appearance of the *Jane Guy*, chapter 23 and the "Note" serve to counteract the sensationalism of Pym's final scrape, providing a semblance of reason and authority.

Although Poe's novel challenges commonsense constructions of the world more significantly than *Blackwood's* thrillers do, it remains a close cousin of the tale of sensation. Even in the latter stages of the narrative, Poe aims for unity of effect—that is, the unity of a brief, terrifying experience on the brink of consciousness and life, where dreamlike visions of the unknown and rational understanding vie for authority. The succession of pseudocrises brings us finally into the vicinity of *ultima Thule*, but we never really leave the world of sensation and reflection. The shape of individual episodes and the retrospective narration of the whole, confirming Pym's return from oblivion and explaining his adventures publicly, anchor us in the known world even as they tend to transport us beyond it. Poe's reiterative tale of effect reaches no *éclaircissement,* no clarification of "real life" or vision of transcendental harmony or chaos; it offers only the shaky "explanation" of narration.

Despite the repetitious action and imagery which produce a tenuous coherence, the form and thematic concerns of *Pym* were not calculated to satisfy the expectations of novel readers in Poe's day for mimetic fiction that confirmed the order and integrity of "real life." Indeed, the sensationalism, ambiguity, and inconclusiveness of the narrative indicate Poe's unwillingness and, perhaps, inability to write the kind of two-volume novel his contemporaries sanctioned. The critical failure of the novel and Poe's subsequent disinterest in it, however, were not unfortunate. The writing of *Pym* was not the making of a novelist. It was the means by which Poe mastered and modified the tale of effect and progressed to his major phase as a short story writer. The tales that followed shortly after the publication of *Pym*, "Ligeia" (1838), "The Fall of the House of Usher" (1839), "William Wilson" (1839), and "The Murders in the Rue Morgue" (1841), are generally regarded as his best thrillers. When he returned to the subject of sensational adventure at sea in 1841, he produced a masterful tale of effect, "A Descent into the Maelström," achieving the "unity of effect" that he preferred and could not sustain in writing *Pym*.

Poe's Reading of Myth:

The White Vision of Arthur Gordon Pym

Carol Peirce and Alexander G. Rose III

 Toward its close, *The Narrative of Arthur Gordon Pym* seems to suffer a sea change. In its early chapters, the work appears a straight, factually oriented account. However, as the novel progresses toward the South Pole and the conclusion, *Pym* seems to many readers to take on redemptive or apocalyptic imagery. Indeed, it has a strange mythic quality all its own—changing from a gripping sea yarn to a revelation of symbolic vision.

Myth in literature is characterized as either having unconsciously survived or being consciously revived.[1] This essay is not concerned, however, with unconscious mythic usage, the province of mythic criticism, but rather with conscious revival—Poe's reading of myth and his possible use of that reading in *Pym*. Poe himself challenges us to find the inner meaning of his works; an attention to his awareness of myth and his borrowings from myth may help to reveal more clearly the ways his imagination is realized through structure and symbolism. Indeed, this approach may show how a straightforward novel about a voyage is, on another level, both profoundly and resonantly about a romantic quest, even the Arthurian Grail quest. This method, involving a concern with a work's mythical nuances, has been said to arise out of "nineteenth-century symbolism with its serious attention to arcane subjects, irrational states, and hermetic meanings."[2] Richard Wilbur speaks of Poe's "symbolic or allegorical method" and concludes that Poe "is the most secretive and difficult of our great symbolic writers. How much of him will permanently elude us, how much we can figure out, we can only learn by trying."[3]

Poe and other writers of the early nineteenth century were both knowledgeable about myth and involved in using it. Not only did they read mythology itself, but they also read about it in the work of recent mythographers and commentators. Burton Feldman and Robert D. Richardson point out that many English and American writers, including Poe, were actively interested and well versed in current developments in the study of myth: "The meaning of mythology, the origins of mythology, the connections suggested by comparative mythology, and above all, the romantic urge to create new myths and whole new mythologies were subjects of central concern to these writers; they were powerfully aware of the importance of myth to their work, and their experiments with myth in literature were conscious, deliberate, and sophisticated."[4]

Early nineteenth-century writers read about myth in the works of such philosophers and mythographers as Augustus and Friedrich Schlegel, Augustus arguing that one might either "work in the spirit of myth, creating new stories," or recast the old myths within one's poems or tales.[5] Accordingly, many American writers "began to look to myth to provide the vital force for a new heroic literature."[6] And Noah Webster, drawing together his own "Origin of Mythology" in 1810, refers to two mythologists, Jacob Bryant and George Stanley Faber, as the outstanding authorities in the field.[7]

We know that Poe read both the Schlegels and Bryant, and he seems in *Pym* to have drawn on the work of Faber, as well. He makes two references in his works to Friedrich Schlegel, eleven to Augustus, and five to Jacob Bryant, but their influences may have been considerably larger.[8] The last he refers to as "Bryant, whose authority we regard as superior to any" (*H* 14:113). Kent Ljungquist bases his analysis of the ending of *Pym* firmly upon Bryant's mythology, stating that "Poe's exposure to Bryant has long been known."[9] Poe does not directly refer to Faber, but Bryant and Faber are often associated. In 1832, Isaac Cory refers to "the very curious dissertations by Bryant and Mr. Faber,"[10] and Charles Anthon, the classical scholar and author of the *Classical Dictionary*, uses both throughout, incorporating their exciting new theories.

Poe apparently became acquainted with Bryant's *New System*[11] through Anthon.[12] Although the *Dictionary* did not appear until 1841, Poe met Anthon in 1836 when he consulted him concerning a book review. A correspondence ensued, and, according at least to Ana Hernández del Castillo, "This was the beginning of a friendship that was destined to play an important role in the genesis of *Pym*."[13] She feels sure that Anthon also introduced Poe to Faber's *Origin of Pagan Idolatry*.[14] Both mythographers see the story of Noah and the Ark as central to much "pagan" mythology. Every god or hero is Noah, especially if he undertakes a voyage. The Ark is personified in the goddess he loves, and she is the same "Great" or "White," three-fold Goddess, whatever her nationality or period. Faber especially stresses the relation to the Arthurian story and sees the god-hero as Arthur and the White Goddess as represented in her three phases by Guinevere, the Lady of the Lake, and Morgan le Fay, all together merging in "Gwenhwyvar" (*F* 3:318, 323).

Poe turned to the current language of myth for both interior meaning and symbolic method. Calling his method "mystic," he particularized it as "suggestion" and wrote about it in a number of places.[15] That Poe's understanding of "mystic" is closely related to "mythic" and "symbolic" and to the concepts of the Schlegels is clear upon reading Anthon's comment in his *Dictionary*: "In the treatment of these [articles on mythology], it has been the chief aim of the author to lay before the student the most important speculations of the two great schools (the Mystic and anti-Mystic) which now divide the learned of Europe." And he believes that "the former will appear to the student by far the more attractive one of the two."[16] Rees' *Cyclopaedia* explains the meaning of "mystic" using Scripture as example: "The Bible, they [commentators] contend, is a book written both withinside and withoutside: withinside, in respect to the mystical, internal, sublime and hidden sense; and withoutside, in respect to the literal and grammatical sense immediately expressed by the words."[17]

Poe picks up this very sense of "mystic" in his review of *Alciphron, a Poem* by Thomas Moore: "The term *mystic* is here employed in the sense of Augustus William Schlegel, and of most other German critics. It is applied by them to that class of composition in which there lies beneath the transparent upper current of meaning an under or *suggestive* one" (*H* 10:65).[18] He then turns to "*imaginative*" works and sees them as "remarkable for the *suggestive* character" manifested. "They are strongly *mystic*," he adds and continues: "With each note of the lyre is heard a ghostly, and not always a distinct, but an august and soul-exalting *echo*. In every glimpse of beauty presented, we catch, through long and wild vistas, dim bewildering visions of a far more ethereal beauty *beyond*" (*H* 10:65–66).

Poe's "mystic" suggestiveness beneath the surface of *Pym* seems possibly, or even probably, to come from ideas that he has gleaned from his reading of mythologists and Arthurian "matter." He seems throughout to follow some of the lines of that legend, drawing on its many-layered turnings in his own creative process. The connection is worth consideration, for there are many intriguing relationships.

The cluster of legends concerning Arthur and the Grail, with its sources in Celtic mythology and fairy lore, its reminder of the primordial White Goddess, its central concern with the shadowy history of Arthur, and its branchings into a multitude of high medieval quests certainly fascinated thinkers of the early nineteenth-century. Emerson, for instance, in his first lecture on English literature, introduces early Welsh poetry, including a poem of Taliesin, and concludes that much of it is devoted to the adventures of Arthur. He goes on to discuss the Arthurian legend more thoroughly in the next lecture, "The Age of Fable," comparing Arthur's exploits to those of the Greek gods. He speaks of the "vast collections of tales" that have been printed and retold and of their popularity "in the abridgments of Morte d'Arthur, Lancelot du Lac" and others.[19]

That Poe was very much aware of Arthurian myth seems evident not just from the wide availability of retellings and reissuings but from a variety of other sources. The *Encyclopaedia Britannica* and Rees' *Cyclopaedia of Arts, Sciences, and Literature*, both of which he used, treat of Arthur and related subjects. An admirer of Ossian, Poe surely knew Percy's famous and popular *Reliques of Ancient English Poetry*, which devotes a whole section to ballads concerning Arthur.[20] Poe himself writes of "a sense of dreamy, wild, indefinite, and he would perhaps say, indefinable delight" that he finds in the "old bards" (H 12:139). Poe also speaks often of his love of Tennyson's early Arthurian poetry, writing that the "Morte D'Arthur" and "The Lady of Shalott" (among others) "are not surpassed" (H 11:176). He is familiar with Scott, and he quotes from Spenser's *Faerie Queen*.[21]

In his own work, Poe creates the author Sir Lancelot Canning in "The Fall of the House of Usher" (M 2:413–15), and he often sets his stories or poems in "saintly days of yore" (M 1:366). Burton R. Pollin identifies Poe himself as the questing knight in "Eldorado" and shows how this poem parallels "The Lady of Shalott."[22] Finally, in two specific references, Poe reveals his delight at the thought of the ancient legend and, further, his reading knowledge of its historical connections and background. In a review of Howitt's *Visits to Remarkable Places*, Poe writes about "A Day-dream at Tintagel": "The old castle of King Arthur seems once more to lift its massy battlements above the thundering surf below, and from its portals go forth the heroes of the Round Table, with hound and hawk, and many a fair demoiselle" (H 10:113). In a second piece, "Some Account of Stonehenge, the Giant's Dance," in giving a description of the place then connected closely to Druidism, Celtic myth, and Arthurian legend, he says: "The earliest account of them [the Stonehenge monuments] occurs in Nennius, who lived in the eighth century. He says they were erected by the Britons to commemorate a massacre which took place at the spot. The Historical Triads of the Welsh refer their origin to the same cause. . . . Modern authors have been profuse in speculation, but no more. The general opinion seems to be in favor of a Druidical Temple" (*H* 14:112).[23]

Poe's interest is revealed clearly in a quotation from Bryant in *Pinakidia*: "Mr. Bryant in his learned 'Mythology' says that although the Pagan fables are not believed, yet we forget ourselves continually and make inferences from them as existing realities" (*P* 2:50). Among all the possible sources, however, for Poe's use of Arthur, Faber's study offers the closest analogues. Faber sees much myth and romance as related to initiation rites and a "remembrance of the diluvian Mysteries." For him, Arthur exemplifies the pattern that repeats itself through many recastings of myth: "The entrance of the great father into the Ship" (*F* 3:315).

In fact, to all the mythographers, Arthur was composed of two beings: a historical man and a sort of Celtic god. The *Cambrian Biography* begins (and Rees approximates it): "ARTHUR, the most remarkable name among the Britons; as a hero and a consummate warrior, he appears illustrous in our history; but as a being of romance his splendor has dazzled the world."[24] Of these two, it is the "being of romance" on whom Faber concentrates (*F* 3:314–23).

Faber further juxtaposes to Arthur the "gigantic White goddess" (*F* 3:328), of whom he declares: "All the Goddesses of Paganism will be found ultimately to melt together into a single person who is at once acknowledged to be the great mother and the earth" (*F* 1:21), whether she is "Anna-Purna" or "Isi" or "the White Goddess." Both Bryant and Faber see the Goddess as born from the seas, having as Faber puts it, "assumed the form of a ship when the mighty waters of the deep universally prevailed" (*F* 1:21). Bryant concludes "that the Ark, by the mythologists, was spoken of as the mother of mankind. The stay in the ark was esteemed a state of death, and of regeneration" (*B* 3:168).[25] She became eventually "venerated by the old Britons under the names of *Ceridwen, Ked, Sidee, Devi, Andrastè,* and *Esaye* or *Isi*," as she is "the Ceres of the classical writers." Her "mystic circle is declared to be the circle of the World" (*F* 3:3–5).

The very beginnings of the Arthurian legend exist in Celtic tales of voyages by water to an Otherworld to find a magic cauldron. In an early Arthur story, "The Spoils of Annwfn," Arthur sails to find the cauldron of rebirth.[26] In time, this first cauldron becomes related to two others, one of these containing creative inspiration and wisdom, the other an endless supply of food. In Celtic mythology, these cauldrons belong to three goddesses, each a version of the White Goddess, and one of them, Ceridwen, is identified by Faber as identical with Morgan le Fay (*F* 3:318). In later Grail literature, the cauldrons are merged with the cup and plate or "stone" of the Last Supper and with the vessel which caught Christ's blood; thus the Grail, the stone, and the cauldron become connected. Though the Grail comes and goes mysteriously, it is always associated with a miraculous and dreamed-of quantity of food and drink. The knights, physically and spiritually hungry and dry, seek its magical fulfillment. Pym, too, and all his fellows, thirst and starve and dream of food throughout.

In the later Grail myth, the knightly hero undertakes a journey across water to a wasteland ruled by a Fisher King, who is deficient physically or spiritually. On the way, the hero also faces physical and spiritual trials and finally must pass through the Chapel Perilous, an initiation site. If proven worthy in courage and character, he may attain the Grail vision. But for each seeker, the way is marked by blood, terror, mystery, and marvel: "Here is the Book of thy Descent / Here begins the Book of the Sangreal, / Here begin the terrors, / Here begin the miracles."[27] So reads the thirteenth-century *Perlesvaus*, in words redolent of Arthurian romance. And, in the "Preface" to *Pym*, Poe begins to describe "the extraordinary series of adventure in the South Seas and elsewhere" which "were of a nature so positively marvellous" that Pym feared they would be disbelieved (*P* 1:55). This, he says, in a possible first suggestion, is due to their "air of fable" (*P* 1:56)—or of "myth," as the words are used almost interchangeably in Rees' *Cyclopaedia* under "Mythology" and elsewhere. Pym's very first adventure on the *Ariel* arouses terror, an "intense agony of terror" (*P* 1:60), followed by a rescue by the *Penguin*—a rescue Pym sees as "miraculous" (*P* 1:65). He continues throughout to use the words "terror," "miracle," and "marvel."

There are a number of suggestive connections of names early in the narrative. The hero's first name is Arthur. On the *Grampus* he meets Dirk Peters, who later becomes his close companion. Peters' name, as Harry Levin points out, "bespeaks his nature, a sturdy combination of knife and rock."[28] It is not far from "knife and rock" to "sword and stone" or to the sword Arthur draws from the stone. Another companion is Pym's dog, Tiger. In early Welsh stories, Arthur is connected especially to his sword Excalibur, his dog Cabal or Horse,[29] and his ship *Prydwen*. Provocatively, each dog bears the name of another animal. Arthur's ship name *Prydwen*, meaning in Welsh "Fair face," is not unlike *Penguin*, which *Johnson's Dictionary* derives from the Welsh as "white head"[30] and which is seen by Richard Kopley especially as foreshadowing the white vision at the end.[31] The name *Pym* itself may well come from "pilgrim," as used in quest stories and in Shelley's phrase for Byron, "the Pilgrim of Eternity."[32]

In another, perhaps significant, hint, Poe mentions in regard to the *Penguin*'s "small jolly" that it "was fitted, as I have since had reason to believe, with air-boxes, in the manner of some life-boats used on the coast of Wales" (P 1:63). Pollin comments that "Poe had no reason to attribute such boats to the 'whaling service' or 'the coast of Wales'" (P 1:223). But, if Poe were thinking of Arthurian legend and the fabled *Prydwen*, this is just such a connection as he might make.

Another tantalizing relationship is implied by datings in *Pym*. In Arthurian myth, many of the stories, such as the story of *Sir Gawain and the Green Knight*,[33] move in time according to Celtic or Christian festivals; seasonal symbolism is unmistakable. Pym's whole journey is carefully dated (as were the nineteenth-century sea chronicles), but the dating of Pym's voyage carries an undercurrent of seasonal suggestion as well. Arthur and Augustus sail from Nantucket on the *Grampus* on 20 June, Midsummer's Eve, at the summer solstice (P 1:69–70). Midsummer's Eve is one of the high fêtes of Celtic Faërie, and Midsummer's Day one of two main feasts of the White Goddess. On this day, her "complementary moods of creation and destruction" join, as her yearly oak-king is sacrificed and translated to the Corona Borealis, the symbol of her northern throne, while she takes a new young lover.[34] Her high seasons are spring, summer, and winter, and her power is strong on their turning days. In the development of *Pym*, Captain Guy decides to "push on towards the pole"; on 21 December, the winter solstice, he sets sail on that determined course (P 1:158). But the spring equinox marks the beginning of the Goddess's highest power, and on 21 March, Pym approaches the cataract "having all the wild variations of the Aurora Borealis" (P 1:203, 205). On 22 March, he sees his white vision (P 1:205–6). Critics have noted the date; thus Sidney Kaplan asks, "Is it worthy of note that it is on the opening day of spring that Pym is taken by the white god?"[35]

Developing the theme of the White Goddess, Faber explains that Arthur had three wives, each named Gwenhwyvar or "*the Lady on the summit of the water*" (F 3:318). This name, from the Welsh, can be translated as "white phantom" and is undoubtedly an allusion to the "Three Great Queens" of the *Welsh Triads*.[36] (Curiously, the name may be suggested in *Pym* by the etymologically related name, *Penguin*.) In connecting two other women to Arthur—The Lady of the Lake and Morgana, the darkest of the three—Faber identifies them as sisters. But he really seems to see them, along with the real Guinevere, as the springtime, summer, and winter manifestations of the White Goddess—like Isis, Maiden, Woman, and Crone. Together they appear to represent the triune goddess whom Arthur loves, and who loves, betrays, and saves him, carrying him in the end to the magical White Island (F 3:318–21).

In *Celtic Myth and Arthurian Romance*, Roger S. Loomis writes about Guinevere as one of the representations of the Celtic Goddess and sees her in her varied abductions as another version of Kore or Persephone.[37] For him, the Arthurian Grail story represents a seasonal myth of the young god going through a "series of initiations" involving the gaining of talismans and the marrying with the springtime Goddess.[38] This myth is tied both to Eleusinian mysteries of Demeter and Persephone and to the celebration in Samothrace, where the Goddess is seen as Demeter, Persephone, Hecate, and Cybele together. He quotes Strabo: "There is an island near Britain where they offer sacrifices to Demeter and Kore like those in Samothrace."[39]

Among the main characteristics of the White Goddess in both the Greek mysteries and Arthurian romance is her ability to change shape. Demeter as Hecate (her darker self) was capable—as are both the Grail Messenger, who is either hideous or radiantly beautiful, and Morgana especially, according to Faber—of taking on a mixed form such as that of a woman with a dog's head or "a gigantic old woman, with serpents in her hair, her legs ending in a dragon's tail."[40] Taking her form from "the Irish lamia, the Morrigan" and coming from the sea, Morgana could play strange roles and assume the most diverse aspects.[41] But, whatever her particular manifestation, the Celtic Goddess or Fairy Queen, "untouched by time," is, ultimately, immortally beautiful. A combination of hostility and love characterizes her nature, as in Morgana's relation to Arthur, and, should the lover escape her power, she will pursue and bear him back to the Otherworld: "In the fairy mythology of romance the law is invariable, that for the mortal who once has experienced the fairy control there is no true release."[42]

Faber says that very early as a child or youth the hero is borne in a boat, cast into the ocean, but brought safe to land. But "occasionally the idea of infancy is dropped; and the hero of romance, at an adult age, performs some extraordinary voyage" (*F* 3:317). In fact, we see both voyages in *Pym*, youth and adult, first in the *Ariel* and then in the *Grampus* and *Jane Guy*. So Arthur sailed on "a wonderful voyage over the ocean" on his ship "called *Prydwen*, which signifies *the lady of the World*" and is thus the Goddess herself (*F* 3:318). Though Pym, feeling a sense of impending doom, has visions "of shipwreck and famine; of death or captivity among barbarian hordes; of a lifetime dragged out in sorrow and tears," he cannot resist the journey. He regards the visions "only as prophetic glimpses of a destiny which I felt myself in a measure bound to fulfil" (*P* 1:65).

In another of the *Welsh Triads*, Arthur is held "three nights in prison in Caer Oeth and Anoeth, and three nights imprisoned by Gwen Pendragon, and three nights in an enchanted prison under the Stone of Echymeint."[43] Faber refers to these as three nights "in the inclosure of wrath and the remission of wrath; three nights, with the lady of Pendragon; and three nights, in the prison of Kud or Ceridwen under the flat stone of Echemeint." He sees this story as borrowed from the enclosure of an initiate "within the mystic stone cell of Ceridwen which typified the womb of the ship-goddess." This enclosure under the stone is "his [Arthur's] allegorical bed or sepulchre" (*F* 3:318). So, too, Arthur Pym as a stowaway, hidden in the hold of the *Grampus* by his friend Augustus, is imprisoned in his "iron-bound box," "nearly four feet high, and full six long, but very narrow," where he remains "three days and nights" (*P* 1:69).[44] Afterwards he goes through horrible dreams and fever and winds his way through a maze of passages among the stowage by means of a whipcord left by Augustus. These "dismal and disgusting labyrinths" (*P* 1:74–75), as Pym calls them, have much in common with the maze that was part of the journey to be made in ancient initiation rites in both Greece and Britain.[45] Pollin writes, "Poe's source has often been assumed to be the thread given Theseus by Ariadne as a guide through the Cretan labyrinth" (*P* 1:230). Ariadne was one of the brilliant personifications of the Goddess, "the daughter, or younger self, of the ancient Cretan Moon-Goddess"; Geoffrey of Monmouth refers to her among "Merlin's Prophecies."[46]

Pym's dreams of demons, of deserts limitless, of tall trees scream-ing in agony, may well reflect the enchanted medieval wasteland. And those "immense serpents" that "held me in their embrace, and looked earnestly in my face with their fearfully shining eyes" (*P* 1:72) may be symbols of the Goddess; Faber says that Merlin called Morgana "*the white serpent*" (*F* 3:321). And Bryant writes: "In most of the antient rites there is some allusion to the serpent" (*B* 2:198).[47] Thus it seems that Pym spends some time in the womb of the *Grampus* in a proleptic dream of her. He tells us that "a dull humming sound, which reached my ears as if from an immense distance, convinced me that no ordinary gale was blowing" (*P* 1:71). The Goddess often manifests herself first by "some mysterious agency" that may "benumb the senses" and is "a sign that the mortal is feeling the bewildering fairy influence."[48] And Pym's watch stops; time seems to stand still, as it often does in Celtic Faërie. Pym says, "I began to suppose that I must have slept for an inordinately long period of time" (*P* 1:71). When he hears Augustus call, he feels "redeemed from the jaws of the tomb" (*P* 1:83).

Later, after coming out of the hold, in defeating the mutineers with Augustus and Peters, Pym disguises himself, splotching his face with blood like that of a dead crewman with erysipelas, whose eye looked as if streaked "with a band of red velvet" (*P* 1:107, 109). Now Arthur in "Triad 20" is described as one of the "Red Ravagers of Britain."[49] Owen, in the *Cambrian Biography*, says, "He was joined to form the triad of blood-stained sovereigns."[50] Graves translates the phrase as "one of the Three Crimson-stained Ones of Britain" and adds, "To be 'crimson-stained' is to be a sacred king." Such kings had face and hands stained red as a sign of royalty.[51]

In the tempest that follows, Pym dreams again, this time pleasing dreams of "green trees, waving meadows of ripe grain, processions of dancing girls, troops of cavalry, and other phantasies." He remembers afterwards that "*motion* was a predominant idea" (*P* 1:118)—as it is an attribute of the Goddess, "white raiser, red reaper, and dark win-nower of grain," Queen of the whirling elements and of the "Circling Universe."[52] Apuleius describes Isis rising from the sea, bearing her sistrum, a mirror or moon in the center of her forehead, supported "on either side by serpents that seemed to rise from the furrows of the earth, and above it were blades of corn set out." Freed from enchantment, Lucius joins her procession, which is led by floral-crowned women, scattering flowers. Temple pipers announce the Goddess; "And then came the great company . . . which were initiate."[53] One face of Isis—and of Gwenhwyvar—is that of Persephone, goddess of the green spring; another is that of Demeter, goddess of corn and earth, Persephone's mother.

However, in her next appearance, it is her third face—of Hecate or Morgana, of darkness and death—that she shows, coming with deadly motion. For then occurs the meeting with that "hermaphrodite brig . . . painted black, with a tawdry gilt figurehead"—the death ship (*P* 1:123). But the strange boat passes them by; or perhaps Pym passes another challenge of the mysteries. Faber writes that "the redoubtable knights of the round table are sometimes fabled to man the infernal ship and to ferry the souls of the dead over the lake of Hades" (*F* 3:318).

The passing of the ship leads straight to the bloody cannibal feast, almost a parody of the Eucharist, the sacred ritual of the Grail mysteries. Pym shrinks in horror but presides over the lots and ultimately participates, as Graves says the new king partakes of the body of the old in the primitive mystery of the White Goddess.[54]

Augustus dies on 1 August, the day of Lugnasadh, the main summer festival of the Celtic Cycle.[55] The "Lugnasad" in Ireland celebrated the marriage of the sun-god Lug to the earth-goddess.[56] In Greek and Celtic myth, the new king eats some "royal" part of the dead king's body; through "this alternate eucharistic sacrifice," he makes "royalty continuous, each king being in turn the Sun-god beloved of the reigning Moon-goddess."[57] The day thus celebrates the beginning of the second half of an even more ancient year, the year after the death of the White Goddess's king, "as soon as the power of the sun" begins "to decline in the summer."[58] Another young man, "his twin, or supposed twin," then becomes the queen's lover: "His tanist or other self . . . succeeds him for the second half of the year."[59] Sometimes a substitute is made for the hero-king, a "mock-king" who dies in his place, allowing him to reign a whole year—or longer. This may throw some light on Poe's comment on the relation of Arthur and Augustus, so close in "state of mind": "It is probable, indeed, that our intimate communion had resulted in a partial interchange of character" (*P* 1:65).

The character of Dirk Peters too receives illumination from Arthurian material, where an ugly and terrifying dwarf as guide may become in the end a selfless savior and friend.[60] Celtic dwarfs sometimes are "grotesquely ugly" and frightening, and they command unusually great strength. Their moods are various, ranging from hostile and surly to helpful, jocular, and even noble. And their characteristic roles include "gracious host, combative opponent, truculent servant, supernatural helper."[61] In more than one romance, the dwarf conducts the hero to a supernatural realm. Also, a close relationship exists between Morgan le Fay and a number of dwarfs, often portrayed as her servants or messengers.[62] Dirk Peters is described as a half-breed Indian, notable for "the natural ferocity of his countenance" and his warped stature, "four feet eight inches high," but with limbs "of the most Herculean mould" and the merriment "of a demon" (*P* 1:87). He has "prodigious strength" (*P* 1:87); when he stabs Parker from behind, the condemned man falls dead immediately (*P* 1:135). But Peters befriends Pym and Augustus, and toward the end he saves Pym's life in a near superhuman effort.[63] In a real change for that time, Pym refers to them together as "white men" (*P* 1:185).

Faber, as he relates the myth, turns from Arthur's own story to consider his knights riding "enchanted boats" that convey them on "some desperate adventure." The knight, he says, "steps into the vessel: and, in an instant . . . is wafted . . . full three thousand leagues to the precise scene of action" (*F* 3:320). Such seems to be the case with the rescuing vessel, the *Jane Guy*, as she wafts Pym and Peters southward toward the pole. Surviving another terrible gale, Captain Guy, using a central word of the story, calls the escape of his vessel "little less than miraculous" (*P* 1:148–50). Pym himself seems marvelously to have grown in authority; at every chance he urges the captain on: "(For in some way, hardly known to myself, I had acquired much influence over him)" (*P* 1:170). Soon they will be making decisions together (*P* 1:172).

On and on to real islands with suggestive names they sail, and they seek the vanishing islands of the Auroras (*P* 1:156–58). In discussing their visit to Tristan d'Acunha, Pym refers to an Englishman by the name of Glass (mentioned in Morrell's original account), a corporal in the British artillery who claimed to be the governor (*P* 1:156), and he later mentions "the search for Glass's Islands" (*P* 1:162). It is intriguing to think that Poe again may be hinting with his use of "British" and the name "Glass." The Otherworld island of Celtic myth, later called Avalon, the modern Glastonbury, to which Arthur once sailed and returned at the end, was the Isle of Glass or the hidden Glass Island—

the White Island of the White Goddess. A second intriguing point is Poe's introduction of the Auroras, for one of the Goddess's signs was the aurora or veil, and at the end of Pym's voyage we do find the aurora, and Pym speaks of white birds flying from "beyond the veil" (*P* 1:206).

Near this point, indeed, the *Jane Guy* seems to sail out of reality into the realm of pure myth—and on to Tsalal Island. On the way, the seamen have a series of suggestively symbolic encounters with what Burton Pollin terms a "melange of animal life" (*P* 1:317). First flies by "a large bird of a brilliant blue plumage" (*P* 1:164), reminiscent of Isis in Egyptian art, shifting her shape to a bird with outstretched wings, sometimes of a wonderful blue color. Then the men meet "a gigantic creature of the race of the Arctic bear" (*P* 1:164–65), reminding us that both the *Cambrian Biography* and Rees' *Cyclopaedia* say that, "Arthur is the Great Bear, as the epithet literally implies," and both works continue by stating that the Bear is a constellation "so near" the North pole.[64] The *Britannica* repeats the story told by Giraldis Cambrensis of the finding of Arthur's "grave" in 1189 "encased in a hollow oak." Cambrensis reports that his bones "were so huge. . . . And the skull was so large and capacious as to be a portent or prodigy."[65] The oak-tree burial may have either suggested or been suggested by the legend of Arthur carried to the island of Avalon in a barge. Further along, Pym and his fellows come on a "low rocky islet" where they find "a piece of wood, which seemed to have formed the prow of a canoe" (*P* 1:165).

Next they pick up "a bush, full of red berries, like those of the hawthorn, and the carcass of a singular-looking land-animal" (*P* 1:167). In Celtic legend the white hawthorn is a sacred bush. The red berries, however, suggest the magical rowan, beloved of the White Goddess and guarded by a dragon. Its berries were, along with the apple and the "red nut" of the hazel, "the food of the gods," "the food of dead heroes," planted near "oracular places" and "in the neighborhood of ancient stone circles" such as Stonehenge.[66] The strange "land-animal" with cat's head, dog's ears, silky white hair, the tail of a rat, and scarlet claws and teeth, recalling Demeter-Hecate's and Morgana's transformations and tree guardianship, suggests that what Arthur Pym encounters may involve not only symbolism, but also shape shifting.[67] Here possibly is another manifestation of the White Goddess's magic, soon to call forth through this beast such fascination and hatred by the islanders of Tsalal (*P* 1:190).

On Tsalal Island, the seamen find that the black inhabitants have some strange symbols of their own. Their canoe bottoms are full of egg-sized black stones, and a small rock guards each hovel in their village. Bryant says that the Egyptians "shewed a reverential regard to fragments of rock, which were particularly uncouth and horrid: and this practice seems to have prevailed in many other countries." He goes on to refer to the Celts and Stonehenge (*B* 5:200–201). The stone, in fact, is one of the four talismans of their Otherworld.[68] Later a stone is seen as the Grail itself; Percival is told that it is called "lapsit exillis," "a stone falling from heaven" with marvelous powers of regeneration.[69] It is related to sacred rocks like the Black Stone of Mecca.[70] And, when the Romans began to worship Cybele, they brought from Phrygia "the small black stone which embodied the mighty divinity."[71] So Tsalal may be the once-fertile wasteland itself, degenerating with a degenerating king, no longer aware of the meaning of its stones or of their connection to the White Goddess and to the Grail.

Related to all this is the islanders' seeing the *Jane Guy* as "a living creature" (*P* 1:169).[72] Later, after murdering her seamen, the natives drag the ship ashore and set it afire in a sort of pyre. When the vessel explodes, throwing the strange white beast among them, they swarm about it pointing and crying "*Tekeli-li! Tekeli-li!*" (*P* 1:190), words seemingly associated with their abhorrence of whiteness. Perhaps they recognize the ship as the personification not just of all things white, which they abominate, but of the White Enchantress herself.

On the island, one or two formidable serpents, reminders of the Goddess, cross Pym's path, and fish and wild fowl crowd the streams, an echo of the Fisher King (*P* 1:173–74). The water is veined in purple like "changeable silk," the life blood of the Goddess, or the wine of the Grail cup (*P* 1:172).[73] Bryant tells of a temple and statue of Isis "situated near some hot springs." And he adds, "One reason for holding waters so sacred arose from a notion, that they were gifted with supernatural powers" (*B* 1:255–56). Pym, in one of the most striking passages of the whole book, states: "The phenomena of this water formed the first definite link in that vast chain of apparent miracles with which I was destined to be at length encircled" (*P* 1:172).

There are other suggestions that the islanders see the boat as the Goddess. Among the puzzling clues offered by Poe is the language of the islanders; specifically intriguing are the words called out at the approach of the ship, "*Anamoo-moo!* and *Lama-Lama!*" as well as later, "*Tekeli-li! Tekeli-li!*" (*P* 1:168, 190). These have been attributed to languages from Maori-Polynesian to Hebrew (*P* 1:318). Hernández del Castillo, however, sees "*Anamoo-moo!*" and "*Tekeli-li!*" as compounded from basic "radicals," which Bryant draws up and from which he says most names in mythology have been compounded (*B* 1:1). "Ana" recurs in ancient mythologies as the Mother Goddess, and Hernández del Castillo sees the "*moo-moo*" as suggesting the moon.[74] Anthon says that in Rome Ana became Anna Perenna, whose festival was on 15 March. She "reposes for ever in the river Numicius, and runs on for ever with it. She is the course of the moons, of the years, of time." Graves says she is a sister of Belus, or Bel, who was a masculinization of the Sumerian Goddess Belili.[75] "*Tekeli-li,*" as Hernández del Castillo points out, resembles her name closely, as it does that of Ishtar Kilili, "a twofold goddess, the creator and the destroyer."[76] Interestingly, *tek-* is an aorist stem of the Greek word *tikto,* meaning "to bring forth, to bear," and the verbal noun *tekousa* means "mother."[77] Anthon, though not mentioning Ishtar, does discuss Astarte of Syria. Anthon sees Astarte as a form of the Great Goddess, "precisely the same as the Cybele . . . by some called Juno, by others Venus, and by others held up to be nature."[78] Poe was very aware of Astarte, we know, using her name to identify the evening star, Venus, in "Ulalume" (*M* 1:416–17). And in *Pinakidia* he refers to the temple of Belus (*P* 2:87).

Cybele, one of the strongest of these goddesses, achieved her greatest fame through her love of Attis. Her spring festival, beginning on 15 March, reached its height with the coming of her lover on the 22nd and continued through his castration, death, and resurrection on the 25th. In the frenzied celebration, her followers slashed and even castrated themselves to appease the Goddess. Regarding the amputated penises, Frazer suggests, "These broken instruments of fertility were afterwards reverently wrapt up and buried in the earth or in subterranean chambers sacred to Cybele," probably to regenerate the land.[79]

Finally, there is a distinct possibility that the phrase "*Lama-Lama!*" too relates to the White Goddess and may be a contraction of *lamia.* Liddell and Scott's *Greek-English Lexicon* identifies the word *lamia* in Greek as "a fabulous monster" from *lamos,* meaning "yawning, profound, voracious, coquettish."[80] Morgana herself is connected with "the lamia, Morrigan." Closer even to Poe and Pym are the recreations of the creature, part woman, part serpent, in Coleridge's "Christabel" and Keats' *Lamia.* All her characteristics—the sea habitat, the serpents, the shape shifting, and her beauty versus her deadly whiteness—seem to suggest that she is a third version of the Goddess in the language of Tsalal.

At length, as the natives ambush the seamen, Pym and Peters turn aside into a "fissure in the . . . rock" (*P* 1:181).[81] This cavern gives evidence of being at once the Chapel Perilous and the White Goddess's grotto from which only a hero need try to escape.[82] Bryant speaks at length of caverns and hollows which were thought to be the residences of gods, saying "that the Deity had always a rock or cavern for his temple" (*B* 1:269, 277). He adds that these caverns served as sites of mysteries and initiations (*B* 1:286).

The mazelike passages in which Pym and Peters find themselves entombed contain certain images suggestive of the mysteries. There is the strangely marked wall ("To be shady," "To be white,") with the figure seeming to point toward "the south"—a figure with extended phallus, related to Cybele's strange rites (*P* 1:192–96, 207–8). Most important, there is "a vast heap of sharp flints somewhat resembling arrowheads in shape," again described as "white arrowhead flints" (*P* 1:194). Graves points out that the arrowhead in Roman Brittany was used only for funerary or for magical purposes. In magical rites, the flints were sacred to the Goddess in her third, darker persona—"the Moon-goddess as hag." In the story of Attis, a sharp flintstone is the instrument of castration.[83]

Fallen from the wall "among the powder" are "several large flakes of the marl" (*P* 1:195). As Pollin says, "The mysterious powder will become a theme in the rest of the work" (*P* 1:342). Graves tells us that the White Goddess's most widespread emblem is the *omphalos,* or round white rock at Delphi, originally, perhaps, a "raised white mound of tightly-packed ash," later identified with a "mound of sea-shells, or quartz, or white marble, underneath which dead kings were buried."[84] This then could be her white powder, these her white bolts on the cavern floor. Perhaps both the black rocks and this black granite passage represent her opposites, but perhaps, as the dark Morgana, she still rules within these caves.

Outside, beneath the cliff, the ground is strewn with "huge tumuli, apparently the wreck of some gigantic structures of art"—like ancient Stonehenge (*P* 1:198). Rees' *Cyclopaedia* connects Stonehenge through the *Welsh Triads* to Merlin, speculating that it was a center of Celtic mystery rites and sacrifices.[85] Close to the cavern grow hazel bushes with their deep red filberts, as they are said to grow near the magical circles of the Celts. Nearby are two deep holes—wells, Poe suggests (*P* 1:196). The passageways of the White Goddess to and from her underground labyrinths are streams and wells; at both Delphi and Mycenae, deep wells still mark her ancient presence. Her loveliest white mansions, though, those "splendid illusive palaces," Faber says, "float upon the surface of the sea" (*F* 3:321).[86]

Fulfillment comes as Pym and Peters flee the island, descending by the steep cliff. Pym's whole soul is "pervaded with *a longing to fall,*" but "a shrill-sounding and phantom voice screamed within my ears; a dusky, fiendish, and filmy figure stood immediately beneath me; and, sighing, I sunk down with a bursting heart, and plunged within its arms." His loathsome guide has become the saving spirit. Reborn, like Perceval, through journey and sacrifice, Pym says simply, "I felt a new being" (*P* 1:198). He too is finally ready in the rites of romance to glimpse the Grail, to meet the Goddess.

Near the end of his quest, Sir Galahad attains the Grail and partakes of its marvels. He then leaves the sinning wasteland for the Grail castle, setting sail with Perceval and Bors in the magical small "Ship of Solomon," which once belonged to that king and which now bears the body of Perceval's sister.[87] So, in a variant form—or in coincidence—Pym sets sail with Peters and the dying Nu-Nu, a native who tells them that the islanders "were governed by a common king, named *Tsalemon* or *Psalemoun*" (*P* 1:203). Now, "a fine white powder, resembling ashes—but certainly not such" falls over the canoe, and the aurora streaks the sky (*P* 1:204–5).

Twenty-two March fast approaches. Emma Jung says that the Arthurian Grail legends belong to the "springtide of the spirit" because they are identified with spiritual awakening. In the legends, there often occurs "*a numinous experience of this inner psychic wholeness . . .* usually accompanied by profound emotion."[88] So in *Pym* the vast aurora—"a limitless cataract," a "gigantic curtain," like the *ventum textilem,* "woven air," "woven snow," of Isis that Poe mentions in other works—looms ahead and a chasm opens "to receive us" (*P* 1:205–6).[89] Then the vision comes—perhaps only a mirage like those that came to the wasteland wanderers, or perhaps the real saving prowhead of a vessel like the *Penguin*. It is an ambiguous figure. And in the Grail vision, "In looking at the idea *behind* the symbol, we seem to catch a glimpse of a dual natured Grail figure . . . contained within a single image of wholeness, the Grail."[90]

But there is one other face, one other myth that rises even beyond the ideal of the Grail in Pym's white figure. At the end of Arthur's life, Malory tells us, there comes "a queen," with many fair ladies. He writes, "'Now put mee into the barge,' said the king . . . and there received him three queenes with great mourning, and so these three queenes set them downe, and in one of their laps king Arthur laide his head."[91] Other accounts tell us that they included the Lady of the Lake and Morgan le Fay. They do not tell us the name of the third, but our own voyage of exploration has given us that name also—Guinevere. The three are but varying manifestations of Gwenhwyvar, the lady of the waters—the White Goddess, who has come to carry Arthur to the White Island at the end of the world.

And so perhaps Arthur Pym glimpses, too, that ancient, eternal figure embodied anew in Arthur's Gwenhwyvar. Here is her southern throne, attended by her symbols of white ashy powder, white birds, and luminous aurora. As in Celtic Faërie, drawn by the Enchantress, Pym feels "a *numbness* of body and mind—a dreaminess of sensation—but this was all" (*P* 1:204). One of the strange beasts drifts by, and many "pallidly white birds flew continuously now from beyond the veil" (*P* 1:205–6). The spring equinox has come. And so Gwenhwyvar rises again for a new young Arthur. She is—in myth, legend, and fable—fresh and youthful, yet older than time, the queen of both life and death—her skin "of the perfect whiteness of the snow" (*P* 1:206).

Thus it seems possible that Poe drew deeply from past literature and myth in creating *Pym*. It seems, indeed, very possible that somewhere in his reading about the journey into light of "this wild and beautiful fiction" of the Arthurian Grail quest (*F* 3:319), Poe caught the glimmer of his own white vision. "Here begin the terrors. / Here begin the miracles," writes the Grail poet. The mystery at the heart of *The Narrative of Arthur Gordon Pym* may in the end be most nearly understood in its most enigmatic statement, that one by one links were being forged "in that vast chain of apparent miracles with which I was destined to be at length encircled" (*P* 1:172).

Pym, the Dighton Rock, and the Matter of Vinland

Joseph J. Moldenhauer

 Among the verifiable and possible sources for *The Narrative of Arthur Gordon Pym*, exhaustively summarized by Burton R. Pollin in his introductory essay and annotations to the first volume of *Collected Writings of Edgar Allan Poe*, we find no mention of a group of works belonging to what might be called "the matter of Vinland"—works dealing with the discovery of America by Scandinavian navigators in the late tenth and early eleventh centuries. These texts, falling variously into the genres of historical writing, anthropology, folk epic, exploration literature, and nautical adventure, enjoyed a perennial interest for American readers and received a strong infusion of publicity at precisely the time Poe was readying his novel for the press. The coincidence of Poe's completion of *Pym* with the conspicuous debut of an edition of the sagas relating to Vinland, accompanied by scientific arguments that Vineyard Sound and Narraganset Bay were the sites of the Norsemen's bases, invites a close study of parallels between that work and the novel. The parallels range from broad similarities of theme, plot, and character representation to local matters of imagery and symbolism—especially in the Tsalalian episodes and in the concluding "Note." In particular, Poe's exploitation of hieroglyphic and secret writing, of archaic tongues, and of the enigmas of interpreting obscure texts finds a stimulus and antecedent in the debate over the so-called Picture Rock on Assonet Neck in the Taunton River near Dighton, Massachusetts—a debate revitalized by a newly published antiquarian effort to use the rock as physical confirmation of the Viking presence in America. (See figure 1.)

My argument for the influence of this Vinland material presupposes that the text of *Pym* was not fixed at the time Harper and Brothers registered the title for copyright in June 1837 but rather that Poe continued to modify it and to add material, especially to the concluding episodes, during the thirteen months that intervened before the novel was published in July 1838. I share this assumption with Pollin, Joseph Ridgely, and Richard Kopley.[1] Alexander Hammond effectively ques-

Figure 1. View of Dighton Rock, based on a sketch by Thomas H. Webb, Albert G. Greene, and John R. Bartlett, in *Antiquitates Americanae*. Courtesy of Bucknell University Library.

tions certain aspects of logic and evidence in Ridgely's essays on the composition of *Pym* but falls short of establishing that the text reached its final state by the time of the initial copyright registration.[2]

It would be difficult to exaggerate the potential interest to Poe, in the last months of 1837 and the first half of 1838, of a publication sharing so many characteristics with the final form of his novel. The story—or rather the series of related stories—concerns adventurous and culturally advanced white men from a far northern clime, journeying southward through uncharted seas to new lands: first, a place of icebergs and barren rocks; next, a forested region; and, finally, a land of extraordinarily mild climate and luxuriant vegetation. In two of the tales, the expedition's leader and hero is accompanied by outlandish retainers. The white explorers encounter in the southernmost region a dark, ugly, and hostile race of hunters who live in caves and holes. These savages display a naive and dangerous curiosity about metal edge-tools; eager to trade their native goods for weapons, scraps of bright cloth, and cow's milk, they are readier yet to come in a flotilla of canoes for a concerted attack upon the pale strangers. A reconnoitering party, shipwrecked on a deserted stretch of coast, erects a broken keel as a memorial. Add to this the taking of native captives in one of the narratives and the rumor, in another, of an even earlier advent of Europeans to the new continent, one of whom is regarded as the patriarch of a native tribe.

In each of the major Vinland sagas, the Northmen return to their homes in Greenland or Iceland when they obtain a cargo of rare wood or fruit or furs, or when harassment by the aborigines weakens their resolve or deprives them of their leader. According to hints in some of the lesser documents, a sporadic commerce and missionary efforts are maintained on the North American littoral for three centuries after the initial discovery. Thereafter, until the eighteenth century, knowledge of the new world is preserved only in the oral traditions of an isolated people and in a few ecclesiastical manuscripts founded on those legends. In the 1837 publication, the Vinland tales, now treated as valid historical records, are collected for the educated world at large, with a scholarly apparatus intended to settle definitively the questions of who discovered America and when and where the sightings and landings took place.

Announced in the periodical press and in prospectuses from the editor for several years in advance, this work was issued in the autumn of 1837 under the title *Antiquitates Americanae, sive Scriptores Septentrionales Rerum Ante-Columbianarum in America* (American antiquities, or writings by northern authors about American matters prior to Columbus). The Danish Royal Society of Northern Antiquaries, Copenhagen, was the publisher of record,[3] and in the United States the book seems to have been distributed by the reputable New York publisher William Jackson. The project's editor and moving force was Carl Christian Rafn, secretary of the Royal Society and an indefatigable advocate for the claims of Viking influence in both the Eastern and Western Hemispheres. *Antiquitates Americanae* consisted of portions of eighteen ancient narratives and geographical writings, edited from medieval manuscripts. The sagas were presented in the original Icelandic, modern Danish, and Latin. An editor's preface (in Latin)

authenticated the manuscripts and summarized prior published translations and paraphrases. The forematter included a lengthy English
"Abstract" of the main historical, geographical, and ethnographic par-
ticulars of the Vinland sagas. Following the texts, which bear footnotes
on manuscript collation and linguistic detail, Rafn and his principal collaborator Finn Magnusen described archaeological remains in
Greenland and New England, deciphered the Dighton inscription, reasoned out geographical equivalents between the saga place references
and modern maps, calculated the latitude of Vinland from a sentence in
one saga, speculated on the etymology of place names, and presented
Rafn's correspondence with American antiquaries. There followed a
group of beautiful facsimiles of the codices and then plates showing
known Norse runic inscriptions from Greenland, Iceland, and Scan-
dinavia, and depicting New World petroglyphs. These last, chiefly a
series of transcriptions of the Dighton Rock, are construed as verify-
ing a sojourn by one of the Viking parties in the vicinity of Taunton
River, in what is now southeastern Massachusetts. Rafn's volume concludes with maps of Iceland, Southwest Greenland, the North Atlantic
perimeter, and the coast of Massachusetts and Rhode Island, illustrat-
ing the Northmen's maritime sphere and outposts.

The bulk of the narrative material in *Antiquitates Americanae* derives from two manuscripts: a life of Eric the Red in the Flatey Codex
and a "History of Thorfinn Karlsefne" in the Arne Magnusson collection. In the following paraphrase, I will add parenthetically Rafn's assignment of modern geographical equivalents for the places described
in the sagas. I will refrain from detailed commentary on parallels between the topography, climate, and natural productions of lands visited
by the Northmen and Poe's *Jane Guy,* between the Northmen and Pym
and his white companions, between artifacts found on shore by the two
groups of travelers, between the Vinland savages (Skrellings) and the
Tsalalians, between the Skrelling and Tsalalian traditions about their
own people and about distant folk with advanced skills, and between
the "foreign" attendants of the Norse heroes and the anomalous Dirk
Peters; these should be reasonably evident to readers of *Pym.*

In 986 A.D., Biarne the son of Heriulf, on his way to the young
Greenland colony, was blown far off course to the southwest; he
sighted, but did not explore, three new regions. Eager to win fame,
Leif, the son of Eric the Red, bought Biarne's ship in 1000 and went to
sea with a crew that included a German named Tyrker. Leif landed first

on the coast Biarne had last seen (Newfoundland), a land of icy mountains and flat stones that he named Helluland. Farther south he put ashore on a low, timbered coast with white sand cliffs (Nova Scotia), which he called Markland. After sailing two more days before a northeast wind, he and his men came to an island (Nantucket) just south of a long promontory (Cape Cod). Cruising westward through shallow seas, they landed at a place where a river (the Taunton), draining a lake (Mount Hope Bay), entered the sea. The party ascended the river and built "booths" or shelters for the winter. In this land of warmth and plenty, salmon thronged the stream, the frosts were so mild that the grass hardly withered, and one day Tyrker returned ecstatically from a scouting excursion with a report of wild grapes—hence, Vinland the Good. (For a map of Vinland, see figure 2.) Leif's brother Thorwald next felt the roving instinct. In 1002, using Leif's ship, he voyaged to Vinland and wintered in Leif's booths. The next summer he dispatched a sea party southwestward (perhaps as far as Delaware) which found no trace of man apart from a vacant shed on an island. Then Thorwald explored the coast to the east and north. Caught in a storm, his ship was driven aground on a remarkable headland (Cape Cod), shattering its keel. This broken timber was erected as a landmark when the company had repaired the vessel. Continuing round to the west (into Massachusetts Bay), they found a handsome wooded point at the mouth of a firth (probably the Gurnet in Plymouth Bay), where Thorwald decided to settle. On a nearby shore, the Northmen surprised nine Skrellings or Eskimos concealed beneath skin canoes. They captured and killed eight; the ninth escaped and brought a horde of his fellows to attack the strangers; and Thorwald incurred a mortal arrow wound. His people returned to Greenland.

In 1007, Thorfinn Karlsefne mounted a large expedition of 160 men, with livestock, in three ships, touching at Helluland and at Markland, where they killed a bear on an island. Far to the south, they found the ship's-keel memorial of Thorwald, and they called the long headland Wonder-strands (the beaches of Nauset, Chatham, and Monomoy). Rounding the southernmost point of the Cape, they set on shore two Scots, prodigious runners. This odd couple returned in three days, bearing grapes and ears of wild grain. Continuing westward, they came to a deep inlet (Buzzard's Bay) at whose mouth was an island crowded with nesting fowl (Martha's Vineyard, or Egg Island off the entrance of Vineyard Sound). Here the party divided, a small

Figure 2. Map of Vinland in *Antiquitates Americanae*. Courtesy of Bucknell University Library.

group under Thorfinn's companion, Thorhall Gamlason, sailing back along Wonder-strands (where a westerly gale blew them to Ireland), and Thorfinn and 150 settlers continuing to a tidal river draining a lake, which they called Hop (Mount Hope Bay, the site of Leif's booths). Finding abundant fish, grapevines, and wild grain, they built dwellings and pastured their cattle in the open field year-round. Savages in great numbers came in canoes to barter furs for red cloth and milk, which they obtained at exorbitant rates, though Thorfinn wisely forbade the trading of weapons. The bellowing of the Northmen's bull terrified the natives and they fled but returned presently with slings and a strange engine of war like a ballista, wounding and almost routing the Europeans. In a later engagement, Thorfinn killed five Skrellings dressed in skins, who ate a paste of animal blood and marrow; in a third encounter, one of the Northmen was slain by a uniped(!) armed with bow and arrows. After investigating the landforms of Vinland, Thorfinn captured two Skrelling boys in Markland on the return voyage, taught them Norse, and learned from them the political organization and the customs of their people. According to their report, a distant region was occupied by men who wore white clothing and carried poles and banners (perhaps masts and sails); the Northmen thought this was "Great Ireland" (the coast south of Chesapeake Bay), where, according to another saga, the Icelander Are Marson lived as a chief after having been driven across the sea by a tempest in 983 A.D. A number of minor narratives and geographical commentaries, from ancient vellum codices, fill out the original Vinland material in Rafn's volume.

Even if Poe failed to read *Antiquitates Americanae* in book form, he is highly likely to have known its narrative and scholarly substance through a number of derivative publications. William Jackson reprinted the English abstract as a 32-page pamphlet, *America Discovered in the Tenth Century*, in January or February 1838.[4] Several lengthy, analytic reviews of *Antiquitates Americanae* appeared between January and May in journals that Poe routinely examined. The earliest and most influential review was by Edward Everett, the famous orator, former congressman, and current governor of Massachusetts, in the *North American Review* for January.[5] (Poe repeatedly cited the staid *North American* and its editors, usually in disparagement and sometimes parodically, e.g., "North American Quarterly Humdrum" [M 2:622].)[6] This journal had given a preliminary notice to *Antiquitates Americanae* as early as July 1836, citing a prospectus dated 1835 and reporting that the work was "about to be published at Copenhagen."[7] In March 1838, the *Knickerbocker* began an installment on "Scandinavian Literature and Antiquities" with a quotation from Everett's essay and a favorable reference to the Danish Society's studies relating to America. A short literary notice of *Antiquitates Americanae* later in the same issue of the *Knickerbocker* also showed the influence of Everett's review.[8] The book was the occasion of a two-installment article in the *Democratic Review* for April and May.[9] In April it was covered in the *New York Review*, the magazine to which Poe had contributed his October 1837 piece on Stephens' *Incidents of Travel in Egypt, Arabia Petraea, and the Holy Land*, another source for the final chapters and "Note" of *Pym*.[10] Like the *Knickerbocker* and the *North American Review*, this magazine makes reference to the long-announced and long-expected publication of the book; the reviewer observes at the outset that the volume "did not reach our hands in season to receive a notice in our last [January] number." It had, however, reached Everett in time for him to prepare his thoughtful appraisal prior to the final printer's deadline (about 1 December) for the January *North American*. ("It has fallen into our hands," Everett wrote, "while the last sheets of this number of our Journal are passing through the press.")[11] Another April review, also containing a reference to Everett's, appeared in the *American Monthly Magazine*, which in January had noted the publication of the volume and its availability in the United States.[12] If the April issue of the *Foreign Quarterly Review* (London) was received in New York before the publication of *Pym* at the end of July, Poe could have seen the long review there—one which would be reprinted in the *Museum of Foreign Literature* (Philadelphia) in August.[13] Although my search of American and foreign magazines has been far from exhaustive, I should mention finally the more interesting of two items on *Antiquitates Americanae* in Horace Greeley's *New-Yorker*: a review (31 March 1838) of a series of *lectures* on the Northmen and their voyages to America, lately delivered by George Folsom to a large audience at the Stuyvesant Institute.[14] This account dominates the front page and includes a conspicuous cut of the supposed Romano-Runic inscription on the Dighton Rock. The petroglyph was "perhaps the most important evidence" in support of the Danish antiquarians' "recently published" theory, a theory evidently accepted without reservation by Folsom and the *New-Yorker* columnist, as it was by most reviewers.

The tradition that the northern coasts of America had been visited by Northmen had been ingrained in New World historiography since before Poe's birth, affording matter for poets as well as historians throughout the first half of the nineteenth century. First proposed by Ortelius in 1570, the notion that Columbus had been anticipated by Norse voyagers five centuries before 1492 was elaborated by Paul Henri Mallet and John Reinhold Forster in influential histories translated into English in 1770 and 1786.[15] Their sources for the Vinland journeys include the very rare treatises of the Icelandic scholar Torfaeus (1705, 1706), based on ancient manuscripts; Jonas Arngrim's earlier history of Greenland; and the eleventh-century ecclesiastical history by Adam of Bremen. A passing allusion to Vinland in Snorri Sturluson's thirteenth-century *Heimskringla*, or chronicle of the kings of Norway, was supplemented, in Peringskiöld's Swedish translation (1697), by eight chapters about the Vinland voyages from an indeterminate manuscript.

Among the earlier American historians, Jeremy Belknap devoted the first chapter of *American Biography* (1794) to Biarne and Leif.[16] Using Forster as his source, Washington Irving reports the traditions of Vinland in an appendix to *Life and Voyages of Christopher Columbus* (1828), the next appendix of which Poe used in a "Marginalia" item (1846).[17] Another of Irving's sources is the geographer Malte-Brun, who suggests (following Ortelius) that Columbus heard about Vinland when he visited Iceland in 1477. *A System of Universal Geography* (in the abridged 1834 Boston translation of the *Précis*) has been proposed as a source for a detail in *Pym* (P 1:352), but it should be observed that Everett summarizes Malte-Brun's remarks from the full French text in his review of *Antiquitates Americanae*. Everett also speaks of Humboldt's defense of Columbus against the discredit implied in Ortelius' comment, citing the German savant's *Examen critique de l'histoire de la géographie du nouveau continent*. Furthermore, Forster, Belknap, William Robertson in *Discovery and Settlement of America* (1777; reprinted by the Harpers throughout the 1830s), Irving, and the American Henry Wheaton in *History of the Northmen* (1831), in addition to the older Scandinavian sources such as Torfaeus, likewise fall within the range of Everett's citations. He observes that in the first edition of *The History of the United States* (1834), a book Poe knew, George Bancroft conjectures that Vinland was merely a southern region of Greenland.[18] The same hypothesis was asserted by Hugh Murray in *Narrative of Discovery and Adventure in the Polar Seas*, a work coauthored with John Leslie and Robert Jameson, reprinted by the Harpers in 1831, and offered, together with Morrell's *A Narrative of Four Voyages* and other pertinent works of discovery and marine adventure, in a bound-in advertising section of *Pym* (P 1:215).

Even before the publication of *Antiquitates Americanae* and its reviews, Poe probably came up against the "problem" of Scandinavian claims to priority over Columbus in his study of historical and geographical authorities whom he respected, like Humboldt and Malte-Brun. Until Rafn, however, no scholar had attempted to prove those claims systematically and scientifically. In the absence of precise nautical documentation, like that for Columbus' landfalls at San Salvador Island (Samana Cay) and Cuba on his first voyage, the notion of Norse precedence had remained safely vague and legendary.

Poe's English and American contemporaries were touched in manifold ways by enthusiasm for Scandinavian subjects. Besides prose translations of sagas, histories, and modern travel books, there were such literary uses as Carlyle's first lecture in *Heroes and Hero-Worship* (1841); Tegner's verse rendition of an Icelandic narrative called *Frithiof's Saga* (1835, widely reviewed in journals read by Poe, including the *North American*, where the notice was by Longfellow);[19] Longfellow's own metrical and substantive adaptations of sagas and "The Skeleton in Armor" (1841)—a ballad, admired by Poe, whose thesis is the Viking identity of a body exhumed at Fall River; Whittier's "The Norsemen" (1841), which accepts as a fact "now very generally admitted" that the ancient Scandinavians visited New England; Thoreau's incorporation of matter from Rafn in *Cape Cod*; James Russell Lowell's parodic treatment of the Dighton Rock, Rafn, and the processes of scholarly decipherment in *The Biglow Papers*, first series (1848), no. 7, and second series (1867), nos. 3, 4, and 5; and Lydia Sigourney's *Scenes in My Native Land* (1845). Sigourney devotes a poem and two pages of commentary to the old tower at Newport (claimed, in the years immediately following *Antiquitates Americanae*, to be a Viking construction), mentions the skeleton in armor, cites Rafn, implicitly chides Irving for his skepticism in the *Columbus* appendix, and takes the Vinland hypothesis as a matter of "grave history."[20]

A desultory survey of major American magazines in the eighteen months immediately preceding the publication of *Pym* also attests to the burgeoning lay interest in North and Central American anthropology and archaeology. The bearing of such articles on *Pym* and on the cultural environment for the reception of *Antiquitates Americanae* is clear. Early in Poe's tenure as editor, the *Southern Literary Messenger* for February 1836 printed a piece called "Sketches of Lake Superior," with references to the "Pictured Rocks." The reviews in the July 1836 issue, probably all by Poe, include *Life on the Lakes*, a book about a trip to the "Pictured Rocks of Lake Superior," illustrated by an "abominable" plate of the pictographs.[21] The *American Monthly Magazine* for January 1836, in an article on "American Antiquities," considered the armored skeleton found at Fall River in 1834; provided an engraving of the skeleton, breastplate, and arrowheads; and conjectured that the bones were those of a Phoenician.[22] The *Knickerbocker* for 1837 printed a three-part series on "American Antiquities"—a piece that concentrates on pre-Columbian Mexican structures but also makes passing reference to the "repeated discovery" of America "by the 'North-men,' and probably by others, from the ninth to the twelfth centuries."[23] Another essay on Mexican antiquities in the *Democratic Review*, October 1837, alludes to the southwestward excursions of the Northmen from Greenland as among the many stories and reputed evidences of knowledge of America by the European ancients. The essay mentions "tumuli"—a term used in *Antiquitates Americanae* and in *Pym*—as well as glyphs, and refers to the myth of "Quetzalcoalt [*sic*]," "the white and bearded man . . . whom the Mexicans traditionally revered."[24] The earlier-mentioned March 1838 *Knickerbocker* essay on "Scandinavian Literature and Antiquities" expatiates on "inscribed rocks" in many parts of America, particularly in the northern states. If the antiquaries can decipher Scandinavian runes, writes the author in phrases anticipating *Pym*, "why have we not reason to hope that those of our own country may yet be unravelled, and their contents made known? . . . A wide field for antiquarian research . . . is still open; and we trust that the growing interest in these subjects may yet lead to important discoveries. [Compare *Pym*, "a wide field . . . for discovery" and "a wide field for speculation and exciting conjecture," P 1:162, 208.] The vast tumuli and mounds of the West, the ancient fortified places, the numerous relics of a demi-civilized people, and the sculptured rocks, are yet involved in the most impenetrable mystery."[25]

The North American artifact most often mentioned in writings on Indian antiquities is the "celebrated" or "famous" Dighton Rock, to give it its customary epithets. Discussions of this petroglyph occur in nine of the eleven contemporary announcements, reviews, and citations of *Antiquitates Americanae* that I have examined, in a *North American*

Review essay (April 1837) on Drake's *Biography and History of the Indians*,[26] and in the *American Monthly Magazine*'s January 1836 archaeological piece. The last of these, for example, says the Dighton Rock is "famed for its hieroglyphic inscription, of which no sufficient explanation has yet been given"; reviewing *Antiquitates Americanae* two years later, the same magazine mentions the "Writing Rocks" on the Taunton drainage and holds the skeleton in armor to be "undoubtedly one of the Northmen who came over in these expeditions."[27]

The Dighton Rock inscription, pecked into the boulder with a tool of metal or hard stone, had been copied or transcribed repeatedly since the seventeenth century. Published drawings include those by John Danforth (1680), Cotton Mather (1712), Isaac Greenwood (1730), Stephen Sewall ("Sewell") (1768), James Winthrop (1788), and the English traveler Edward Augustus Kendall (1807).[28] These six drawings are reproduced in *Antiquitates Americanae*, together with those by "Dr. Baylies and Mr. Goodwin" (1790)—actually Joseph Gooding for Judge William Baylies and others—and Job Gardner of Dighton (1812); also included is an illustration based on a drawing made in 1834 (mistakenly reported as 1830), at Rafn's request, by Thomas H. Webb and two other members of the Rhode Island Historical Society. (See figures 3, 4, and 5.) Plates representing the markings on inscription rocks at nearby Portsmouth and Tiverton, as drawn for Rafn by the Historical Society in 1835, are also provided.

John T. Irwin has observed in *American Hieroglyphics*[29] that Humboldt devotes two pages to the Dighton Rock and its probable lack of hieroglyphic significance in *Researches, Concerning the Institutions & Monuments of the Ancient Inhabitants of America* (1814), a work which deals extensively with Aztec inscriptions. Irwin considers the Humboldt passage as a possible source for Poe's letter-shaped pits, ambiguous petroglyphs, and hermeneutic speculations in *Pym* but neglects the journalistic context in 1836–38. The magazines frequently exhibited the Dighton Rock as a puzzling curiosity and, in reviews of *Antiquitates Americanae*, variously endorsed or questioned Rafn's use of the rock as an archaeological proof of Viking settlements in southern New England. Everett, for instance, remarks that the facsimile transcripts "differ materially from each other, some of them so much so as with difficulty to be recognised as copies of the same original." Rafn and Finn Magnusen read the inscription as a monument of Thorfinn's visit in 1007–9; as Everett summarizes their interpretation, "The [human]

figures represent the personages of his family; . . . certain characters supposed to be numerals, express the number CXXXI, to which
his party was reduced after the departure of Thorhall; and . . . other
characters, deemed Runic, record the occupation of the country by
him and his followers." Acknowledging that many of the carvings are
rude delineations of men and beasts, Everett cites alternative explanations to convey his skepticism about the meanings assigned by Rafn:
"By some persons the characters are regarded as Phenician [sic]. The
late Mr. Samuel Harris, of [Boston], a very learned Orientalist, thought
he found the Hebrew word *melek* (king) in those characters, which the
editor of the work before us regards as numerals signifying CXXXI.
Colonel Vallancey considers them to be Scythian, and Messrs. Rafn and
Magnussen think them indubitably Runic. In this great diversity of
judgment a decision is extremely difficult."[30] After paraphrasing Rafn's
"highly skilful and ingenious geographical commentary" and examining certain fabulous elements in the Vinland sagas, Everett reverts to
the Dighton Rock:

> We remain wholly unconvinced in reference to its interpretation by
> the learned and ingenious commentaries of our friends at Copen-
> hagen. The representations of the human figures and animals appear
> to us too rude for civilized artists. . . . They greatly resemble the
> figures which the Indians paint on the smooth side of their buffalo
> skins. The characters supposed to be numerals certainly resemble the
> Roman signs for unity and for ten; but every straight mark resembles I,
> and every cross resembles X. In the characters supposed to be Runes,
> we behold no resemblance to the only specimens of Runes we have
> ever seen.[31]

Everett here touches the central issue of hermeneutics, and although his purpose is to question the inferences drawn by the zealous
Danish antiquaries as they pursue their theory, he incidentally stresses
the ambiguities attending any interpretation of ancient characters.
Both Rafn's confident decipherment of the Dighton Rock and Everett's
view that it contains nothing but Indian pictures are highly pertinent to
chapter 23 of *Pym* and the etymological "Note." We will recall that Poe
compounds the difficulties of exegesis by having Pym demonstrate to
Peters that the "indentures" on the wall of the final chasm are of natural
rather than intelligent origin—that "the . . . rude . . . representation
of a human figure" is not "intentional" (*P* 1:195)—while the anonymous philologist of the "Note" shows that in Arabic and Coptic char-

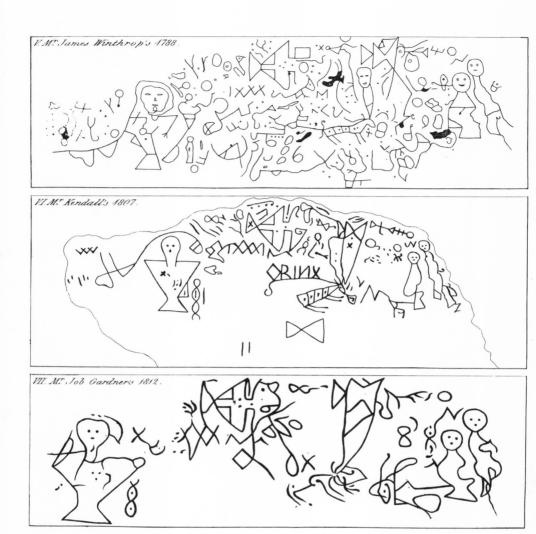

Figure 3. Drawings of the Dighton Rock inscription, in *Antiquitates Americanae*. Courtesy of Bucknell University Library.

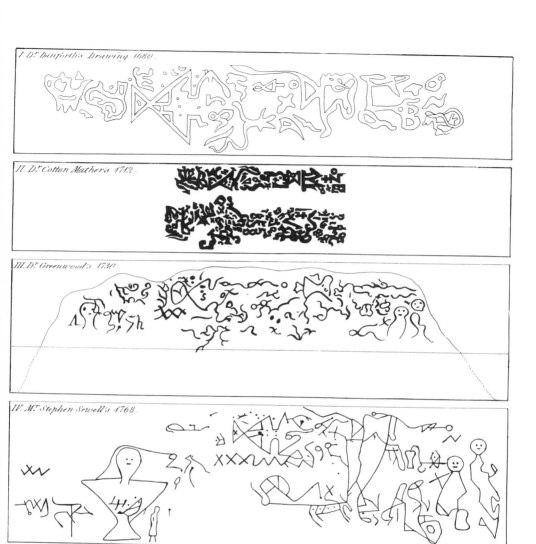

Figure 4. Drawings of the Dighton Rock inscription, in *Antiquitates Americanae*. Courtesy of Bucknell University Library.

Tab. XII.

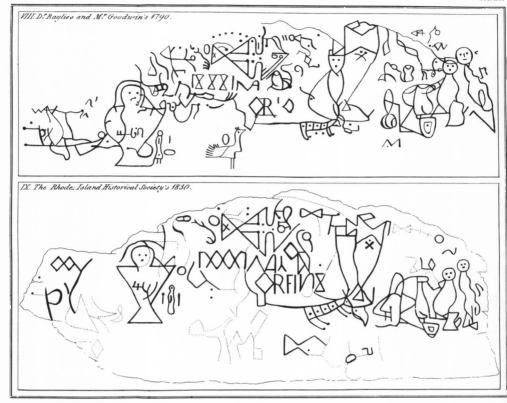

Figure 5. Drawings of the Dighton Rock inscription (the Rhode Island Historical Society illustration is actually based on a detailed Webb-Greene-Bartlett representation of 1834), in *Antiquitates Americanae.* Courtesy of Bucknell University Library.

ΓXXXI ΛΛ   † ΓXXXI ΛΛ
    ÞORFINꟄ   ÞORFINꟄ

Figure 6. Cuts representing part of the Dighton Rock inscription, from the *New-Yorker* and the *New York Review.* Courtesy of General Libraries, the University of Texas at Austin.

acters these indentures, and the "Ethiopian" pit-shapes themselves, have meanings that are both internally coherent and consistent with the geography, ethnography, and mythology of Poe's fictional Tsalal (*P* 1:207–8).

With one exception, other reviewers of *Antiquitates Americanae* were more prone than Everett to accept Rafn's reading of the inscription. The report of Folsom's lectures in the *New-Yorker* offers a visualization of the graphic elements isolated by the antiquaries.[32] The same illustration, with one additional mark, appeared in the *New York Review* simultaneously with the *New-Yorker* and was probably taken from the same drawing.[33] (See figure 6.) Rafn had supplied the thorn (þ) inferentially, assuming this symbol had been eroded from the rock's surface. Reading the first character (Γ) as an Icelandic form of C, which could mean either ten tens or a "greater hundred," twelve tens, Rafn takes the marks to signify "Thorfinn with 151 took possession here." But as Everett noted, the design as drawn by the Rhode Island scholars does not necessarily reduce to these characters, and earlier copies show even less resemblance to the pattern abstracted by Rafn. It might almost be said that the design becomes more definite in these copies with the passage of time, even while the Dighton Rock itself deteriorates under the forces of wind, rain, frost, and daily tidal immersions. Like the "hieroglyphics" on Tsalal, the "glyphs" on Dighton Rock begin as a nearly random and apparently meaningless set of marks and end as a deliberate message. While Everett takes care not to impugn the integrity of the Scandinavian researchers or to question the objectivity of his learned colleagues in Providence, he manifestly thinks the "ingenious" Rafn's thesis has dictated his perception. The *Foreign Quarterly Review* expressed disbelief more forcibly, ironically comparing Thorfinn's men with greenwood swains "[cutting] their names on bark of trees, / With true-love-knots and flourishes." The reviewer found that the "antiquarian absurdities" in Rafn's decoding weakened his generally "good case" by overstatement.[34]

That good case rested, for the *Foreign Quarterly*'s critic, on two considerations. The first was the excellent geographical correlations Rafn showed between the saga descriptions and places on the northeastern seaboard. The other was the nature of the sagas themselves. The very naiveté and fancifulness of the narratives—for instance, the anecdote of Tyrker becoming *inebriated* by wild grapes—furnished "strong evidence of the genuineness" of the stories; "The amount of fiction . . .

does not exceed what may be allowed for as the inevitable colouring of facts preserved by tradition." (Everett was likewise amused, but not rendered more doubtful, by these instances of extravagance and credulity.) The Icelandic accounts have "the substance and the colour of reality. Nothing can be more plain, natural, or vivid; [they are] even, in some respects, remarkably circumstantial." Therefore, despite or even because of palpable distortions and improbabilities in the tale, "no one possessing common sense . . . can harbour a suspicion of its genuineness and general truth."[35] We may here recall Poe's strategy of counterweighting bizarre events in *Pym* with masses of concrete, mundane information. The critic's rationale also strangely prefigures the logic of the *Pym* "Preface," where Arthur initially refrains from publishing his "true" story because he fears it will be received as an "impudent and ingenious fiction" due to his lack of literary talent and to the extraordinary nature of his experiences, but instead allows "Mr. Poe" to publish it as a "pretended fiction"; whereupon the public, endowed with "shrewdness and common sense," sees through the "air of fable" and recognizes it as veracious. Both Arthur's account and the sagas in the reviewer's estimation "carry with them sufficient evidence of their own authenticity" (*P* 1:55–56).

Everett subjects to critical scrutiny two other key features of Rafn's argument pertinent to the hermeneutic issues of *Pym*. One is the Danish antiquary's circuitous equation of "Mount Hope"—the English name of the hill in the vicinity of Dighton—with the Icelandic name "Hop" or "Hopi" (haven, estuary) given for the site of Thorfinn's camp.[36] The second involves the translation and interpretation of a sentence in the Eric saga relevant to the location of the land Leif called Vinland: "Meira var thar jafndaegri enn a Graenlandi ethr Islandi; Sol havthi thar eykterstad ok dagmalastad um skamdegi," or, literally rendered, "There is a greater equality of the days there than in Greenland or Iceland; the sun there on the day of the winter solstice has *eykterstad* [an obscure term] and *dagmalastad* [day-meal or breakfast time]." Since the shortest day of the year is a constant, if one knows the relative significance of the two italicized terms in clock time, one can determine the length of the day and hence, by astronomical calculation, the latitude of Vinland. The sentence had exercised the philological skill of Scandinavian scholars and translators for 150 years prior to Rafn. These exegetes arrived variously at days lasting six, eight, nine, and ten to twelve hours. Rafn's acceptance of the nine-hour interval of the sun's stay above the horizon allowed him to locate Vinland at the latitude of 41 degrees, 24 minutes, 10 seconds, or almost exactly the latitude of Sakonnet Point at the mouth of the river below Dighton, Tiverton, and Portsmouth, and of Conanicut Island in Narragansett Bay just opposite Newport on the west. As Everett's and the *Foreign Quarterly Review's* notices imply, this calculation, based upon an extremely equivocal set of linguistic assumptions, is too neat. It proves nothing so clearly as it proves Rafn's zeal to place the Northmen in the region of "Mount Hop" and the Dighton Rock. "It appears to us," Everett concludes, "a matter of doubtful criticism. Farther light seems to us necessary, before any of the interpretations [of the periphrastic sentence about daylight on the solstice] can be confidently relied on."[37]

I hope to have established the strong likelihood that Poe read *Antiquitates Americanae* or publications deriving from it. The concluding sections of *Pym* seem to owe as much to this historical cause célèbre as they owe to proven nineteenth-century sources like Irving's *Astoria*, Stephens' *Incidents of Travel*, and Keith's *Evidence of the Truth of the Christian Religion*. The Vinland sagas, the learned commentaries on obscure expressions in ancient tongues, and the controversy about the deciphering of the Dighton Rock harmonize with narrative elements, philosophical themes, and hermeneutic issues in those other sources. The Dighton Rock, especially, afforded just such a "wide field for speculation and exciting conjecture" and just such opportunities for "minute philological scrutiny" as the scholarly persona of the *Pym* "Note" claims for the place names, chasms, and hieroglyphics of Tsalal (*P* 1:208). The "great problem [of] the discovery of America," in Everett's phrase,[38] resonates sympathetically with the contemporary excitement about prospective discoveries by the U.S. Exploring Expedition in the higher southern latitudes—an excitement on which Poe capitalizes with Pym's promises of "solving the great problem in regard to an Antarctic continent" (*P* 1:166). Everett, whose suspicion of Rafn's archaeological proofs and geographical calculations was borne out by later research, conceded that it was "almost impossible" that daring navigators like the Northmen should *not* have touched on some parts of the northerly American coasts, if only Labrador or Newfoundland. The sagas commanded assent to their general truth; Columbus, a figure second only to Washington in the American pantheon, was probably anticipated by the roving Greenlanders, though they lacked the Admiral's motives and vision.[39] Whatever southern marvels Wilkes might encounter, he would have been fictitiously scooped by Pym and Peters, who had themselves been preceded by the boat builders and inscription writers now situated south of Tsalal in Tekeli-li-land. Rafn's sensational volume on the Northmen in the New World posed a challenge to American historiography. It must also, I believe, have propelled Poe imaginatively and intellectually toward the peculiar ending of *Arthur Gordon Pym*.

Poe's Life Reflected through the Sources of *Pym*

Burton R. Pollin

 The extraordinary scope and variety of the sources intrinsic to the text of *The Narrative of Arthur Gordon Pym* clearly reveal many aspects of Poe's life and thought at a most formative stage of his career. Several of these sources relate to his literary associations and reviewing emphases, his salient personal experiences, his home life, and his underlying concerns and goals. Major elements of these sources are the popular and classical novels that he read for the *Southern Literary Messenger*; the books of travel that were then firing the imagination of Americans; the sea chronicles and romances—by Daniel Defoe, Michael Scott, Frederick Marryat, J. F. Cooper, and others—that evoked his own boyhood sea experiences; and the works of biblical prophecy, discovery, and speculation raising issues of belief and also of geographical exploration. Throughout the protracted writing of the twenty-five chapters plus addenda (1836–38), Poe shows changes in his preoccupations, personal contacts, and even literary aims, reflecting also his shift of household from Richmond to New York.

Starting with the two years before his published poems of 1827 and ending with 1849, Poe's writing career encompasses two dozen years, with the year and a half devoted to *Pym* at the very midpoint. Steadily gaining more status in the Poe canon since his death, the novel now claims an authoritative role, even summoning a large conclave to the remote island of Nantucket as a tribute to its importance. Yet it still has to parry the charge of incorporating more source material than any other Poe work, save for the incomplete "Journal of Julius Rodman." Of its two hundred pages, perhaps one-fifth represents texts either copied or loosely or closely paraphrased from other writings, while perhaps one-third to one-quarter of its 328 paragraphs show distinct traces of his readings. In fact, for the number and variety of published books lending to it ideas and language, *Pym* clearly stands first. On the other hand, we now assert the extraordinary originality and individuality of Poe's only novel, which seem to transcend both his reliance upon a peculiar assortment of stimuli and the seemingly adventitious and even mercenary motives which produced the novel in four stages. Indeed, at this central stage in his productive life, the book reflects a set of meaningful experiences, leading master-images, and prepossessions that could be called a roster of the essential aesthetic, or what Coleridge might call the esemplastic elements of Poe's creativity.

For the critical, fully annotated edition of the novel (*P* 1:xiii–xix, 1–363), which exacted almost ten years of unremitting editorial labor, I followed up almost every possible avenue of Poe's journalistic and literary activities which stimulated and irradiated his lively and sensitive imagination. Efforts were made to record everything previously or newly discoverable in the annotations and commentaries and to classify and group, in the introduction, all sources with reference to early and contemporary studies and to indicate the locus in the text and notes. The research over the years led me to observe that there is a growing and widespread academic misconception regarding Poe's relationship to his own world of culture and of ideas. To state it very simply: Poe himself was not an academician, with large libraries at hand or numerous book-laden shelves along the walls of his abode and a population of stimulating colleagues nearby. I note a relevant comment in Saul Bellow's novel *Humboldt's Gift.* When Humboldt's ex-wife Kathleen says of her former husband, "He used to say how much he would like to move in brilliant circles, be a part of the literary world," the narrator Charles Citrine responds: "That's just it. There never was such a literary world. . . . In the nineteenth century there were several solitaries of the highest genius—a Melville or a Poe had no literary life. It was the customhouse and the barroom for them."[1]

This, at least, was true before Poe's entrance into New York's social circles, years later, after the publication of "The Raven." Nor was Poe, up to 1838, a denizen of any city which had a public library or even a cheap private subscription library, able to provide him with ample reference tools or volumes on wide-ranging, varied topics. In Baltimore and in Richmond, before his shift to New York, only the bookshops and the home libraries of friends could furnish him with reading material—nor do we have the impression of any intimacy with a cultured, book-lending circle of friends, like the Duyckincks of New York during the late forties. There is no evidence of well-filled book shelves at Mrs. James Yarrington's house, where Poe and his wife and mother-in-law boarded during most of their stay in Richmond.[2] In view of the Poes' meager existence and finally their 1837 move to New York in penury, can we expect Poe himself to accumulate and preserve a personal library? The bookseller William Gowans wrote that in New York City Poe had only periodicals, and current books, given to him, which he sold cheaply.[3] Even much later, in 1846, we have the report or reminiscence, by a visitor, of a single, small hanging bookshelf in his Fordham cottage.[4] T. O. Mabbott believed that Poe owned very few books and scarcely dared to mark up and devaluate the review copies that he regularly received or used. Hence in his edition of Poe's tales and sketches, Mabbott included as a piece of fiction the November 1844 preface to the "Marginalia," which Poe intended to employ also to begin a hoped-for volume gathering these short pieces; in this essay, Poe talks about annotating his own collection of books—which was largely mythical (*M* 3:1112). Poe probably did retain copies of Isaac D'Israeli's *Curiosities of Literature,* Jacob Bielfeld's *First Elements of Universal Erudition*, and a few more such compendia, apt for quotation and expansion of their nuggets of learning.[5]

As for the numerous books that he received as editor of four magazines for reviews (ninety-four in a nine-month period of 1835–36),[6] selling them to the local book shop (as Gowans noted) provided a small supplement to his income. This resort is later indirectly shown through the mishap over the William Duane, Jr., copy of the *Messenger*, borrowed by Poe through Henry Hirst in Philadelphia and inadvertently sold by "Muddie" Clemm to Leary's bookshop; Duane had to retrieve his very own copy from a dealer who had bought it, while Poe gave him a totally fabricated, haughty explanation.[7]

Also to be borne in mind is another reason for Poe's habit of borrowing literary materials,—that is, the limited time, in 1835–36, 1839–42, and 1845, available to editor Poe for research and properly meditative and well-wrought, imaginative composition. The business of editing and reviewing certainly consumed his time for reading, aside perhaps from the time spent on the columns and pages of exchange papers and current magazines.[8] It was time well spent, to judge from the possible use of the name Ariel and shipwreck details afforded to his first chapter by a disaster reported by two survivors in the Norfolk papers of early 1836, while a New York *Mirror*'s hitherto unpublished journal account by J. N. Reynolds, early in 1838, may have contributed to the conclusion of the book.[9] Sometimes, as in his later tales, Poe makes specific reference to these contemporary ephemerae, as in "The

Premature Burial" (*M* 3:954–61, 969–71) and "The Angel of the Odd" (*M* 3:1099, 1101, 1111). Aside from the editorial summaries that they provided for his own columns, they helped to enrich his critical and fictional texts and gave him a keen sense of changes in the taste of the public for current writing.

As for available repositories of source materials for *Pym* and other works—we should note that the major bookshops in American cities, large and small, devoted to used or antiquarian books and also to new works, were a substitute, although a poor one, for our present free library systems. In Richmond, Poe was a frequent visitor at R. D. Sanxay's Book Store at 120 Main Street, from which he often borrowed books during the periods of his residence there.[10] In Baltimore in the early 1830s, he is said to "have haunted" the store of E. J. Coale on Colbert Street.[11] Fresh from Richmond, in February 1837, in New York City he soon became a close friend of the aforementioned William Gowans, a very knowledgeable and reputable bookseller with a very large stock, who actually boarded with the Poe family for eight months.[12] It was he who caused Poe to be invited to the famous City Hotel dinner of 30 March 1837, given by the city's book dealers for prominent writers. Poe's toast to "The *Monthlies* of Gotham—Their distinguished Editors, and their vigorous Collaborateurs" was an obvious bid for employment, fruitless at that time of deep economic depression.[13] Surely Poe had free access to Gowans' extensive collection, possibly for such a costly book as the Gesenius Hebrew-English lexicon (see below).

Now to return to Richmond—late in 1836, we find Poe, although brilliant as an officiating but unofficial editor of the *Messenger*, conscious of the ominous "handwriting on the wall" inscribed by Thomas W. White, who so often wrangled with him over his drinking habits and his sharp criticism, even of White's personal friends. Stung by the *Mirror*'s rejoinder to his attacks on *Norman Leslie*, Poe was trying to arrange for his new "successful" book to be published through a major publisher, such as Harper and Brothers, after the rejection of his "Folio Club Tales" proposal.[14] He would therefore follow the benevolent advice of James Kirke Paulding about issuing a single work with "humor" and "satire" in its makeup.[15] As I have maintained, Poe tried to blend adventurous and exotic elements derived from *Robinson Crusoe*, a new edition of which he had lauded in a review early in 1836, and from other works that he had reviewed or received (*P* 1:5–7, 21, 24).[16] These included the sea novels of Captain Marryat, such as *Peter*

Simple (1834) and *Mr. Midshipman Easy* (1836); Cooper's *The Pilot*; and Michael Scott's gory, horrifying sea tales, first published as long installments in *Blackwood's Edinburgh Magazine* (namely, *Tom Cringle's Log* and *The Cruise of the Midge*); Mrs. Hofland's *The Young Crusoe*, which was number 12 in the Harper and Brothers' "Boys' and Girls' Library"; and also the books by "Uncle Philip," pseudonym of the Reverend Francis L. Hawks, whose *Ecclesiastical History* of Virginia was extravagantly praised by Poe in the *Messenger* (H 8:239–51).[17]

In the installments of *Pym* that were originally published in the *Messenger*, initially Pym and Augustus were fourteen and sixteen years old; these ages were augmented by two years in the 1838 book publication to appeal to a more mature readership and to make the characters capable of scientific and exploratory fervor. But the tone of fun and frolic, the puerile deception, and the boyish dialogue persist. So do the grotesqueries of the names and of the tricks of the plot:[18] Robert and Emmet Ross (comprising one Irish patriot's name), the "scream or yell" of the *Penguin's* crew that stuns Pym into fainting, numerous details about the dog, the nomenclature applied to parts of the brig *Grampus*, the inept stowage, the strange hiding place, and the many errors and incredibilities of the events in Tsalal.[19] Poe must have intended to banter the mature readers and to gull the juvenile. He had done this more openly in several of his mocking and satirical "Folio Club" tales.[20]

Apparently feeling committed to this tone and this double aim, after leaving Richmond Poe continued similarly through the rescue in chapter 13, that is, during the second stage of composition in New York early in 1837. Now Poe needed some readily available sources to lend "authenticity" and flesh to the exciting episodes designed for those who survived on the derelict wreck of the *Grampus*—the two beleaguered lads, Augustus and Pym, and two seamen, Peters and Parker. We remember Poe's bookless state upon arriving in Gotham—his lack of a personal library, of public reading rooms, and his general isolation. For a few shillings Poe could pick up a half dozen of the battered, cheaply printed "true tales" or "mariners' chronicles" that delighted children, apprentices, sailors, and workmen. It is possible to trace in *Pym* the language of textual passages and unmistakably related descriptions and plot details from thirty-six of these short narratives of dangers and wrecks, narratives available in five collections of nautical chronicles (P 1:22–23). Purporting to be written from actual experiences, these accounts were published in numerous editions in

America from 1806 through 1836 (reprinted from their London firsts): for example, R. Thomas' *Remarkable Shipwrecks*, Duncan's *Mariner's Chronicle*, and a *Mariner's Library*, among others. Most of the passages lie in chapters 4 through 13 of *Pym*, concluding with a long footnote quotation from the "Loss of the Polly" (found in *Remarkable Shipwrecks*, *Mariner's Chronicle*, and *Mariner's Library*); this quotation is Poe's tacit admission of considerable earlier borrowing from "Loss of the Polly" and other chronicles. But the rest of the book continued to benefit from the nautical lore taught to Poe by these volumes.

Probably Poe made arrangements with Harper and Brothers, as was true of John L. Stephens in writing his account of his Mideast travels; Poe as contracted author was permitted to acquire many of the firm's publications that would help him to fill out the atmosphere and the details of the disasters on the *Grampus* as well as the route and episodes of the *Jane Guy* in the third section.[21] These works included Barrow's detailed version of the *Bounty* mutiny[22] and the three works of the much admired Jeremiah N. Reynolds, all reviewed in the *Messenger* (two of the reviews being articles by Poe himself).[23] These reviews demonstrated the keen current interest in the long-delayed exploring expedition which finally left on 19 August 1838 for Antarctic and South Seas exploration, under the lead of Lieutenant Wilkes instead of Poe's favorite, Reynolds. Poe contrived to incorporate a reference to "the governmental expedition now preparing for the Southern Ocean" into the third paragraph of his mystifying "Note" attached to the main text of *Pym* (P 1:207; related comment, 360). Another utilized work of exploration, but with a setting on land, was Washington Irving's *Astoria*, which had been reviewed by Poe. It contributed the figure of Dirk Peters, the deceptiveness of the natives, and the explosion of the ship the *Jane Guy* (via *Astoria*'s Tonkin episode).[24]

But most important of all, Harper and Brothers could give Poe carte blanche to use Benjamin Morrell's *Narrative of Four Voyages* (the last voyage being to the Solomon Islands, prototype of Tsalal).[25] This long piece of trumpery was the firm's first book to be ghostwritten— actually from rough notes of Captain Morrell—by Samuel Woodworth, a jack of all trades: magazine editor, poet of the song "The Old Oaken Bucket," and a dramatist; he would soon adapt a section of Morrell's notes of the last voyage for an 1833 play, *The Cannibals; or, Massacre Islands.* Note the parallelism of this title with elements in Poe's subtitle, which in turn much resembles a portion of the subtitle of Morrell's book.[26] The ghostwriter Woodworth inserted into the *Narrative* many of his own borrowings from other lurid and vivid accounts of exotic voyages to fill out the natural history details and to display various incredibilities to create this large best-seller, which the publisher reprinted into the 1850s. Poe gladly helped himself to this repast of falsities, utilizing Morrell's *Narrative* in more than sixty-six paragraphs scattered over eleven chapters.[27]

In this third phase of *Pym*, from the summer of 1837 to the end of the year (chapters 14 through 22), Poe infused a new tone—of serious nautical doings, of true scientific curiosity satisfied as to details of flora and fauna borrowed from David Porter, Morrell, Reynolds, Washington Irving, James Riley's *Authentic Narratives*, and J. L. Stephens' *Incidents of Travel in Egypt, Arabia Petraea, and the Holy Land* (stony, craggy Edom being much like Tsalal).[28] The mature reader can enjoy the pseudoscientific details while the young or naive can relish the violence and narrow escapes. How could a public being courted by tales of the natives of the South Seas and darkest Africa resist Poe's account of these odd natives in their habitat of curiously colored water and variegated animals of sea and earth, with their fear of mirrors and of all white objects? Attractively mystifying too were the ending and both the "Preface" and the long "Note," author inserted, about the puzzling fate of the two surviving characters and the inexplicably retrieved manuscript. (No contemporary or Victorian-period critic ascribed allegorical or unifying apocalyptical meaning to any aspect of the plot or the "mysteries.")

The fourth stage in the composition of the work involves the obviously late insertion, early in 1838, of the chapter about the gorges, which was created chiefly from a newly available source, the 1836 *Lexicon* of the Hebrew language, written by Gesenius; the glyph was borrowed by Poe from the entry for "tsalal" or "darkness."[29] Actually, Poe found his divine or devilish clefts under the entry for Hebrew "tsalam." He was misled into using the form "tsalal" by an error made by the scholar Charles Anthon in his review article in the *New York Review* concerning the Baron de Meiran's book on comparative language roots.[30] In addition to his use of the "lore" of Anthon's letter of June 1837, Poe derived hints from James Bruce's Mideast travel classic of 1790 and both details and passages from the new best-seller, Alexander Keith's *Evidence of the Truth of the Christian Religion* (an 1832 Harper-pirated reprint).[31] Poe shaped and adapted this graphic, mysterious, and confusing material to suggest supernatural, revelational conclusions about the degradation of the blacks with hints of the southerly destination of the ancient white overlords through the cave-wall figures and the white giant at the end, thanks perhaps to the fantasy novel of *Symzonia*.[32] This stage of composition also features—but more seriously, in a sense—Poe's bantering attitude, since this final stage raises narrative issues that go counter even to the long analytic title under which the work was finally published in July 1838, such as discoveries south of the 84th parallel and the reference to the loss of only two or three chapters.

Very briefly we have noted some of the major source materials at each stage of the writing of *Pym* according to three elements: (1) the underlying interests of Poe himself as a writer and as a man of twenty-eight with a given background and living in a particular social and cultural ambiance; (2) Poe's chief aims for developing the work according to the sales value of a given approach; (3) the availability of source material that could be modified and adjusted to the assumed demands and story line of each section of the work. Of course, there had to be all sorts of convergences, adaptations, and compromises between the interests of the writer and those of the public.

I have included little or nothing about Poe's underlying interest in certain narrative themes basic to each part of the book. By narrative I refer solely to plot, not to implied imports or meanings. We might note, in his review of Hawthorne's *Twice-Told Tales* of May 1842, his rejection of the author's "moral" at the end of "The Minister's Black Veil" in favor of his inferred "*true*" import"—of a crime by the minister against "the young lady" of the funeral scene—an utterly preposterous assumption (*H* 11:111). Yet this is consonant with Poe's involvement with the "intrigue" of detective fiction.[33] Tracing his typical narrative themes, exemplified in *Pym*, would require considerable biographical discussion of data familiar to all students of Poe, such as his prowess in swimming; his riverside activities as a boy; his crossing the ocean; his two-year stint in harborside forts; his life of grim penury; his dabbling in puzzles, hoaxes, and mystifications; his interest in atavism; his weakness of heart and perhaps his vertigo; his sensitivity to alcohol; and so forth. Since *Pym* was produced at the midpoint of his career, it can be regarded as a touchstone or index by which to gauge the old and new directions in his tendencies and his work. The sources that he sought and that he found to aid him in the presentation of his narrative ideas are closely linked to those changing motifs. I suggest that just as Poe tried to stress the predetermination of a worthwhile plot, we might consider the importance of a predetermination of sources, according to the total personality and situation of the master-artist.

Sociohistorical Contexts

Mourning in Poe's *Pym*

Grace Farrell

 When one experiences profound grief over the death of a loved one, the loss can be sufficient to render oneself lost. To lose is to become lost. And mourning is the process of finding oneself again. So it is that Emerson begins his essay on grief with the words "Where do we find ourselves?" This is the problem for the griever: where to find oneself; how to situate oneself within the flux of experience which has been changed utterly by the loss of one person; how to find oneself and go on.[1]

Both Poe and Melville suffered losses which were to haunt them their whole lives long and out of which they were to write fiction which served them as quests for selfhood. Poe's primary loss was that of his mother in 1811 when Poe was not yet three years old;[2] Melville's was that of his father in 1832 when Melville was twelve. Neal Tolchin has written a stunning book which establishes how Melville both accommodates and defies the mourning conventions of his time and, throughout his work, "crafts rites of bereavement"[3] to accommodate his feelings and, if only momentarily, to resolve his grief. Tolchin demonstrates how Melville's adolescent grieving was influenced by the mourning of his mother; her grief linked itself to his and influenced his own resolution of his father's death. It is my premise that Poe, experiencing parental death twenty years earlier and when ten years younger, was denied access to any mourning conventions and excluded from the grieving process altogether.

When Edgar Poe's mother died on 8 December 1811 at the age of twenty-four, after several weeks of illness, possibly with malaria,[4] it may be supposed that Edgar, aged two years and almost eleven months, was there, in close enough proximity to witness her death. It is known that Edgar and his infant sister Rosalie were in their mother's care during her final weeks in a boardinghouse frequented by actors near the Washington Tavern at Ninth and Grace streets in Richmond. Poe's brother William Henry, older by two years, had been left in Baltimore in the care of his grandfather, "General" David Poe, some two years earlier. During the weeks while their mother lay dying, Edgar and Rosalie, "very fretful," were fed "liberally with bread soaked in gin."[5]

Whatever little Edgar Poe witnessed through his gin-soaked haze, it was not the "beautiful death" which would be celebrated by the sentimentality of a slightly later time. The great cover-up which death has undergone since the early nineteenth century, with hospitals and funeral "homes" removing the dying and the dead from the direct and horrified gaze of the survivors, had not yet begun in 1811. In his study of the changing patterns of death and dying in American culture, James J. Farrell documents how dying began to come under scientific control only after 1830 with the rise of scientific naturalism: "Between 1830 and 1920, the denial of death in America took the form of a quest for control, with each instance of control an attempt to keep death out of mind by keeping it out of sight."[6] The usurpation by funeral directors of the care of the dead body and the arrangements for interment was a phenomenon which did not begin to develop until after 1850. Etiquette manuals which imposed control on unleashed emotions by ritualizing public displays of grief became increasingly important in the last two-thirds of the nineteenth century.[7] Sentimentality, which beautified and, as Ann Douglas puts it, "domesticated" death, grew in reaction against Romanticism's focus on death's sublime terror.[8]

Dying in 1811 was more likely to be experienced by the survivors in two ways typical of the Romantic era: one could tame death by interpreting it as part of the organic cycle of the universe, uncontrollable to be sure, but signifying the human correspondence with nature; or one could see death, as Farrell puts it, "as a source of the sublime, an awe-inspiring event that elevated human emotions to peak sensitivity."[9] Not surprisingly, Farrell cites Poe as his prime illustration of those Romantics who

> stressed the horror of death in order to elicit fear, the strongest of human emotions. They considered death an adversary, and the struggle between death and the individual as a battle of epic proportion. They emphasized the horrors of death and the grave, the futile fight with conqueror worm, and the terrible prospect of burial alive. Besides producing a sense of the sublime, this view of death also increased grief for the survivors, who imagined the deceased in the midst of death's horrors.[10]

We can speculate that such a general view of death, which we find embodied in Poe's work, would also characterize his view of his mother's death. And yet, although such a perspective on death serves, as Farrell puts it, to increase grief, in 1811 very young children were supposed not to grieve at all. Although these children were not protected from a close association with the dying, grief was not thought to be a matter touching them. Indeed, the idea that children are incapable of grieving persists even today. Not until late in the first half of the twentieth century, with studies by Anna Freud and others, was there any acknowledgment that young children respond to the absence of their mothers with signs of grief.[11] But even here, the assumption is that children do not proceed through the stages of mourning characteristic of grieving adults, but that they instead soon forget the object of their grief and overcome their sadness. Only more recently, with John Bowlby's landmark studies of children as young as eighteen months who had experienced the death of a parent, especially of the mother, has the conclusion been reached, and not without controversy, that young children experience loss in much the same way as do adults and must go through the process of mourning as do adults.[12]

But the conventions of mourning in 1811 excluded young Edgar Poe from any participation. On 9 December, the day following his mother's death, he was removed to his new home with Frances and John Allan. Hervey Allen describes with sensitivity how that day might have been experienced by Poe:

> Young as he was, Edgar Poe could scarcely have remembered the actual scenes surrounding the final tragedy of his young mother, but even a child of three may be conscious at the time that its own familiar little world has suddenly gone to pieces about it. . . . he must dimly have experienced for the first time, in an emotion without words, the extreme sense of fear and utter loneliness which was to follow him to the grave.[13]

The conclusiveness of Allen's initial statement that Poe "could scarcely have remembered" the scenes surrounding his mother's death may be questioned in light of Piaget's studies of the cognitive development of young children, who, even before the age of two, have achieved object permanence (i.e., the ability to understand that an object or person exists independently of them and to remember that object or person when it or he or she is out of their sight).[14] The achievement of object permanence is thought to be a necessary prerequisite for an apprehension of loss and a response of grief. Nevertheless, Allen's affirmation of Poe's loss and the disruption which that loss caused are prescient in light of Bowlby's conclusions that children do, indeed, mourn, rather than simply forget, their losses.[15]

I would like to reframe in terms of current grief theory the familiar issue of Poe's unrequited search for his lost mother in *The Narrative of Arthur Gordon Pym*. Although Poe was excluded from the conventions of mourning, through his work, he, like Melville, found a medium through which he might mourn, but, unlike Melville, he was not able to resolve his grief. In particular, the endings of *Pym* and *Moby-Dick* may serve to indicate how Melville was able and how Poe may not have been able to come to that resolution which could answer Emerson's question, "Where do we find ourselves?"

Earlier studies of these issues include Edward Davidson's placement of Poe's focus on death within the sociological context of the third and fourth decades of the nineteenth century, emphasizing Poe's use of the century's conventional connection between death and sexual love.[16] Certainly Poe's writing was part of, and partook of, the popular culture of these decades, but, as Farrell's research argues, attitudes toward death and dying were substantially different in pre-1830 America, when Poe lost his mother. J. Gerald Kennedy also situates his discussion of death and Poe's writing in the decades mapped out by Davidson. His argument is cast in a postmodernist context, but he reveals its Freudian roots in his focus on Poe's "relentless effort to probe the nature of modern death anxiety."[17] I agree with Kennedy that Davidson's inclination to "construe death in Poe as sheer convention or as a code for other problems is itself symptomatic of a . . . tendency . . . to repress the reality of death."[18] But so, too, is Kennedy's deconstructive gaze at death, which reads *The Narrative of Arthur Gordon Pym* as Poe's attempt to deny death by deferring it through his writing. Rather, I view *Pym* as Poe's defiance of the conventions which refused acknowledgment of his grief and excluded him from the mourning process and as his attempt not to deny but to face the reality of death.

Richard Kopley maintains that Poe's losses are central to an understanding of *The Narrative of Arthur Gordon Pym*.[19] He argues that the "shrouded human figure" at the end of the novel suggests the reemerging ship the *Penguin*, coming again, as it had in the novel's "Preface," to destroy Pym's vessel and then to rescue Pym. The symmetrical Penguins, self-reflecting icons, mirror the center of the novel: the death of Augustus. It is that moment of death, Kopley says, to which Pym wished to return so that he might die along with his friend. Kopley links the death of Augustus to that of Poe's brother Henry and argues that Poe's focus in *Pym* is through Henry to his mother: "The 'shrouded human figure' is both brother and mother. . . ." "If not in time, at least in manner," concludes Kopley, "Poe did finally manage, through his fiction, to 'lie close' to his mother. By means of this, his only novel, Poe did ultimately attain the cherished 'intimate communion' of mother and son, of which the 'intimate communion' of brother and brother had been an incarnation."[20]

Pym is a novel of mourning: death is its center, and a search for the lost mother is its motivating force. While I would stress that this search is neither pathological nor regressive but is part of the mourning process, a process directed toward finding one's own lost self, other studies emphasize the dissolution rather than the recovery of the self. Marie Bonaparte's traditional psychoanalytic concern is with Poe's Oedipal fixations and regressions to early phases of libido development.[21] In an important essay on the enclosure motif, Paul Rosenzweig argues that the fluctuation between the two extremes of enclosure—one of security and protection, the other of imprisonment and suffocation— involves a "self-destructive strategy inevitably precluding true growth," because the ego keeps regressing to a pre-Oedipal phase of desired union with the mother.[22] While Davidson had stated that *Pym* is "a study of emerging consciousness,"[23] Rosenzweig maintains that the ego-regressions impede any search for self. He views the "Preface" and "Note" as reinforcing the pattern of indeterminate identity by shifting the problem of identity into a literary context. In a little-read but valuable essay, Ana Maria Hernández sees engulfment in *Pym* as engendering a "*mystic* kind of horror, since it brings about the dissolution of consciousness and the return to the all-devouring Void." She adds, "In mythological language, the theme of the return to the origins and the danger of loss of self is presented as the hero's voyage to the Underworld and his encounter with the Magna Mater [which] . . . symbolizes and objectifies the author's anxiety neurosis facing death and dissolution of the body and is projected as a fear of disruption and dissolution of consciousness."[24]

Freud saw regressions, such as Bonaparte, Rosenzweig, and Hernández describe, as part of a pathological mourning process, in which, instead of transferring the libido from the person lost to another, the mourner regresses, drawing the libido inward narcissistically.[25] Bowlby, on the other hand, identifies, as a central phase in the process of mourning—a phase which may last for years—the yearning and searching for the person lost, and he views such a search not as regressive but as appropriate and necessary to the individual's attempt to reorganize his life in a changed world.[26] It is in this context that I view Poe's search in *Pym* for his lost mother not as pathological and not as regressive but, rather, as an attempt to mourn and, in that attempt, to search for the self in order to emerge reborn out of the death experience.

I take as my emblem that aspect of Narcissus which Freud, interestingly, overlooks. In Pausanias' version of the myth, Narcissus is a mourner. He is searching for his dead sister in the pool of water when he gazes in and finds himself instead.[27] His action articulates the mourning process: the search for the Other is prototypical of the search for the self. In "Loomings," Melville links Narcissus' act with the ontological leaps through water into self which Ishmael (and Pym) makes. Narcissus, "because he could not grasp the tormenting, mild image he saw in the fountain, plunged into it and was drowned. But that same image, we ourselves see in all rivers and oceans. It is the image of the ungraspable phantom of life; and this is the key to it all."[28] The phantom of life, the key to it all, is the object of Ishmael's voyaging through Pacific waters into what Ahab terms the "'endless landscapes in the soul,'"[29] and of Pym's voyaging into that concluding chasm which throws itself open as if to embrace.

There is, of course, potential for regression in the mourning process. When one feels bereft by the death of a loved one—abandoned, left behind in a world emptied of meaning—there is a longing to undo the final separation and to be rejoined with the loved one forever. This longing defines a powerful death wish which we find in much of Poe's work and repeatedly in *Moby-Dick*.[30] This wish for death is also a denial of death, because in joining the beloved forever, one both denies separateness—by uniting with the other—and overcomes time—for the union is forever. The psychological literature tells us that such longing, when manifested in the extreme, is symptomatic of a nostalgia for an absolute unity, undying and eternal. And such a feeling is an echo of the first such feeling, the impossible wish to return to the mother, to alleviate the anxiety of separateness, and to immerse oneself in the preconscious comfort of the womb.

The desired regression would indeed impede any search for self, because without the loss of absolute unity with the mother, one cannot conceive of oneself, cannot give birth to oneself as a separate entity.

Consciousness of self is predicated upon this loss. Lacan discusses the formation of the function of the "I" as occurring only when the child discovers his separation from the mother and experiences the gap between self and Other.[31] It is the experience of loss which creates a gap, "a hole in the real," Lacan calls it, which one nostalgically longs to fill with the lost object.[32] Mourning involves a nostalgia for the lost primal unity which is countered in the healthily developing individual by an impulse toward separation: one is attracted to the security of the womb but is repulsed by the death of self implicit in it. If one resists the pain of separation, the birth pangs of the individual coming to be, then one participates in the death of one's own self. Thus, as Julia Kristeva puts it, "Matricide is our vital necessity, the sine-qua-non condition of our individuation,"[33] but everywhere, as Freud pointed out, recurs the *"impossible mourning for the maternal object."*[34]

That impossible mourning for the maternal object—that nostalgia for a lost unity—motivates the journeys of both *Pym* and *Moby-Dick*.[35] For Ishmael, as for Pym, the secret of self-knowledge lies in a death experience linked with a return to maternal arms. Ishmael's nostalgic double, Ahab, conveys this view:

> "Where lies the final harbor, whence we unmoor no more? In what rapt ether sails the world, of which the weariest will never weary? Where is the foundling's father hidden? Our souls are like those orphans whose unwedded mothers die in bearing them: the secret of our paternity lies in their grave, and we must there to learn it."[36]

It is in the mother's grave that the paternal source of self may be found.

Mourning for the maternal object and the development of the self are implicitly touched upon in Michael Vannoy Adams' Jungian study of Ahab.[37] In Jung's theory of the Jonah and the whale complex, the whale is an archetype of the mother in both her aspects: the Good Mother who aids the child in the individuation process and the Terrible Mother who engulfs and thus hinders him in that process. The developing child must separate from the mother but experiences intense nostalgia for an earlier union with her. In the symbolism of the myth, the Terrible Mother is the devouring fish who swallows up the child, while the Good Mother expels the child, as the whale expelled Jonah, casting him off so that he may grow to be himself. The Terrible Mother, on the other hand, encourages regression and does not allow for growth through separation.

Adams focuses his study on Ahab, but his material is relevant to the issues I am raising concerning Ishmael as well as Pym. Ahab is but the nostalgic side of Ishmael. In mourning for all that he has lost,[38] in the intensity of his death wish and his need to return to that terrible whale-mother, Ahab never frees himself from his obsession but instead disappears forever, dragged down into the oceanic abyss. Ishmael, on the other hand, is expelled from the depths of the vortex to find himself alone—an individual—and not a part of that all-consuming mother sea. The dilemma of both wanting individuation and mourning for a lost union is worked through in *Moby-Dick*. By bifurcating his voyager, Melville was able to have the nostalgic child, Ahab, return to the Terrible Mother and to have the maturing Ishmael expelled and alone.

As *Moby-Dick* ends, Ishmael meets a mother. He is picked up by the Rachel in her "retracing search after her missing children."[39] In Jeremiah and Matthew, Rachel is a matriarchal figure, mother of lost tribes, weeping for her children and inconsolable because they are no more, while in Genesis, Rachel dies in giving birth to Benjamin. These images of another archetypal mother convey significant suggestions. First, in an inverted projection, instead of the child searching for the mother, we have the mother, in a "*retracing search,*" that is, in a repetitive, regressive search. She is inconsolable because her children are no more—that is, they are no longer children; she has birthed them; they are separate, dispersed. Second, Rachel the mother is dead. The separation which the mourning child nostalgically longs to prevent has already taken place, and the mourning process is one of recognizing the truth that there are no embracing chasms that can ease this knowledge or undo this fact.

The dilemma of mourning is resolved in *Moby-Dick*. The novel, linear and developmental, concludes with a clear-eyed view from Ishmael. He, buoyed up by Queequeg's coffin, is not allowed any denial of the separateness which death has affirmed. As if in answer to Emerson's question "Where do we find ourselves?" Ishmael leaves behind Ahab—his death-denying, death-wishing alter ego—and finds himself orphaned in vast Pacific waters "whose gentle awful stirrings seem to speak of some hidden soul beneath."[40] With "*orphan*" as the final word of *Moby-Dick*, Melville acknowledges this existential fact of each human life. Orphans are we all—separate and alone—floating on the "dirge-like main."[41]

Pym, on the other hand, in his headlong rush into the apocalyptic embrace of the chasm, is both returned to, and annihilated by, the maternal embrace. The engulfing Mother, in swallowing up the child, disallows his separation from her; she, in effect, kills the individual. And the individual, because of his intense mourning for that preconscious absolute unity, participates in the death of his own self. If the novel ended here, Pym's fall into the self could be regarded as a regressive leap which takes him back to the maternal arms of unity and infantile undifferentiation.

But, of course, the novel does not end here. The end circles around to its beginning. Poe repeatedly saves his protagonist from destruction. Pym is finally subsumed by that maternal embrace, only to be resurrected from seeming death so that he may tell the tale in which he dies and is resurrected to tell the tale in which he dies and so on and so on. Through his series of deaths and rebirths, descents and ascents, engulfments and separations, losses and recoveries, Pym keeps approaching and avoiding absolute unity. This is the creative rhythm of the novel. It is also the rhythm of mourning. It expresses the struggle of the mourner who both longs for primal unity and resists the absorption and negation of self which such a unity implies.

Poe's cosmology is a macrocosmic projection, as it were, of the mourning process. In *Eureka*, Poe theorizes that all Matter is composed of Attracting and Repulsing particles. Matter arises from an original Unity, with a "separative ether" keeping atoms apart, but on what Poe calls "that great day," Matter shall expel the ether and return "into Absolute Unity." As he might have done in the *Narrative*, however, Poe queries the reader, "Are we here to pause?" and answers his own question with "Not so." He explains that the Unity into which all Matter sinks is Nothingness, but a certain kind of Nothingness. Matter, Poe writes, "in sinking into Unity . . . will sink at once into Nothingness which, to all Finite Perception, Unity must be—into that Material Nihility from which alone we can conceive it to have been evoked—to have been *created* by the Volition of God." As Matter sinks into Nothingness, it sinks into that from which it once arose and, presumably, from which it may arise again, reconstituted up out of the creative void. The process, Poe writes, "will be renewed forever, and forever, and forever; a novel Universe swelling into existence, and then subsiding into nothingness, at every throb of the Heart Divine? And now— this Heart Divine—what is it? *It is our own*" (H 16:310–11).

Just as he saves Pym from the destructive absorption of the apocalyptic embrace, Poe saves himself from Nothingness. First, he proclaims it a Nothingness out of which all that is comes; it is the diastole of a throbbing heart. He then incorporates into one statement "*It is our own*" both the longing for and the resistance to that creative void; he merges his identity with the very source of that Nothingness—the Divine Heart—while at the same time forcefully asserting his identity by declaring the Divine Heart his own.

Poe defines Absolute Unity, which "Nothingness" is, as a "lost parent." It is the source of all atoms: "Their source lies in the principle, *Unity. This* is their lost parent. *This* they seek always" (H 16:220). So pervasive is Poe's search for his own lost parent that just such a search becomes central to the very workings of the universe. The entire cosmos is locked in mourning. And so is Poe's Pym—locked in the mourning process, searching still for that lost mother. While circling birds call out "*Tekeli-li!*" (*P* 1:205–6),⁴² he struggles to give birth to his own "emerging consciousness."⁴³

The goal of mourning is to search for the Other in order to find the self—to emerge reborn out of the death experience—but the very inconclusiveness of the text indicates that the process of mourning in *Pym* never reaches closure. Melville was able to bring *Moby-Dick* to a resolution that could proffer a tentative answer to the question Emerson poses, but Poe, denied access to mourning conventions and excluded from the grieving process, never completed his mourning. This is not to suggest, however, that Poe's journey should be read as a regression. On the contrary, it continually resists regression and loss of self and instead renews, again and again, the mourning process. While Poe could not reclose the gap created by his loss, neither did he smooth over the fragmentation and disjunction of experience which express that loss. Instead, the narrative, preventing its own resolution into a closed form, leaves Pym where Poe remained: repetitively poised on the boundary between loss and recovery.

Poe, Antebellum Slavery, and Modern Criticism

John Carlos Rowe

 Mr. Poe is decidedly the best of all our young writers—
I don't know but that I may say, of all our old ones.
—James Kirke Paulding

My argument is on the face of it simple: Poe was a proslavery Southerner and should be reassessed as such in whatever approach we take
to his life and writings. This is by no means an original claim. From
Ernest Marchand in the 1930s to Bernard Rosenthal in the 1970s, the
proslavery case against Poe has been argued again and again, usually on
the very specific grounds of the infamous review of proslavery books
by James Kirke Paulding and William Drayton published in 1836 in the
Southern Literary Messenger under Poe's general editorship (H 8:265–
75).[1] For these earlier critics, Poe's sympathies with the Southern
aristocracy, plantation life, and the institution of slavery have been
treated as personal prejudices which are not consistently displayed
in his literary writings. Marchand, F. O. Matthiessen, and Rosenthal,
among others, have found elements of Poe's racism at the heart of certain key works, notably *The Narrative of Arthur Gordon Pym*, but in
most cases have treated the literary work as an allegory of Poe's antebellum prejudices. My own argument is that Poe's proslavery sentiments
are fundamental to his literary production and thus demand a searching reconsideration of his aesthetic canon. Of equal interest, I think, is
the history of Poe's twentieth-century canonization as modernist and
the ways it has compounded the problem. Thus the reinterpretation
of Poe's writings in terms of his proslavery sentiments involves an
equally comprehensive reconsideration of twentieth-century critical
approaches to Poe, as well as their theoretical assumptions.

My thesis is complicated by several factors that cannot always be
kept clear and distinct, so I shall simply make a preliminary effort
to identify them and then let these factors play throughout the rest
of this essay. First, the critical neglect of the historical circumstances
surrounding Poe's literary production has been the work of both tra-

ditional literary historians and critical theorists. Ironically, the only literary historians who seem to have been *right* about Poe's complicity with antebellum Southern legitimists are those who have been demonstrated to have been factually *wrong* on several scores. In a similarly ironic manner, the vigorous efforts of poststructuralist theorists to "modernize" Poe and thus remove him (and his writings) from any historical context other than our own have had the effect of complementing what I contend was precisely Poe's racist strategy of literary production in the antebellum period. Second, Poe's racism is inextricably entangled with his attitudes toward women and his conception of the literary author as the new aristocrat. Racism, sexism, and aristocratic pretensions, of course, often go together, but in the case of Poe, these prejudices are finely woven into the fabric of his art. Finally, the purposes of this essay are not restricted simply to understanding *Poe* and his writings more accurately or more historically, since the blindnesses many of us have shared with respect to Poe have some serious consequences for contemporary critical theory and its relation to the postmodern societies in which we live.

I will entangle Poe's name and thus meaning in contemporary debates about the psychoanalytical dimensions of literature (or the inevitable literariness of psychoanalysis) with a much-needed review of the historical study of Poe's proslavery sentiments, even as I warn against a narrow reliance on strictly empirical evidence. Such documentary evidence as the review of Paulding and Drayton in the 1836 *Messenger* and the possible sale of a slave by Poe in Baltimore should not be ignored, but it should not be treated in purely archival and historical terms.[2] Treated in a strictly positivist manner, documentary evidence can be easily enough refuted or ignored, as has been the case with these two significant "details" from Poe's life. The ruses by which willful critics separate and discriminate "life" from "letters" are sufficiently familiar to all of us, and the text-bound myopia of literary criticism is by no means restricted to that brief historical moment we have so obsessively monumentalized in the ominous name "Anglo-American New Criticism." Textualists have often done the same work, trivializing biographical and historical "facts," even when they know well enough that such "facts" ought to be incorporated into "rhetorical history" rather than conveniently forgotten.

Literary historians, too, often play their own parts in this work of historical repression. In this regard, let me turn to the fate of the review of Paulding and Drayton in the twentieth century. The misattribution of that infamous review to Poe seemed to be settled decisively by William Doyle Hull II's 1941 doctoral dissertation for the University of Virginia, "A Canon of the Critical Works of Edgar Allan Poe." Arraying an impressive variety of circumstantial evidence, Hull argued that the review was most likely written by Judge Beverley Tucker, the proslavery advocate.[3] Hull's scholarship is in no way concerned with Poe's literary writings, except in their connection with the literary taste demonstrated in his reviews. Hull ignores equally the wider cultural context in which proslavery works appeared in the antebellum period. "Authorship" for Hull is not a theoretical matter; it is simply a question of assessing the surviving empirical evidence to determine the authorship of an unsigned work.

Yet as the recent scandal about Paul de Man's wartime writings for *Het Vlaamsche Land* and *Le Soir* has once again taught us, the moral responsibilities of writing are hardly covered by conventional notions of historical "authorship." Those defending de Man's writings on the grounds that they display only occasional and then debatable anti-Semitic and pro-Nazi sentiments can do so only by ignoring or trivializing the virulent anti-Semitic and vigorously pro-Nazi views published along with de Man's "cultural" reviews in *Le Soir* during the German occupation of Belgium.[4] Wary as we should be of the dangers of charging "guilt by association," we must acknowledge that the "association" of publication in the same newspaper or journal can be the basis for a substantial case.[5]

In the case of Poe, such an "association" with the likes of Judge Tucker, should he in fact be the author of the disputed review, is made even more invidious when we consider Poe's role as editor of the *Southern Literary Messenger* and thus his formal responsibility for what was published in its pages. In 1974, responding in part to criticism that his *Race and the American Romantics* (1971) had mistakenly included the Paulding-Drayton review as the work of *Poe,* thus ignoring the evidence of Hull's doctoral dissertation, Bernard Rosenthal both carefully argued the "guilt by association" thesis and challenged the circumstantial "evidence" of Hull's thesis in "Poe, Slavery, and the *Southern Literary Messenger*: A Reexamination." In that essay, Rosenthal argues the case in historically concrete terms, but he includes as part of that history Poe's deferential correspondence with Judge Tucker, his great admiration for and gratitude to Paulding himself, and Poe's undisputed admiration for Thomas R. Dew in his October 1836 review of Dew's address to the students at William and Mary—the Thomas R. Dew whom Rosenthal calls "the architect of the South's intellectual position in defense of slavery" and who subsequently became President of William and Mary.[6]

Yet, since Rosenthal reopened the debate concerning the authorship of the infamous Paulding-Drayton review, there has been very little scholarly discussion of Poe and slavery, with the exception of interpretations of *Pym* as a "fantasy of white slave-holding paranoia" that have followed the leads of Walter Bezanson and Rosenthal himself.[7] The "modern" or "postmodern" Poe hardly lends himself to this debate, which turns so crucially on historical details and the very regional identification that Poe himself seemed to do everything possible to disavow in his major literary productions. Rosenthal made an understandable, albeit strategic, error in framing his 1974 argument primarily in historical terms. Although he broadened the historical context of Hull's argument, he kept the argument primarily in the archival arena at the very moment Poe was about to reemerge as a major figure in what has come to be termed "deconstruction in America."

Rosenthal's arguments were virtually ignored, even by Poe scholars. When I telephoned him in the spring of 1988, Professor Rosenthal confirmed my sense that there had been very little response to his essay, either formally in journals and books or by way of private correspondence. One notable exception was the distinguished Poe scholar G. R. Thompson, who later told me that he had argued in favor of the publication of Rosenthal's 1974 essay in *Poe Studies* against objections from others that Rosenthal's historical evidence was not entirely convincing. Reviewing Rosenthal's argument in *American Literary Scholarship* for 1974, Thompson concluded: "Although his argument depends on a number of ambiguities and a few improbabilities, he does a good job of showing greater improbability that the review is Tucker's."[8] Such grudging acknowledgment of Rosenthal's challenge to Hull, appearing as it did in the annual *ALS* review of Poe scholarship, was not likely to have much impact on poststructuralists working on Poe, especially since their interest derived hardly from the study of Poe as an American author but from the study of Poe primarily in the context of comparative literature and Continental theory.

Thompson himself seems to have forgotten what he wrote in 1975 about Rosenthal, because in his contribution to the new *Columbia Lit-*

erary History of the United States, Thompson argues in "Edgar Allan Poe and the Writers of the Old South" that "Poe's conception of letters is virtually devoid of regionalist sentiment" and that "the notorious review of two books defending slavery in the *Messenger* in 1836, upon which some critical interpretations of Poe's *Narrative of Arthur Gordon Pym* have been based, was written not by Poe but in all likelihood by Beverley Tucker."[9] Acknowledging that "Poe's Southernness" remains a question "of recurrent critical debate," Thompson judges Poe's "high formalism of prose style, . . . idealization of women, . . . scorn for democracy and the idea of progress, and an uneasiness about the age of the machine" as not "specifically Southern."[10] Further, in his volume for the Library of America, *Edgar Allan Poe—Essays and Reviews*, Thompson pays little attention in his notes to Poe's Southern sentiments, despite his inclusion of Poe's long, admiring review of Beverley Tucker's chivalric romance *Balcombe*. Throughout the reviews and criticism that Thompson selects for this volume, there is frequent evidence of Poe's preferences for Southern literature and the chivalric romance, including Poe's praise for William Gilmore Simms' racist romance *Beauchamp*. In his "Note on the Texts" in this volume, Thompson cites Hull's dissertation as one of his sources for establishing the canon of Poe's reviews and criticism, a reliance which seems to explain why Thompson makes no reference to the Paulding-Drayton review.[11] Yet Hull's thesis alone does not justify Thompson's omission of any discussion of Poe's Southern sentiments in his notes to the volume, an omission especially noticeable in the section devoted to Poe's reviews of American writers.

Thompson's assessment of Poe in the *Columbia Literary History* as a proto-modern cosmopolitan writer without a "specifically Southern" identity in his writings is the place to begin reinterpreting Poe's significance for our own time as well as in the antebellum South. Rosenthal's mistake, like Marchand's and Matthiessen's before him, was to treat the historical Poe and the modernist Poe as different figures, involving drastically different intellectual issues. The consequence has been that the rise of the "modernist Poe" has left the historical Poe in the archives, virtually ignored in our generation and, unfortunately, for the next generation reading the *Columbia Literary History of the United States*.

Let me now try to weave some of these specific historical questions, including Poe's critical reception in the twentieth century, together with the theoretical Poe, whose circulation in the past twenty years has given him a new currency, but one that has strategically ignored his nineteenth-century political affiliations. Since the recovery of Poe by the French Symbolists, "Poe" has been treated as an invention or an occasion for a wide variety of different language games—Symbolist poetry, psychobiography, psychoanalysis, deconstruction—that would seem to have little to do with the historical Poe. Edgar Allan Poe, of course, would have loved this transcendence; he himself never much cared to live in his own age. The translation of his literary works into the language game of psychoanalysis has accomplished precisely what Edgar Allan Poe had hoped: the substitution of an immaterial world for the threatening world of material history. The immaterial poetic world of the language game that Poe worked so hard to distinguish from ordinary reality is in no way an "unreal" or purely "fictional" world. The very appropriateness of post-Freudian psychoanalytical and textualist approaches to Poe's writings argues just the opposite, and I have no intention of attacking their claims according to some specious criteria for "truth" and "falsehood." My contention is that there is a rhetorical and psychoanalytical relation between the immaterial, poetic world of Poe's writing and the material history from which it flees. It is just this differential relation between the material and the immaterial that modern psychoanalytical theories using Poe's writings have missed— not just in Poe, but in themselves.

Lacan, Derrida, Barbara Johnson, Jean Ricardou, I myself—none of these interpreters of Poe, I suspect, would be disturbed by the accusation: "You have not been historical enough." That, it would appear, is beside the point. Even John Irwin's *American Hieroglyphics*, which so brilliantly translates many of the chief issues in the Lacan-Derrida debate into the rhetoric and ideas of international Romanticism, demonstrates this discrepancy between intellectual and material history. The rich history that Irwin offers us is the grand narrative in which Poe is a single chapter: the narrative of Romanticism's defensive substitution of its own text (the Text of texts) for the increasingly unmanageable text of nineteenth-century social life.[12]

Let us be historical. And let us begin in the most improbable place for such work, "The Purloined Letter." Suffice it to say that Lacan and Derrida have so charged the title of this story that I can hardly utter it without invoking the fantastic narrative of twentieth-century psychoanalysis.[13] The analysis is truly interminable. The story is one that encourages just such fantastic narration because it is itself so tenuously connected with any history. A monarchy. Paris. Minister D——. An unread message. In the first paragraph, as if to confirm this ahistorical mise-en-scène, there is a mocking date: "18——" (*M* 3:974). It is as if Poe works here, as in so many other fictive spaces, to make the intrusions of material history as insignificant as possible, serving the barest of technical functions to permit us to imagine what is otherwise unimaginable, unpresentable. Like the furnishings in Minister D——'s apartments, which the Prefect so diligently and futilely destroys, these historical details seem given only to be discarded.

"18——." The date can be uttered only clumsily and with explanations; it is a nearly pure grapheme that emphasizes the space of writing we are entering. Yet, even Poe's textual formalism is still penetrated by history, for this date *follows* the French Revolution in a text that plays with the threat posed to the monarchy by a message stolen by a minister of state. Dupin's clever narrative saves the monarchy from this threat by recourse to two simulated "revolutions." The distraction that allows Dupin to substitute his forgery for the actual message is a "disturbance in the street" occasioned by "the frantic behavior of a man with a musket. He had fired it among a crowd of women and children. It proved, however, to have been without ball, and the fellow was suffered to go his way as a lunatic or a drunkard" (*M* 3:992). We shall have more to say of women and children, as well as of revolutions. The other revolution is the real challenge Poe offers to the French Revolution: the poetic "counter-revolution" (the term is quite precise here) by which he appears to save the monarchy but in fact institutes his own power. It is, quite obviously, the power of rhetoric, of poetry: Poe's power as the "new" nobility of the Author.

In the disputed review of J. K. Paulding's *Slavery in the United States* and [William Drayton's] *The South Vindicated from the Treason and Fanaticism of the Northern Abolitionists*, which appeared in the April 1836 issue of the *Southern Literary Messenger*, we find the following remarks on the French Revolution:

> It should be remembered now, that in that war against property [the French Revolution], the first object of attack was property in slaves; that in that war on behalf of the alleged right of man to be discharged from all control of law, the first triumph achieved was in the emancipation of slaves.

> The recent events in the West Indies, and the parallel movement

here, give an awful importance to these thoughts in our minds. They superinduce a something like despair of success in any attempt that may be made to resist the attack on all our rights, of which that on Domestic Slavery (the basis of all our institutions) is but the precursor. (*H* 8:269)

The "disturbance in the street" is a mock-enactment of a "lunatic" or anarchic act of revolution; it motivates the reasoned act of "counter-revolution": the apparent restoration of the monarchy with the subtler effect of the instantiation of Dupin's power as master of rhetoric.

We must keep in mind a certain biographical interpretation of Poe that can't be detailed here. His own Southern aristocratic pretensions, fueled just as they were frustrated by his foster father John Allan, find here their curious realization in the will to power of the artist, whose "property" is the ultimate defense against "the attack on all our rights" that is the Abolitionist movement.[14] Derrida's critical reading of Lacan may be recalled in general terms here. For Derrida, what marks Lacan's "contradiction," his blindness, is precisely his insistence upon the route by which the psychic narrative of "The Purloined Letter" restores the monarchy, reaffirms the Law-That-Is-the-Name-of-the-Father—the Father, in this case, being the King. For Derrida, this transforms the Signifier of the Unconscious into a Signified, restoring the phallic authority of the King/Father, just as Dupin's "forgery" inseminates that obvious vaginal scene: the clitoral card rack dangling above the yawning, burning opening of the fireplace in the Minister's apartments.[15] For Lacan, Dupin's forgery is a metonymic displacement (his coded message for the Minister's theft, itself a substitution for the original performative of the message to the Queen) that reroutes the letter, only for the letter of the Unconscious to return to its proper service: affirmation of the centered authority of the Father/King in the circuits of psychic signification.[16] For such clever insemination, Derrida substitutes *dissemination,* which is exemplified by Dupin's rhetorical tricks. Dupin's restoration of the purloined letter relies on the linguistic truth that any message can be diverted from its proper meaning. For Derrida, the only law of letters is this diversion or straying from the letters' intended meanings. Even successfully delivered messages are affected by the possibility of errancy. This knowledge is potentially liberating for Derrida because it challenges the titles of those conventionally assumed to command meaning and truth: Kings and Queens, Ministers, Prefects of Police, Authors. For Derrida, it is the subversive, the deconstructive moment, which would align Dupin with a revolution against monarchy, the Minister, the Prefect—all the putative authorities of this world "recentered" in the wake of the decentering of the French Revolution. For Derrida, Dupin would have to be understood as a revolutionary, shadowy precursor to the deconstructor himself, and here, of course, is the dilemma for those interested in claiming Poe as proto-deconstructive writer.

Returning to history, to the proslavery cant in the 1836 *Messenger* (as well as other issues under Poe's editorship), we must pursue a different reading, albeit one that grants the validity of Derrida's deconstruction of Lacan. Poe/Dupin has "seized" a certain "property," and it is, of course, the "property" of language. As we know from Poe, such property must be distinguished strictly from the material property that is finally an illusion for his characters, even from the specious "empiricism" of science and journalism: that is, the properties of a referential language. In the decidedly "immaterial" domain of poetic rhetoric, "possession" is no longer mere theft, the sheer crudity of what Marx would consider the "primitive accumulation of capital." "Possession" is now achieved by ruses that declare the intelligence, even the genius, of the poet. Thus the allusive texture of "The Purloined Letter" culminates in the ultimate "forgery," Dupin's strategic "quotation" from Crébillon (M 3:993), the line itself an allusion to Aeschylus' *Oresteia*, Sophocles' *Electra*, Euripides' *Electra* and *Orestes*, and these classical tragedies themselves allusions to their mythic prototypes. Dupin's "theft" is legitimized by means of literary and mythic history in ways far more subtle and finally subversive than the Minister's crude attempt at blackmail.

Even so, a certain strategic will to power has been enacted, whereby these "literary properties" have been made to conclude in the name of Dupin/Poe. For whom? The reader, of course, whose interest in the story turns precisely on the rhetorical moves by which Dupin solves the puzzle by constituting a new narrative. The very appearance of the "ahistorical" setting for this tale leads us inevitably to an "interest" in literary history: a history far more compelling in this tale than anything that speaks of that despicable aftermath of the French Revolution, that threat to aristocracy and monarchy, that anarchic rebellion against what "the few possess." Again, from that troublesome 1836 proslavery review in the *Southern Literary Messenger*: Man's "prevailing interest" is "Happiness." "Foremost among" the "external means" to happiness, and "the equivalent which is to purchase all the rest, is property. . . . Under such excitement [as prevails], the many who want, band themselves together against the few that possess; and the lawless appetite of the multitude for the property of others calls itself the spirit of liberty" (*H* 8:267–68). I confess that this sounds too crude for Poe, too naively utilitarian, and nevertheless I "quote" it here, in a reading of "Poe."

There is yet another historical detail in "The Purloined Letter," albeit one that requires considerable speculation. It is in *Vienna* that the Minister once did Dupin "an evil turn, which I told him, quite good-humoredly, that I should remember" (*M* 3:993). For those worried about aristocratic privilege in the years leading up to the Paris Commune and to the American Civil War, Vienna has one large significance among others. It was at the Congress of Vienna in 1814–15 that the last desperate effort was made by the European and Russian monarchies to consolidate their powers and territories in the wake of Napoleon's abdication. Even so, the Congress was a reminder that the old order was changing, that monarchy was in jeopardy and royal territories increasingly arbitrary. Admittedly, I can only speculate here, but in ways that make the most of these bare historical traces in a designedly literary displacement of history into the psychopoetic history that is so often the wish fulfillment of the embattled aristocrat, the would-be plantation owner: the apotheosis of "property" into the ultimate property of language. The Congress of Vienna, the great political event of the early nineteenth century, now becomes the "occasion" for Dupin's revenge against a minister of state. "The Purloined Letter" is Dupin/Poe's own "Congress of Vienna," in which the "territory" of Europe is not simply reapportioned, but remapped onto the coordinates of poetry. Crébillon, we ought to remember, was one of the official censors of the French Academy in the first half of the eighteenth century. Dupin has effected his own repetition of such censorship by creating a discursive field in which the materiality of the letter forbids the intrusions of the more threatening materiality of history.

Jacques Derrida is thus the winner of the battle, but perhaps he has lost the war. What war? Well, the Civil War, among others, which brings us to *Pym*, written twenty-four years before the American Civil War and yet addressing all the fears that the Southerner would feel in the turbulent years leading to the necessity of battle. I make no claim for originality here; the interpretation of *Pym* as a thinly disguised allegory of Poe's manifesto "Keep the South White" belongs to others.[17]

I add only a few touches, delicate strokes, as it were, not the least of which involves the entanglement of historical, psychoanalytical, and textuality debates.

The date of *Pym*'s first appearance in the *Southern Literary Messenger* is 1837, but the date of the voyage on the *Grampus* is "June, 1827" (*P* 1:66). Relevant historical events occurring between these two dates may illuminate *Pym*. The significant event on board the *Grampus* is a mutiny, which seems distinguished for its extraordinary brutality and its utter irrationality. Emancipation in the British West Indies was formally declared on 1 August 1834. Three years earlier, Nat Turner's rebellion—the Southampton Insurrection—occurred in August 1831 in Southampton County in southeastern Virginia. Following the much-publicized trial and execution of Nat Turner in November of 1831, much stricter laws regulating Southern slaves (especially laws regarding travel passes) were passed in most Southern states.

The Narrative of Arthur Gordon Pym of Nantucket is not a mere allegory of proslavery values; in this regard, the historical interpretations have been too crude, rather than simply "inaccurate" or falsely "historical," as Thompson by way of Hull would argue. Poe's own repressed fears regarding slave rebellions in the South and the deeper fear that Southern aristocratic life itself might be passing are the psychic *contents* that provoke the poetic narrative. The defense of the poetic narrative against just these fears is its argument that language, the essence of reason, is the basis of all reality and thus the only proper "property." As the "enlightened ruler" of language, its rational governor, the poet works to recontain that savagery—the mob, the black, the lunatic—within poetic form.

In *Beneath the American Renaissance*, David Reynolds shows how Poe "had learned from America's pioneering penny newspaper a lesson in conscious manipulation of sensational themes through a double-sided fiction that possessed both novelty and tact, excitement and control." For Reynolds, *Pym* combines the irrational sensationalist and the pseudoscientific in a narrative that, if "not altogether successful," nonetheless constitutes a defensive parody of such popular styles.[18] Nat Turner's Southampton Insurrection provoked sensationalist journalism of the most hysterical kind, often focusing on Turner's gory use of a broadax to murder his master and the master's wife.

Poe's defensive fantasy about savage, rebellious blacks is not exclusively enacted on the island of Tsalal. The first outbreak of such savagery is on board the *Grampus* during the mutiny. As I argued in "Writing and Truth in *The Narrative of Arthur Gordon Pym*," it is during the mutiny that *writing* assumes the virtual bodily character of the blood Augustus desperately uses to send his warning to Pym in the hold.[19] From this point on, writing will become the primary referent for reality, and it will be represented commonly in metaphors of the body and/or physical reality. Chief among the savages of the crew is the Black Cook, who is a virtual "demon" and executes bound seamen who have not joined the mutiny by "striking each victim on the head as he was forced over the side of the vessel" (*P* 1:86). The Black Cook tells Augustus "that he should never put his foot on deck again 'until the brig was no longer a brig'" (*P* 1:89). As Reynolds points out, piracy was a common topic for sensational literature of the time. In Poe's narrative, this conventional subject is poetically, perversely metaphorized to cross "piracy" as a literary topic with the historical threat of the "theft" of property posed by slave insurrection and Abolition in general. Like Nat Turner, the Black Cook strikes his victims on the head, testifying to the symbolic danger to reason posed by the emergence of the irrational savagery so many Southern whites imagined would accompany slave rebellion or even legal emancipation.[20]

The mutiny unleashes a terrible savagery that belongs for Poe to the uncivilized state. The providential storm that saves Augustus and Pym from butchery seems to argue against Poe's thesis that the "savagery" of the pirate or the black belongs to a "state of Nature" that civilization must control. In the Paulding-Drayton review, the reviewer endorses the extended "family" of the Southern slave-owner as the basis for "the moral influences flowing from the relation of master and slave, and the moral feelings engendered and cultivated by it" (*H* 8:270). In a perfectly conventional manner, the reviewer argues for the happy "patriarchal character" and the essential "clanship" in the extended "family" of the black's childlike relation to his/her benign master. These are typical proslavery views, certainly more compatible with Tucker, Paulding, and Dew on that subject than the subtler, more ambivalent Poe.

Even so, in *Pym* "Nature" is nothing but the site of savagery and precisely what the unnatural family of master and slave, and thus of the institution of slavery itself, are designed to control. The providential storm arrives, however, at precisely the moment that *The Narrative of Arthur Gordon Pym* has been transformed from the pseudorealism of either sensational or scientific "voyages" and "travels" into the *poetic* voyage constituted by Augustus' and Pym's writing and reading. At this very moment, in fact, Pym learns to *impersonate* the dead mutineer, Hartman Rogers. This impersonation will be followed by the *ingestion* of the other surviving mutineer, Richard Parker.

The scene of cannibalism enacted by the survivors on the drifting hulk of the *Grampus* only appears to identify them with the savagery they have miraculously escaped. The "horrible purpose," "the most horrible alternative which could enter into the mind of man," is proposed initially by Parker (P 1:132), who becomes the victim of his own plan. Although Pym's efforts to convince Parker to "abandon his design" or "at least . . . defer it for another day" seem motivated by Pym's reason and humanity, Pym's arguments have the consequence of turning Parker's savage instinct for survival into a rational, even democratic "lottery" (P 1:132–34). In short, Pym tricks Parker into agreeing to a rational choice of victim. Once he is chosen in this manner, Parker is utterly unmanned, mastered by Pym's trick, no less than the mutineers were mastered by the ghostly apparition of Hartman Rogers: "He made no resistance whatever, and was stabbed in the back by Peters, when he fell instantly dead" (P 1:135).

Translated into the rhetoric of the poetic voyage, such cannibalism figures doubly. On the one hand, as empirical event, it represents the savagery exploited by sensationalist literature. Read as poetic enactment, it is the *internalization* of white power, the transformation of the "blood" of Augustus' message into the perverse Transubstantiation of Poe's Poetic Mystery. This event is not simply a defensive enactment of the savage custom of eating an enemy to defeat his spirit, although it certainly partakes of that ritual. Internalizing his power, consuming his body, the poet transforms the threatened body of the White Master into the rhetoric of the White Poet. Without offering a full analysis, I shall merely remind the reader here of the curious rhetoric of *inversion,* of a topsy-turvy world, that characterizes the experiences of the survivors on the capsized *Grampus*. There is yet one more touch that, speculative as it must remain, I cannot help adding to this account. Of the six judges signing the 5 November 1831 order for Nat Turner's execution, one was James W. Parker. Conventional as the name is, the association of these Parkers is at least suggestive. Judge Parker, of course, can hardly be identified with a mutineer in league with that savage executioner with his axe, the Black Cook, but the wayward tracks of condensation and displacement hardly meet the requirements of logic. Even so, if the Parker eaten by Pym is not just his threatening enemy but also the authority of the court in Jerusalem, Virginia, that condemned Nat Turner, then Pym is invested with the power of the law, now transposed into the fictional frame.[21]

The remainder of the *Narrative* hardly needs to be analyzed in such detail; my own overdetermination of the text has introduced a certain inevitability into it. Let me simply repeat here that the Paulding-Drayton review that *Poe published* in the *Messenger* relies centrally on the special qualities of the extended family constituted between Master and slave. Resorting to anecdotes of devoted slaves weeping at the bedsides of ailing masters, of white mistresses doting on ailing slaves, that review repeats most of the perverse clichés of desperate Southern defenses of slavery as a benign, paternal institution.

In *Pym*, the narrative begins in Nantucket as Augustus enchants Pym with stories of romantic adventure at sea, not unlike, we might guess, the sensational stories of pirates that appeared contemporaneously in the popular press. Reborn first in the accident of the *Ariel*, then again from the mutiny and shipwreck of the *Grampus*, Pym and Augustus leave behind the nuclear family of Pym's own family of lawyers and Augustus' family of sea captains. In the place of those conventional forms of bourgeois "control" and "civilization," Augustus and Pym substitute their own friendship, which is based on their adolescent rebellion against family authority (especially various father figures for Pym and Augustus). This friendship is repeatedly linked with storytelling and writing, as if to suggest that this, rather than the bourgeois family, is the real source of social authority. Augustus' wounded arm, which rots disgustingly as they drift on the *Grampus*, has its obvious sexual suggestiveness, which few critics have missed. The threat of castration that Augustus makes sensuously present to Pym provokes Pym's own narrative of compensation. Insofar as the "savagery" of the mutineers—above all, that of the Black Cook—threatens the powers of reason represented by Augustus and Pym, the pencil that Pym wields as he keeps that soggy diary of events following the mutiny becomes a powerful defense. But so does his subsequent companion, Dirk Peters.

As a "half-breed" (P 1:55), Peters offers an alternative to the "savagery" of the Black Cook. Like the black slaves who would serve their masters faithfully and often to the death during the Civil War, Dirk Peters is Poe's fantasy of the faithful and grateful servant. It is Peters, of course, who embodies the "fierceness of the tiger" that grips Pym just before Parker draws the final lot (P 1:135). Peters' savagery is of a fundamentally different character than the Black Cook's, because it enacts what has already been conceptualized by Pym, who is from this moment on Peters' white master.

Peters both resembles and is distinguished from the natives of Tsalal, who "were among the most barbarous, subtle, and bloodthirsty wretches that ever contaminated the face of the globe" (P 1:180). In his July 1835 review of Theodore Irving's *The Conquest of Florida*, by Hernando De Soto, Poe observes that "the Floridian savage was a more formidable foe than his Mexican brother—more hardy of frame, and more implacable in his revenge" (H 8:39). In his favorable review of James Hall's *Sketches of History, Life, and Manners in the West* in the December 1835 *Messenger*, Poe testifies not only to Hall's "undoubted abilities as a writer" but also to his being "excellently qualified to write precisely such a book as he has written," which includes "the policy of our government in regard to the Aborigines" (H 8:108). Peters is from a Missouri tribe, his father a fur trapper, but he resembles these Floridians and the "Aborigines" whom William Henry Harrison, old "Tippecanoe," helped subdue by defeating Tecumseh in 1811. Let us not forget that Poe, along with his friend Frederick W. Thomas, would campaign vigorously for Harrison in the 1840 election.[22] Peters reenacts the fate that the faithful crewmen on the *Grampus* met at the hands of the Black Cook: "We had proceeded some hundred yards, threading our route cautiously between the huge rocks and tumuli, when, upon turning a corner, five savages sprung upon us from a small cavern, felling Peters to the ground with a blow from a club." With pistols in hand, Pym kills two "savages" and frees Peters, who, promptly "seizing a club from one of the savages who had fallen . . . dashed out the brains of the three who remained, killing each instantaneously with a single blow of the weapon, and leaving us *completely masters of the field*" (P 1:199; emphasis added). Like Native Americans who scouted for and fought with the U.S. Cavalry against tribal foes in the course of Manifest Destiny, like the East Indian Sepoys who fought faithfully for the British in India, Dirk Peters exemplifies one common "colonial solution" to the problem of a native population: subjugation by way of ideological conversion. As "half-breeds," either biologically or ideologically, such colonized people are indentured to the colonizers' values. It is an "art" never raised to a higher level than that of the British in their vast Empire, practiced more crudely in the American West and in our recent ventures in Southeast Asia.

The black prisoner, Nu-Nu, whom Peters and Pym take along on their escape from the savagery of Tsalal, wastes away as they advance toward the whiteness of the Pole. Even so, the incomplete "family" of Augustus and Pym is here fully constituted, albeit in appropriately *masculine* form. With the help of the servile half-breed, the white master affirms his mastery and takes possession of the savagery that so threatens him. He does so not by means of legal and economic domination but in and through the poetic domination that is figured in the *writing* in the interior of the island of Tsalal. Like Nantucket, the poeticized Tsalal now becomes a place of civilization, thanks to the powers of reading and, above all, the power of *writing* that has helped insinuate this "fiction"—*The Narrative of Arthur Gordon Pym of Nantucket*—into reality. It should not surprise us that the author of the "Note" tells us that "Peters, from whom some information might be expected, is still alive, and a resident of Illinois, but cannot be met with at present. He may hereafter be found, and will, no doubt, afford material for a conclusion of Mr. Pym's account" (P1:207). I shall not belabor this passage, although I am tempted to do so. Suffice it to say that Illinois is a Free State, and the convenience of Peters' status as "half-breed" (Native American and white) allows Poe's Pym to liberate a savage without succumbing to the Southern heresy of liberating a perfectly good piece of property, that is, a black slave. Having served his murderous purposes—the murder of Parker, the vengeful murder of the natives on Tsalal, the indirect murder of Nu-Nu—Peters has earned his just desserts: the "free state" that only the white slave master, now turned poet and parodist, can award for service against the savagery that threatens him and his kind. That Peters remains a potential "authority" who might verify the authenticity of Pym's posthumous narration (P 1:55) only underscores this point.

Much could still be said of the translation of black and white oppositions into the manageable black letters and white field of Poe/Pym's written text. Even Poe's apparent anticipation of Freud's thesis about the "antithetical sense of primal words" (in Freud's review of Karl Abel's philological work of the same title) seems to confirm Pym's will to power in this instance. If the psychic script has the power to transform opposites into uncanny relations, if black is nothing but the repression of white, then the psychic narrative is little more than a confirmation of Poe's own thesis: that the transformation of material history into poetic history will "save" the reign of Reason from the savage intrusions of the real.

Freud of course, would not stop at such a conclusion, but would reveal, as I have crudely attempted to do, how the "black savagery" so frightening to both Pym and Poe is little other than the repressed contents of their own white psyches. Such an interpretation would matter little to Poe, however, for it would depend crucially upon a reading in which the ego would read the authority of its own unconscious. In fact, Poe has constituted a narrative in which the reader is by no means the ego of Poe/Pym, but yet another Dirk Peters, the faithful "half-breed" who discovers only the "authority" of the white master.

I return finally to those twentieth-century narratives of psychoanalysis provoked by Poe's *Narrative*. In his reading of the uncanny relation between black and white in *Pym*, John Irwin concludes:

> For though Pym says that they "noticed no light-colored substance of any kind on the island" and though the anonymous author of the note adds that "nothing *white* was to be found at Tsalal, and nothing otherwise in the subsequent voyage to the region beyond," Pym himself points out the white arrowhead flints in the chasm. And just as whiteness lies at the core of the dark realm of Tsalal, so darkness must be present in the white realm of Tekeli-li, otherwise there could be no color boundary, no figure/ground differentiation, no signification. The shadow image haunts the lone regions of Tekeli-li—whether Pym recognizes it or not.
>
> . . . What the ending of *Pym* acts out, then, is "a certain *tendency* of the human intellect" (inscribed within it by the very structure of its birth) to try to survive death by projecting an image of itself (the self as image) into the infinite void of the abyss.[23]

In the subtle optical reading he offers of the appearance of the white figure at the Pole, Irwin contends that it is the shadow cast by Pym that establishes the figure/ground relation. Irwin has already made clear that such an "optical" scene is always already a psychic scene of representation, that the "shadow" of Pym is nothing other than his fear of death, the ghostly "double" of Freud's "Uncanny." Without for a moment disagreeing with this reading, I would supplement that shadow— the shadow of the White Man as Poet—with the corpse of Nu-Nu: the black body that as slave chattel or as "soulless" corpse is the necessary shadow for the poetic representation of *Pym*. The "whiteness" found at the heart of the chasms is, after all, that of "arrowhead flints," which are instruments of the kill. As images of the savage threat posed by the black natives and by black slaves, they are metonymies for their targets: not animals of the hunt, but the whites tabooed in the cry, "Tekeli-li!" Poetically repossessed both by the White Poet and the "half-breed" with whom arrowhead flints are so conventionally identified, the "white arrowhead flints" become the "invisible bullets" of Poe's poetic mastery, his poetic of postmodern colonialism.

Such a reading is thus not the radical "other" of the psychoanalytical debate, occasioned by Poe's writings, between Jacques Lacan and Jacques Derrida, unless that "other" is the uncanny double of just what psychoanalysis threatens to consolidate as the "law" of psychic signification. In her account of that debate, Barbara Johnson summarizes the consequences for the reader of the Poe text and the psychic signifier of the unconscious:

> The reader is comprehended by the letter: there is no place from which he can stand back and observe it. Not that the letter's meaning is subjective rather than objective, but that the letter is precisely that which subverts the polarity "subjective/objective," that which makes subjectivity into something whose position in a structure is situated by an object's passage through it. The letter's destination is thus *wherever it is read:* the place it assigns to its reader as his own partiality.[24]

The "letter" thus quite by design "takes dominion everywhere," so constituting the reader's relation to his psychic text that he can find nothing but the letter's dominion, its specular *shadowing-forth* of his own identity. In this way, Lacan, Derrida, Barbara Johnson, and I myself (among other textualist readers of Poe) would institutionalize the "domain of language," both as psychic and literary landscape, as the ineluctable field of our historical acts. The appropriateness of these gestures to Poe's own intentions is thus perfect; the textualist has read, even as he or she has disregarded Poe's own historical situation, in a manner that perfectly realizes Poe's very contemporary poetic purpose. Johnson continues:

> The opposition between the "phallus" [Lacan] and "dissemination" [Derrida] is not between two theoretical objects but between two interested positions. And if sender and receiver are merely the two poles of a reversible message, then Lacan's very substitution of *destin* for *dessein* in the Crébillon quotation—a misquotation that Derrida finds revealing enough to end his analysis upon—*is,* in fact, the quo-

tation's message. The sender (*dessein*) and the receiver (*destin*) of the violence which passes between Atreus and Thyestes are equally subject to the violence the letter *is*.[25]

Once again, we can find no fault with this reading, insofar as we stay within the "frame" of psycholinguistic reference. The revenge cycle of the ancient struggle between Atreus and Thyestes, which turns upon the subtle arts by which each attempts to destroy the lineage of the other's house, is precisely the incestuous violence initiated by this postmodern poetic: that of Poe's art and of psychoanalysis itself. Internalizing the violence of material history, the immaterial history of poetry and psychoanalysis transforms such violence into the very principle of its perverse power.

My conclusion, then, is that the modernist (postmodernist?) Poe and the antebellum proslavery Poe are far more intricately connected than we want to believe. Spiller and Thorp's 1947 *History* and Arthur Hobson Quinn's 1941 *Edgar Allan Poe—A Critical Biography* treat Poe as a Southern writer, whose ambivalence toward his own "Southernness" is treated both literarily and psychobiographically. They are history and biography respectively that are perfectly "readable" in the context of Ernest Marchand's 1934 essay, "Poe as Social Critic," which uses a wide variety of materials other than the disputed Paulding-Drayton review to make the proslavery case against Poe. I have for sheer histrionic effect not mentioned the author of "Edgar Allan Poe" in the 1947 *Literary History of the United States*, edited by Spiller et al. I myself could not remember as I quickly looked back through my copy. Reading it again, I am struck powerfully with how much it appears to represent G. R. Thompson's primary antagonist in the *Columbia Literary History*. The author writes: "To be sure, he [Poe] sometimes betrayed a provincialism of his own. He was so eager to prove himself a Virginian that he followed Allan's tradition, which was that of Marshall and not that of Jefferson. Poe went so far as to deplore the French Revolution, to defend slavery as 'the basis of all our institutions,' and to assume the scorn held by the propertied classes for the democratic 'mob.' "[26] The references are obviously to the infamous Paulding-Drayton review, but they are also to Poe's general politics and his psychobiography. The author was F. O. Matthiessen, often the target of critics intent on establishing Poe's centrality to American literature. Is it any wonder, then, that Matthiessen should have so neglected Poe in *American Renaissance*?

The answer to that rhetorical question is not as clear as I have implied. At the end of his article on Poe in the *History*, Matthiessen concludes: "In opposition to the romantic stress on the expression of personality, he insisted on the importance, not of the artist, but of the created work of art."[27] And then, as if fearing we had missed his reference to Eliot's "Tradition and the Individual Talent," Matthiessen writes: "He stands as one of the very few great innovators in American literature. Like Henry James and T. S. Eliot, he took his place, almost from the start, in international culture as an original creative force."[28] There it is: Poe the precursor to the international modernism of James and Eliot that is the very center of *American Renaissance*. Six years later is Matthiessen changing his mind, or is this earlier work merely an explicit address to the "Poe" otherwise pushed to the margins of the book *American Renaissance*, whose theoretical boundaries welcomed him and accounted for him perfectly? No. Matthiessen simply didn't know what to *do* with Poe in that context. Poe's Southernness, his pro-slavery arguments and regional sentiments, "queered the geometry" of Matthiessen's Modernism. Matthiessen, then, was wrong as well, and he let himself do just what G. R. Thompson and subsequent Poe critics have done: repress the subtle complicity of literary Modernism with racist ideology, which now Poe may be said to represent both in his antebellum historical context and his modern "revival."

But just what *is* the complicity of "Literary Modernism" with the proslavery sentiments we have tried to impute again to E. A. Poe, now in his proto-modern as well as antebellum identities? Poe's prose and poetry is, of course, full of abused, murdered, dismembered women, of native peoples represented as the embodiment of primitive evil, of visionary aristocrats, of royalty "saved" by poetic manipulation, of the hateful "masses." Such literary thematics, although we should not neglect their evidence, will take us only so far in the direction of a re-valuation of Poe's aristocratic pretensions and slaveholding mentality. Behind these obsessive themes in Poe's writings is the gnostic ide-alism, together with its hatred of the material and the temporal, of the body and its decay, that found such powerful resonance in the Symbolists, Decadents, and High Moderns. It is a virtual Nietzschean *ressentiment*—that hatred of time, change, and becoming—that Nietz-sche attributes to the "priestly abnegation of life" he finds so central to Romantic Idealism.

Its characteristics are, Nietzsche knew well enough himself, the very predicates of a Modernism from which Nietzsche would work futilely to distinguish himself: contempt for history, disdain of labor, disgust with the body, avoidance of the crowd, abhorrence of Nature. Out of such negativity, aesthetic modernism constructed its own anti-terra, a Laputa that seemed once populated only by harmless Swiftian cranks. Its geography is perfectly mental or verbal, and it can be traveled only by those clever enough to follow its precharted paths. Access to this territory can be gained only by a certain literacy, defined by competency in those ideas and texts that in our own age have challenged the status of the landed estate and other signs of privilege marking the ruling class.

This critique of the ideology of Modernism is familiar enough by this late date, but it has generally led merely to an indictment of aesthetic modernism—and of idealism in general—as powerless, reactive, or narcissistic. We need to recognize the will to power that is involved in such modernist negativity in the larger context of the new class configurations that have emerged in our own postindustrial age. Poe's contempt for the material world enables his glorification of the imagination, visionary experience, and the ultimate transcendence of the alienated body. Even in *Eureka*, Poe's sublime is language, but only when it is employed in very specific ways. Only in its poetic, self-referential, metamorphic dimensions does language escape the instrumentality of everyday life. And such poetic language demands a special literacy, a competency of poetic reading and writing that would develop into the sorts of *institutions* of sophisticated interpretation that have their origins in aesthetic modernism. For all their avant-gardism, the modernists yearned for a new aristocratic order, a secret society, whose signs and symbols could be read only by those initiated properly and strictly.

However powerless, irrelevant, or insignificant the institutions of academic criticism might seem in the larger context of our postindustrial age of information, they have helped legitimate hierarchies of language use that are today the structural foundations for what I would term a "hermeneutics of class." The calls for "cultural literacy" are only the most recent echoes of this modern appeal for the reorganization of human activity along the lines of signifying authority. Abolitionists like Frederick Douglass knew well enough that the postbellum fight for genuine economic and social freedom would have to be conducted at all levels in terms of verbal authority—in politics, in the courts, in the press, as well as in literature. Those with *access* to language, both in terms of their educations (the capabilities to speak in technically proper ways) and the availability to them of actual media (control of the presses of papers, journals, and the book-publishing industry), control the political economy. The rest constitute the "mob," which Poe fears as profoundly as any of his literate contemporaries. Like Poe's "Man of the Crowd," the mob represents all that which "does not permit itself to be read," a fearful collective unconscious.

Yet, it is just this "unconscious" that the *flaneur* of Poe's story, "amusing" himself with a cigar, a newspaper, and the comings and goings of the London crowd, does read, translating the apparently indiscriminate mob first into a carefully articulated hierarchy of classes and then into a single figure, the "Man of the Crowd" himself, whose passage from downtown London to the Gin Palace at the outskirts of the city and back again seems to describe the senseless repetition of the mob's apparent "industry" (*M* 2:506–15). It should not surprise us that Poe's *flaneur* reads the unconscious of London in a manner that recalls the interpretation in the "Note" of the "writings" of and in the chasms on the island of Tsalal in *The Narrative of Arthur Gordon Pym*, published two years before "The Man of the Crowd." What remains unreadable to Pym and simply a part of the natural environment of the Tsalalian natives is for "Mr. Poe" a complex "text," whose origins are the same as those of our own Western, literate, rational tradition and whose "end" is, as Jean Ricardou has argued so eloquently, the signature of the Author.

Poe's insistence upon a new *authority* capable of reading what remains profoundly "unconscious" either to the malevolent Tsalalian native or to the London mob becomes his warrant for a new class system predicated on linguistic competency. The new "property" of words may have seemed to have little practical value for the Poe harassed by money worries and dependent on his Southern patrons, whose capital was counted in human beings and acreage. But today we may conclude, as we so often have, that Poe was profoundly clairvoyant, even if we must insist that his was a perverse vision. Today one's class identification and one's virtual earning power are tied intimately to the "Power of Words." If we hope to revive the important historical question of Poe's antebellum politics, then we will have to reconsider its continuity with the postbellum politics of aesthetic language and its powerful hierarchies of verbal competency and cultural "literacy," which is to say we must rethink the entanglement of the antebellum Southern writer with his shadowy other, the modern, cosmopolitan trickster, Edgar Allan Poe.

Prefigurings

"Postmodern" or Post-Auschwitz:

The Case of Poe

David H. Hirsch

 I wish to examine that quality in Poe that enables us to think about him in so many different guises, and I would like to speculate on what it is specifically that may link Poe to "postmodern" criticism. We may think of Poe as a wholly antiquated eighteenth-century gothic writer in the Monk Lewis tradition, who somehow blundered into mid-nineteenth-century liberal, Enlightenment America. Vernon L. Parrington, it will be recalled, in *Main Currents of American Thought*, found that "the surprising thing is that such a man should have made his appearance in an America given over to hostile ideas"—by which Parrington meant that nineteenth-century Enlightenment America was hardly the kind of society one would expect to give rise to gothic extravagance and effete aestheticism. It is also tempting to think of Poe as a writer distinctly of his time, sharing with fellow great mid-nineteenth-century writers, like Hawthorne and Melville, leanings toward dark Romanticism and "the power of blackness." Harry Levin, of course, includes Poe in the triumvirate making up *The Power of Blackness*, and G. R. Thompson has edited a collection of essays on Poe, entitled *The Gothic Imagination: Essays in Dark Romanticism*. Paradoxically, we may also consider Poe as a writer who was anachronistic not so much in looking back to eighteenth-century gothic traditions as in looking forward to French symbolism and Modernism (as has been amply demonstrated by Patrick F. Quinn and Charles Feidelson, Jr.). We can also think of Poe as a writer who anticipated the post–World War II despair of the Existentialists, as I tried to demonstrate in an analysis of "The Pit and the Pendulum."[1]

And now, in an age of critical movements designated variously, and in rapid shifts, as semiotics, poststructuralism, deconstruction, and postmodernism, it is possible to look at Poe as a deconstructionist who deconstructs one of his own poems in "The Philosophy of Composition." But in the present essay, I want to think about Poe in terms of what has come to be called postmodernism, except that I should like to jettison this indeterminate, pseudo-historicist term and replace it with what I believe is the more focused and more accurately historical designation, the post-Auschwitz age. For though I cannot say what is meant by postmodern, except that it is somehow antithetically related to Modernism, I believe I can identify what I mean by post-Auschwitz. In brief, the post-Auschwitz age is one in which the nineteenth-century prophecies of Marx and Nietzsche have been realized in the Soviet Gulag, on the one hand, and in the Nazi death camps, on the other. As George Steiner put it in an essay published in the *Times Literary Supplement*: "The doctrines or pseudo-doctrines of nineteenth and early twentieth-century chauvinism, of Marxism-Leninism, of Fascism and of National Socialism were . . . European. . . . Auschwitz and the Gulag, the systematic incineration from the air of great cities evolved from inside the politics, the technologies and the vocabularies of European culture."[2]

Whatever postmodernism may be, the post-Auschwitz age is one of total war, mass murder, and genocide; an age of the death of God and of the eclipse of Western culture and Judeo-Christian values; an age that has witnessed the end of illusions about human potential and about the indomitable goodness of the human spirit; an age of the breakdown of the Renaissance concept of the human form as that Judeo-Christian fusion of flesh and spirit so eloquently described by Shakespeare's Hamlet in his speech to Rosencrantz and Guildenstern: "What a piece of work is a man, how noble in reason, how infinite in faculties, in form and moving, how express and admirable in action, how like an angel in apprehension, how like a god! the beauty of the world; the paragon of animals" (2.2.303–7).

Although Poe obviously could not have known the writings of either Marx or Nietzsche, his imagination somehow gained access to a vision of the disintegration of the human form that was enacted in the death camps and the Gulag, a disintegration to which we, in the latter half of the twentieth century, have been witness. While Emerson was preaching what became the mainstream American message of the glories of the organic unity of form, and the infinitude of the human spirit and of human potential, Poe had already perceived the beginnings of the disintegration of the self. In fact, I cannot take credit for being the first to notice this phenomenon. Allen Tate showed himself to be not only a most penetrating New Critical close reader but a historically conscious one when he wrote as early as 1951, without specifically making the connection to events of the Nazi era, that "Poe is . . . a man we must return to: a figure of transition, who retains a traditional insight into a disorder that has since become typical, without being able himself to control it." I should like to note one more lucid insight in Tate's deservedly influential, enabling essay that I shall return to later in discussing *The Narrative of Arthur Gordon Pym*: "He [Poe] was a religious man," Tate wrote elsewhere in the essay, "whose Christianity, for reasons that nobody knows anything about, had got short-circuited."[3] Poe, then, is postmodern because he gave us not only the earliest but also some of the most powerful descriptions of human beings in the process of disintegration: human beings who are forced to survive *in extremis,* as, of course, Pym himself is required to do again and again.

D. H. Lawrence was, as far as I know, the first to perceive this strain in Poe. But as was often the case with Lawrence, his dislike of everything he thought Poe stood for led him to blame the messenger for the message. Poe, he asserted, "is absolutely concerned with the disintegration-process of his own psyche."[4] Having knowledge of the Nazi death camps and the Soviet Gulag, as Lawrence did not, we can see, now, that Poe was not recording "the disintegration-process [only] of his own psyche" but also of the collective psyche of Western culture. The uncanny accuracy of Poe's prophetic vision is attested to by the witness of Bruno Bettelheim, a Viennese psychologist who spent a year in Dachau and Buchenwald (before 1939). The "most dedicated followers" of the Nazi state, he wrote,

> were destroyed as persons in our sense, as may be seen from . . . the story of [Rudolph] Hoess, commander of Auschwitz. Hoess, because of the total dominance which the state imposed on him and to which, true Nazi that he was, he expected himself to submit without question, so laid aside his personal existence that he ended a mere executor of official demands. While his physical death came later, he became a living corpse from the time he assumed command of Auschwitz. That he never became a "moslem" was because he continued to be well fed and well clothed. But he had to divest himself so entirely of self respect and self love, of feeling and personality, that for all practical purposes he was little more than a machine functioning only as his superiors flicked the buttons of command.[5]

It is commonplace for European critics and men of letters to trace the beginnings of contemporary literature, and the depiction of the postmodern condition, to Baudelaire or Mallarmé. The following statement from José Ortega Y Gasset's "The Dehumanization of Art" is typical: "Poetry had to be disencumbered. Laden with human matter it was dragging along, skirting the ground and bumping into trees and housetops like a deflated balloon. Here Mallarmé was the liberator who restored to the lyrical its ethereal quality and ascending power. Perhaps he did not reach the goal himself. Yet it was he who gave the decisive order: shoot ballast."[6] Harold Bloom, in reviewing the Library of America volumes of Poe, edited by Patrick Quinn and G. R. Thompson, diminishes Poe's importance as a writer and thinker in the context of world literature: "Poe's mythology, like the mythology of psychoanalysis that we cannot bear to acknowledge as primarily a mythology, is peculiarly appropriate to any modernism, whether you want to call it early, high, or postmodernism. The definitive judgment belongs to T. W. Adorno, certainly the most authentic theoretician of modernism, in his last book, *Aesthetic Theory*."[7] Bloom goes on to quote Adorno at length, but I will pick up only the last two Adorno sentences: "Baudelaire marks a watershed, in that art after him seeks to discard illusion without resigning itself to being a thing among things. The harbingers of modernism, Poe and Baudelaire, were the first technocrats of art." Bloom adds that "Baudelaire was more than a technocrat of art, as Adorno knew, but Poe would be only that except for his mythmaking gift." That is a very large "but," especially when one considers that Bloom did not find "mythmaking" so negligible a virtue when he wrote the book *Shelley's Mythmaking* some twenty-five years earlier. In a final burst of pique, Bloom asserts that "Poe is a great fantasist whose thoughts were commonplace and whose metaphors were dead."[8]

In fact, one could only wish that Bloom were right about this, because if Poe's metaphors had been less alive and his thoughts not so uncannily prophetic, we would be living in a more peaceful and less threatening age. But nothing could be farther from the truth. Poe's thoughts were far from commonplace for his time, and his metaphors were more alive than he could have hoped and than humanity could have feared. As has been more than amply demonstrated by Patrick Quinn, Poe's thoughts and metaphors not only were alive when Poe uttered them, but quickly found new life in France. "In *L'Art romantique*," Quinn writes, Baudelaire

> calls Poe simply "the most powerful writer of the age." . . . the sincerity underlying it [this statement] may be inferred from the allusion, in *Journaux intimes*, to his morning prayers to God and to Edgar Poe

as his intercessor in heaven. For Mallarmé also, Poe was a writer altogether unique, *the* poet, as we know from "Le Tombeau d'Edgar Poe." For him as for Baudelaire the stature of Poe was evidently that of a literary deity.[9]

In his powerful, authoritative account of the historical, cultural, sociological, psychological, and literary developments that led up to the Nazi death camps, Eric Kahler cites Baudelaire as having started a chain of literary events, carried on by Rimbaud, Laforgue, and Mallarmé, among others, that formed "the bridge to the *hommes absurdes et révoltés* of our own age, and in all of whom we can observe the symptoms of the same psychic disease." Of the European authors who formed the late nineteenth-century and early twentieth-century links in this chain, including Nietzsche, Ibsen, and Dostoyevski, Kahler writes:

> None of these men stood for their countries alone. What else did these great authors express, most of them with the help of a newly developed psychological perception, but the deep unrest, uneasiness and alarm at the effects of our modern middle-class civilization: the increasing hollowness and precariousness of conventional values, the derangement of human relations? What else did they voice but the rumbling of revolutionary forces, of a whole underground level of reality that burst into the open in the various crises of the twentieth century? [10]

Certainly in the cases of Baudelaire, Mallarmé, and Dostoyevski, the "newly developed psychological perception" owed something to Poe. But the questioning of values is also a basic strain in Poe's writings: "the deep unrest, uneasiness and alarm at the effects of our modern middle-class civilization: the increasing hollowness and precariousness of conventional values, the derangement of human relations." And of course we can see this uneasiness in Pym. As Quinn points out, Pym keeps running away from the traditional family and from middle-class culture, as represented by his family.[11]

In addition to the new psychology and the questioning of values, Poe established for the Romantic poets a new relationship between nature and consciousness. In describing the qualities that make Mallarmé both a Romantic and a postmodern writer, Paul de Man writes that for Mallarmé

> Nature, far from representing the satisfaction of a happy unproblematic sensation, evokes instead separation and distance; nature is for him the substance from which we are forever separated. . . . The sym-

bols of failure and of negativity that play such an important role in his poetry must be understood in terms of the underlying polarity between the world of nature and the activity of consciousness.[12]

I think there can be no doubt that Poe, who in this was so different from the British Romantics, is also at the root of this particular strain in Romantic poetry, an "underlying polarity between the world of nature and the activity of consciousness" that we can translate into the term "alienation." In fact, Gaston Bachelard makes just this point in talking about *The Narrative of Arthur Gordon Pym*, asserting that Poe hears the call of the ocean " 'because this call comes from the most dramatic of solitudes, one in which man has for his antagonist the elemental world itself. There man is alone . . . faced with a universe of monstrous forces.' "[13] I would say, further, that it is the fusion of this sense of alienation with Poe's inversion of values that results in what is perhaps Poe's most post-Auschwitz quality, his vision of the dehumanized person.

As is well known, D. H. Lawrence refused to accept the validity of Poe's vision of the dehumanized person, attributing Poe's perception to his personal sexual dysfunction and to what Lawrence took to be American Puritan attitudes toward sexuality: "All Poe's style," Lawrence observed, "has this mechanical quality, as his poetry has a mechanical rhythm. He never sees anything in terms of life, almost always in terms of matter, jewels, marble, etc."[14] But it was the nineteenth-century writer Poe who was right about the fateful path on which Western culture had embarked and Lawrence who was rowing against the tide in trying to reassert a Romantic organicism.

Poe's vision of dehumanized man may be found even in a relatively verisimilitudinous work like *The Narrative of Arthur Gordon Pym*, a work that Poe wrote out of a multitude of both literary and documentary sources, as is definitively established in Richard Kopley's recent essay "The '*Very* Profound Under-current' of Arthur Gordon Pym."[15] Poe's vision of dehumanization is apparent in the last two journal entries in the novel. As Grace Farrell Lee has demonstrated in "The Quest of Arthur Gordon Pym," the ending is a culmination of a descent into Hell and into the subconscious.[16] But it is also, I believe—on a less positive note than Farrell Lee—a return to chaos and a disassembling of the Judeo-Christian construct of the human form, an unraveling, so to speak, of the divine creation: "We were evidently approaching it [the cataract] with a hideous velocity. At intervals there were visible in it wide, yawning, but momentary rents, and from out these rents, within which was a chaos of flitting and indistinct images, there came rushing and mighty, but soundless winds, tearing up the enkindled ocean in their course" (P 1:205). Though Poe's novel may count among its themes a return to chaos, nevertheless *Pym* remains a work of art in which Poe scholars have traced a number of thematic and structural patterns.

These patterns, however, are often parodic. As Farrell Lee puts it, in speaking about the death and rebirth pattern, Poe's "parodic vision creates a mock communion from a scene of cannibalism by interfusing it with allusions to the last supper of Christ."[17] But it is not only that they are parodic; the patterns of conventional Judeo-Christian (which is to say the fusion of Hellenic-Roman and biblical) culture are ruptured. The conventional unifying symbols and consolidating metaphors of the culture are shattered. For example, the narrator describes his state of mind just before the four survivors are to draw lots to decide who will be cannibalized. "Even then," he writes, "I could not bring myself to arrange the splinters upon the spot, but thought over every species of finesse by which I could trick some one of my fellow-sufferers to draw the short straw, as it had been agreed that whoever drew the shortest of four splinters from my hand was to die for the preservation of the rest" (P 1:134). Here the crucifixion as a symbol of God's redemptive power is returned to an absurd physicality, as the purely physical term "preservation" is used to portray the salvation of the cannibals.

It may also be of value to call attention to the parallel and disjunction between the drawing of lots here and the skill involved in playing the game of "even and odd" as it is described in "The Purloined Letter," a skill which has been exhaustively commented on by the two postmodern Jacques, Lacan and Derrida.[18] They have been able to convert the game itself into an eternal circle precisely because Poe knew that he was describing a game that in its purest form is infinitely circular. The schoolboy who "'attracted universal admiration'" for his skill in the game has converted the pure game of guessing into a test of psychological acumen. But the way in which the boy explains this acumen is itself a mockery of the human form: "'"When I wish to find out how wise, or how stupid, or how good, or how wicked is any one, or what are his thoughts at the moment, I fashion the expression of my face, as accurately as possible, in accordance with the expression of his, and then wait to see what thoughts or sentiments arise in my mind or heart, as if to match or correspond with the expression" ' " (*M* 3:984).[19] The schoolboy has mastered a guessing game by converting it into a psychological game. But in *The Narrative of Arthur Gordon Pym*, the game of lots is in earnest, and Poe knows it. James W. Gargano has reminded us that Poe's narrators are not always the same narrator and are not always Poe.[20] In this instance, we have a confirmation of Baudelaire's observation that *Arthur Gordon Pym* was "a purely human book."[21] Here the game of drawing of lots, which is a variant of the game of "even and odd," is not only in earnest but a matter of life and death. And here, as we can see, Poe takes an attitude toward the game that is quite different from that taken by Dupin in "The Purloined Letter."

Poe, of all people, recognized that death was not a game, a fact which seems to have escaped the two Jacques. Poe was, as all his readers quickly perceive, obsessed with thoughts and fears of death. And this is no less true of his "purely human book" than of his "mechanical" tales. It is not just death that Poe described, however, but violent death and murder, in *Pym* as in many of the tales. But here again, Poe had moved into the post-Auschwitz (or postmodernist, if one prefers) consciousness, leaving his more optimistic fellow Romantics in the dust. While the British Romantics were still ephebes struggling with the shadow of their great precursor, the author of *Paradise Lost*, trying to make some sense of the heroic grandeur of evil as personified in Milton's Satan, Poe had already arrived at the post-Auschwitz recognition of what has been called (controversially) the banality of evil. In his preface to *Prometheus Unbound*, Shelley declared, obviously with Milton in mind, that "the only imaginary being resembling in any degree Prometheus is Satan."[22] As we can see in the lot-drawing episode, Poe had passed beyond the belief that there was some epic grandeur in evil.

I cannot, therefore, agree with Walter Bezanson, who finds a "solemn rhythm" in the description of the cannibalistic act.[23] Indeed, the description, following the narrator's earlier protestations of disgust and revulsion, is all too matter-of-fact:

> Let it suffice to say that, having in some measure appeased the raging thirst which consumed us by the blood of the victim, and having by common consent taken off the hands, feet, and head, throwing them, together with the entrails, into the sea, we devoured the rest of the body piecemeal, during the four ever memorable days of the seventeenth, eighteenth, nineteenth, and twentieth of the month. (*P* 1:135)

Moreover, the very next sentence is so offhand as to make the reader almost forget the horror that has just been described: "On the nineteenth, there coming on a smart shower which lasted fifteen or twenty minutes, we contrived to catch some water by means of a sheet which had been fished up from the cabin by our drag just after the gale" (*P* 1:135).

We need not look far in the canon of Holocaust literature to find an analogue to Poe's prophetic fiction. I shall cite here two entries from the diary of Johann Kremer, doctor of medicine and philosophy, who kept part of this diary while serving as a physician in Auschwitz. The entries are dated 5 and 6 September 1942. The first entry reads: "This noon was present at a special action in the women's camp ("moslems")—the most horrible of all horrors. Obersturmfuhrer Thilo, military surgeon, is right when he said today to me we were located here in '*anus mundi*.' In evening at about 8 p.m. another special action with a draft from Holland. Men compete to take part in such actions as they get additional rations." The editor of the diary has appended Kremer's explanation of the 5 September entry, given in a deposition to a war crimes tribunal:

> "Particularly unpleasant had been the action of gassing emaciated women . . . I remember taking part in the gassing of such women in daylight. I am unable to state how numerous that group had been. When I came to the bunker they sat clothed on the ground. . . . I could deduce from the behaviour of these women that they realized what was awaiting them. They begged the SS men to be allowed to live, they wept, but all of them were driven to the gas chamber and gassed. Being an anatomist I had seen many horrors, had to do with corpses, but what I then saw was not to be compared with anything seen ever before."

In the next day's entry, Kremer writes, "Today an excellent Sunday dinner: tomato soup, one half of chicken with potatoes and red cabbage (20 grammes of fat), dessert and magnificent vanilla ice-cream. After dinner we welcomed the new garrison doctor, Obersturmfuhrer Wirths."[24]

The dissociation of sensibility and the atrophy of human conscience detectable in the Nazi Kremer's matter-of-fact depiction of the atrocity and of his own "horror" are anticipated by Poe in the narrator's description in "The Tell-Tale Heart" of why he has murdered his victim: "Object there was none. . . . I loved the old man. He had never wronged me. He had never given me insult. For his gold I had no desire"

(*M* 3:792). The narrator's consciousness, here, reflects one of Tate's observations about Poe that can be applied, without missing a beat, not only to Kremer but also to "postmodernist" criticism: "We get the third hypertrophy of a human faculty: the intellect moving in isolation from both love and moral will, whereby it declares itself independent of the human situation in the quest of essential knowledge."[25] But Poe, to do him justice, knew that his narrator was mad. Kremer, like the narrator in Poe's story, thinks he is sane.

The concluding sentences of Pym's final journal entry remain a challenge to Poe scholars, and I do not hope to resolve them here. I would, however, for my own purposes, like to point out that they embody two disfigurations of the human form, one a physical disfiguration and the other a disfiguration of color: "But there arose in our pathway a shrouded human figure, very far larger in its proportions than any dweller among men. And the hue of the skin of the figure was of the perfect whiteness of the snow" (*P* 1:206).

The closing sentence evokes echoes of Isaiah 1:18, in particular, "Though your sins be as scarlet, they shall be as white as snow." In the biblical verse, the whiteness of snow is equated with moral purity. But in *Pym*, the image of whiteness has become—not terrifying, I believe, as Melville makes it in "The Whiteness of the Whale"—but repulsive, perhaps because it is associated with the disfigured human form in the previous sentence. Poe's inversion of the symbol of purity into an image of disgust is, once again, an anticipation of the inversion of values that characterizes our post-Auschwitz age.

Figuration

Consumption, Exchange, and the Literary Marketplace:

From the Folio Club Tales to *Pym*

Alexander Hammond

 In *American Romanticism and the Marketplace*, Michael T. Gilmore argues that the economics of authorship and publication underwent a profound transformation in this country between 1820 and 1850 as a mass market emerged and "authors lost most of their earlier control over publication" to "highly competitive publishing houses"; by the end of this period, "publishing had become an industry, and the writer a producer of commodities for the literary marketplace."[1] According to Gilmore, this transformation of literature into "an article of commerce" had a "profound influence" on such figures as Hawthorne, Thoreau, and Melville, an influence that can be traced in the "themes and form of their art," in their ambivalent "accommodation and resistance" to "dependency on the market," in the defeat of "their hopes for certain kinds of authority or for closeness to their readers," and in the reconstruction of "the alienation they criticized in modern society" in "their relations to their audience."[2]

Although Gilmore mentions Poe only in passing, his generalizations clearly recall Poe's ambivalent attitudes toward authorship and audience as described in such studies as Michael Allen's *Poe and the British Magazine Tradition*, Bruce Weiner's *The Most Noble of Professions: Poe and the Poverty of Authorship*, and Michael Williams' *A World of Words: Language and Displacement in the Fiction of Edgar Allan Poe*.[3] Furthermore, the kinds of self-conscious reconstructions of writer/audience/marketplace relations that Gilmore finds in the fiction of Hawthorne and Melville are characteristic of Poe's canon generally and of *The Narrative of Arthur Gordon Pym* in particular, as readings of the novel by such critics as John Carlos Rowe, Paul Rosenzweig, and J. Gerald Kennedy directly or indirectly demonstrate.[4] A general interpretation of *Pym* from Gilmore's perspective would, I think, ground much of the text's concern with the problematics of authorship and audience in Poe's response to the conditions of its production. My concern here. however, is limited to outlining such an approach to only selected features of the novel, with an emphasis on how they reflect Poe's characteristic formulations of the writer's relationship to the marketplace in his early literary career. The argument focuses, as will be seen, on a tropic language for literary exchange involving food, consumption, and cannibalism that *Pym* shares with Poe's "Tales of the Folio Club," particularly the 1833 version of that never-published collection.

Fundamental to this essay's approach to *Pym* is the familiar fact of the narrative's transfer, in mid-composition, from one marketplace to another. Poe began the work as a magazine serial for the relatively elite audience of the *Southern Literary Messenger*, which published two installments of the story early in 1837; he subsequently completed the bulk of it for Harper and Brothers of New York, a publishing firm dealing with the general reader in a much more profit-oriented market-place, particularly in its travel books and fiction.[5] As Joseph V. Ridgely notes, Harper and Brothers had explicitly set forth that marketplace's standards for fiction when the firm rejected a collection of Poe's Folio Club tales in the spring of 1836 (*P* 1:31). It refused publication be-cause, as James Kirke Paulding reported to Poe, his tales demanded "a degree of familiarity with various kinds of knowledge [,] which [ordi-nary readers] do not possess, to enable them to relish the joke; the dish is too refined for them to banquet on"; accordingly, Poe was advised in future submissions to "lower himself a little to the ordinary com-prehension of the generality of readers."[6] In June of 1836, when the Harpers' reader wrote the author directly, he reiterated that Poe's Folio Club tales "would be understood and relished only by a very few— not by the multitude"—and made it clear that the "multitude" deter-mined what the firm could publish: "Readers in this country have a decided and strong preference for works (especially fiction) in which a single and connected story occupies the whole volume, or number of volumes, as the case may be; and we have always found that republi-cations of magazine articles [as many of Poe's Folio Club tales were by this time] . . . are the most unsaleable of all literary performances."[7]

Two points in these characterizations of the Harpers' marketplace are important here. First, the writer's role is framed, to use Gilmore's terms, as a producer of commodities for a marketplace controlled by the preferences of the mass readership; second, the commodity sup-plied by the writer in this exchange is rendered metaphorically as food served up for the readers' consumption—thus, Poe's tales, a warmed-over meal at best, are a "dish" "too refined for [ordinary readers] to banquet on." While the immediate occasion for this food metaphor may have been the banquet setting of Poe's Folio Club collection,[8] the trope itself is both long-standing in Western literature and common in the literary discourse of Poe's era.

In her study of the reception of fiction in antebellum America, Nina Baym finds that "drinking and eating were the activities most compared [by reviewers] to novel reading." Such tropes, she suggests, are generally linked to assumptions about readers' sensual appetites and share "a conception of the novel as a substance taken into the body, there to work an effect [for good or ill] beyond the reader's control."[9] Although the linkage of food and literature is an ancient one, as the classical tradition of the literary banquet indicates, a recent semiotic study of post-Revolutionary French culture and fiction by James W. Brown suggests that conjunctions of gastronomy, commerce, and writing may especially mark Poe's era; in particular, Brown notes that both the restaurant, with its democratizing of the consumption of artfully prepared food, and cooking as a professionalized art form arose in the context of nineteenth-century bourgeois commerce.[10] These phenomena suggest obvious parallels to the changes in the literary marketplace that Gilmore traces. That American writers and reviewers were aware of such conjunctions seems clear: in the *Southern Literary Messenger* for May 1835, for example, Nathaniel B. Tucker offered the following assessment of the increasingly "French" literary diet available to nineteenth-century American readers:

> Men can no more read every thing than they can eat every thing; and the *petits plats,* that are handed round hot-and-hot, leave us no room to do honor to the roast beef of old England, nor to the savory Virginia ham. But these are the food by which the thews and sinews of manhood are best nourished. They at once exercise and help digestion. Dyspepsia was not of their day. It came in with *French Gastronomy.* Are we mistaken in thinking, that we see symptoms of a sort of intellectual dyspepsia, arising from the incessant exhibition of the *bon bons* and *kickshaws* of the press? (*H* 8:15)[11]

When in February 1836 Poe justified a lengthy review of a Harper and Brothers novel because it was "a portion of our daily literary food" (*H* 8:179); when a junior editor for the *United States Telegraph* explained his inability to review the August 1836 *Messenger* because his superior had probably "cabbaged it, and sits up after his dinner of politics, to take tea upon cakes of literature"; when Lewis Gaylord Clark in August 1838 mocked any "gentleman" possessing a "capacious maw" big enough to "swallow" *Pym*'s improbable contents [12]—all were using a shared tropic language that casts the literary marketplace as a restaurant or banquet hall in which readers dine, choosing among and consuming literary works variously served up as appetizers, main courses, and desserts. Both Poe's "Tales of the Folio Club" and *Pym* share this language of literary consumption. In the 1833 collection in particular, a young, unknown, and, one suspects, ill-fed Poe elaborated gastronomic tropes into a satiric conceit for author/reader/marketplace relationships that both anticipates and, I will argue, illuminates how Poe self-consciously scripted such relationships in the text of *Pym*. In the interests of clarity, what follows is a brief summary, from surviving manuscripts and letters, of the framework of the 1833 collection.[13]

The basic metaphor of the literary marketplace as banquet hall is central to the Folio Club design, as Benjamin Fisher's study of its insistent drinking imagery implies.[14] In it, a comic literary club holds a monthly banquet to which its eleven members "come prepared with a 'Short Prose Tale'" to read "to the company assembled over a glass of wine at [a very late] dinner" (*M* 2:204). The commentary on this literary menu was intended, Poe explained, as a "burlesque upon criticism" (*O* 1:53, 104). The banquet climaxes with a vote:

> The writer of the 'Best Thing' is appointed President of the Club *pro tem:*, an office . . . which endures until its occupant is dispossessed by a superior *morceau*. The father of the Tale held, on the contrary, to be the least meritorious, is bound to furnish the dinner and wine at the next similar meeting of the Society . . . an excellent method of occasionally supplying the body with a new member, in the place of some unfortunate who, forfeiting two or three entertainments in succession, will naturally decline . . . the 'supreme honour' and the association. (*M* 2:204)

The frame story itself concludes when its narrator, a new member whose "morsel" is "adjudged to be the worst[,] demurs from the general judgment, seizes the . . . M.SS. upon the table, and, rushing from the house, determines to appeal, by printing the whole, from the decision of the Club, to that of the public" (*O* 1:104).

In order for me to gloss Poe's gastronomic language here, it is necessary to emphasize that the Folio Club frame story dramatizes what Michael Williams has called Poe's "anxieties of authority" about loss of control of the written text to its readers: "On the one hand [Poe] fears the failure to gain a readership; yet on the other he resents the interpretive appropriation of his texts once they are out of his direct control."[15] Citing Gilmore, Williams calls attention to Poe's persistent use of "economic figures" in descriptions of his struggle to control "'literary property.'"[16] Williams notes, for example, that as early as the "Letter to B——" written in preface to his *Poems* of 1831, Poe defensively counterpoints the reader's "ownership" of the physical text as commodity against the author's "originating authority" over that text's signification: "A man [will] call a book his, having bought it; he did not write the book, but it is his" (H 7:xxxv).[17]

Featuring not only images of economic appropriation of the text, Poe's "Letter to B——" offers the following characterization of the "great barrier" faced by the unknown American writer in the marketplace: "He is read, if at all, in preference to the combined and established wit of the world. I say established; for it is with literature as with law or empire—an established name is an estate in tenure, or a throne in possession" (H 7:xxxvi). The institutional metaphors here cast the possession of a literary reputation as akin to inherited property or regal office, a foundation for power and income, because most readers, like tenants and subjects, pay uncritical fealty to those with "established" names and continental or British birthrights, which constitute "so many letters of recommendation" in this form of commerce. In 1831, Poe's position on the literary marketplace was clearly ambivalent: he condemns yet implicitly envies the power of established authors, who function in the marketplace with the detachment of landed aristocrats standing above mere "trade"; and he laments his own lack of access to that trade even while he damns the readers in it for possessing derivative, uncritical tastes and for presuming illegitimate authority over texts purchased as mere commodities.

In his 1833 Folio Club framework, Poe recasts these various marketplace relationships in gastronomic terms. He elaborates in particular on the combined power of authors with "established" names by imaging them as a closed eating and drinking club that displays its influence, first, by restricting table access to an elite few; second, by "dining" on and critically evaluating only the contributions of its own membership; and, third, by keeping itself both literally and figuratively supplied with fresh meals and new members by "using up" one of its current authors at each banquet. The newest member of this comic literary establishment, the narrator of the frame story, initially expresses "profound sentiments of admiration" for the "remarkable men" whom he lists by name at the club's table (M 2:203, 205). When his contribution to the evening's menu is judged worst, his theft of the manuscripts constitutes a reappropriation of his literary property in order to appeal from the "taste" of the elite few to that of the many. In effect, he calls on the mass reading public to resist the authority of established authors (and critics) by asserting independent judgment and thus control over the menu at the literary world's dining table. (The ironic distance between this character's naive faith in the judgment of the mass reading public and Poe's own skepticism about it may be traced in Weiner's *Most Noble of Professions*.)

The struggle for interpretive authority over the Folio Club menu introduces an initial parallel with *The Narrative of Arthur Gordon Pym*. When Poe moved the text of *Pym* from an elite to a mass marketplace, he explicitly scripted the transfer into the novel's "Preface," which purports to account for the replacement of his signature on the *Messenger* text with Arthur Gordon Pym's on the Harpers book. In this "Preface," I would suggest, Poe recapitulated a version of the Folio Club frame story, with "Mr. Poe" cast in the role of the established author, Pym in that of the novice newcomer. As J. Gerald Kennedy has argued, the "Preface" elaborates a variety of ironies around Mr. Poe's advice to the hesitant Pym to "trust to the shrewdness and common sense of the public—[Mr. Poe] insisting, with great plausibility, that however roughly, as regards mere authorship, [Pym's] book should be got up, its very uncouthness . . . would give it all the better chance of being received as truth" (P 1:55–56). Trust in the public's shrewdness seems confirmed when readers overrule the authority of "the name of Mr. Poe . . . affixed" to the narrative in the pages of the *Messenger* by refusing to accept as "fable" what that "gentleman" published "*under the garb of fiction*" (P 1:56). We have here a struggle for interpretive control of a text in which, just as the Folio Club narrator would hope, the independent judgment of the "public" wins out, a fact that gives Pym a similar confidence to reclaim control of his literary property and to offer it under his own name to the judgment of the mass audience. In reference to the latter marketplace, of course, the ironic implication is that Pym, the unskilled amateur, not Mr. Poe, the "gentleman" who edits a literary journal from Virginia, is clearly the more appropriate author to produce and sign a book for the Harpers reader, who will not object to "uncouthness" in a "roughly . . . got up" text.[18]

Poe's ironic gesture here may be largely self-protective, particularly in light of his sloppy assembly of the novel's patchwork text (as Burton Pollin amply documents in *P* 1:12–13, and passim). Indeed, Poe's concern about hasty craftsmanship on this novel, which he apparently produced very rapidly for Harper and Brothers during a period of precarious family finances,[19] is implicit in another self-referential passage in *Pym* that, like the "Preface," deals with the transfer of its text between marketplaces: the well-known digression on the "proper stowage" of a ship's cargo. This digression appears in the text shortly after the *Messenger* section ends and employs a nicely turned variation on the language of literary consumption. In it, Pym documents the problems attendant on poor "management" of the cargoes of trading vessels that carry either foodstuffs—flour and grains—or two uniquely Southern products, tobacco and cotton; ships that fail to give "proper attention to stowage" of these cargoes capsize when they encounter rough seas and "heavy gales" of wind (*P* 1:97–99). Because no direct source has been found for the material here, Evelyn Hinz reasonably argues that "stowage" in this digression functions as a "metaphor for literary composition," that wind and sea serve as images for reception and audience, and that the whole passage is an "extended comment on the problems of the writer in general and on the technical features of [*Pym*] in particular."[20]

In the process of expanding his unfinished *Messenger* narrative, Poe evidently scripted into his text an ironic meditation on the critical risks he faced in taking his inexpert sea narrative north on a voyage for profit. As in the *Grampus*, certainly "stowage . . . was most clumsily done [in Poe's text], if stowage that could be called which was little better than a promiscuous huddling together of oil-casks and ship furniture" (*P* 1:99). Such a narrative would indeed be at risk from "readers who may have seen a proper or regular stowage" (*P* 1:97); furthermore, it could well suffer the fate of "the schooner Firefly, which sailed from Richmond, Virginia, to Madiera, with a cargo of corn, in the year 1825." The schooner's captain, appropriately surnamed "Rice," "had never before sailed with a cargo of grain, . . . [and] had the corn thrown on board loosely, when it did not much more than half fill the vessel" (*P* 1:99). In the language of literary consumption, the naive Captain

Rice's departure from Richmond with a partial, ill-stowed cargo of corn implies the author's recognition that he was both inexperienced in this mode of literary commerce and bringing to market insufficient material with which to prepare, or perhaps distill, a "meal" for the Harpers' readers. The drinking imagery (cf. Fisher, *Very Spirit of Cordiality*, p. 11) also suggests that the contents of this "vessel" had already been partially consumed before it left Richmond, as indeed the narrative itself had been through prior serial publication of two installments in the *Messenger* in early 1837.

Once at sea, the schooner continues to function as a self-referential emblem for Poe's in-process narrative: the *Firefly* meets only "light breezes" on the "first portion of the voyage" but goes "down like a shot" when the "corn was . . . heard to shift bodily" after the captain is forced to "lie to" by "a strong gale from the N. N. E." (*P* 1:99). In light of the harsh notices that Poe had given to various works by Northern authors during his years with the *Messenger*, in 1837 he might well anticipate a hostile reception for his sea story from reviewers in the "N. N. E." Thus, in Pym's account of the fate of this ship, its captain, and its cargo of grain, Poe seems to be encoding his own sense of professional peril about bringing an inexpert, partially published, as yet unfinished narrative into a new marketplace. And the fact that many similar "vessels" were launched ill-prepared to risk stormy critical receptions was apparently not reassuring:

> No seaman who knows what he is about will feel altogether secure in a gale of any violence with a cargo of grain on board, and, least of all, with a partial cargo. Yet there are hundreds of our coasting vessels, and, it is likely, many more from the ports of Europe, which sail daily with partial cargoes, even of the most dangerous species, and without any precautions whatever. The wonder is that no more accidents occur than do actually happen. (*P* 1:98–99)

As I gloss Poe's food tropes for literary exchange, it is important to stress that those shared by *Pym* and the Folio Club tales are not simply transparent analogies for the commodity and authority relationships that Poe reconstructs in these texts. When Poe deals with the literary marketplace in the Folio Club collection, for example, his tropic language casts the writer's "self" as the commodity that is expended, sold, and consumed—thus rendering literary exchange as a kind of cannibalistic commerce in which readers feed upon authors and for which authors sacrifice parts of the self. An oblique use of such language informs the 1833 Folio Club introduction, which describes the club as a "body" that discards old "members" and "supplies" itself with new ones; thus, after joining the club, the narrator terms himself "a member of that body" (*M* 2:204), as if the price of becoming an insider were trading separate corporeal existence for that of an appendage. This pattern is replicated in the court of drunken wine tasters featured in "King Pest," a key tale in the 1833 collection. In it, the Folio Club's function as a collective assembly of critics is mirrored in a grotesque banquet scene wherein individual participants become separate anatomical parts (mouth, nose, eyes, and so forth) of a single head—a head that critically evaluates wine served in fragments of human skulls. As Fisher implies, Poe's references to drink and drinking in this and other Folio Club tales tend to literalize "inspiration" as wine, ale, and liquor.[21] In the image of a collective self in "King Pest," who consumes wine from "a portion of a skull, which was used as a drinking cup" (*M* 2:248), we have one of Poe's most disturbing metaphors for readers, or perhaps more precisely for critics, as cannibalistic feeders on the contents of the writer's skull.

The motif of literary exchange as bodily commerce figures in other Folio Club tales as well. "Lionizing" features an author who becomes a literary celebrity by turning his nose into a "pamphlet," only to lose his renown to "a Lion with no proboscis at all" (*M* 2:177). And the title character of "The Duc de L'Omelette" is both the "Prince de Foie-Gras" and "author of the 'Mazurkiad'" (*M* 2:34), his names suggesting that writers are indeed consumable "dishes" for their readers. After dying in disgust at an improperly served meal, the Duc is served up in turn as an emblematic "meal," delivered "per invoice" to Satan in the latter's chambers in Hell. The Folio Club tale that most directly treats literary commerce as cannibalism of the author, however, is "Bon-Bon."[22] The title character is a philosopher, author, and *restaurateur* who believes "the powers of the intellect" hold "intimate connection with the capabilities of the stomach" (*M* 2:97). His café literalizes the trope of author as producer of meals for sale to readers: it bears as its sign a "vast folio" volume of Bon-Bon's own writings inscribed with a bottle on one side, a paté on the other—thus, in the narrator's words, "was delicately shadowed forth the two-fold occupation of the proprietor" (*M* 2:100). In a corner of the café that serves as both "kitchen and . . . *bibliothèque*," "volumes of German morality were hand and glove with the gridiron—. . . Plato reclined at his ease in the frying pan—and contemporary manuscripts were filed away upon the spit" (M 2:101).

A customer in the form of a devil who dines on the souls of writers appears in the restaurant, convinces Bon-Bon that the soul is no mere " 'shadow' " of the corporeal self (" 'Only think of a fricasséed shadow!' " [M 2:113]), and comments on the taste of previous meals made from the souls of various classical authors and philosophers. (Like those to whom Harper and Brothers market their books, Satan dislikes meals that are not fresh—" 'a pickled spirit is *not* good' " [M 2:111].) True to his name and calling, Bon-Bon attempts the sale of his own soul, insisting that it would make an excellent " 'Stew,' " " 'Soufflée,' " " 'Fricassée,' " " 'Ragout and fricandeau,' " but he finds the market overstocked, his customer " 'supplied at present,' " and his offer refused (M 2:113–14).

Joan Dayan has argued that "convertibility" of "shadow and substance" is central to the language of this tale, built as it is around the premise that "all souls . . . are physicalized as food."[23] This insight helps characterize Poe's language of literary consumption generally: in this language, I would argue, tropic convertibility operates among meals, texts, and materialized souls, all of which become commodities in metaphorically equivalent exchange relationships. In an impressive analysis of "The Gold-Bug," Marc Shell demonstrates such tropic interaction between the processes of literary and monetary exchange involving texts, paper money, and coinage.[24] Such interactions operate in "Bon-Bon," which features three parallel commercial exchange relationships that interact with, and are essentially convertible into, one another. The first of these exchange relationships involves cooks who convert foodstuff into meals sold to and eaten by customers. The second encompasses the writing, selling, and reading of texts and is implied when, at the beginning of the tale, Bon-Bon retouches "a voluminous manuscript, intended for publication on the morrow" (M 2:102). And the third, a variation on the classic Faustian exchange, is made explicit when, at the end of the tale, Bon-Bon offers to convert his soul into a "stew" to be sold to the devil. At the middle of each of these relationships, the exchangeable commodity—a meal, a text, a "physicalized" soul—can be metaphorically substituted one for another, as can the more mysterious conversion and consumption processes at the extremes. The tropic interactions among these exchanges are not, I would stress, merely analogical or metonymical; the substitutions are, to borrow John Irwin's phrasing, simultaneously either/or and both/and.[25]

It should be clear that various substitutions across these three exchanges yield an array of the kind of figures that this essay has been examining. To illustrate briefly, libraries can become kitchens, writers can become cooks and Faust figures, and literary markets and reading scenes can become restaurants and dining halls and rooms with cannibal and devil figures in them. Such an array clearly informs "Bon-Bon," as it does the Folio Club framework in which Poe images the literary marketplace as both an eating club and a "diabolical association" (M 2:203) that, as noted above, consumes its own members.[26] Writing, partaking of both the cooking of food into meals and the rendering of soul into substance, implicitly involves a loss, an expenditure by the author of self/mind/spirit "stuff" that is converted into the physical commodity of the text;[27] because the exchange of that commodity is economic, writing for the marketplace thus becomes both a kind of Faustian bargain with those who would buy and control the author's work and a commerce with the cannibals who "dine" on it.

In Poe's early use of this figurative array, the writer's return for expenditure varies. Had the title character of "Bon-Bon" succeeded in selling his soul as a meal for the devil, his payment would obviously have been fame, as was Voltaire's in that tale (M 2:113, 117, 95). By contrast, in such Folio Club stories as "The Duc de L'Omelette," the author figure struggles to escape the control of the Prince of Hell who has had him delivered, as noted, "per invoice" from his coffin (M 2:34). The Duc evades the devil by cheating him at cards, a defense of the authorial self that recalls, I would suggest, Poe's characteristic hoaxing strategies with readers; in terms of Poe's tropic array, such strategies function as efforts by the writer to avoid being owned, controlled, or consumed by the marketplace and its readers (cf. Williams, *World of Words*, p. 48). In 1841, Poe said of literary exchange, "To coin one's brain into silver, at the nod of a master, is to my thinking, the hardest task in the world" (O 1:172). Whomever Poe was thinking of in the category of "master" here, whether readers, editors, or publishers, by this date he clearly felt that the return in silver did not compensate for either the expenditure of self or the loss of control involved in the exchange.

In *The Narrative of Arthur Gordon Pym*, Poe's use of this figurative array for literary exchange is fairly obvious. In the much-discussed episode in the hold of the *Grampus* in which Pym reads a note written by Augustus, clearly Pym as reader is figuratively a long-suffering diner, while Augustus plays the part of makeshift restaurateur (the latter's cabin recalls Bon-Bon's café, featuring as it does both "hanging shelves full of books" and, in a "kind of safe or refrigerator," "a host of delicacies, both in the eating and drinking department" [*P* 1:68]). Augustus begins his role by supplying Pym with the following stores, from which I delete only the blankets: "some books, pen, ink, and paper, . . . a large jug full of water, a keg of sea-biscuit, three or four immense Bologna sausages, an enormous ham, a cold leg of roast mutton, and half a dozen bottles of cordials and liquers" (*P* 1:69). The conjunction of food, drink, and texts is clear, as is the linkage of eating and reading in Pym's later consumption of these stores (presumably they are not served from the "fine earthenware" [*P* 1:69] that his reading/dining room once contained). Pym ignores the writing materials but for three days contentedly samples the mutton, the water, and, just before falling into his first extended sleep, "the expedition of Lewis and Clarke to the mouth of the Columbia" (*P* 1:70). After Pym awakes, the eating/reading parallel is reinforced: the mutton spoils, the sausages make him thirsty, the water runs low, and he "could no longer take any interest in [his] books" (*P* 1:71). As John Carlos Rowe has observed, the book title on Pym's menu mirrors the character's own narrative, thus doubling the scene of literary consumption below with that of the reader of Pym's text "above," as it were.[28] As far as I have been able to determine, Poe's version of Lewis and Clarke's title is unique to *Pym*; the phrasing is singularly appropriate, because in Poe's tropic array all books take journeys, as in this scene, to the mouth of some reader.

The sole addition to Pym's diet before Augustus returns in person with water and "three or four cold boiled potatoes" (*P* 1:83) is, of course, the note that the latter scrawls in his own blood; appropriately enough, Augustus uses a "toothpick" for a pen (*P* 1:92). In light of recent analyses of Pym's various efforts to read this note—analyses by Rowe, Kennedy, and G. R. Thompson[29]—there is no need to discuss this scene at length. As Evelyn Hinz observes, Augustus turns his blood into "the word," the kind of expenditure of self that writing in Poe's tropic array often involves.[30] Pym's famous response to the word "blood" in the text is a variation on Poe's characteristic figure for the threat that literary consumption poses to the author: Pym is implicitly troubled by cannibalistic feeding on what Rowe has called a "synecdoche for the body of Augustus."[31] After the *Messenger* section of the text ends, Pym will have another, more literal opportunity to make a meal of the author of this note when starvation forces the remnant of the *Grampus'* crew into cannibalism; by the luck of the draw, Augustus escapes in the latter instance from having both blood and body consumed (P 1:134–35), but shortly thereafter, like the leg of mutton he earlier supplied to Pym, his flesh spoils and his rotted body becomes food for the sharks:

> It was not until some time after dark that we took courage to get up and throw [Augustus'] body overboard. It was then loathsome beyond expression, and so far decayed that, as Peters attempted to lift it, an entire leg came off in his grasp. As the mass of putrefaction slipped over the vessel's side into the water, the glare of phosphoric light with which it was surrounded plainly discovered to us seven or eight large sharks, the clashing of whose horrible teeth, as their prey was torn to pieces among them, might have been heard at the distance of a mile. (P 1:142)

Unlike Pym, who had had some difficulty in finding light to decipher a note written in Augustus' blood, these sharkish "readers" seem to have no problems with illuminating the meal that they make from the body of the author of that note.

To sum up, it would appear that, after Poe arranged to transfer his narrative from the relatively elite *Messenger* to a marketplace catering to a mass readership, and thus presumably after he composed the textual digression on "proper stowage" of foodstuffs being shipped to market, he created a variety of episodes informed with elements of the tropic array for literary exchange in the Folio Club collection, especially those that emphasize cannibalism of the authorial self. In doing so, Poe was evidently scripting into the text figures for the threat he felt from the new marketplace in which he labored. In such a reading, the fate of the corpse of Augustus, object of the sharks' feeding frenzy, becomes an extreme image of the fate of authors who must market "parts" of the self as commodities for audience consumption. One might speculatively link this image with the scene in which Pym leads a countermutiny by masquerading as the corpse of Rogers. In the latter episode, Poe can be said to be mapping out strategies for facing threatening audiences by disguising the self as an "unappetizing" body within the text, as John Irwin's reading implies.[32] Finally, I would also note that the obverse of this episode is enacted in the scene in which the *Grampus* encounters the death ship: here, Pym as audience confronts a corpse masquerading as a living seaman, one who apparently gestures to him across the gap between their vessels. The cannibalistic center of Poe's tropic array for literary exchange is starkly dramatized when a seagull transfers a bloody piece of human flesh from the corpse to the deck at Pym's feet. Here, no text mediates the exchange between "author" and "reader" as it does when Tiger delivers Augustus's note; the seagull carries to Pym not an inscription in authorial blood but rather a "horrid morsel" from the body of the "author" himself—an explicit invitation to cannibalism that Pym rejects in horror (*P* 1:125).

This essay must necessarily remain open-ended and tentative until its readings are more firmly grounded in Poe's texts, in his ideological assumptions about "democratic" audiences,[33] in the conditions of literary production to which he was responding, and in nineteenth-century cultural codes involving food and commerce. It does seem reasonable to conclude, however, that in the process of composing *The Narrative of Arthur Gordon Pym*, Poe self-consciously scripted into the text his concerns both about how to make a meal for himself and his readers out of his *Messenger* material and about how to avoid being "cannibalized" in the new marketplace for which he wrote.

Pym Pourri:

Decomposing the Textual Body

J. Gerald Kennedy

 We cannot be sure whether Poe or some nameless functionary at Harper and Brothers constructed the elaborate subtitle for *The Narrative of Arthur Gordon Pym of Nantucket* which summarizes the novel's sensational elements. But the sixteen-line inventory—which promises "mutiny," "atrocious butchery," "shipwreck," "horrible sufferings," "famine," "capture," and "massacre," as well as "incredible adventures and discoveries"—must have amused the author, who well understood the exchange value of sensation (*P* 1:53). In "How to Write a Blackwood Article" (published a scant four months after the novel's appearance), Poe's fictional magazine editor, Mr. Blackwood, advises the aspiring writer Psyche Zenobia to "pay minute attention to the sensations" because they will be worth "ten guineas a sheet" (*M* 2:340). Unfortunately for Poe, his grisly novel did not yield so handsome a return, but *Pym* nevertheless betrays his unrelenting effort to wring sensational effects from its material. Indeed, in a body of fiction pervaded by morbid themes, the narrative marks what Poe might have called the ne plus ultra of bad taste. Except for the closing paragraph of "The Facts in the Case of Monsieur Valdemar," or perhaps the fiery violence of "Hop Frog," nothing else in Poe rivals *Pym* in its representation of disgusting scenes.

Now, a century and a half after its publication, this "silly book" (as the author called it [*O* 1:130]) threatens to replace "The Fall of the House of Usher" as the central Poe text, the crux of current critical discussion. This is the case largely because its ambiguous central events both compel and resist analysis, depicting interpretation itself as a species of self-delusion in which the young narrator repeatedly posits mistaken inferences and theories. *Pym* has thus emerged as a fable of misreading, eliciting an unusually wide range of explanations for its flawed form and cryptic images. But its irresistibility compels us to ask whether on some baser level we are also drawn to *Pym* (as Poe predicted) by "its very uncouthness" (*P* 1:55–56), by its projection of the scandalous, the revolting, and the unspeakable. In a tale which turns on the violation of a taboo—the intrusion of white men into the black world of Tsalal—Poe seems intent on violating the literary taboos of his time and place by representing murder, mutilation, canni- balism and—in noisome detail—human decomposition. In this brief essay, I want to consider the interpretive implications of putrefaction, drawing upon certain anthropological theories to flesh out the issues. My title plays both on the idea of a pot pourri—suggesting a mixture of perspectives on the novel—and on the more common signification of *pourri,* which in French means "rotten" or "stinking." What follows, then, is a reflection on *pourriture* (or putrescence), both its place in *Pym* and its broader cultural implications.

Decay figures in four principal scenes in *Pym* and in each instance points toward related cultural attitudes or practices. As if to offer a foretaste of horror, Poe depicts Pym in chapter 2 settling into his little "apartment" beneath the deck of the *Grampus* with an array of tooth- some provisions. After nibbling some cold mutton, Pym falls asleep, only to discover upon awakening that the mutton is "in a state of absolute putrefaction." His "great disquietude" seems prompted by the supposition that he has slept an unnaturally long time; since his watch has also run down, Pym realizes that to slumber in the total darkness of the hold is to risk falling out of time altogether into timeless and end- less sleep (*P* 1:69–71). Yet the threat is more immediate than that: the decomposing mutton, which was to have sustained his life, has become a sign of death—a sign which, in the process, subverts the slumber metaphor to suggest that death is less a big sleep than a big stink, a fetid disintegration of matter.

Georges Bataille enables us to place this scene in a broader context when he suggests (in *Erotism: Death and Sensuality*) that the horror of death is the "mainspring" of desire. Among primitive people, he observes, "the moment of greatest anguish is the phase of decomposi- tion." This is so because decaying flesh exposes not simply the skeletal structure but biological disorder—"the sickening primary condition of life." Bataille explains: "That nauseous, rank, heaving matter, frightful to look upon, teeming with worms, grubs, and eggs, is at the bottom of the decisive reactions we call nausea, disgust, or repugnance." In effect, the power of decomposition lies in its revelation of the crude, organic basis of life which culture seeks to idealize and deny. The living bury the dead, Bataille implies, less to keep the body safe than to escape the contagion associated with decay. However irrationally, survivors "perceive in the horror aroused by corruption a rancor and hatred projected toward them by the dead man which it is the function of the mourning rites to appease." Decaying flesh invariably prefigures one's annihilation and return to seething life. Bataille claims that he thus lives "in expectation of that multiple putrescence that anticipates its sickening triumph in my person."[1]

The rotten shank of mutton lying beside Pym epitomizes the process of corruption and portends his own return to "rank, heaving matter." It also prefigures his subsequent encounters with increasingly threatening embodiments of decay. The second such confrontation occurs after the bloody mutiny; in chapter 7, Poe's narrator recounts the death of Hartman Rogers, who has apparently been poisoned by the mate who leads the mutineers:

> Rogers had died about eleven in the forenoon, in violent convulsions; and the corpse presented in a few minutes after death one of the most horrid and loathsome spectacles I ever remember to have seen. The stomach was swollen immensely, like that of a man who has been drowned and lain under water for many weeks. The hands were in the same condition, while the face was shrunken, shrivelled, and of a chalky whiteness, except where relieved by two or three glaring red splotches, like those occasioned by the erysipelas: one of these splotches extended diagonally across the face, completely covering up an eye as if with a band of red velvet. (*P* 1:107)

Since Pym elsewhere indicates that he was below decks when Rogers died, his eyewitness account of the condition of the corpse "a few minutes after death" raises serious questions about his reliability. But the very impossibility of the account implies the obstinacy of Pym's fascination with decay: Rogers' death seems a "horrid and loathsome" spectacle because his body resembles that of a bloated drowning victim. Like Valdemar, Rogers undergoes instantaneous decomposition; this corruption is scandalous precisely because it takes place out in the open, under the gaze of men, rather than in the privacy of the grave, or in this case, in the ocean depths.

Pym's obsession with the appearance of Rogers, however, goes beyond voyeuristic curiosity. In a subsequent scene, after the victim has been tossed overboard, Pym contrives to "represent the corpse of Rogers" by donning the dead man's shirt, stuffing it with bedclothes to simulate "the horrible deformity of the swollen corpse" (*P* 1:108–9), and then applying white chalk to his face along with a few dabs of blood. By this impersonation, he aims to terrify the mutineers so that he, his friend Augustus, and their ally Dirk Peters can overwhelm the rival gang. Despite the makeshift nature of the disguise, Pym has transformed himself so successfully that when he passes before a mirror, he experiences a "violent tremour" at the very recollection of that "terrific reality which [he] was thus representing" (P 1:109). In this act of imposture, Pym has *become* Rogers, effecting an identification with the dead man which implies his symbolic consanguinity. The mutineers, meanwhile, construe Pym's appearance as the "revivification of [Rogers'] disgusting corpse" (P 1:112) and succumb to their own fears; indeed, the guilty mate falls dead upon the spot.

Both Pym's "tremour" and the rival gang's dread of a "disgusting" yet reanimated body partake of the "terror of decomposition" elucidated by Edgar Morin. In his analysis of funerary practices and the psychic "disruptions" underlying them, Morin notes that the most violent *purturbations funéraires* prolong themselves in the institution of mourning, which is shaped and ordered by "the horror of the cadaver's decomposition": "The 'impurity' of death is its putrefaction, and the taboo of impurity which strikes the parents, who are obliged to cover themselves with a distinctive sign or to hide themselves, is mourning itself, that is, the placing in quarantine of the family where the contagion reigns." For Morin, the crucial meaning of decay resides in its immediate, personal threat:

> The terror of decomposition is none other than the terror of the loss of individuality. It is not necessary to believe that the phenomenon of putrefaction in itself brings dread, and now we can specify: where death is not individualized, there is only indifference and simple stench. Horror ceases before animal carrion or that of the enemy, of the traitor, which one deprives of burial, which one leaves to "burst" and "stink" "like a dog," because he is not recognized as a man. The horror is not the carrion, but the carrion of a counterpart, and it is the impurity of this cadaver which is contagious.

Unlike Bataille, who emphasizes the horror of creatureliness, Morin grounds this elemental disgust in a shock of recognition, the perception of the rotting corpse as "mon semblable—mon frère." Decomposition marks "an irreparable loss of individuality," literally the dissolution of that which comprises one's irreplaceable essence.[2]

When Pym assumes his disguise, he becomes the literal counterpart of Rogers and in the mirror confronts a double loss of individuality: he is no longer himself, and his dissimulation exposes him to the wrenching truth that death itself—the death he presumes to mock—entails just such an effacement of self. Pym gazes at a momentary image of his own inevitable decomposition. For the mutineers, however, Pym as Rogers evokes primal fear through the supposed "contagion" of corruption. The mate and his cohorts dread what Morin calls the "taboo of impurity," the contamination which extends to those close to the deceased (and who are in this case responsible for his death). As Bataille notes, the decomposing corpse is believed to project a hatred or rancor toward survivors who have failed to perform rituals of mourning. The superstitious mutineers perceive the disguised Pym as the intrusion of that contagion which by its very presence marks them for death. In part, the "horror and utter despair" of the gang as they perceive the bloated figure derives, Poe explains, from "the deep impression which the loathsomeness of the actual corpse had made in the morning upon the imaginations of the men" (*P* 1:112).

Pym thus exploits the "taboo of impurity" associated with decomposition to wrest control of the *Grampus* from the mutineers. To some extent he displaces his own fears through masquerade in the way that children dress as witches or monsters at Halloween: protection through mimesis. But in a subsequent episode, when Pym and his comrades encounter a ship of death, the problem of putrefaction can be avoided no longer. Suffering from hunger and thirst and lashed to the hulk of the wrecked *Grampus*, the survivors hail an approaching brig and imagine that their rescue is at hand. "Of a sudden, and all at once," Pym redundantly notes, "there came wafted over the ocean from the strange vessel (which was now close upon us) a smell, a stench, such as the world has no name for—no conception of—hellish—utterly suffocating—insufferable, inconceivable." As the brig passes by, Pym observes "twenty-five or thirty human bodies, among whom were several females . . . in the last and most loathsome state of putrefaction" (*P* 1:124). The tall figure on the bow, initially thought to be smiling encouragement to the survivors of the *Grampus*, proves to be the chief horror: "The eyes were gone, and the whole flesh around the mouth, leaving the teeth utterly naked. This, then, was the smile which had cheered us on to hope!" (*P* 1:125). Pym concludes from the "saffron-like hue" of some of the corpses that the entire crew has fallen victim to yellow fever (*P* 1:126). But apart from the gothic *frisson* imparted by this evocation of the *Flying Dutchman* myth, what purpose does the episode serve? Why does Poe insist on elaborating the repugnant details?

In one sense, this repugnancy is the very point of the scene. Poe compels us to consider why it is that the sight and smell of decaying human flesh occasion such profound aversion. Is it nature or culture which teaches us to perceive decomposition as a disgusting process?[3] After all, the huge sea gull "busily gorging itself with the horrible flesh" (*P* 1:125) treats the corpse of the tall sailor as a great delicacy. Yet for Pym, the stench of death produces an instant recoil; as he gasps for breath, he notices that his companions are "paler than marble" (*P* 1:124). In effect, the approach of death induces a deathlike pallor in the living; here Pym, no longer masquerading as a corpse, finds himself exposed to the contagion of decay. In *Violence and the Sacred*, René Girard speaks of the disruptive and violent effect of death upon the community in which it occurs; the phase of physical decay marks its most violent threat—that of a formlessness which erases the distinction between life and death. "The crisis assumes the form of a loss of difference between the living and the dead," Girard writes, "a casting down of all barriers between two normally separate realms."[4] This appears to be the literal situation in *Pym* when the decomposing figures on the deck of the phantom ship—and especially the tall stranger on the bow—present a ghastly parody of living sailors; indeed, so radically has Poe effaced the distinction between the quick and the dead that Pym and company find themselves madly "shouting to the dead for help" even after they have observed that "not a soul lived in that fated vessel" (*P* 1:124).

But Pym's difficulty in the face of decomposition is still more complicated, for he experiences a virtual loss of language; even in retrospect he can find no name for the insufferable smell wafting across the waves. The communal breakdown prefigured by the disintegration of the corpse has its parallel in discourse; Girard remarks that "language itself falters in describing the 'remains.' The rotting corpse becomes, in the words of Bossuet, 'cet objet qui n'a de nom dans aucune langue.' "[5] The spectacle of corruption exposes the inability of speech or writing to signify the "inconceivable" or to conventionalize and regulate the attendant disgust. This sense of decomposition as a defiance of language comes closest to the radical, theoretical implications of *Pym*. For Poe's recurrent staging of human decay leads even the obtuse narrator to admit the failure of language, to realize that the odor from the brig was "a stench, such as the whole world has no name for." This smell that cannot be signified, which is itself the sign of an object that cannot be named in any language, discloses not only the inadequacy of language but the incapacity of intellect and culture to normalize—and neutralize—the reality of putrefaction. What the unspeakable reality of the corpse ultimately exposes is an elemental breach between words and things, a gap which is customarily ignored by the conventions of discourse but which nevertheless inheres in the phenomenal structure of experience. In a novel singularly preoccupied with the difference between fact and fiction, illusion and truth, appearance and reality, the perception of this abyss has more than incidental importance. Through decomposition, Poe calls attention to the provisional nature of language and hints through his hoaxical narrative that all discourse participates in the archetypal hoax which assumes that language confers mastery or control over the phenomena which it names. By resisting such domestication, *pourriture* exposes that breach concealed by the hoax of language.

The fourth instance of decay in *Pym* enables us to see more clearly its unsettling metaphorical implications. In chapter 13, just after the gruesome episode of cannibalism in which Parker, the last surviving mutineer, has been slaughtered and devoured, Pym records the death of his friend Augustus, who has succumbed to gangrenous infection from a wound sustained in the skirmish with the mate's gang:

> About twelve o'clock he expired in strong convulsions, and without having spoken for several hours. His death filled us with the most gloomy forebodings, and had so great an effect upon our spirits that we sat motionless by the corpse during the whole day, and never addressed each other except in a whisper. It was not until some time after dark that we took courage to get up and throw the body overboard. It was then loathsome beyond expression, and so far decayed that, as Peters attempted to lift it, an entire leg came off in his grasp. As the mass of putrefaction slipped over the vessel's side into the water, the glare of phosphoric light with which it was surrounded plainly discovered to us seven or eight large sharks, the clashing of whose horrible teeth, as their prey was torn to pieces among them, might have been heard at the distance of a mile. (P 1:142)

This scene, which follows closely upon the dismemberment of Parker, enacts yet another deconstruction of the physical self. The detachment of the putrefied leg evidences both the rapidity of decomposition and the tenuousness of human identity and essence. By depicting the swift, Valdemar-like dissolution of Augustus, Poe problematizes the concept of self, effacing with a sudden authorial gesture the individuality and importance of Pym's closest friend. Indeed, Pym had earlier alluded to an "intimate communion" and "a partial interchange of character" between himself and Augustus (*P* 1:65). Now he must witness the actual coming apart of his companion and double, a spectacle which in its grotesque detail literalizes the disintegration and loss of selfhood noted by Morin.

In its almost ludicrous abruptness, the corruption of Augustus moreover reveals the metaphorical function of decomposition in *Pym* —as a trope of erasure or self-cancellation. Putrefaction signals the various erasures effected by the narrative itself in its relentless decomposing of the myths and pieties of nineteenth-century culture. The contradictions between the "Preface" and the concluding "Note," for example, cast doubt upon their own credibility and the believability of any text claiming to represent the "truth." Poe simultaneously throws into dispute the authorship of the text and the authority guaranteeing its veracity. The novel itself calls into question the notion of a benevolent deity controlling human destiny; it implicitly questions the legitimacy of colonial exploitation; it may even be said to question, in its depiction of savage behavior by American and British sailors, the racial superiority assumed by Pym in his representation of the Tsalalian natives. The novel's repeated disconfirmations of Pym's rational observations problematize the efficacy of human knowledge, and its recurrent staging of deception and revolt moreover puts in doubt (like Melville's *The Confidence-Man*) the possibility of human goodness. Finally, in its insistent depiction of bloodshed and horrific decay, the narrative subverts the nineteenth-century tendency to fetishize "the beautiful death" and to conceal the work of corruption.[6] In a culture preoccupied with idealizing mortality, Poe understood decomposition as a taboo subject, always denied by and excluded from polite discourse. Yet it afforded him the perfect trope for his own revolting and revolutionary project. *Pourriture* signaled his covert desire to represent the unspeakable and his determination to inscribe the disruptive power of that object which has no name in any language.

The Quincuncial Network
in Poe's *Pym*

John T. Irwin

There is probably no serious reader of *The Narrative of Arthur Gordon Pym* who hasn't felt puzzled by Pym's lengthy description, in chapter 14, of the nesting habits of the albatrosses and penguins he encounters on Desolation Island. The usual explanation of this passage is that it forms part of a larger description of the flora and fauna peculiar to the island, that Poe has culled the details from narratives of voyages to the region (almost certainly from Benjamin Morrell's *A Narrative of Four Voyages*), and that its inclusion is meant to give a greater air of authenticity, of convincing local color, to Pym's account. What puzzles the reader, what makes this local-color explanation less than satisfying, is the length and level of detail of the passage. The account of the visit to Desolation Island takes up four and a half pages in the Pollin edition, and two and a half of these are devoted to the nesting habits of the birds. Poe is, of course, essentially an artist of the short form—a writer of short stories, poems, and essays—and economy of means remains his watchword, even in a longer work of fiction like *Pym*. Any knowledgeable reader of Poe senses that the passage in question is simply too long and too detailed to be just a bit of startling local color meant to make the narrative more authentic. Clearly something else is going on here.

Recall that in describing the various species of birds on Desolation Island Pym is particularly struck by the fact that though "the albatross is one of the largest and fiercest of South Sea birds," there exists "between this bird and the penguin the most singular friendship." This friendship is manifested by the fact that "their nests are constructed with great uniformity, upon a plan concerted between the two species—that of the albatross being placed in the centre of a little square formed by the nests of four penguins" (*P* 1:151–52). Having chosen a level piece of ground suitable for nesting, "the birds proceed, with one accord, and actuated apparently by one mind, to trace out, with mathematical accuracy, either a square or other parallelogram, as may best suit the nature of the ground, and of just sufficient size to accommodate easily all the birds assembled" (P 1:152). After smoothing out a pathway six to eight feet wide around the encampment, the birds "partition out the whole area into small squares exactly equal in size. This is done by forming narrow paths, very smooth, and crossing each other at right angles throughout the entire extent of the rookery. At each intersection of these paths the nest of an albatross is constructed, and a penguin's nest in the centre of each square—thus every penguin is surrounded by four albatrosses, and each albatross by a like number of penguins" (P 1:152). I would suggest that this geometric pattern in the arrangement of the birds' nests is the whole point of the lengthy passage on the two species' mutual nesting habits. We know that Poe was familiar with the works of the seventeenth-century English polymath Sir Thomas Browne (the epigraph to "The Murders in the Rue Morgue" [M 2:527] is taken from Browne's essay *Urn Burial*), and no reader who knows Browne's work well could fail to recognize that the geometric pattern which Pym describes is the quincunx, the subject of the essay that is the companion piece to *Urn Burial—The Garden of Cyrus*.

Browne published the two essays together in one volume in 1658, the two pieces joined in a Janus-like relationship in which *Urn Burial* looks toward the past and *The Garden of Cyrus* toward the future. Commenting on the structural link between the two works, Frank Huntley observes that the essays "form a Platonic dichotomy: two parts opposed yet conjoined, with a rising from the lower or elemental *Urn Burial* (death) to the higher or celestial *Garden of Cyrus*, the 'numerical character' of reality (life). . . . That Browne intended us to read the two essays in the order he gave them is seen most obviously in the deliberateness of their opposition in subject matter. One concerns death, the other, life; one the body, the other the soul; one passions, the other reason; one accident, the other design; one substance, the other form."[1] In the dedicatory preface to *The Garden of Cyrus*, Browne himself comments on the linking of the two works: "That we conjoyn these parts of different Subjects, or that this should succeed the other; Your judgement will admit without impute of incongruity; Since the verdant state of things is the Symbole of the Resurrection, and to flourish in the state of Glory, we must first be sown in corruption. Beside the ancient practice of Noble Persons, to conclude in Garden-Graves, and Urnes themselves of old, is to be wrapt up in flowers and garlands."[2]

The full title of Browne's essay is *The Garden of Cyrus or, The*

Quincuntiall, Lozenge, or Net-work Plantations of the Ancients, Artificially, Naturally, Mystically Considered. The initial subject of the essay is "Cyrus the Younger's method of planting trees by fives in the shape of a quincunx" (Huntley, p. 204), that is, in the shape of an X (a tree at each corner of a rectangle and one in the center), so as to produce a continuous plantation whose form is a network of lozenges or rhombs.

Figure 1.

Later in the essay, Browne evokes the quincuncial network as a microcosmic symbol of the world when he points out that in the Egyptian hieroglyphics "*Orus*, the Hieroglyphick of the world, is described in a Net-work covering, from the shoulder to the foot" (Browne, p. 188). Indeed, Browne spends most of the essay's five chapters demonstrating that the recurrence of the quincuncial network (or its component shapes) throughout the human, animal, vegetable, and mineral worlds constitutes in effect the intelligible continuity of the universe.

Now it is not hard to see how a net, with each of its strands linked to every other strand in a single unbroken fabric, is an appropriate figure of continuity, but what is perhaps less clear is its appropriateness as a figure of intelligibility. How does the image of a net present the world as an object whose shape is compatible, whose form meshes, with the shape of the mind? To ask this question is in effect to ask why or how the network's component figures are appropriate schematic images of specular self-consciousness, for it is simply the repetition of these component figures that produces the network pattern. The two most obvious components of the network pattern are the lozenge or diamond (the shape enclosed by two intersecting sets of oblique parallel lines) and the decussation (X) or hourglass figure (the figure that represents the actual method of planting the group of five trees in the quincuncial arrangement).

Figure 2.

These two figures are in turn composed of a still more basic figure, one that, I would suggest, visually represents the physical basis of the functioning of human intelligence—the V shape.

To understand how this simple shape evokes the physical ground of intelligence, we must examine the connection that Browne makes in *The Garden of Cyrus* between numbers, letters, and geometrical shapes, specifically between the number five (the number of trees in the quincuncial pattern), the letter V (the Roman symbol for five), and the geometrical decussation (the X shape in which the five trees are planted, one at each corner of a rectangle and one in the center). Clearly, Browne views the quincuncial network of lozenges as an "Originall figure," that is, as the geometrical form of an orderly disposition of the physical world that is far older than simply the garden of Cyrus. Browne speculates that this pattern dates from "the Prototype and originall of Plantations," the Garden of Eden, for "since even in Paradise it self, the tree of knowledge was placed in the middle of the Garden, whatever was the ambient figure, there wanted not a centre and a rule of decussation" (p. 169). And the implication is that if the God-given design of man's original plantation was a quincuncial network, then this design must express the basic relationship between man and the world, the basic link between knower and known, subject and object—which is to say that this formal design, imposed on physical nature, schematizes the interface of mind and world in that it contains within itself the various modes of ideation, of intelligible representation of the world (i.e., mathematics, language, geometry), joined together in the homogeneousness of their physical inscription as numbers, letters, and geometric shapes.

If Browne believes that the quincuncial network is a God-given design expressing the original relationship between mind and world, then its shape must in some way be the root at which the branches of intelligible representation are joined. It must be the spot at which numbers, letters, and geometric figures share a common medium, reduce to a single physical shape that allows them to be converted directly (and visibly) into one another. Browne indicates both the connecting point and the conversion mechanism in the network figure when he notes that the quincunx pattern owes its "name not only unto the Quintuple number of Trees, but the figure declaring that number," that is, the Roman letter V, "which being doubled at the angle, makes up the Letter X, that is the Emphaticall decussation, or fundamentall figure" (p. 165). Thus the Roman letter V, the written sign for the number five in Latin, by "being doubled at the angle" (by having a second, inverted V projected downward from the angle of the first), produces the geometrical figure for the quincunx plantation, the decussation or X shape whose five places (four end points and central intersection) embody the meaning of the number five. The Roman V is at once, then, a letter, a numeral (the signifier of a number), and a geometric shape whose manipulation both embodies the meaning of that number (in its five places) and displays that arrangement of objects by fives which, through its repetition, unfolds the network pattern. And this sense of a necessary correspondence (as evidenced by the convertibility) of letter, number, and geometric shape is reinforced by the fact that the X produced by doubling the sign for the number five is itself the sign in Latin for the integer that is five doubled. The ultimate root of the word "decussation" is, of course, the Latin word for ten, *decem*. We might note that Browne bases the numerical structure of his two essays on the figure of the quincuncial decussation considered as "the Roman X, the perfect number, made of two fives—Roman V's—joined at their apices" (Huntley, p. x): *Urn Burial* and *The Garden of Cyrus* are each composed of five chapters and "each essay is dated 'Norwich, May 1,' the fifth month" (Huntley, p. x). Moreover, if the trajectory of *Urn Burial* is downward, toward death and the grave, and that of *The Garden of Cyrus* upward, toward resurrection and the celestial sphere, then the decussation is an even more appropriate figure for their linking, since, according to Browne, in "Aegyptian Philosophy . . . the scale of influences was thus disposed, and the geniall spirits of both worlds . . . trace their way in ascending and descending Pyramids, mystically apprehended in the Letter X" (p. 204). Browne has, then, designed the conjunction/opposition of his two essays so that each of them is composed of five chapters but with the trajectory of one essay downward and the other upward in imitation of the two V's (fives) joined at their apices with the angles pointing in opposite directions.

The V shape which, as letter, number, and geometric design, brings together in a single figure three modes of representation, is, as we noted earlier, the basic shape which composes the lozenge and the hourglass or X figure in the network. The hourglass or X is simply the Roman V "doubled at its angle" and the lozenge the Roman V doubled at its open end.

Figure 3.

But now the question that was deferred from the network pattern to its components (the lozenge and the hourglass or X), and then deferred again to their component, the V shape, arises once more. What makes the V shape an appropriate image of intelligibility? Which is to ask, why or how does this shape visually represent the physical basis of the functioning of human intelligence? Browne starts us in the direction of the answer by noting the connection between the V shape and vision itself. He points out first that the V shape governs the path of light rays to the eye's lens and then from the lens to the retina (Fig. 4). He then notes a second decussation associated with sight in that intersection of the optic nerves known as the optic chiasma (Fig. 5). Just as Browne associates the decussation formed by the V shape doubled at its angle with the path of vision that runs from outer to inner, from object to brain, so he associates the reciprocal of this figure—the lozenge or rhomb formed by the V shape doubled at its open end—with the path that runs from inner to outer, the path by which an internal image is projected into the external world in the painting of a picture, for example (Fig. 6). Browne notes that "perspective picturers, in their Base, Horison, and lines of distance, cannot escape these Rhomboidall decussations" (p. 172).

The reciprocity of the decussation and the lozenge—a function of the reciprocal doubling of their component V shape at its angle and its open end—can be seen again in the geometric figures which

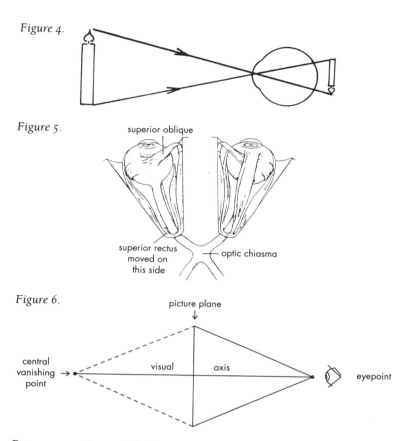

Figure 4.

Figure 5.

superior oblique

superior rectus
moved on
this side

optic chiasma

Figure 6.

picture plane

central
vanishing →
point

visual   axis

eyepoint

Browne associates with the conjunction/opposition of body and soul. On the one hand, he finds the decussation present "in the whole body of man, which upon the extension of arms and legges, doth make out a square, whose intersection is at the genitals," not to mention "the phantastical Quincunx, in *Plato*, of the first Hermaphrodite or double man, united at the Loynes, which *Jupiter* after divided" (pp. 188–89); while on the other hand, he reminds us that "the Noble *Antoninus* in some sense doth call the soul it self a Rhombus" (p. 209), though he notes elsewhere that in their operation the powers of the soul describe the reciprocal shape: "Things entring upon the intellect by a Pyramid from without, and thence into the memory by another from within, the common decussation being in the understanding as is delivered by *Bovillus*" (p. 203).

Browne's schematic figurations of intelligence and its associated structures—vision, imaginative projection, the interaction of under-standing and memory, and of mind and body—are all ultimately based on a single figure, the V shape, doubled either at its angle or its open end. And if we interpret this V shape as the simplest possible geometric representation of a fold or hinge that doubles an entity back upon itself by folding it in half _ ↑\/↑ _, then this doubling (at angle ✕↓, or at open end ◇↑) of a shape (V) which is itself a representation of halving and doubling produces a structure which figures specular self-consciousness as the mirror doubling of the mirror-image halves of the bilaterally symmetrical human body, that is, as the intersection of the mirror fold between the right and left sides of the body by the mirror fold between the body and its reflected image. Indeed, it is precisely in the context of the right-hand/left-hand mirror fold of the body that the special appropriateness of the V shape as a figure of the physical basis of the functioning of human intelligence becomes clear, the clue being the V shape's association with the number five. For in being both a sign for the number five and a simple visual representation of the fold or hinge, the V shape points to its origin: the conjunction of these two signifieds in the hingelike structure of the five digits of the human hand—that fold, formed by the four fingers and opposable thumb, that is the physical (i.e., necessary) embodiment of the essentially oppositional character of human knowledge. This fold of the hand is doubled in turn by the fold of the opposing hand, the opposition between the right and left hands being at once a replication of the oppositional structure of the thumb and fingers of each hand and a function of the mirror fold between the right and left halves of the body. One might diagram this arrangement of opposable thumb and fingers, of opposing hands and arms, as the branching of a V-shaped fold into other V-shaped folds.

Figure 7.

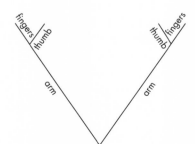

And if we move from the level of touch to that of sight, we find that the V shape, variously oriented, also describes the operation of binocular vision, in that the activities of scanning and focusing (the visual analogues of opening and closing the hand in order to grasp an object between thumb and fingers) can be geometrically figured respectively by a V whose open end represents the field of vision in the scanning mode and by an inverted V whose angle represents the intersection of the axes of vision of the eyes in the focusing mode. The reciprocity of scanning and focusing would then be evoked either by the lozenge or by the decussation depending upon the order in which the related activities are represented.

Now what all of this ultimately suggests is that the V-shape (considered as a geometric representation of the fold of the hand, i.e., of that opposition between fingers and thumb that constitutes the hand's grasping power) is an appropriate figure of intelligibility precisely because the basic metaphor of human knowledge—"basic" because derived from the givenness of the body's structure, the physical basis of the functioning of human intelligence—is one which figures thought as the mental grasping of an object. (Recall that the roots of the word "intelligible" are the two Latin words *inter,* meaning "between" or "among," and *legere,* meaning "to gather, choose, pick," an origin that evokes the handling and selection of objects as the model of intellection.) In this context, then, to say that a thing is "intelligible" means that it exists as an object for the mind, an object of knowledge, by being grasped between the poles of a differential opposition in a manner directly analogous to that in which a physical object is grasped between the opposing poles of finger and thumb. And this sense of intelligibility as the grasping or enclosing of an object between opposing sides, a sense symbolized by the V shape, is carried through all the figures which the V shape composes—the forcepslike decussation, the enclosure of the rhomb, and the network pattern which images the world's continuous intelligibility as its containment or capture within a net whose structure is an endless repetition of the structure of the hand. Indeed, we can see, within the pattern of the quincuncial network of lozenges, that geometrical figure which we employed earlier to show how the oppositional structure of thumb and fingers within the hand is replicated in the structure of the opposing hands and arms, as if a V shape branches into other V shapes.

And if we take the image of a net literally as an openwork pat-

Figure 8.

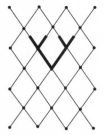

tern of loosely knotted cords—that is, as a pattern whose basic linking element, the knot, is a self-opposing, self-interfering structure in
which a line, looping back to grasp itself within itself, is thereby able
to grasp some other thing within that loop—if we give it this literal
interpretation, then the net is a particularly appropriate figure of self-
consciousness, of that self-opposing structure which grasps itself by a
process of simultaneous projection and introjection, by a loop which
runs from the self into the world and then back to grasp the self and in
so doing grasps the world within this loop as that physical other *from
which* and *by means of which* the self is differentiated.

Fine, so whatever happened to Pym and the birds' nests? Returning to the description of the albatrosses and penguins on Desolation
Island, we can see that what probably attracted Poe's attention to the
passage in Benjamin Morrell's *A Narrative of Four Voyages*, on which
this description is based and which thus led him to give the description the length and prominence it has in his own narrative, was more
than likely Poe's recognition, in the pattern of alternating penguin and
albatross nests described by Morrell, of the quincuncial network that
Browne discusses in *The Garden of Cyrus*. But what is particularly revealing is the difference in inflection that Poe as compared to Morrell
gives the passage and the implicit difference in inflection that he as
compared to Browne gives the quincuncial pattern. For Browne, of
course, the quincunx is a God-given design that orders the universe, a
pattern made up of component shapes that are in effect the geometric
building blocks through whose endless repetition in nature God creates the universe as a continuously intelligible whole. And Morrell's
response to the pattern of the birds' nests is in a similarly religious vein.
Commenting on the way "these creatures of the ocean so faithfully dis-

charge the various duties assigned them by the great Creator," he says, "A moral philosopher could not, perhaps, be more usefully employed, for a few days, than in contemplating the movements and operations of a South Sea rookery, and marking the almost incredible order and regularity with which every thing is performed. Such a spectator could not fail to confess, that so wonderful an instinct must be 'the Divinity which stirs within' them."[3] But Pym's comment on the significance of the pattern of the birds' nests and their nesting habits is much more equivocal in its brevity. He says, "In short, survey it as we will, nothing can be more astonishing than the spirit of reflection evinced by these feathered beings, and nothing surely can be better calculated to elicit reflection in every well-regulated human intellect" (*P* 1:153).

In *American Hieroglyphics* I suggested that Poe intends this remark of Pym's to be an ironic comment on the lack of reflection that Pym consistently demonstrates when faced with traces of intelligent design in the desolate regions near the Pole, design that would seem to indicate a previous human presence. In chapter 17, for example, when the crew of the *Jane Guy* discover on an uncharted island "a piece of wood, which seemed to have formed the prow of a canoe . . . half buried in a pile of loose stones" and Captain Guy observes that the carving on the prow resembles "the figure of a tortoise," Pym in effect dismisses this evidence of a previous human visitation by remarking, "We had now advanced to the southward more than eight degrees farther than any previous navigators" (*P* 1:165–66). And again, in chapter 23, when Pym and Peters in exploring the caverns on Tsalal come upon a series "of singular-looking indentures in the surface of the marl," which "might have been taken for the intentional, although rude, representation of a human figure standing erect, with outstretched arm" and for two groups of "alphabetical characters," Peters actually takes them as such, while Pym dismisses the markings' intentionality, claiming that they were caused "by some convulsion from the surface where the indentures were found . . . thus proving them to have been the work of nature" (*P* 1:195). One can see how the lengthy description of the birds' nests on Desolation Island fits into this pattern of nonrecognition. Morrell in his *Narrative* describes the interlocking design of the nests but doesn't seem to recognize the design as a quincuncial network (at least he doesn't identify the pattern as the quincunx, and one would certainly expect that he would have, given that the moral which Browne draws from the universal recurrence of this pattern matches that with which Morrell ends the passage). Poe, on the other hand, in reading Morrell's text, does recognize the quincuncial pattern in the passage and as a result gives the passage prominence in his own text. And it is precisely the situation of a reader's recognizing a design inscribed in a text which the writer himself does not recognize that Poe reproduces in *The Narrative of Arthur Gordon Pym* when he has Pym report the design of the birds' nest without seeing that it forms a quincuncial net-work—a pattern which Poe expects that the reader *will* recognize. Just as he also expects the reader to recognize that Pym's remark, about "the spirit of reflection evinced" by the birds evoking "reflection in every well-regulated human intellect," is an ironic comment (whose irony its speaker does not himself perceive) on Pym's ongoing blindness in such situations. This scenario of a reader's recognizing a design within a text which the author of that text does not himself recognize is, of course, given a comic fillip in the novel's concluding "Note." The note's anonymous author points out that the figures on the chasm walls in Tsalal (which Pym reproduces in the text, though he denies that they are alphabetic characters) are in fact words in Ethiopic, Arabic, and Coptic writing, and he adds that not only did Pym not recognize them but "the facts in question have, beyond doubt, escaped the attention of Mr. Poe" (*P* 1:207) as well.

As I argued in *American Hieroglyphics*, Pym's continuing lack of recognition culminates in his not recognizing that the gigantic white figure in the mist at the end of the narrative is his own shadow, a kind of literal nonrecognition of reflection, a nonrecognition that he is seeing his own shadow image. In opting for this interpretation, I was also im-plicitly arguing for the essential indeterminacy of the figure's meaning, arguing that the figure is indeterminate precisely because it is over-determined, that Poe's text permits, indeed fosters, so many different readings of the figure's meaning that one cannot be absolutely certain from the evidence of the text what the figure is. In effect, in interpret-ing the figure in the mist as Pym's unrecognized shadow image, I was opting for a single meaning that would undermine the very notion of the figure's having a single meaning. Which is to say that if the misty figure is Pym's own unrecognized shadow, then the relationship be-tween Pym and the figure is an image of the relationship between each reader and the figure: when one opts for a particular meaning for the figure—whether it be the shadow of death, the Ancient of Days, the mother in a fantasized return to the womb, the resurrected Christ, or

Pym's unrecognized shadow, to name only a few—when one finds one absolutely certain meaning in a situation where the overdetermined-ness of the text makes meaning essentially indeterminate, then the reader is likely not to recognize how much that single meaning is a function of self-projection, how much any given meaning in such a case is determined by an unperceived shadow which the reader's own self casts upon the text. Confronted with an apparently meaningful repetition or design in nature, man has several choices: either he can decide that it is not meaningful, that it is an accident, a mere random "convulsion from the surface," as Pym says of the markings in the cavern; or he can decide that it represents the workings of intelligence. In which case he must decide whether the intelligence at work is his own or another's, whether it represents " 'the Divinity which stirs within' " nature or represents simply the unrecognized structure of the human mind projected on the world in the act of knowing, a structure which in meshing with physical nature finds some recurrences meaningful and others not. In one way or another, what man adds to any landscape is meaning, no matter how empty or desolate that landscape may be—an insight enacted again and again in American literature, whether in the form of a figure in the South Polar mist, in the image of a jar on a hill in Tennessee, or, as in the present case, in the pattern of birds' nests on Desolation Island.

The Arabesque Design
of *Arthur Gordon Pym*

G. R. Thompson

 The devices of aesthetic fantasy may be conventional
or otherwise. In the opinion of Jorge Luis Borges,
the most ubiquitous devices of fantastic literature are four:
the double, the voyage back in time, the contamination of
reality by irreality, and the text within the text.
—John Barth, "Tales Within Tales Within Tales" (1981),
reprinted in *The Friday Book*, (1984)

Early in his career, Poe conceived of an interrelated sequence of experiments with generic forms of popular literature. One of the earliest
of these framed-tale collections was called "Eleven Tales of the Arabesque" (1833). With the addition of fourteen more tales, Poe was able
in 1839 to publish a volume of narratives as *Tales of the Grotesque and
Arabesque*. Critics have (generally though not uniformly) assumed that
the latter title indicates a division between comic stories (grotesques)
and serious stories (arabesques). But each term has a double meaning,
and each definition shares some of the properties of the other. The term
grotesque has both a comic and a sinister meaning, and frequently the
word is defined as a conjoining of humor and horror into an aesthetic
unity. Its history confirms such a sense of the fusion or interpenetration
of normally discrete realms. The word comes from Italian, *grottesco/
ca,* indicating "grotto" paintings discovered on the walls of ancient
Rome below the modern street level. These grotto paintings showed
human heads growing out of tangled vines and other fusions of plant
and animal, organic and inorganic. The implication of entanglement,
of looping and twisting lines, is especially strong in grotesque design;
radically different elements entangle and accommodate one another.
In this effect, *grotesque* shares connotations with *arabesque,* the root
meaning of which is "Arab-like." But the basic denotation suggests an
important difference between grotesque and arabesque: namely, the
difference between hopeless entanglement and orderly symmetry (even
if of chaos), total indeterminacy and controlled or contained indeter-

minacy. Poe's *The Narrative of Arthur Gordon Pym* (1838) conforms in general and specific ways to the tradition of the arabesque. Its design evokes both Arabo-Oriental art forms and the European genre or mode named for those forms—the latter closely linked to theories of "romantic irony."

Arabesque Tradition

The Koran prohibits reproduction in graphic art of natural forms that may be considered to have a soul. This prohibition reinforced in Arabic and Arabic-influenced art the development of highly intricate patterns of geometric designs, of structurally repeated, symmetrically developed lines, loops, and concentric and interpenetrating curvilinear, triangular, and rectilinear structures. An often-repeated version of the rectilinear pattern is the interlineated quincunx, a figure with five points of reference, four outer points forming a square or parallelogram, the fifth point in the center. In the quincuncial designs, often an outer rectilinear frame will be doubled or trebled, and grotesque curvilinear patterns will decorate or inhabit, symmetrically, the four interior corners and envelop the visual middlepoint—as in an "Arabesque" or "Persian" carpet. The basic carpet design components are borders, corner elements, and a central medallion (plus pendants top and bottom)—nearly always in a quincunx design. Although the central field can become so filled (or cluttered) as to obscure the basic structuring shape, the quincuncial (or arch variation) can still be discerned beneath the proliferated ornamentation.

Within the double or infinite implication of the quincunx exists the archetypal arabesque leaf, symbol of the garden, earthly symbol of paradise—or of a *glimpse* of paradise through the *gateway* to paradise.[1] The basic symbol is repeated within repeated patterns within repeated borders to suggest infinity. The question of the function and symbolism of borders gets to the heart of East/West oppositions and perceptions. Put simply, the question is: Are borders limiting or limitless?

Michael Craig Hillmann writes that "the traditional division of design elements on Persian carpets into border and field areas is often viewed as the mere framing of the field pattern by border material that in addition serves as a transition to the space beyond the carpet." He cites the *Encyclopaedia Britannica* on the analogy between the border of a carpet and a cornice on a building or a frame to a picture, each a corresponding feature which emphasizes limits and controls the implied movements of the interior pattern. But Hillmann suggests that the primary function is almost the reverse: "Such a view fails to take into account differences between border and field areas in terms of motifs and patterning in many Persian carpets and may be the imposition of a Western conception of framing upon a visual art form to which the concept may not always apply" (*Persian Carpets*, p. 57). In a tradition that dates back at least to thirteenth-century Turkish carpets, the border frames a detail of "the infinite." The infinite pattern flows on freely without beginning or end. When the border cuts through single motifs of the central field, it implies that the field is to be imagined as endless.

The framed floral and calligraphic patterns of architectural decoration, carpets, and book illustrations, reflecting "traditional Islamic aversion to the representation of animal forms and human figures," also symbolize "the denaturalization of nature." Denaturalization in this sense is the attempt to represent the supernatural via abstraction of natural forms into mathematical and geometrical relationships. The arabesque design becomes a representation of the dissolution of matter into a perception of infinity through abstract representation that reveals the mind of God. Into this rarified void the observer also dissolves. Self disappears into the great Void: the "journey's end" is to be found in God's "Infinity"—the voyager is from "snares of self set free" (see Hillmann, *Persian Carpets*, pp. 59–61).

The concept of framing also predominates in Arabic literature as introduced to the West at the end of the seventeenth century from Arabic-speaking countries of the Middle East. This literature includes the many fragments of poetry gathered into collections or shaped into wholes, like the *Rubaiyát* attributed to Omar Khayyám and the collection of serious and humorous framed-tales known as the book of *A Thousand and One Nights*. The *Arabian Nights* became enormously popular in Europe in the Galland translation (1704–12), generating in the eighteenth century a flood of Turkish, Persian, Indian, Chinese, and Tartar tales and a craze for "Oriental" fiction in general. The trend persisted into the nineteenth century; Byron's *Turkish Tales* and Thomas Moore's *Alciphron* and *Lalla Rookh* (favorites of Poe's) became best-sellers. Poe imitates the Arabesque tale in his "Thousand-and-Second Tale of Scheherazade," "The Domain of Arnheim," "Al Aaraaf," "Siope" ("Silence"), "Some Words With a Mummy," "A Tale of the Ragged Mountains," and other works.[2]

It is not just in the usual, general sense of an "Oriental tale" but especially in the sense of elaborately and/or subtly *framed* design—in which one pattern picks up and transforms another into a new pattern, in which one exterior pattern duplicates and multiplies (directly or inversely) another—that the term *arabesque* enters Western literary theory from art history. By analogy to a sense of elaborate symmetrical yet open-ended design in carpets, replicated in framed narratives, *arabesque* as a European literary term early came to indicate (1) deliberate inconsistencies in the handling of narrative frames and of the conditions of interior narrative for a larger ironic and aesthetic design, and (2) intricate interrelationships among many tales within a frame or series of frames which may themselves be contained within a frame. The concept of arabesque design foregrounds design itself, whether or not the patterns symbolize anything beyond themselves. The arabesque became the norm of a "pure" standard of beauty for Immanuel Kant: "abstract design," structures and patterns with no "inherent meaning" in themselves.

Irony and Arabesque: Romantic Dialogics

In the early German romantic period in particular, Friedrich Schlegel and others appropriated the term *arabesque* to indicate an intricate geometric or abstract design of narrative into which incongruity in detail and antithesis in character and structure are consciously insinuated. In the arabesque, the relationship between a framing narrative and one or more narrative strands severely strains or calls into question the overt narrative illusion, which may be further undermined through involuted narrative conventions, complex digressions, disruptions or incongruities, and the blurring of levels of narrative reality. The writer of the arabesque calls attention to the narrativity of the text, the fiction of its mimesis, the artifice of its conventions—and then frequently turns all these conventions on their heads, beginning at the end or in the middle, or failing to end the narrative in the expected way. Such arabesque attributes are now conventionally categorized under such labels as "metafiction," "postmodernist fiction," "self-reflexive fiction"—modes partaking of "romantic irony."

"Romantic irony," writes Raymond Immerwahr, "is most commonly applied nowadays to the drastic violation of illusion by reference within a literary work to its author and the process of its creation, to the transgression of the boundary which separates our level of reality as readers of a book or as audience in a theatre from the reality of the characters in that book or play."[3] But when Schlegel praises literary works that abound in direct violation of illusion, he tends to speak "not of irony but of the arabesque" (Immerwahr, *Romantic Irony*, p. 83), that is, of a form rather than an abstract idea. Taking as his supreme examples the novels of Sterne, Diderot's *Jacques le Fataliste*, and (with reservations) the novels of "Jean Paul," Schlegel "uses the term 'arabesque' to denote a *form* characterized by involutions, complex and seemingly aimless digressions, and wandering back and forth between temporal and spatial settings as well as between levels of narrative reality" (p. 84, emphasis added). Although Immerwahr remarks that romantic irony is a "device" that constitutes "one element of what Schlegel terms the arabesque," the term "irony" is also understood to mean "all the ways . . . by which a creative writer calls attention to the paradox and flux inherent in the universe."[4] The romantic ironist acknowledges and embraces contradiction, opposition, paradox. Romantic irony privileges the idea of the *interplay* between and among norms, forms, genres, themes, voices, languages. Moreover, to generate "dialogue" between the "two romanticisms"—the light and the dark, the positive and the negative, and the redoubled binary within each of positive and negative—is in part the function of the arabesque.

The special theory of the arabesque and the *Roman* developed by Friedrich Schlegel defines a more specific generic category, the *arabesque romance,* that simultaneously illuminates *Pym* and positions it relative to analogous modes of contemporary literary discourse. After Kant, such writers as Schiller, Schelling, Novalis, Fichte, Solger, and Friedrich and August Wilhelm Schlegel (in differing ways) wrestled with the idea of an "absolute idealism" wherein all *objective* "reality" is arbitrated, if not created, by the *subjective* individual. This view makes of the individual almost a God-in-oneself. And this Godlikeness is especially true of the Artist, a supreme "puppetmaster" or "stage manager" analogized in God the Creator of the World as the Author behind or within the Text. Yet Schlegel was aware, as perhaps no one else in his time, of the dialogical voices of the "selves" constituting the "self" of the text—and thereby aware of the frequently naive assumptions about and conceptions of "truth" and "unity" in a text. A simplistic concept of determinate "unity" in a text, Schlegel recognized, is in danger of denying the "true" voice of the text, namely, its "medley" of (sometimes competing) voices, or its "ensemble" of voices. To say that Poe's *Narrative* is characterized by a "medley" of voices and intentions is not, in this theoretical perspective, necessarily to voice a negative criticism.

For Schlegel, the lesson (if there is one) of "romanticism" is dual: first, to acknowledge multiplicity and indeterminateness; and, second, in the acknowledgment of multiple claims upon our sense of unity, including those of competing genres, to come to an aesthetic accommodation—that is, a quasi-resolution in the aesthetic, not the empirical, or even logical, realm. The arabesque, according to Schlegel, not so much "reconciles" as "elevates" contradictions and oppositions into a *higher unity of consciousness* for the artist—in a text that explores and embodies the continuity of *various* intentionalities. It is no accident (even of tradition) that Schlegel's major critical pronouncement is titled *Gespräch über die Poesie*: the Dialogue on Poesy (1800). This work comes out of a traditional critical dialogue that grapples with a redefinition of *dialectic*. Even though it does not duplicate the twentieth-century conception of the *dialogic* of fiction as articulated by Mikhail Bakhtin, it struggles toward (and comes very close to) that conception.

In his formulation of the dialogical and the monological, Bakhtin echoes the theories of Friedrich Schlegel and Adam Müller, the latter of whom seems to have been the first in the Romantic era to have specifically introduced the terms *monological* and *dialogical* as mutually interdependent opposite tendencies of thought and language. Summarizing much of the general overview of language and genre argued by Schlegel in the late 1790s, Müller in 1804 and 1806 emphasizes the concept of "mediation" rather than "synthesis" in the "dialectical" doctrine of "contradiction." Employing Schlegel's term *irony,* Müller suggests in his *Vorlesungen über deutsche Wissenschaft und Literatur* that the dialectical aspect of irony results from the interplay of the "monological" (*monologisch*) and "dialogical" (*dialogisch*) and (as in Schlegel) "mediates" without absorbing and annihilating oppositions. This early romantic concept of dialectic as expansive accommodation of dissonances undergoes considerable narrowing (monological constriction) in the hands of Hegel and Marx as the nineteenth century wears on. The original open-ended quality of romantic dialectics was specifically dialogical rather than dialectical. The dialogical was a concept that was itself a reaction to the overly restrictive and thesis-oriented interpretation of Platonic dialectics by the neoclassicists.

Ernst Behler, in a brilliant essay on "The Theory of Irony in German Romanticism," locates Schlegel in the history of aesthetics and distinguishes between an early romantic concept of Platonic dialectic as open-ended dialogue and Hegel's more closed concept of dialectic as thesis-antithesis-synthesis in which the oppositions of thesis and antithesis "disappear."[5] The key to understanding the distinction lies in a close resemblance between Schlegel's general orientation and that of Bakhtin—in Schlegel's antipathy to repressive authority (political or artistic) and his love of the human "freedom" (represented for Schlegel by ancient Greek literature). Freedom at its most exalting is to be found in Art—the Romantic Artist being the freest of all beings. Schlegel speaks of the highest incarnation of the Romantic Artist as "the Poet" in terms of a process of "self-creation" (*Selbstschöpfung*) and counteracting "self-destruction" (*Selbstvernichtung*). These movements of the creative self and the critical self alternate or oscillate until "developed to irony." Irony does not "destroy" creativity but mediates between earnestness and skepticism. The result of "alternation between self-creation and self-destruction" is creative "self-restraint" (*Selbstbeschränkung*). In this large sense, irony is the beautiful "self-mirroring" or "artistic reflection" of the author, embodied in the text as a whole. Irony has the potential to raise poetic reflection "to higher and higher powers and can multiply, as it were, in an endless array of mirrors." The works of Shakespeare and Cervantes, Schlegel writes in the *Dialogue on Poesy*, especially represent this pervasive and permeating irony, "this artistically arranged confusion, this happy symmetry of contradiction, this wonderful eternal exchange of enthusiasm and irony."

In his romantic dialogics, Schlegel emphasized the evolution of increasingly superior versions or texts of the self in the artistic perception or creation of a succession of contrasts—between the ideal and the real, the serious and the comic, the sinister and the absurd—through which the "transcendental ego" can mock its own convictions and productions from the "height" of an ever yet higher "ideal." The process is on one level a dialectical transaction, but there is less an "ultimate" synthesis, or reconciliation, than an aesthetic *framing,* a dialogical incorporation of a multiplicity of voices, perspectives, selves. The Self is a kind of library of books, an "encyclopedia" of voices, a multiple figure of figures in the carpet, a potentially infinite reflective and refractive mirroring of subject and object as one.

Socrates as supreme ironist represents for Schlegel the ideal "mind" of the Romantic Artist, in the sense of a union of apparently antagonistic elements held together by a mind characterized as consummately (divinely) ironic. In the classic *Lyceum* "aphorism" or "fragment" of 1800, Socratic irony is seen as all-pervading—constituting the persona of the artist as well as the work. "Socratic irony" is the "only entirely involuntary *and* nevertheless completely conscious dissimulation" (emphasis added). Schlegel writes:

> In it, everything must be jest and yet seriousness, artless openness and yet deep dissimulation. . . . It contains and incites a feeling of the *insoluble conflict* of the absolute and the relative, of the *impossibility and necessity* of total communication. It is the freest of all liberties, for it enables us to rise above our own selves. . . . It is a good sign if the harmonious dullards [i.e., smug, commonplace people] *fail* to understand this constant self-parody, if over and over again, they believe and disbelieve until they become giddy and consider jest to be seriousness, and seriousness to be jest.[6]

In works produced by such a mind, we find embodied a certain continuing reversibility, so that those whom Schlegel contemns as self-satisfied bourgeois readers—addicted to conventional notions of transparent language and linear narrative and familiar plots, of verisimilitude based on a naive notion of mimesis—do not know how to read the romantic text. It is an elitist aesthetics aimed at those who can see the "secret" irony of composition. As Raymond Immerwahr succinctly puts it, for Schlegel, both irony and the arabesque are frequently "centered in the generally playful treatment of artistic form," which emerges most obviously as "discussion within the work of the form or medium along with the actual object of portrayal" or as the "portraying of this form or medium instead of the object."[7] This self-reflexivity is designed to frustrate the preconditioned genre expectations of "linear" narrative held by the "bourgeois reader."

Roman and Romance

Schlegel's terms for the "new literature" are *Roman* and *romanisch*. In English, *Roman* is almost always translated as "the novel" despite the fact that its obvious linguistic affinities are with the romance (cf. French usage). In a once famous statement, Schlegel declared: "*Ein Roman ist ein romantisches Buch.*"[8] The standard English translation of Schlegel's dictum is "The novel is a romantic book." A more accurate translation, closer to the spirit of the utterance, would be "The romance is a romantic book," highlighting the tautological potential. But the new *romance* is, for Schlegel, a more highly charged concept than indicated by the old term *romance,* which had been used for centuries to designate such works as the *Song of Roland* or *Le Morte D'Arthur.* The modern *romance* is a mixture of the new and the old, sometimes designated the new *nouvelle* or *novella* or *Novelle* or *novel.* The modern *romance* belongs in a special way to *romant*icism. Schlegel is situating it philosophically, culturally, and historically.[9]

In his *Notebooks* of 1797–98, as well as in the opening section of the *Dialogue on Poesie*, Schlegel sees the origin of *Roman* or *Arabeske* in the "mixed forms" of the late middle ages, "compendia" that for him are "encyclopedias" of the "thinking life" of an individual, in particular of an artistic genius in the midst of an aesthetic and philosophical quest.[10] He adds that the realistic depiction of the "inner life" of the "individual" will obviously have to include false starts and digressions, for that is a true picture of the workings of the mental life as an actual living process. The "self-consciousness" of the artist depicting his self-consciousness will be characterized, even in fictive narrative, by an ever-recurrent digressiveness on the part of the author, especially as he speaks directly to the reader about the process of the narrative (as in *Tristram Shandy*). The *Roman*—this alternative but not quite synonymic word for "arabesque"—is characterized not only by tensions among narrative frames but also by illusion-breaking addresses to the reader and by other self-conscious encodings of the artistic process into the narrative of mental process. Thus the new conception of the romance is of a self-reflexive, intellectual-intuitive quest, focused on the interweaving processes of living and writing. The romantic book is a book with a "thesis" as its central "character," and that thesis represents the central coherence of the mental processes of the "author" writing the book. In this way, all the characters become *the* character, and the author his book.

The dynamic "unity" realized by foregrounding the mind of the author is, as Schlegel recognizes, no simple thing and is itself an illusion—or a useful fiction. He writes of an absolute "chaos" of character wrought into a primal unity that is "a formed, artistic Chaos": "ein gebildetes künstliches Chaos." It is this framed indeterminacy or "*formed* chaos" representing a central informing *mind* that *is* the book. The central character and process of a romance/novel is the dialectical/

dialogical relationship of the putative author and assumed reader, so that *Roman* becomes a complex and multilayered "Socratic dialogue" between these two "characters" who comprise the single doppelgänger that is the dynamic of the book as living artifact.

In contemporary terms, the book itself is the central and original character formed self-reflexively out of the author-reader dialectic in which the author imagines his reader into existence in order to define or redefine his own existence in the text. A text is *self*-reflexive in this sense of the congruence of multiple selves or multiple voices in dialogue. The dialectic of author-reader over the text gives way to a dialogic form of the novel similar to that later proposed by Bakhtin. Schlegel exhibits an unreconciled desire for reconciliation into unity, even if the only "unity" possible involves the incorporation of chaos or indeterminacy in the artist's consciousness as represented by the artistically framed text. It is *gebildetes* (imagined, developed) and *künstliches* (artistic, formed, framed).

A quality of *Roman* especially pertinent to Poe's *Narrative* is Schlegel's idea of the "elliptical" structure of the modern romance. In an essay on *Wilhelm Meister* in 1798, Schlegel observes that the *Roman* has a "progressiveness" that is "organic" rather than "linear" in terms of conventional plot lines. Each book of the *Roman* "takes up what is achieved in a previous book and also contains the germ of the next book," as Eric A. Blackall paraphrases it, so that the "magic" of the whole volume is a constant "hovering between forwards and backwards" over some kind of *Mittelpunkt* and succeeds only from its organic wholeness, not from its individual parts.[11]

Considered as a formal term, *Mittelpunkt* suggests two things: (1) the midpoint in a linear line and (2) the center of a concentric field. Here the term applies in both senses; as well as involving a symmetrical narrative line (freed from mere chronology), the middle point also recalls a series of Chinese boxes. Like a labyrinth, the structure framing the *Mittelpunkt* may give a first impression of confusion and chaos, but it is in fact formed, shaped. (This does not mean that it necessarily reflects any metaphysical reality.) A labyrinth is a chaotic puzzle that (as in Poe or Borges) is yet artificed, designed, framed—in some way or another—as in the center frame of a series of frames, or the middle point of an interlocking quincunx design in an arabesque carpet. In this elliptical way, the text equilibrates around a center or more than one center.

Schlegel's *Roman*, Eric Blackall insists, is not a specific genre like the novel but a romantic mode: a "romantic book," an "encyclopedia," a "compendium" of all genres in one, made coherent by *Witz*. The term *Witz* (loosely, "wit") means many things, but principally it is the faculty of imagination and intellect that perceives similarities and makes connections among hidden likenesses in seemingly disconnected or unconnected things. It is another form of irony, most often combined with dry humor and parody (including self-parody). *Die Arabeske* is an expression of *Witz,* that power of the living author's "mind" to perceive discrepancies and to hold all contradictions within a coherent whole or frame, the "essence" of which is aesthetic design. Herein is a "secret irony" of narrative, or in contemporary terms, a fundamental "textuality." [12]

The Arabesque Narrative of *Arthur Gordon Pym*

The generic term *arabesque* describes Poe's most puzzling extended work of fiction, significantly titled *The* Narrative *of Arthur Gordon Pym*, which is neither exactly a novel nor a conventional romance. More than just a journey to the South Pole, Pym's adventures symbolically suggest a journey within the self and back in time, a quest for origins and ends. But the narrative breaks off; the revelation of an ultimate secret is withheld. The "apocalyptic" conclusion of the main narrative veils rather than unveils.

The concept of the arabesque as a literary form or genre answers many of the usual questions about the "unity" of *The Narrative of Arthur Gordon Pym*. For one thing, in a large-writ TRAVEL-ADVENTURE to the END OF THE WORLD in quest of the ULTIMATE DISCOVERY, the omission of the end of the quest does not *have to* be seen as merely a hastily or badly contrived conclusion. The truncation of the genre of the travel-adventure narrative could be seen as deliberate foregrounding of a major genre deformation. In *Pym*, the narrative quest becomes less for conventional dénouement or any ultimate "truth" (and less and less for "verisimilitude") than for the *astounding* as a kind of permanent penultimate apocalypse. The narrative to the end of the world is deliberately regressive and indeterminate: Pym seems to die at the end of his (interior) narrative as he plunges toward a gigantic white figure rising out of the Antarctic but comes back to finish his memoirs, left unfinished by "Poe"; but Pym then "really" dies, leaving them unfinished, to be (partially) finished (and therefore unfinished) by the "editor/publisher."

This editor/publisher makes tantalizing suggestions regarding an astounding revelation buried in "indentures" in rock walls and in letter-shaped chasms that seem created by some unseen hand—but no final revelation is offered. More than mere hoax, these framing conjectures evoke themes of infinite regression paralleling the act of writing a narrative to a series of infinitely regressive "adventures." The "Truth," in the (fictive) reality purportedly mimed in the text, is elusive. Or, to put it in a way that reflects the spirit of both romantic aesthetics and contemporary theory, the "Truth" of the narrative is dependent on the interrelation of foregrounded narrativity and the fiction of reality, on the dialectic of object and subject—or on the dialogic of many subjects and planes.

One of the unifying motifs of what seems to be a loose, overly episodic, fragmented narrative is the experience of the inner mind. In its fragmentation and suggestion of the deep interior movement of thought processes, the narrative exhibits distinctive features of Friedrich Schlegel's definition of the "arabesque romance," including the feature of multileveled quest: instinctive, unconscious, intellectual, or philosophical. The infinite regression that opens up in *Pym* when the mind contemplates the mind is reminiscent of other romantic works that partake of the self-reflective character of arabesque romance, such as Ludwig Tieck's drama *Die verkehrte Welt* (1799), literally "The reverse world" (or The world turned topsy-turvy or inside out). In this work, characters in a play contemplate themselves as characters in a play contemplating themselves as characters in a play, so that (in Tieck's phrase) the mind "spins into the inwardness." Poe's controversial narrative of a series of stuttering journeys to the end of the world is also a narrative of the possibly infinite journey into "the inwardness." Pym's journey inward also includes the idea of multiple texts in Schlegel's sense of multiple texts of the self, although the journey, as in Tieck, may be a good deal less self-affirming than in Schlegel.

The imagery of Pym's narrative suggests that Pym travels regressively, as though in a dream within a dream, from the complex world of social institutions toward a world that is increasingly "simple." But the basic affirmative connotation of romantic "simplicity" is reversed. The seeming multiform and multicolored world becomes simplistically elemented into black and white and the mixture of the two as gray. At the same time, the steady increase of whiteness to all things suggests an original, primeval unity that is both oneiric and mythic. Whatever the implications of the ambiguous "allegory" of black versus white may suggest about racial tensions in an accursed America,[13] Pym's incomplete recovery of mythic history suggests that there is a fundamental opposition of black and white in the primal schism that was the Creation, when God spoke the light from the dark.

Whether this division is negative or affirmative is neither asked nor answered explicitly in the text, although Poe's critics have variously addressed the issue. When Pym sails nine months later into warm and milky waters at the end of the world, does he journey an amniotic sea toward reabsorption in the womb of the great mother earth? Does he journey toward burial in eternal unbeing? Does the rising up of a gigantic human figure in a "shroud" of perfect whiteness at the "end" signify a beatific vision, at the moment of symbolic and transfiguring death— what one critic calls the negative, blank white light of revelation and another a manifestation of Christ? Or is it a vision of pale void reflecting or inscribed with the vague figure of the observer-perceiver?[14] In the main narrative, these seemingly opposed possibilities, and others, are balanced one against another. Just as the final revelation at the end of the world and the end of the main narrative is about to be given, the narrative abruptly breaks off, without conventional closure.

In this frustration of carefully planted genre expectations, Poe's *Narrative* conforms to the European definition of the arabesque: it uses genre conventions and conventional narrative to go *against* the grain of narrative convention. Furthermore, in its incorporation of satiric and ironic elements, especially those that seem to be calculated contradictions or absurdities, into the seemingly serious quest narrative (itself contained within a simultaneously serious and joking metafictional frame), Poe's *Narrative* suggests not so much a "Menippean satire," as some have argued, but an encompassing "romantic irony" central to Schlegel's sense of the romantic arabesque.[15] For while the text *Pym* and the journey of Pym ineluctably suggest a religious or metaphysical allegory which we are invited to read and *challenged* to decipher, at the same time such meanings are repeatedly withdrawn (or forever "deferred") and even mocked.

Aesthetic Framing and the Metaliterary

The *Narrative* is ironically framed by complexly self-referential commentary about the text and its authors that simultaneously calls into question the authority of the text and earnestly suggests that it is redolent with meanings. In addition to the ironic metafictional joking in its frames, from the perspective of conventional narrative, the text breaks all contracts with the reader; in particular, it defeats reader expectations of linear plot development and conventional resolution. The narrative hovers elliptically back and forth between apparent beginnings and endings, increasingly edging toward questioning the very assumptions behind one's belief in fixed beginnings and endings. Perhaps the ultimate revelation is the romantic-ironic perception of the fictiveness of all things. In the editorial "Note" appended at the end (*P* 1:207–8), we are told that the last chapters are missing and that "Mr. Poe" has declined the task of filling the "vacuum" because he is disturbed by the "general inaccuracy of the details" and holds a "disbelief in the entire truth of the latter portions of the narration." The words "entire" and "portions" stand in obvious conflict here, ironically undercutting each other. But exactly what the phrase "latter portions" signifies is not clear. Conventionally, in a narrative, the "latter" holds a privileged position over the "former" because what is latter normally clarifies what has gone before and thus is more authoritative. Poe does not necessarily remove that privilege, but he certainly inverts those conventional reasons for privileging latter over former.[16]

The concluding editorial frame refers to the opening editorial frame but emphasizes its distinctness from it. The "editor" observes that Pym had described the figures of the chasms on Tsalal "without comment" and had spoken of certain "indentures" found at the extremity of one of the chasms as "having but a fanciful resemblance to alphabetical characters." Although "Mr. Pym" is obviously in "earnest" in his opinion, the editor thinks that there are certain "facts" about the configuration of the chasms and indentures that "beyond doubt, escaped the attention of Mr. Poe" (*P* 1:207). The editor then makes a number of teasingly enigmatic suggestions about the resemblance of the shapes of the chasms and the inscriptions on the walls to Ethiopian, Arabic, Egyptian script with Hebraic meanings; and the reader is asked to entertain the possibility that they have been written in the earth by some gigantic hand. The linked chasms suggest to this editor an ancient word for shadow or darkness and, the indentures suggest, simultaneously, ancient words for whiteness—and for the "south." The reader is now invited to regard this speculation in terms of some of the "most faintly-detailed incidents of the narrative," though "in no visible manner is this chain of connexion complete" (P 1:207–8). The editor suggests that the contrast between the black island of the chasms and the steady increase of whiteness, linked with the cry ("Tekeli-li!") of the sea birds flying overhead and the ejaculations of the natives, be conjoined with some "philological scrutiny" of the name "Tsalal" itself. In the final paragraph, the final words are given as a "quotation" without transition: " '*I have graven it within the hills, and my vengeance upon the dust within the rock*' " (P 1:208). The reader is implicitly invited to piece together the meaning of this echo from Genesis, Isaiah, Job, and Deuteronomy (along with other biblical echoes throughout the narrative) and the words "Tekeli-li," "Tsalal," and "Tsalemoun."

Other clues to the metaliterary nature of *Pym* are found in Pym's recurrence to the "narrative" he is telling; in his reading of other narratives of exploration; in the contrived junctures of the narrative episodes; in the multiplication of messages, letters, texts; in the obsession with words, inscriptions, and encryptions in the text; in the imagery of graven letters; and even in the imagery of blackness and whiteness. Whatever else it is, Pym's journey is overtly metafictional.[17] That is, *Pym* may be read in part as a narrative about the process of artistic creation (of a text, of a self) that increasingly marginalizes reference to the objective world: a subjective fiction about fictionality. (Schlegel would say that such subjectivity thereby becomes objective, for the creation of fiction is part of the definition of the self.) The tyranny of the WORD takes its form not only in utterance or "indentures," but also in the black and white that constitute pages of text, like the physical form of the book *The Narrative of Arthur Gordon Pym* itself. The progress through the text of *Pym*, and through the narrating of Pym's adventures, is a recurrent journey to the white margin at the end of the page. The margin at the bottom of the last page is the not-quite-final silence, a resonant silence, a palpably present absence, suggesting that the text is incomplete, always requiring completion.[18]

The Quincuncial Design

In addition to the "episodes" in which both Pym and the frame editor attempt to decipher the suggestive but vague inscriptions of rock and chasm, there are at least three major symbolic scenes or incidents (I would call them icons) that exemplify the interpretative problems presented by efforts to stabilize "meaning" in a romantic arabesque such as Poe creates. These are Pym's partial reading, in the dark hold of the *Grampus,* of Augustus' note in the third chapter; his analogous efforts to "read" and "describe" the black and white rookery of albatross and penguin in chapter 14; and the facing mirrors aboard the *Jane Guy* in chapter 18. Space permits consideration here of only one: the quincunx structure of the Christmas Harbor rookery. It is also an icon of the *Narrative* as a whole.[19]

In chapter 14, Pym "reads" a natural "text" (the rookery of penguin and albatross on Desolation Island) seemingly without full comprehension, foreshadowing the natural/preternatural/supernatural texts in the rocks at Tsalal. Pym describes the pattern of the rookery formed by two separate species of birds that are "actuated apparently by one mind, to trace out, with mathematical accuracy, either a square or other parallelogram" (P 1:152). At first he says that the nest of each *albatross* is "placed in the *centre* of a little square formed by the nests of four penguins" (emphasis added). Then he comments that "one side of the place thus marked out runs parallel with the water's edge" and is "left open." The two species of black and white birds have (more or less) "defined the limits of the rookery" by creating a wall of stone and rubbish "on the three inland sides"; and "just within this wall a perfectly level and smooth walk is formed" as a "general promenade." Thus we have a doubly framed "arabesque" design of repeated quincunxes within a quincunx with an open-ended border or margin on one side. The question is: What is the "text" of the "page"? Or what is the "figure in the carpet"?

With Pym, we look at the rookery design a second time. The text tells us that the birds partition the whole area "into small squares exactly equal in size," formed by narrow paths "crossing each other at right angles throughout the entire extent of the rookery. At each intersection of these paths the nest of an albatross is constructed, and a *penguin's* nest in the *centre* of each square—thus every *penguin* is surrounded by four albatrosses" (P 1:152; emphasis added). In other words, the pattern is described in terms that seem the "reverse" of Pym's first description—though actually the pattern is the "same." The effect anticipates and parallels that of the double "reversing" mirrors of chapter 18, which leave the imaged pattern the same while reversing it, and parallels in another way the two sides of a letter, each of which can communicate information even when (and because) there is nothing to read on one side. The rookery symbolically mirrors the *same* epistemological problem as the writing and reading of Augustus' message in total darkness. Here, in the rookery, the *difference* lies in what is taken as the center and what is decentered, and the center of the design of the open-ended rookery as a whole cannot be determined.

Pym's second description is accurate for a perspective that focuses on the penguin as the center object, but it is not entirely accurate as a description of the dual pattern of the *whole,* for "each albatross" is also surrounded "by a like number of penguins" (*P* 1:152). The mirror-like quality of Pym's syntax—"every penguin is surrounded by four albatrosses, and each albatross by a like number of penguins"—suggests that Pym is in the presence of some revelation, the significance of which he does not understand. The question of whether penguins are surrounded by albatrosses or albatrosses surrounded by penguins in a framed but indeterminate rookery of nests within nests of alternating types is, on one level, moot. Both observations are equally correct and equally false, much like the question Melville raises about the two kinds of coral at Mardi (*Mardi,* bk. 1, chap. 82). What is clear is that there *is* a pattern, but this natural pattern, contrary to optative romantic reasoning, has "no inherent meaning," being an arabesque. Any "meaning" or interpretation of center and margin is imposed by the perceiving Self. Moreover, the absurdity of setting the reader to meditate (scholastically) whether penguins surround albatrosses or albatrosses penguins is a consummate romantic-ironic joke, simultaneously serious and silly.

The foursquare pattern, with the addition of either albatross or penguin at the center, along with the whole field of such abstract design, forms the ancient quincunx as a figure-five of one-within-four. In his description, which closely follows the lines of his travel-book sources (see *P* 1:295–98), was Poe invoking the tradition of the quincunx? The matter is not something that can be determined with any certainty—although the symbolism of the quincunx was well known in Poe's time. For example, in some of Sir Thomas Browne's writings, the quincunx is the master trope, and Poe himself twice quotes from chapter 5 of Thomas Browne's *Urn-Burial* (once as the epigraph to "The Murders in the Rue Morgue" [*M* 2:527] and once in his review of *The Quacks of Helicon* [*H* 10:189], both 1841). Bracketed with *Urn-Burial* and bearing an inverse parallel relationship with it—the one text on death and dissolution, the other on life and immorality, in a Janus-faced (mirror variant) relation—is Browne's *The Garden of Cyrus* (published with *Hydriotaphia, or Urn-Burial* in 1658). *The Garden of Cyrus* is a meditation on the global symbolism of the underlying design of the ancient "arabesque" garden; for, in addition to being the basic design of arabesque carpets, the quincunx was common in ancient agriculture as a basic unit of infinite reduplication in a field. There are striking resonances in *Pym* with the natural, the supernatural, and the epistemological significations of the quincunx as set forth by Browne in this work.[20]

In a discussion of the symbology of the "Quincunciall Lozenge, or Net-Work Plantations of the Ancients, Artificially, Naturally, Mystically Considered," Browne attributes a providential and mystical signification to the ever-varying but constantly manifest pattern of the squared figure-five. (Compare the word "quintessence," the fifth essence: the pure, highly concentrated essence of something, the purest or most typical; in ancient and medieval philosophy, the fifth and highest essence after the four elements of earth, air, fire, and water, thought to be the substance of the heavenly bodies and latent in all things.) Arabesque agriculture traditionally required the planting of trees in this pattern. The Persian king Cyrus the Great—who "delivered" Babylon from Belshazzar and Nabonidus (implicated in the biblical-historical-mythic mists of *Pym*)—was, as was Cyrus the Younger, famous for systematic cultivation of the desert.[21]

The agricultural arabesque becomes for Browne, two thousand years later, an archetype for the five stars lowest in the horizon, the five senses, the five wounds of Christ, and so on. He makes of the quincunx network a global and cosmic symbol of universal significance, of meaning and order, citing for example the underlying form of crosses and crucifixes, both angular and rounded, and the Egyptian symbol of "*Orus*, the Hieroglyphick of the world," who wears a "Net-work covering, from the shoulder to the foot" (p. 87). Taking the V shape as fundamental, Browne particularizes the diamond (or lozenge) shape ⬦ and the X (or decussation) shape as doublings of the V, which is, in addition to a geometrical shape, both a letter and a number. He notes the various V shapes of the relation of internal organs, of the neurological avenues of vision and the supposed angles of rays of light entering the eyes and brain, and the V shape of the hand made by thumb and fingers—so that the fundamental pattern is an icon of the organization of the world (object) and of our means of knowing the world (subject) as a *network* of such shapes (interaction of object and subject). But it is more; it is the basic component of the mythic significance of Logos and religious aspiration, forming not only the basis for the cross of Christ but also (doubltess, he says) the design of the Garden of Eden (pp. 59–64, 104–7) and the cabalistic "name" or "letter" for God himself (pp. 109–10). In addition to sheer repetition of the pattern, the quincunx design in a network also lends itself to incorporating smaller versions within larger versions of itself, as it were endlessly concentralizing itself by framing itself. The multiplication of patterns gives rise to a plentitude of seemingly endless signification that ends in emptying design of meaning—while framing that process meaningfully.

Whether Poe read Browne's quincunxiamania this way or not must remain speculative, but the implication is not uncommon in the nineteenth century. The fifth edition of the *Encyclopaedia Britannica* (1815–17) defines the "QUINCUNX *Order*, in *Gardening*" in a way that suggests its doubleness of meaning and meaninglessness: "a plantation of trees, disposed originally in a square, consisting of five trees, one at each corner, and a fifth in the middle; which disposition, *repeated again and again,* forms a regular grove . . . *or wilderness*" (emphasis added). Is it orderly, or is it a wilderness?

A further association of the quincunx with the problem of determinacy and indeterminacy in the romantic arabesque yields some rather startling possibilities for the partially withheld or faintly intimated patterning of *Pym*. The fifth edition of the *Britannica* further defines the quincunx as a word that "in Roman antiquity, denotes any thing that consists of five-twelfths of another; but particularly of the *as*." The *as* was a general symbol of something entire or whole, an integer (cf. "ace"), and in particular a weight of twelve ounces, "being the same as *libra,* or the Roman pound." "AS was also the name of a Roman coin," continues the *Britannica*, and the decussation X was the symbol for ten *asses*. But the *as* was of four "different weights and different matter in different periods of the commonwealth." Its quantity was so frequently redefined over the centuries (being reduced after the first Punic War to two ounces, and then by half, and half again down to half an ounce) that its signification became indeterminate, and eventually the Roman coin signifying the *as* (and its quincuncial subtext) came, after the time of the emperors, to carry the symbol of "a Janus with two faces" on one side and "on the reverse the rostrum or prow of a ship."

The suggestive quality of the *as* in terms of *Pym*, a coin linked with the quincunx, involves indeterminacy of meaning and the etymological origin of the word "symbolize" from a token or coin. The image of "a Janus with two faces" appearing on one side of the *as* parallels Browne's famous paired "books" on death and life that, like shadow and light, "mirror" each other. The doubleness suggested by the *as* is evident in *Pym* in such elements as the emblem of a ship's prow and the rookery in a quincunx pattern near a harbor named "Christmas" on an island named "Desolation," attained after a long sea voyage, in a narrative about dualities of meaning and life and death—a narrative suggesting illusion and hallucinatory regress as much as a journey of DISCOVERY. The pattern of oppositions and doublings of meaning, within a multiplicity of meanings in the full text of *Pym*, is heavily implicated in the scene of the black and white rookery.

The congruence of this network of symbols is too fortuitous not to pursue a little further. One of the standard methods of navigation in Poe's time involved the quincunx. Under the heading "Geography," the fifth edition of the *Britannica* notes that using curved lines of latitude and longitude, one seeking a "location" on the "globe" of the earth can "estimate" the spot between "what two parallels of latitude and longitude the place lies, and consequently by what four lines it is bounded, to find the place by trial, by considering the proportional distance of it from each line" (Navigational "Problem II"). The "proportional distance" (a kind of abstract, intellectualized dead reckoning) results in no less than the following figure of "estimation" for the patterned lines enabling circumnavigation of the earth:

The point of reference, the center of a quincunx, provides the sight line for the course of the ship, as it tacks back and forth through a network of repetitions of this image. The nearly infinite multiplication of this pattern enables the charting of the journey to the end of the world, for it represents order. It also represents in the multiplied duplication of itself both wilderness and oversignification. The global network of such parallelograms (Orus), through which, and by means of which, we chart our course, is, like the rookery of penguin and albatross and albatross and penguin, an arabesque design.

X Marks the Spot

Indeed, the general configuration of the four voyages in *Pym* approximates the pattern of the rookery and the quincunx of the navigation parallelogram. Consider the configuration of the double journeys of the *Grampus* from Nantucket in the west and of the *Jane Guy* from Liverpool in the east—to the middlepoint at the island rocks on the equator (in the 30th meridian of western longitude, between the continental promontories of South America and Africa)—thence east to the Kerguélen Islands (at the 70th meridian of eastern longitude), and then west to the Falkland Plateau in search of the disappearing Auroras (in the 50th meridian of western longitude)—and thence ever southward into the Filchner Ice Shelf in the Weddell Sea. The key points on this course describe a long, lazy, four-pointed parallelogram, or a not quite completed Arab X, or a more curved Greek χ.

Browne, in fact, remarks in chapter 1 of the *Cyrus* on the ever-implied X of the quincunx, calling it the "Emphaticall decussation, or fundamental figure" (p. 60) of the doubled V. He weaves together in an intricate pattern images of darkness and light, vision, doubleness, and symmetrical replication, focusing especially on the variations of X and V as quincuncial. In chapter 4, he comments on the "sacred" meaning of the figure, a figure which corresponds to the Egyptian X that signifies one of the ten sacred animals, the stork, whose "open Bill and stradling Legges" were "imitated by that character" (p. 106). This observation follows a discussion of how "darknesse and light hold interchangeable dominions," and how "light that makes things seen, makes some things invisible" (like the noble creation of the stars), which leads him to ruminate on "sight" and the double V-shaped refraction of "rays," one V without, the other within, thus forming an X, as a doubled or self-reflecting V. Vision and doubleness, of course, are the common motifs of all three of the icons of indeterminacy in *Pym* mentioned here: the writing/reading of the letter in the dark, the discerning of the "pattern" of the black and white rookery, and the two facing mirrors and their variants.

The X pattern that Browne conjoins with black and white, dark and light, is highly suggestive regarding the latent, "faintly-detailed" patterning of *Pym*, so vividly represented by the iconography of the rookery, which anticipates (actually adumbrates) the shadow meanings of black and white in the hieroglyphic rock writings at the end of the *Narrative*. The "greatest mystery of Religion," Browne writes, "is expressed by adumbration. . . . Life it self is but the shadow of death, and souls departed but the shadows of the living. . . . The Sunne it self is but the dark *simulachrum,* and light but the shadow of God" (pp. 104–5). The upper and lower shapes of the letter X he calls "ascending and descending Pyramids, mystically apprehended" (p. 106), and he cites Plato's use of the Greek X, turned in a circle, to represent the "double aspect" of the "soul of man." Browne observes that, in Justin Martyr's reading of Plato's reading of X for T or a cross, "this figure hath had the honour to characterize and notifie our blessed Saviour" (p. 107), and he concludes with a comment on the "other mysteries not thoroughly understood in the sacred letter X," thus leaving the significance of the whole with a resonant undercurrent of indeterminacy.

In this context, it is important to note the placement of the center in the journey pattern of *Pym*—that is, the fifth point, or *Mittelpunkt,* of a quincunx cross that has degenerated along one axis. The text gives a series of fairly precise longitude and latitude readings, inviting the curious reader to plot out the courses of the ships. If the reader will, in fact, take the trouble to plot these courses according to the arbitrary grids of navigational parallelograms, it will be discovered that the exact *Mittelpunkt* of latitude and longitude of the whole journey is at the twin jutting rocks called *St. Peter* and *St. Paul* in the mid-Atlantic, halfway in the long journey to *Christmas* harbor rookery and the end of the world. The configuration is another "faintly-detailed" suggestion of overall signification—like the Figure 4 drawing of chapter 23, suggestive, like so much else in the *Narrative*, of a meaning just out of reach, of some Messiah come to deliver the afflicted, stretching out a hand or pointing the way, but disappearing in the act.

Geometry of Void: Symmetry and "Meaning"

The arabesque patterning of Poe's *Narrative* suggests a "postmodernist" question regarding the reading of the text. What emerges from contemporary critical attention to the narrative is the recurrent perception that there is a coherent, stable, and symmetrical structure of repeating elements. This framing or structuring pattern, however, has no "inherent meaning" in itself. It generates an evocative ambiguity, in which oversignification leads to undersignification and purposeful textual collapse.

Like Schlegel's conception of *Roman*, like the quincunx which Poe makes its symbol, the *Narrative* is structurally symmetrical around a *Mittelpunkt*. Harry Levin notes the "almost symmetrical" pattern of the framing preface and endnote enfolding Pym's narrative, within which are the framing episodes of the small boat *Ariel* at the beginning and of the canoe at the end, within which are framed the voyages of the larger vessels *Grampus* and *Jane Guy*, the transition from the one ship to the other occurring in the middle of the narrative.[22] Indeed, the two halves of the *Narrative* stand in a mirror relation to each other. Harold Beaver writes that the two halves of the book structurally replicate each other with "perfect symmetry"; they are "split down a central spine which (geographically) proves to be the equator and (fictionally) Pym's rescue by the *Jane Guy*."[23] In chapter 13, the middle chapter of twenty-five total chapters, the intervention of the *Jane Guy* occurs at the end, which is the arithmetical middle of the narrative. The initial treachery and mutiny on the *Grampus* is mirrored by the treachery and revolt on Tsalal. The murderous Black Cook on the *Grampus* is paralleled by the unscrupulous black chief Too-wit on the *Jane Guy*. Pym's confinement in the hold of the *Grampus* is transmuted into his confinement underground in the hills of Tsalal. The opening incident of the small boat *Ariel* is paralleled by the closing journey of the small canoe. And, of course, the overt editorial frames enclose the whole.[24]

John P. Hussey takes the symmetry even further. Noting that Pym's journeys take precisely nine months, from the end of spring to the beginning of spring in the succeeding year, he identifies nine episodes to the whole narrative—and finds a central sequence of twenty-seven pages bracketed on either side by four episodes of development precisely equal to one another in the design.[25] From the *Mittelpunkt* outward toward both the beginning and end simultaneously, we find a double pattern of four around either side of a fifth central point. Recognition of affinities of the romantic arabesque (with its use of patterns of no "inherent" meanings in themselves) with postmodernism suggests a question about the symmetries of *Pym*. The question is not whether these *are* patterns but whether they are meaningful and necessary, or arbitrary and gratuitous. My contention is that they are, simultaneously, both. Our inability to determine the matter either way underlies the postmodernist affinities of *Pym*.

Once regarded as an unfinished or hastily and awkwardly finished mistake, the arabesque romance of *Arthur Gordon Pym* exemplifies Poe's method of resonant indeterminateness. The foregrounding of epistemology in contemporary readings of *Pym* leads to an important observation: the basis of what we may call Poe's philosophical romanticism is not epistemology as conventionally understood; rather it is the *question* of epistemology—the question behind the question. In this questioning of the very foundations of Western metaphysics and modes of observation, the *Narrative* looks forward more (insofar as a distinction is valid) to postmodernist than modernist aesthetics.

The indeterminacy of meaning in Poe's arabesque fictions parallels Poe's themes of the paradox of human existence. The vision not so much of void as of the *possibility* of void haunts Poe's characters (even more so than Ishmael in *Moby-Dick*). The rhetoric of his philosophical essay on the universe, *Eureka*, is largely an elaborate conceit on the word *nothing,* treated both seriously and playfully within a multiplicity of meaning, a plenitude of oversignification finally signifying nothing. As I have elsewhere pointed out, at one juncture in *Eureka* the birth-death-resurrection cycle of the universe is analogized to an "imperfect plot" in a "romance."[26] Poe's analogy confirms again, I would say, the Schlegelian conception of *Roman* as an imperfect emulation (whether from within or without) of God's imperfect text titled *World* or *Universe*. Nevertheless, Poe suggests, the universe (whether or not it exists apart from us) may yet have an aesthetic design. But of what kind? Poe proposes a system of expanding and collapsing cycles of *nothingness.*[27]

For Schlegel and Poe, the very recognition of the possibility of nothing leads to a recognition of the importance of the "as if" as a necessary qualification to every statement, thus suggesting the refracted and metaphoric quality of all perception: one thing in terms of another rather than absolutes. The arabesque in Schlegel's theory and in Poe's practice is an *attempt* at an *aesthetic* resolution (by means of framing romantic irony) of such philosophical-epistemological matters as faith and doubt, affirmation and denial, and of intellectual confusion. This "resolution" is attempted by embodiment of the conflict in an artistic text: by framing chaos (Schlegel's "gebildetes künstliches Chaos"). The *recognition* that, rather than conventional absolutist pronouncements, the "as if" really constitutes reality is in itself the first step toward higher consciousness for Schlegel and Poe. The second step is to *embody* that suspected nothingness (or the apprehension of infinitely regressive dislocatedness) in something like a being or like a world. For the limited, earthly artist, this embodiment, of course, would be a fictive text, that text being itself a world or a being. The liberating paradox (to speak in Schlegelian terms) is the recognition of the fictiveness of the constructs. John Barth in "Tales Within Tales Within Tales" observes that the cabalists ("whom writers as different as I. B. Singer and Jorge Luis Borges have found to be a rich source of literary metaphor") urge that "reality, our reality, is God's text, his significant fiction." He adds, "Arthur Schopenhauer . . . declares that our reality, whether or not it's God's fiction, is our representation, as it were *our* fiction: that relations, categories, concepts such as differentiation, time and space, being and not-being—all are ours, not seamless nature's.[28]

It is significant that Barth recurs to a philosopher of the Romantic period to gloss the concept of the dissolution of subject and object in an as-if game. The romantic God-Artist is the architect of the abyss, the geometer of designs of no inherent meaning. "How can Nothing have a structure?" is a crucial Schlegelian question. The ironic *perception* of the *structures* of nothingness that constitute our cosmos and our selves constitutes our sanity as we structure the formless and empty void. For Poe, the origin of the universe lies in nothingness, its present material state is but a variation of that nothingness, and its final end is a reconstitution of the original nothingness. This void can have shape only if it is consciously and continuously regenerated as a structure, conceived as a Kantian aesthetic design—that is, what Kant and Schlegel, in different ways, defined as the "arabesque."

Here then is the insistent structuring impulse of the romantic in the arabesque. Even so, infinite regression opens up. The abyss yawns. Knowing that the world has order, coherence, and meaning only by means of the imposition of these human constructs, the self-conscious romantic artist yet continues to generate the text, even though he knows, or suspects, that the text will collapse. In Poe's writings, the deceptive perversity of the universe (if we can posit the "as-if" personification) and of the mind is transcended by the romantic-ironic imagination of the Artist of the Arabesque. It is the romantic artist who achieves—through the simultaneous detachment and involvement embodied in the new aesthetic, through the creation of the new artwork of the *Roman*, through the highly conscious but deeply felt act of writing the "as if"—a liberating vision of the paradoxical order of indeterminacy: "ein *gebildetes künstliches* Chaos." The act of writing becomes the supremely ironic weaving of a tapestry signifying the paradoxical journey through Cosmos/Chaos. The journey's "end" is to be found in "the inwardness," in God/Self as infinity, paradoxically from "snares of self" set "free." The merely mortal Israfel becomes the God-Artist writing and rewriting the always dissolving text of the world/self. Read as an arabesque of romantic irony, Poe's 1838 *Narrative* becomes a comprehensible and significant text, exemplifying an important romantic vision of world and aesthetic form that shares a number of features with postmodernism. Read without this reference to a particular tradition and genre (or mode) of the arabesque, I would say with Poe that the *Narrative* is "a very silly book," hardly worth all the attention it has received from contemporary academic critics.

A Writer's View

"Still Farther South":

Some Notes on Poe's *Pym*

John Barth

 Gatherings of experts sometimes entertain themselves by inviting a nonexpert to hold forth: one whose own expertise is either refreshingly outside theirs (as when a specialist in the physiology of dreaming looks at *Finnegans Wake*) or refreshingly inside (as when Kafka's ape reports to the Academy).

My late acquaintance Italo Calvino was once commissioned by the publishing house of Ricci in Milan to write a short novel involving the Tarot cards, to accompany a facsimile edition of a medieval Tarot deck in the Morgan Library, fully annotated by a scholarly tarotologist. Calvino told me that his first artistic decision in this instance was to purge his imagination altogether of the cards' traditional significances; to look at those famous icons as if he knew nothing whatever about them, like an intelligent visitor from an alien culture. The happy result was his novel *The Castle of Crossed Destinies*, on the facing pages of Ricci's beautiful volume *I Tarocchi*.

That is the spirit in which, on this conference's commission, I have lately taken another look at Edgar Poe's *The Narrative of Arthur Gordon Pym of Nantucket*. The task of purging my imagination of 150 years of critical commentary on that novel—beginning, I suppose, with Poe's own remark that it is "a very silly book"—was made immeasurably easier for me by the circumstance that I have read virtually none of that commentary. Indeed, though the author died where I live, and though I feel certain other connections with him as well, I happen not even to have read his first and only voyage upon the bounding main of the novel until maybe ten years ago, when I had conceived and was in the early gestation of my own sixth novel: one called *Sabbatical: A Romance*, published by Putnam's in 1982.

It is because of that novel that I'm here: more particularly because the story of Poe's *Pym* drifts in and out of it like a bit of saltwater flotsam on the brackish tides of Chesapeake Bay. I propose to review in abbreviated form the three principal offending passages, then tell you briefly, as best I can this far after the fact, how Edgar and Arthur came to be involved in my story, and finally venture some innocent observations upon the novel itself—Poe's, not mine.

The time of the present action of *Sabbatical: A Romance* is the last weeks of spring 1980. Susan Rachel Allan Seckler, a young professor of classical American literature on sabbatical leave (to finish a study of Poe's *Pym*), and her husband, Fenwick Scott Key Turner—an ex-CIA agent turned exposeur and aspiring novelist—have just returned to the Chesapeake from a nine-month sailing cruise to the Caribbean in their 33⅓-foot cutter. In the course of this sabbatical adventure they have confronted but not yet successfully dealt with various big-ticket problems and questions in their recent past and their present—including the question whether to beget children at this possibly late hour of the world. Their sailboat's name, *Pokey,* is among other things an amalgam of the surnames of one each of the couple's real or putative ancestors: in Fenwick's case, Francis Scott Key, of whom Fenn is a lineal descendant; in Susan's case, Edgar Allan Etc.: an obviously more problematical genealogy, which gets addressed midway through their narrative in the course of a chapterlet called "Your 19th Is Susan's Century, Your 18th Fenn's, Or, Was Edgar Allan Poe Jewish?":

Susan stretches out against the cockpit bulkhead and glumly surveys our wake. Her mind obviously elsewhere . . . she supposes that we haven't really explained yet to the reader, who must be wondering, what all this Poe-Key/*Pokey*/Kepone business is about, beyond our putative ancestries, the name of our boat, and Allied Chemical Corporation's deliberate, criminal, and perhaps irremediable poisoning of the noble James River, site of the first permanent English settlement in America.

Fenwick encourages her: Keep on.

Aye yi. Well. Ma says Da believed that E. A. Poe was as Jewish as I am and that the Secklers are related to him through the Allans of Virginia, who were only Poe's adoptive bloodline anyhow, but the connection's lost because Grandma never understood it when Grandpa Allan used to explain it, and Ma never believed it. John Allan, who adopted Poe, was a Richmond merchant; does that make him Jewish, I ask you?

Keep on.

There's an Uncle Artie Golderman back in the line—Grandpa Allan Seckler's great-uncle, I think—that Jack Seckler claimed was the model for Poe's Arthur Gordon Pym. Never mind that Edgar Allan Poe sounds more like Arthur Gordon Pym than Artie Golder Man does: Great-Uncle Artie was in corset stays and whale oil in Boston before the bottom fell out of the business when petroleum was discovered in Titusville P A in Eighteen Fifty-nine. . . .

Susan.

I need to talk. Anyhow, the world *is* a seamless web.

Onward, then. Upward.

Yeah. Be all the foregoing as may—and there's more to it, but who cares?—your irrational, romantic, overreaching Nineteenth is my fucking century, and Crazy Edgar is my alma pater, Jewish or not. Nervous. Unstable. Frenetic.

Brilliant, Fenwick hastens to add. Energetic. Intuitive.

Susan's eyes are wet again. Fatherless. Childless. Self-tormented. Half hysterical. And doomed to an early, unquiet grave.

Susele . . .

She quotes unsmiling from [last night's flashback] dream: Quoth the raven: Baltimore.

Enough, honey.

She's still slouched on the [cockpit] cushion . . . looking where we've been. . . . Her eyes close. The Overwhelming of the Vessel.[1]

The woman is obviously distraught. A hundred pages later, having shared that flashback dream just mentioned, the couple experience separate but equal "flashforward" dreams—waking up from which, Susan will acknowledge her unilaterally resolved-upon abortion (by vacuum aspiration). Fenn's dream has had to do with forks in the road, or the channel, of the couple's imaginable future. Susan's dream involves Poe and Pym:

[Her] cry wakes him: Reynolds! Reynolds!

What?

Her night's mare has flashed forward from the night before's, and is for the most part impersonal. Our marriage having failed along with the Democratic coalition, the NATO alliance, the U.S. dollar, and Fenwick's heart, to the strains of "The Star-Spangled Banner" Susan witnesses the physical collapse in turn of the continental United States (which splits anticlimactically at the San Andreas Fault), of the hemisphere (when that fault connects with others), then of the solar system, the galaxy, the universe—for some reason all because she and Fenn will have no children. From [Fort] McHenry's ramparts, which are also *Pokey's* cockpit, Susan sees the West sink into the sun, the sun into the galactic vortex like Odysseus's ship-timbers into Charybdis, or whatever-it-was into Poe's Maelstrom. *Pokey* himself is now become our galaxy, now our universe, rushing headlong into one of its own Black Holes like that legendary bird that flies in ever-diminishing circles until it vanishes into its own fundament; like Pym's canoe rushing into the chasm at the foot of the cataract at the southern Pole: a black hole aspirating, with a cosmic shlup, us, U.S., all.[2]

Finally, at the novel's close, catharsed by literal as well as figurative tempests and safely at anchor behind an uninhabited little Chesapeake island called Cacaway, Fenwick pops champagne to toast their survival and says to his emotionally exhausted wife:

Now . . . tell me something new about Arthur Gordon Pym.
Susan begs his pardon?
Fenwick thinks he's got F. S. Key and E. A. Poe sorted out, at least enough to get us started. They . . . fit! But Poe's queer story still nags at him. It was a voyage, sure, but so was Odysseus's and Ishmael's. Here you go, darling Susan:

TO OUR STORY.
. . . He has drawn her onto his lap, on the starboard settee berth. . . . Tell him something new about the voyage of Edgar Poe's Arthur Pym, he lovingly recommends her; he has the feeling that whatever Susan says just now will, you know, fit.
The cabin is storm-darkened, cozy with the putter of light and rain. [Fenn's] familiar hand calmly takes her breast; [Susan] feels like a confident Scheherazade, hundreds of nights after that first, upon the lap of her long-since conquered king.
She . . . breathes; begins. In the Nineteenth century, lots of people believed that at each of the earth's poles there was a great abyss. These twin abysses continuously swallowed up the ocean and continuously disgorged it somewhere along the Equator, maybe at the sources of the Amazon and the Nile, just as matter swallowed up in a Black Hole might reappear from a White Hole somewhere else in the universe.
Mm hm.
We feel her nipples rise. Well. Pym's log of his voyage breaks off on March Twenty-two, Eighteen Twenty-eight, the vernal equinox, just as his canoe approaches the South Polar abyss . . . and now as his little boat sweeps along through the cataract toward the chasm he sees a giant white shrouded human figure—and his narrative breaks off.

FENN'S LISTENING.
People have taken that figure to be everything from Jesus Christ to a giant penguin to the author himself, but never mind that. The

interesting thing is that what we've been reading is supposedly Pym's own account, written back in New York after he somehow survived the voyage. . . . [But] Pym's written account breaks off just as he's about to be vacuum-aspirated—

What?

Never mind. Just as he and Dirk Peters and the canoe are about to be swallowed up, the story breaks off without our ever learning how Pym survived and got back to New York City to write it. . . . Maybe he popped up in Uganda and floated down the Nile to the Mediterranean and back to the U.S.A.—but we'll never know how he managed it, because he gets killed or something back home in Eighteen Thirty-eight just when he brings the log of his voyage up to the abyss ten years before. . . . Are you listening?

I really am. Also.

Well, the point of my story* is that the point of Poe's story is that the point of Pym's story is this: "It is not that the end of the voyage interrupts the writing, but that the interruption of the writing ends the voyage." Would you make love to me now?[3]

Okay: a little love interest there, a little sex, even, to toast this conference, since there's none of either in Pym (at least not literally) and Lord only knows how much and what kind in the hectic life story of its young author. Susan Seckler is alleged to be descended from Edgar Poe, but she can't account for the allegation since Poe had no known children, as neither will she. Similarly, the narrative that she shares the lead in can be said to be a maverick, recycled descendant of *The Narrative of Arthur Gordon Pym*, at least in a few respects—and I can't really account for that, either, except to say that like many another American writer, no doubt, I think of Poe as among my literary forebears, for better and worse: not my great-grandfather, but a brilliant though erratic great-uncle, maybe. There have been in my literal genealogy a couple of sharp-tongued maiden aunts, more or less dotty, in whom (as in all the fish in one's gene pool) I have seen alternative, cautionary versions of myself. When I contemplate the famous face of my fellow Baltimorean, my Great-Uncle Edgar, I never fail to be struck by the certain familiar looniness in it: that flaky-Romantic strain most uneasy-making to me not in his overtly gothic fictive preoccupations—live

---

*A point made by Professor John T. Irwin of The Johns Hopkins University in his book *American Hieroglyphics* . . . which memorious Susan goes on now to quote verbatim. [Footnote from *Sabbatical: A Romance*]

burial, putrefaction, sibling crypto-incest, and the rest—but rather in his more apparently calm and reasoned productions. Hugh Kenner has remarked that nothing looks more Victorian than a Victorian pagoda, for example; just so, I think I hear my great-uncle's half-hysteria most clearly when he's trying to keep it out of his voice: in his reasoned refutation of Maelzel's chess-playing automaton, for example, or his prescient explanation (in *Eureka*) of why the night sky happens to be dark instead of white with the aggregate luminosity of stars, whose number is infinite and one of which must therefore occupy absolutely every line of sight from Earth.[4]

If, like Fenwick Scott Key Turner in the novel *Sabbatical*, I myself feel more affinity for Henry Fielding's and Laurence Sterne's eighteenth century than for Susan's and Poe's "self-tormented, half-hysterical" nineteenth, there is in that feeling an element of prophylaxis, or exorcism. Susan no less than Fenn c'est moi, in this regard; both registers of their coupled voice are mine, and I feel honored that the venerable house of Putnam's, which published *Eureka* (though not *Pym*), was also the publisher of *Sabbatical: A Romance*.

As for *Pym, Pym, Pym, Pym, Pym, Pym, Pym*: God knows it is, if not "a very silly book," a very odd duck of a novel, as impossible in its way as Melville's *The Confidence-Man* (though mercifully shorter) and as likely to be overvalued, I fear, by ingenious readers for its real or projected ingenuities in the teeth of its patent tiresomeness, its gothic preposterosities, and its dramaturgical shortcomings. And yet . . . and yet, by gosh and by golly, the thing works, sort of—especially the four opening paragraphs of chapter 1 and the magical last chapter (25), if the nonspecialist reader has, with young Pym, survived the 23 chapters between. Captain Edgar manages after all to skipper his maiden (and final) novel out of some fairly shaky heavy-weather realism, down through gothic Doldrums into latitudes of rather more plausible irrealism, and finally "STILL FARTHER SOUTH" (as Poe's subtitle advertises in boldface caps) into a realm where I too have done some narrative navigation: a realm whose resistless current I recognize and, reading *Pym*, give myself over to at last, whether or not I have ever attained it in my own novelistic expeditions. I shall address that climactic or at least culminating leg of Pym's odyssey after some passing remarks on the course of Poe's voyage: remarks made not as an expert critic or scholar but as a fairly seasoned fellow novelist and, by the way, a not-inexperienced amateur sailor.

Echoing the astronomer Edward Harrison's comment on *Eureka*, I report to you that I find *The Narrative of Arthur Gordon Pym* sometimes less credible in its more realistic stretches and more so in its less. I won't speak here to its metafictive narrative frame, which Susan Seckler and many another contemporary critic have spoken much to. What most impresses me about the opening paragraphs of the story proper is the tone of the camaraderie of the two boys' escapade in Pym's little sloop *Ariel* that October night in 1825. Young Augustus Barnard's drunken postparty oath—that he will not lie in bed like a dog for any Arthur Pym in Christendom when there's such a glorious breeze out of the southwest—and young Pym's counterboast that he too is tired of lying in bed like a dog and is as ready for any fun or frolic as any Augustus Barnard in Nantucket—these and the other details of their setting out I find as refreshing as a breeze out of the English eighteenth century: out of a scapegrace-*roman* by Fielding or Smollett, say. I don't recall anything elsewhere in Poe, certainly not in *Pym*, quite as appealing and convincing in this line. God forgive me, I myself have undertaken such reckless, not-quite-sober late-night sails in years gone by (it's always a southerly or southwesterly that promotes them), and Poe has got it right: the little sloop chafing against the dock piles, the boys' underestimation of the wind and overestimation of their abilities after Substance Abuse, the fast-sobering scariness, for Pym anyhow, of the night-sea out there, from which one is lucky to return intact. Poe even supplies, somewhat belatedly, the bright moon normally required, along with a glorious southerly, to inspire such lunacies. Yo, Poe!

Already by the fifth paragraph, however, I'm having trouble, as are the young night-sailors. In keeping with his temporarily realist mode, Poe has described *Ariel* in some detail as a sloop, under whose unreefed main and jib sails the boys have set out. She will have been one of those small, cuddy-cabined, gaff-rigged jobs of the sort pictured in Currier & Ives' *Trolling for Bluefish* or Winslow Homer's *Breezin' Up*, except that *Ariel* is rigged as a *sloop*—one mast, two sails—instead of a single-sail catboat. But when an accidental downwind gybe in paragraph 5 "carrie[s] away the mast short off by the board" (that is to say, the apparently unstayed mast breaks off just above deck level, where it goes through the cabin top to its step on the keel, and is lost over the side along with the boom, the gaff, and the mainsail), Arthur and his passed-out buddy roar along downwind "under the jib only," without Poe's troubling to tell us from what—on a single-masted boat which is now a no-masted boat—that jib is flying.

Okay: Sometimes even good Homer nods, and in a novel whose principal characters zonk out as often and completely as do those in *Pym*, it would be a miracle if the author didn't blink from time to time—particularly in the realistic passages of his voyage, which have about them the clenched-jawed metonymity of a driver determined to stay awake on a long and featureless stretch of Interstate. I certainly find this lapse more acceptable as a simple lapse than as a deliberate challenge to the "merely proairetic reader," as one recent critic has called the likes of us low-tech Pymophiles. In the same spirit, I don't fret overmuch at my question marks in the margins of *Pym*'s jury-rigged chronology, such as the narrator's declaration in his preface of July 1838 that he returned to the United States "a few months ago" from "the South Seas and elsewhere" and met Poe in Richmond, etc., when his return would seem to have to have been closer to two *years* ago to jibe with the publication of those first installments in the *Southern Literary Messenger* in January and February 1837—dates that "Pym" verifies. Never mind, while one is at it, that my most meticulous reconstruction of the schooner *Jane Guy*'s movements in chapters 14 and 15, in the neighborhood of Christmas Harbor, doesn't quite add up (Try it; you'll hate it: The schooner first arrives there on 18 October 1827, and her crew explore the neighborhood in the schooner's boats "for about three weeks." Then on 12 November she sets out in search of the Aurora Islands and "in fifteen days" [i.e., on 27 November] passes Tristan da Cunha en route, but manages nevertheless to reach the reported area of the Auroras a whole week *before* that, on 20 November). Let it go: Who among us novelists has not had such gaffes pointed out by sharp-eyed readers? The important thing about *Jane Guy*'s log is that it picks Pym up from the drifting hulk of the brig *Grampus* on 7 August somewhere off Brazil's Cabo de San Rocas—about 7° South latitude by my calculations, of which more presently—and delivers him on the winter solstice (summer solstice down there) to the 60th parallel of latitude and Captain Guy's decision on that portentous date to push on Still Farther South.

I wouldn't even have mentioned *Ariel*'s mastless jib (which has also been noted by Professor Burton Pollin of this conference and by Herbert F. Smith of the University of Victoria, a fellow sailor) if not that it foreshadows my first more serious crisis of belief, just as the dismasting itself foreshadows the sloop's being run down in the dark by the Nantucket whaleship *Penguin*. Three paragraphs later, after Pym revives from the first of his many, many losses of consciousness, we learn that the crewmen of the *Penguin*, having risked their lives valiantly to look for survivors, had turned back in the ship's jolly-boat. The whaler rolls in the heavy seas, and along with First Mate Henderson we see our hapless and unconscious young hero . . . *bolted through the neck?* Yup: bolted through the neck (and through the collar of his jacket) to the vessel's coppered bottom, alternately buried at sea and resurrected, like a funhouse corpse, as the ship rolls.

I know: The shot symbolizes A, B, and C and foreshadows D, E, and F later on in the movie. But I groan all the same at its sensational implausibility: the first of many such groans to come from this "proairetic reader." *Bolted through the neck,* and so securely that all that slow-rolling and dunking in a gale of wind doesn't dislodge him! Yet he neither drowns nor requires so much as a suture for his wound! The *end* of chapter 1 charmingly wears its portentousness up its sleeve rather than on it—I mean the boys' coming down to breakfast at Mr. Barnard's as if their night-sea adventure had not happened, and getting away with it—but I am not deceived by Poe's winning observation that "school-boys . . . can accomplish wonders . . . of deception." I know now that it's to be the Rocky Horror Picture Show after all; I sigh and settle in with my popcorn, and take not a word of the story straight thereafter, not even the mesmerizing last chapter. So you scared those hard-case mutineers out of their wits by making like a zombie? Sure you did. And later on you saw a shipload of deadies under full sail with seagulls chewing on the crew, and later yet you cannibalized old Parker there, and after that your dead pal Augustus' leg came apart in your hands like a . . . oh, like a putrefied leg of mutton from chapter 2, let's say, and you could hear the sharks chomping him up from a *whole mile away,* and on the island of Tsalal you were reburied alive and re-resurrected for the fifth time out of six in 25 chapters? Right, right.

The documents of the days of sail are rich in actual such horrors, which in our time the Vietnamese boat people could doubtless match. In Poe's hands, alas, they almost invariably turn, not into "challenges to the proairetic code," but into genre effects. And for all Pym's elaborate subsequent logging of his psychological weather, as a credible, palpable novelistic character he goes down with the *Ariel* in chapter 1 and never resurfaces. Even in proto-metafiction, that's a casualty to be regretted.

Yet even through the barfiest of ghoul-flicks the deep myths sometimes speak, more or less, and through the tellings of a canny and intuitive though erratic genius like Poe they may speak strongly, how-evermuch or little their "medium" (in the spiritualist sense) might be conscious of them. Autodidact Edgar was unpredictably knowl-edgeable as well as plenty smart; the paradigmatic image of him in Dominick Argento's opera *The Voyage of Edgar Allan Poe* is surely not the whole story, though it seems a fair piece of it: I mean the tenor zapped flat onstage by his *daimon* after every second aria, the vessel of his rational consciousness overwhelmed. As I tour Great-Uncle Edgar's floating gothic funhouse, my own authorial consciousness respectfully notes that the shipwright managed some admirable and not so obvious formal touches along with the more conspicuous gee-whizzers; and something "still farther south" in my sensibility rides on the undercur-rent of myth, stronger and stronger as we descend the parallels of south latitude. Umberto Eco reports that the last words of his friend Italo Calvino were "*I paralleli! I paralleli!*": It's a better exit line for a writer than Poe's "Reynolds! Reynolds!" and regarding certain of *Pym*'s *paral-leli* I shall speak next as the author not of *Sabbatical: A Romance* but of certain earlier fictions inspired by the Wandering Hero myth: the Ur-Myth, which my imagination once upon a time became possessed by after critics pointed out to me that my imagination was possessed by it.

Inasmuch as every literary person nowadays knows at least the outlines of that myth, I don't doubt that Poe's commentators in our time have long since noted its parallels in *Pym*. The *Ariel* episode prefigures it in miniature, even down to the time-zapping and the returned hero's appearing as if nothing remarkable had happened, as if he'd never been away—in short, as if he were not who he is, the man who has come through. The voyage proper (serial voyages, rather, in serial vessels) incorporates literally or figuratively most of the cyclical myth's classic features: in its first quadrant, the reputable ancestry, with a particu-lar role for the maternal grandfather and a mother so royal-virginal in this case that she's not even mentioned; the undetailed childhood in "another country" (New Bedford, where Pym is sent to school—by his maternal grandfather); the nocturnal summons to adventure; the sidekicks and helpers, tokens and talismans; in its second quad-rant, the threshold crossings, the initiatory ordeals, disguises, contests, riddles, trips-out-of-time, incremental divestitures and subterranean (or submarine) weekends, all culminating in mysterious, even mysti-cal passage from the Twilight Zone to a *coincidentia oppositorum* at the Axis Mundi: the transcension of categories; the "oxymoronic fusion" of dark illumination, winter and summer, et and cetera. And from there, from the edge of the South Polar Abyss itself (a place as spookily, equivocally white as the icy center of Dante's Inferno leading to the white-rose peak of Paradiso, or the Whiteness of the Whale and for that matter the white white room on the far side of time in Arthur Clarke's *2001*), our hero is cycled *still farther south* into the Quadrants of Return and Death. . . .

To which *I* shall return after nodding Yes to my fellow skipper's large-scale calendrics and making a point about his structural navigation, so to speak. I mean in the former instance that rhythm of equinox and solstice, for example, a common feature of such myths, which my Susan Seckler (among other readers) has already remarked upon. I confess to having done that sort of calendar-diddling myself in more novels than one, even before I understood why. Ditto Poe's scheduling the death of Pym's "first-stage" helper, Augustus, not only on the first day of his eponymous month but at the formal center of the novel: chapter 13 of the 27 narrative divisions, with 13 units before it (the prologue plus 12 chapters) and 13 after (12 chapters plus the epilogue). Indeed, it's very nearly at the center of the center: Augustus dies at 12 noon on Day 9 of the 15 journalized days which comprise that central chapter, adrift in the hulk of the *Grampus*. The *very* center of the center would be Day 8 of the 15 (July 31), and if nothing special is noted in Pym's log of that pivotal day, it's because the desperate survivors are in no position to know at the time what Pym could have calculated in retrospect but didn't, quite, though I daresay his author did: that it will have been on that day that our hero drifted across the equator into the Southern Hemisphere of the novel.

The necessary numbers are all given in chapter 14: The survivors were rescued by the *Jane Guy* on 7 August "off Cape St. Roque" in longitude 31° west: that is to say, comfortably off the nose of Brazil, which extends from Cabo de San Rocas (at latitude 5° south) nearly 200 miles down to Recife (at latitude 8° south), its eastmost tip being at about the 7th parallel. Given the instruments of the time, the schooner's positions are approximate indeed, the longitude more so than the latitude, since sextants back then were more reliable than chronometers. Even so, young Pym reckons after the fact that the *Grampus* must have drifted south "*not less than twenty-five degrees!*" (italics and exclamation mark his; distance 1500 nautical miles; probability nil, since in fact the prevailing ocean currents in those latitudes set inexorably west instead of south, but never mind). Conveniently for us armchair navigators, that drifting began on 14 July: 25 days in all, which comes neatly to 1° (60 nautical miles) per day. That's a 2.5-knot current, almost a Gulf Stream in reverse, and though it does not exist in fact (until you get well *below* the nose of Brazil), we know where it's going. As for where it's coming from, if we dead reckon from a rescue at latitude 7° south and plot backward (which is how both novelists and navigators often do their plotting), we'll find the *Grampus* to have been at latitude 20° north back there on Bastille Day (i.e., just under the Tropic of Cancer) and smack on the equator of the globe smack at the equator of the story. Another symbolic threshold crossed: one with its own initiatory traditions, as sailors and cruise-ship passengers know.

Way to go, Poe. Back to the myth now, and then on with the novel:

The first half of the generic wandering hero's night-sea journey (or whatever) ritually fetches him to the heart of mystery. The second half, as I read it, fetches him from mystery to tragedy and then recycles him. What there is of this latter half-cycle in Poe's novel is in "Pym's" preface and, glancingly, "the editor's" afterword. The wanderer returns "home" from the bright heart of darkness in the netherworld unrecognized or unrecognizable, bringing something precious with him. He manifests himself, routs the usurpers, and delivers his message or whatever, which, being ineffable, must always be more or less garbled in transmission. He reigns peacefully for a time (about eight years, says Lord Raglan in *The Hero*) and then leaves his city to meet his mysterious end. No one knows for sure where his grave is; several cities claim him as theirs; one day he may return.

On the vernal equinox of 1828, when he goes down the hole, Arthur Gordon Pym is still a very young man—nineteen years old—though he seems to have been initiated out of boyishness back there between the Tropic of Cancer and the equator (his senior shipmates Parker and Peters never refer to him as "the kid"). By my calculations, the median age for these things is 33⅓; like his author, Pym's precocious. Eight blank years later he pops up in Richmond, and in the ninth and tenth years he endeavors to truthify his message, which has been cordially usurped and betrayed as fiction by "Mr. Poe"; when he dies in July 1838 immediately after writing his preface, in circumstances even more equivocal than those of his author's death eleven years later, he's still only in his thirtieth year to heaven, a threshold more poetical than mythical. In the epilogue, at second or third hand, his creator disclaims the factuality of the bottom line of his creature's account, and the vertiginous paradox of that passing disclaimer at once betrays and affirms the ontological status of Arthur Gordon Pym and of the narrative: They are factual in the fiction but in fact fictional; what truth is in them is the truth of myth.

Yet despite "*i paralleli*," every professional intuition tells me that Poe's novel is *not* a systematic and pointed reorchestration of the myth of the wandering hero. There are about as many and significant disanalogies as analogies (including the compass directions, which are all wrong), and lots of missing pieces. Some of those are supplied by Pym's sidekicks (it's Dirk Peters who makes the Odysseus-like inland trek at the voyage's end), and several more can be supplied from the author's biography—the late-adolescent setting out for his "true" home, the shrines to his memory in several cities, etc.—but surely that's cheating. More important, the *sense* of the great myth is absent from *The Narrative of Arthur Gordon Pym*, as it is not from the stories of Odysseus, Aeneas, Oedipus, Perseus, Jesus, and even Paul Morel of D. H. Lawrence's *Sons and Lovers*. Poe's novel rides on the myth the way the *Grampus* and then the canoe ride on that current, but it is not a rendition of the myth, nor is it sensibly about the myth. Beyond the metafictive paradoxes of its framing text, which I find to be of real though not unlimited interest, and beyond, in the story proper, the sundry contaminations of reality by irreality (as Borges puts it) and vice versa, I think I don't after all know quite *what* the presenting sense of Poe's novel is: I mean its situational premise, its thematic center, and its moral-dramatical bottom line, apart from its symbolical razzle-dazzle and any encrypted messages about its author. Pym, and therefore his narrative, has no mainspring. As we say in fiction-writing workshops, his story is all "vehicle" and no "ground situation," and therefore his actions (on the several occasions when he *takes* action rather than passively enduring what befalls him) seem to this reader meaningless, dramaturgically speaking, however resonant they may be from our experience of myth and of initiation novels. Moreover, as I have said, after that fine opening of the *Ariel* episode he is scarcely apprehensible as a character. To compare Pym and company with Billy Budd and company or Roderick Random and company or even Odysseus or Sindbad and company is to be reminded how little gift Poe had for the "realistic" aspects of characterization, even as we find them in fantastical mythographers like Dante and Scheherazade. And this de-fect is more conspicuous in a pseudorealistic narrative like *Pym* than in the flat-out gothics of "The Cask of Amontillado" or "The Fall of the House of Usher." Indeed, I think I know Fortunato and Roderick Usher better than I know Dirk Peters and Arthur Gordon Pym. Poe's gifts, like Borges', simply lie elsewhere.

In short, I confess to sharing the reservations of Henry James and Robert Louis Stevenson concerning our subject. The way I would put it is that the young hero of *Pym* is altogether without the moral-dramatic voltage required of protagonists in particular and desirable even in metafiction if it is not to become mere metaphysics. Pym is not a dramatic character but rather the simulacrum of a dramatic character, and Poe's novel ought to be regarded as some sort of simulacrum of a novel: not a counterfeit but an isomorph; not a hoax but a mimicry. *Pym* echoes the *Bildungsroman* and the Ur-Myth and mimes the contours of dramatic action the way a praying mantis mimes a green twig but is not a green twig. I am less than confident that Poe understood the difference (and his own motives) as clearly as the mantis may be said to understand them; novels were truly not his métier. I believe, however, that the reader who approaches *Pym* as if it were a bonafide novel, like the fly who approaches the mantis thinking that *lean* plus *green* plus *stationary* equals *twig,* is in for difficulties—less consequential ones, I trust.

I trust too that the readers gathered here in conference, on the island where Pym's voyage began and on the sesquicentennial of Poe's novel about it, are of all readers the least likely to make so innocent an approach. I have to hope, on the other hand, that in distinguishing the mantis from the twig, they don't mistake it for an eagle or a bird of paradise. Who ever heard one of those cry "*Tekeli-li!* "?

A Bibliographer's View

Tracing Shadows:

Pym Criticism, 1980–1990

David Ketterer

 At this stage, to attempt a complete survey of *Pym* criticism, with its pattern of well-nigh exponential growth, would be both a daunting and a redundant task. In 1978 Shoko Itoh in Japan published "A Bibliographical Survey of the Studies of *The Narrative of Arthur Gordon Pym*."[1] In 1981 Frederick S. Frank's "Polarized Gothic: An Annotated Bibliography of Poe's *Narrative of Arthur Gordon Pym*" appeared; it is a useful listing but for Frank's odd decision to omit parts of books.[2] The following year saw the publication of Douglas Robinson's "Reading Poe's Novel: A Speculative Review of *Pym* Criticism, 1950–1980." Robinson's article is a model of its kind, and, in what follows, I propose simply to bring his review up to date. However, unlike Robinson, I include doctoral dissertations, and overall my summations of the individual critical works are rather more detailed than his. My starting date is 1980 rather than 1981 both because Robinson missed 1980 articles by Frederick S. Frank and Burton R. Pollin while including a 1980 book on Poe which does not treat *Pym*[3] and because one of the things which is unique about the 1980–90 period of *Pym* criticism is the presence of two commentaries which give *Pym* and Poe's work generally more-or-less preeminent status in the canon of American literature. The first of these, that of John T. Irwin in *American Hieroglyphics*, appeared in 1980; the second, that of Douglas Robinson in *American Apocalypses*, in 1985. Not since 1925 and the publication of William Carlos Williams' *In the American Grain* have comparable claims been made for Poe's and *Pym*'s American importance.

There is another aspect of Irwin's book that signals something new for the 1980s in *Pym* criticism. Irwin is the first critic to identify the gigantic, white human figure at the narrative's conclusion as a shadow, specifically Pym's own unrecognized white shadow—a natural optical illusion associated with temperature inversions that Poe would have read about in David Brewster's *Letters on Natural Magic* (1832). Robinson, whose analysis of *Pym* in *American Apocalypses* is very much a response to Irwin's, agrees that the mysterious figure is a paradoxical white shadow but argues much more positively that it is "a god-shadow cast . . . by Christ" (p. 118)[4] or the Blakean perfected body of Pym.

Such is the exemplary excellence of Robinson's "Review of *Pym* Criticism" that, rather than reinvent the wheel, I am forced to adopt its organizational procedures, albeit with some minor amendments. In rough chronological order, Robinson lists "six major foci, six key issues around which commentators have oriented themselves":

1. The text's relation to its author
2. The text's relation to its author's world
3. The symbolic status of the narrative
4. Narrative unity
5. The narrator's relation to the author
6. The meaning of the problematic frame (p. 47)

There should, I think, be two additional foci. The first of these, to be inserted after focus 2 above, "The text's relation to subsequent works by other authors," would allow for influence studies. My second additional focus, "The text's relation to its author's other writings," might be inserted directly after the first. This second addition would allow, for example, for reading *Pym* (pace Richard Wilbur) as an adumbration of *Eureka*, an interpretation that Robinson does not specifically instance in spite of the fact that it arises in a 1973 article by Paul J. Eakin.[5] Parallels with other Poe texts might, of course, produce quite different readings. Since the last three foci involve matters of coherence (unity), credibility (the narrator's relation to Poe), and plausibility (the meaning of the frame), *Pym* criticism has become increasingly concerned with the rhetorical question of "the novel's success as *persuasion*" with the result, noted by Robinson, that "it necessarily begins to point back up to the top of the hierarchy, to questions of self-projection (the author-text relation) and external reference (the text-world relation)." Thus "critics have essentially curved the hierarchy around into a *circle*" (p. 47). It would seem to follow that the period of my review should be characterized by both deconstructive, problematic-frame-inspired approaches and by historical or factual approaches focusing on Poe and his world.

In introducing his 1984 and 1985 reviews of Poe scholarship, Kent Ljungquist does indeed note the increasing conflictual presence of deconstructive and historical approaches. In the 1984 review, speaking of Poe criticism generally rather than *Pym* criticism in particular, Ljungquist writes, "Whether Deconstructionists and Historicists will engage in a pitched battle—the Poe of Francophile theory pitted against the Poe of literary history—remains to be seen."[6] Again, speaking generally in his 1985 review, Ljungquist sees this "radical split between theoretically minded criticism and historically oriented scholarship" continuing, but he also observes that "the best studies covered" show "that historicists and theorists can learn from one another."[7] Certainly Robinson sees the possibility of an emergent "critical consensus on *Pym*" through a reconciliation of deconstructive and historical approaches, although he does not use those terms. He speaks rather of "an attempt to fuse transcendental vision and romantic irony in a far more thoroughgoing fashion than the visionary critics offer" ("Review of *Pym* Criticism," p. 52). But since the visionary critics return to a first-level focus in seeing "*Pym* as the intentioned creation of Poe" and since "deconstruction" is described as "the most influential ironic reading of the novel" (p. 51), it is clear that what Robinson anticipates is some kind of rapprochement between historicism and deconstruction.

In the world of criticism generally, this rapprochement, to some degree, is taking the form of what is often called the "new historicism," basically the historical approach (often Marxist in tendency) of those who have absorbed the lessons of structuralism and poststructuralism. With the realization that "facts" are "always already" interpreted, gone is the old opposition between solid facts and shadowy fancies. The shadowy status of so-called facts, their inevitable ideological and epistemic coloration, now figures in the writings of the new historicists. I would project that in the area of *Pym* criticism, it is a reconciliation of deconstruction and the new historicist approaches that is most likely to be productive. But, contrary to rumor, traditional scholarship is not dead, and it too may be expected to prosper.

However, like present readings, all future readings of *Pym* will adopt one or more of Robinson's six or my eight foci. Since Robinson was writing at a time when the circle of possible foci had been completed, he suggests that *Pym* criticism inevitably "will continue to travel" that circle ("Review of *Pym* Criticism," p. 52). During the period 1950–80, these foci generated "over ninety studies" (Robinson actually lists ninety-three) and "ten radically distinct readings" of *Pym*, plus what Robinson describes misleadingly as "three non-interpretive approaches" (p. 47). The first "non-interpretative approach," contemporary reviews (which I have termed *reception studies*), appeared, of course, way before Robinson's 1950–80 period, and two studies of the novel's reception were published in the 1980–90 period. In fact, the three approaches (the other two being *source studies* and *influence studies*) and ten distinct ways of interpreting *Pym* are all represented in the one hundred eighteen studies that have appeared between 1980 and 1990 (including eight dissertations—out of twenty-three—that over-lap with published versions of, or extracts from, the dissertations, and three 1980 items that overlap with Robinson's checklist). The interpre-tations implicit or explicit in Robinson's "non-interpretive approaches" can be assigned to one or more of the distinct readings. There is no rea-son why the eight foci (let's agree on that number) should not spawn additional distinct readings, and one such, as I shall indicate, may be in the process of emerging. The only extant reading that I would wish to specify as an addition to Robinson's ten is that of viewing *Pym* as an ad-umbration of *Eureka*, a consequence of the focus that Robinson neglects to specify, "The text's relation to its author's other writings." Since this focus has generated one dissertation, one article, and various aside arguments during the 1980–90 period, in the survey below of eleven distinct readings—which follows a survey of the three approaches and which retraces Robinson's readings in the roughly chronological order that he adopts—I have inserted the *Eureka* reading of *Pym* in its ap-proximate chronological place. To the objection that the *Eureka Pym* is generally a variant of the visionary reading, I would argue that while the visionary reading can be generated by one or more of Robinson's six foci, the *Eureka* reading deserves to be distinguished since it depends solely on the author's-other-writings focus. Of course, if *Eureka* is read ironically or deconstructed, then *Eureka*-inspired readings of *Pym* do not belong in the visionary category at all.

There is one further distinct reading of *Pym* (making for a total of twelve) that Robinson fails to mention—the literal one (*Pym* as a strange adventure story in the imaginary voyage tradition)—in spite of the *Pym* chapter in William C. Spengemann's *The Adventurous Muse: The Poetics of American Fiction, 1789–1900* (a 1977 work listed in Robin-son's checklist and somewhat oddly instanced in his text as an example of deconstruction). The majority of *Pym*'s readers (those people who do not write scholarly articles) would surely interpret the novel in this manner. Thus J. R. Hammond notes in passing in his *Edgar Allan Poe Companion* (1981) that *Pym* is "an exciting tale of adventure in the vein of Marryat or Fenimore Cooper" (p. 125). But since the literal reading is not generally the stuff of criticism and since in the 1980–90 period no study of *Pym* has treated its literal level at any length, I have not included this distinct reading in my survey.

Approaches

(1) *Reception studies.* Burton R. Pollin's "Poe 'Viewed and *Reviewed*': An Annotated Checklist of Contemporaneous Notices" (1980) includes thirty-eight reviews and notices for *Pym* (and cites three earlier such *Pym* studies). I. M. Walker's introduction to his edition of *Edgar Allan Poe: The Critical Heritage* (1986) includes a short section on the nature of the reviews that *Pym* received. Of these reviews, Walker reprints edited versions of six from American publications and five from British publications.

(2) *Source studies.* The earliest source study of *Pym* appeared in 1895.[8] For the period under review, Burton R. Pollin's 1981 magisterial edition of *The Imaginary Voyages* (volume 1 of *Collected Writings of Edgar Allan Poe*) must be considered the prime exhibit. Pollin's authoritative text of *Pym* is buttressed by 149 pages of "Notes and Comments." From these notes and Pollin's introductory essay on sources, a clear sense emerges of the extent to which *Pym* is a virtual pastiche of sources, albeit sources most of which had been identified in the early days of Poe scholarship. Source studies depend upon foci 1 and 2, the text's relation to its author and its author's world, and constitute a species of historical criticism, generally speaking the old historicism rather than the new. But Pollin's edition does illustrate the extent to which source studies are inevitably interpretive and, however unintentionally, does support a new historical awareness of the absence of innocent facts. In his search for *the* truth, Pollin, no less than Pym, is ultimately pursuing a chimera, a shadow. In his review of Pollin's edition, Patrick F. Quinn notes that Pollin's glosses stress the narrative's numerous flaws. By Quinn's count, Pollin points to at least two hundred errors of fact in *Pym*. Pollin interprets many of these "errors" as "planned absurdity" or "whimsical" method on Poe's part. But how are these to be distinguished from simple errors? When is an error not an error? When is a fact not a fact? Pollin apparently believes that Poe wrote *Pym* with two audiences in mind, but, as Quinn observes, Pollin himself would seem to be the only example of the truly "informed" second audience.[9] And what are we to make of Pollin's own "errors"?

Is it possible that Pollin's reference to Augustus' "death on July 31" (*P* 1:282) on a page immediately preceding a reference to the correct date, "August 1" (*P* 1:283) is just a simple mistake? Finally, of course, Pollin's interpretation of *Pym* is a variant of the hoax reading, a reading more often arrived at via a focus on the problematic frame.

On five occasions, Pollin notes details in *Pym* that suggest that Coleridge's "Rime of the Ancient Mariner" was an important source (*P* 1:268, 270, 271, 283, 284). In a 1985 article, Shoko Itoh traces Poe's development, in three poems ("Al Aaraaf," "Fairyland," and "The Raven") and in *Pym*, of Coleridge's albatross image.

Pollin makes two references (*P* 1:334, 357) to a new source, J. N. Reynolds' "Leaves from an Unpublished Journal," that Richard Kopley argues for in "The Secret of *Arthur Gordon Pym*" (1980), an article derived from his 1982 dissertation then in progress. The third chapter of this dissertation makes a renewed case for *Robinson Crusoe* as providing the blueprint for *Pym* in terms of plot, themes (particularly the references to the Providential tradition), language, and structure. In the last of Kopley's escalating trilogy of *Pym* articles, "The '*Very* Profound Under-current' of *Arthur Gordon Pym*," an article that goes beyond the dissertation, Kopley proposes a new source for the *Ariel* episode, a mid-February 1836 account in the *Norfolk American Beacon* and the *Norfolk and Portsmouth Herald*, by seamen William Wiseman and J. Mann, of the loss of a vessel named the *Ariel*.

Four other dissertations should be noted here. In "The Lockean Tradition in the Gothic Fiction of Brown, Poe, and Melville" (1979), Beverly Rose Voloshin, anticipating somewhat Joan Dayan's *Fables of Mind* (1987),[10] considers the relation of the isolated mind to the order of nature. Particular attention is given to *Pym*, "Poe's most extreme Gothic fiction in the Lockean mode" (*DAI*). The first part of Joan Tyler Mead's 1982 dissertation on *Pym* discusses the novel's complex interweaving of borrowed materials. The final three of the eight chapters of James Louis Berta's dissertation, "Poe and the West" (1986), offer explications of *Pym* and "The Journal of Julius Rodman" as works whose "thematic resources" "emerged from Poe's reading in western literature" (*DAI*). In her 1986 dissertation, "Edgar Allan Poe and the Rhetoric of Science," Susan Welsh shows how scientific rhetoric influenced Poe's narrative practice in *Pym*, the Dupin tales, and *Eureka*. Her second chapter discusses the ways in which *Pym* experiments with the context of exploration narratives as affected by Alexander von Humboldt's *Per-*

sonal Narrative of Travels to the Equinoctial Regions of America during the Years 1799–1804.

The *Pym* source speculation in Kent Ljungquist's *The Grand and the Fair* (1984) recycles his 1978 article, which draws on the work of Susan and Stuart Levine.[11] Ljungquist believes that Jacob Bryant's *A New System; or, An Analysis of Antient Mythology* and Charles Anthon's revision of Lemprière's *A Classical Dictionary* provided Poe with information about a mythic race of Titans that Poe hints at toward the conclusion of *Pym.* Since these Titans descended into degenerate blacks, "Pym's sublime vision thus penetrates the mists of time in his ability to see, in one appalling image, the sway of history from man's origins in harmony to his degeneration into savagery" (*The Grand and the Fair*, p. 67). The narrative amounts to an "allegory of white ancients dispersing into shady remnants" (*The Grand and the Fair*, p. 71). Ljungquist's interpretation of what he believes to be the crucial sources for the conclusion of *Pym* leads him to a variant of the visionary reading. In a later article, " 'Speculative Mythology' and the Titan Myth in Poe's *Pym* and Melville's *Pierre*" (1985), Ljungquist adds to Bryant and Anthon Francis Wilford's "Essays on the Sacred Isles of the West" (1809), which includes a description of the White Island. Ljungquist concludes that "almost all elements of *Pym*'s fantastic conclusion are contained in the works of the 'speculative' mythologists" (p. 252) and that these elements enhance the seriousness and elevate the status of *Pym*'s quest. Incidentally, Ljungquist does not take account of Ana Hernández del Castillo's 1981 argument that, while Poe became acquainted with the theories of the syncretists largely through Anthon, "a number of symbolic allusions and names of deities in the last section of *Pym*" (*Cortázar's Mythopoesis*, p. 59) may derive from a source for Anthon's *Dictionary*, George Stanley Faber's *On the Origins of Pagan Idolatry.*

In *Beneath the American Renaissance* (1988), David Reynolds argues for sources in popular culture for various aspects of *Pym*, including the cannibalism episode. He writes, "The novel as a whole can be seen as an attempted fusion of two modes—Dark Adventure [and Subversive] fiction, featuring savagery and nightmare imagery, and the scientific social text, featuring mimetic reportage of intriguing facts." Hence the novel's "weirdly bifurcated [ultrairrational and ultrarational] conclusion" (p. 242).

In a 1989 article, Selma B. Brody treats the influence of Sir David Brewster's *Letters on Natural Magic* (1831) on a number of Poe's works including *Pym*. There are possible sources in *Natural Magic* for *Pym*'s white slip of paper that is best seen "by surveying it slightly askance" (*P* 1:78) and the word-shaped ravines. In addition, Brody supports Irwin's contention that the white figure may be indebted to Brewster's lengthy discussion of the Spectre of the Brocken phenomenon, a diffraction image (*not* a genuine shadow) which moves when the person who is the source of the image moves. Brewster tells an anecdote of a *third* gigantic figure witnessed by *two* alarmed men and provides an illustrative sketch of two men and three images. Roberta Sharp provides a complementary account of *Natural Magic* and *Pym* (and other Poe works) in her 1990 article; she credits Brewster for Too-wit's terror at his reflection in two mirrors, Pym's askance survey of the piece of paper, the spectral white figure and other spectral phenomena, Peters' ventriloquism while Pym masquerades as a corpse, and the veined water of Tsalal.

In an aside in *Sexual Personae* (1990), Camille Paglia relates the ashy white powder at the end of *Pym* to the flakes of fire that Dante compares to Alpine snow (*Inferno*, 24.28–30). And in a 1990 note, Charles Swann relates the last line of *Pym*—"'I have graven it within the hills . . .'" (*P* 1:208)—to "written mountains" (quoted p. 425) in Maturin's *Melmoth the Wanderer* (1820).

(3) *Influence studies.* No more interpretively innocent than source studies, influence studies involve an interpretation of both the influencing work and the work influenced. First to be observed were the influences of *Pym* on the work of Jules Verne and H. P. Lovecraft, and on Melville's *Moby-Dick*.[12] And, in fact, these relations have all recently been further explored. The *Pym*/Verne connection has recently been reexamined in articles by Di Maio (1982), Gouaux (1988), and Picot (1988), while in a 1986 article Jules Zanger discusses Verne's and Lovecraft's *Pym*-inspired works along with the lesser known sequel by Charles Romyn Dake: *A Strange Discovery* (1899).

In a 1989 article, "Melville's Gam with Poe in *Moby-Dick*," Michael Hollister speculates that, through *Moby-Dick*'s Bulkington, a Virginian member of the *Pequod*'s crew late of *Pym*'s *Grampus*, Melville acknowledges his debt to Poe's *Narrative*. Interpreting Bulkington as an allegorical exemplar, a seeker after Truth, Hollister argues that, because "Bulkington prevails over Ahab" (p. 283) in his soul, Ishmael, unlike Pym, attains a yin/yang unity. Because Pym is just as polarized and narcissistic as Ahab, "His development is arrested at a Gothic pole, without the transcendence Ishmael attains through Queequeg, Bulkington, and Pip" (p. 285). Hollister concludes that "Poe is a proto-Postmodernist in *Pym*, a predecessor of Thomas Pynchon deconstructing his narrative . . . and imbuing it all with a spirit of hoax" (p. 288), while Modernist Melville rejects Poe's vision. Just as speculatively, perhaps, I suggest, in the context of a 1988 article dealing with *Moby-Dick*, that its enveloping structure parallels the enveloping structure of *Pym*.[13]

During the 1980–90 period, the names H. G. Wells, Julio Cortázar, and Carlos Fuentes are prominent among those added to a rapidly growing list of writers influenced by *Pym* and Poe's work generally.[14] *Pym* looms large in Catherine Rainwater's 1983 discussion of Poe's influence on Wells, "Encounters with the 'White Sphinx.'" The "white god" of *Pym* suggests the "white sphinx" of *The Time Machine* (p. 35). "Like the 'editors' of *Pym*," the narrator of *The Time Machine* "argues for the 'veracity' of a report designed specifically to challenge all traditional notions of narrative veracity" (p. 40). Much the same situation applies in *The Island of Doctor Moreau* where Prendick's disorienting experiences are like Pym's, Moreau's island is like Tsalal, and the death boat is like the death ship in *Pym*. Wells' *The First Men in the Moon* features an underground world comparable to the chasms of Tsalal and a message from Cavor in blood that is only partially intelligible, like Augustus' message to Pym. Rainwater concludes that for both writers language cannot communicate the mystery at the heart of life. *Pym* also figures significantly in the part of Rainwater's 1987 article dealing with Wells' re-visioning of Poe in *Mr. Blettsworthy on Rampole Island* (1928). Contrasting Poe's concern with transcendence and Wells' with transformation leading to an ideal *earthly* realm, Rainwater elucidates a number of parallel concerns in *Pym* and *Blettsworthy* (mutiny at sea, Tsalal/Rampole Island, and language) and argues that in *Blettsworthy* Wells reconciles his concern with rationality with a Poean nonrationality. She was apparently unaware, however, that J. R. Hammond had earlier (1981) noted startling similarities between the title pages of, and several incidents in, *Pym* and *Blettsworthy*.

Connections between Poe and the magic realists of South America seem to be a topic of growing interest. We presently await John Irwin's *The Mystery to a Solution: Poe, Borges, and the Analytic Detective Story*, scheduled for publication in Fall 1993.[15] In the meantime, we have *Keats, Poe, and the Shaping of Cortázar's Mythopoesis* (1981) by Hernández del Castillo, and Susan and Stuart Levine's article on "Poe and

Fuentes" (1984). Hernández del Castillo demonstrates, largely via a Jungian comparison, the extent to which Cortázar's first two novels— the unpublished "El examen" (written 1948–50) and the published *Los premios* (1960)—are indebted to *Pym*, read as a negative quest that ends in madness. She also notes comparable mythic structures in *Pym* and Cortázar's novel *Rayuela* (1963) and concludes that Poe's influence on Cortázar surpasses, by far, that of Keats. As for Poe and Fuentes, the Levines write: "Fuentes is trying to subvert the certainty of what he feels is an unacceptable reality; he explores the other possibilities, as he feels Poe had done" (p. 40). In Fuentes' *Terra Nostra* (1975), which is about Spanish history and the colonization of the New World, there are extended allusions to Poe's sea narratives. The specific *Pym* parallels include the blend of metafiction and marvelous adventures, a discussion of the interrelationship of black and white, and the passage from a region of blackness to whiteness when the protagonist descends into a volcano. And, of course, to view *Pym* through the lens of Fuentes has interpretive consequences: "Seeing him [Poe] as a modern writer of metafiction means seeing him as ironic transcendentalist, skeptical of himself and of his transcendent vision" (p. 52).

In a note (1987) heralding a full-length study of *Pym*'s influence on Italian literature, Roberto Cagliero instances works by Ugo Iginio Tarchetti (1839–69), Emilio Salgari (1863–1911), Enrico Novelli (1876–1945), and Luigi Motta (1881–1955). In a 1987–88 article, Lynette C. Black adduces parallels between the opening and closing chapters of *Pym* and Baudelaire's poem "Le Bateau Ivre." Written when Baudelaire was sixteen, the poem describes his visionary awakening in the metaphoric terms of being drunk with wine or poetry on an ocean-voyaging small boat. Thomas S. Hanson in a 1988 article documents the indebtedness of Arno Schmidt's novel *Zettels Traum* (1970) to Poe's work generally and to *Pym* in particular, while Thomas Immelmann (1987) notes parallels between a passage in Schmidt's "Kaff auch Mare Crisium" and Pym's fall from a precipice into Dirk Peters' arms.

Back in the United States, in chapter 3 of his dissertation "The Paradoxical Structure of the Sea Quest in Dana, Poe, Cooper, Melville, London, and Hemingway" (1979), James Ronald Black identifies a tradition and at least implies that *Pym* may have influenced Cooper's *The Sea Lions* (1849) to the extent that both works stress man's metaphysical relation to the universe. And Hanjo Berressem, in his 1982 article "Godolphin . . . ," argues convincingly for *Pym* (and Captain Symmes' "holes at the Poles" theory) as the source of the underground realm of Vheissu in Thomas Pynchon's *V.* (1964). Pynchon's appropriation, it is claimed, "stresses the fictitiousness of [*Pym*]" (p. 15).

And what of the influence of *Pym* on the work's illustrators and vice versa? Richard Kopley's 1985 article pioneers this topic; Burton R. Pollin's rich bibliography, *Images of Poe's Works* (1989), provides chapter and verse.[16]

Distinct Readings

(1) *Psychoanalytical readings*. Here the goal is to understand the conscious or unconscious motivations of Poe himself. Marie Bonaparte's detailed reading of *Pym* in her 1933 study translated into English as *The Life and Works of Edgar Allan Poe: A Psycho-Analytic Interpretation* (1949) remains the model. Robinson observes, "It would hardly be unfair to say that whatever was said about *Pym* before 1950 was said by Marie Bonaparte; and her contribution to later criticism is central, as virtually the entire first decade of serious *Pym* criticism was conceived as various forms of reaction to or expansion of her reading" ("Review of *Pym* Criticism," p. 48). Paul Rosenzweig's discussion of jawlike images in *Pym* (enclosures threatened by penetrating sharp instruments, enclosures with teeth) in a 1980 article obviously owes something to Bonaparte's identification of the *vagina dentata* theme in Poe's work, but since Rosenzweig seems more concerned with Pym's psyche than Poe's, this article more properly belongs in the category of *psychological* studies.

Richard Kopley's exciting work on *Pym*—certainly one of the more important contributions made in the 1980s—must ultimately be placed in the *visionary* camp, but Bonaparte's identification of Augustus with Poe's brother Henry and the return to the mother quest in *Pym* (itself a visionary motivation) clearly provided the inspiration for Kopley's second *Pym* article, "The Hidden Journey of *Arthur Gordon Pym*" (1982). Kopley's essentially New Critical textual focus (Robinson's foci 3 and 4) corroborates Bonaparte's psychoanalytical findings. For Kopley, the "spirit of reflection" in *Pym* (P1:153) refers particularly to the way in which the penguin figurehead in the first and last chapters of *Pym* (Kopley ingeniously argues in his previous article [1980] that the mysterious white figure is the figurehead of the ship the *Penguin*) constitutes a set of double mirrors infinitely reflecting the death of Augustus who, like Poe's brother Henry, died on 1 August. Finally the *Penguin* figurehead reflects Poe's desire to be reunited with both his brother and his mother, his mother being suggested by the cry of the white birds, "*Tekili-li*" (P 1:190, 191, 203, 204, 206, 208), since she played the role of a young bride in the play *Tekili* (1806, 1809) by Theodore Edward Hook.

Sybil Wuletich-Brinberg's unconvincing Freudian approach in *Poe: The Rationale of the Uncanny* (1988) elaborates a struggle for integration between Poe's knowledge-hungry affirming self and his fearful negating self, and considers this struggle's relationship to Poe's characters. Wuletich-Brinberg maintains that *Pym* is an unsuccessful work because Pym himself is too shallow a character to be aware of such a struggle. Consequently, he fails "to accept diversity and contradiction as the essence of the universe" (p. 195). The concluding images of whiteness and the white figure (Pym's double), then, signify "abstraction, repression, mental blindness and thus a repudiation of evil and pain" (p. 196).

(2) *Mythic readings.* Robinson notes that the mythic readings of *Pym* offered by Gaston Bachelard (1944) and Leslie Feidler (1960) developed directly from Marie Bonaparte's work.[17] This brand of *Pym* criticism might seem to have exhausted itself, but there are five recent examples. Hernández del Castillo's Jungian archetypal approach to both *Pym* and Cortázar's works leads to her discussion of initiation into manhood structures and her identification of the white figure in *Pym* as the Magna Mater. Uusur Al-Madani argues in his 1982 dissertation that the pilgrimage to the center in the work of Thoreau, Poe, and Melville "constitutes a quest for spiritual rejuvenation and initiation into the mysteries of the world," whether the journey is outward to a paradisal center situated in the American West or inward and downward to the abyss (*DAI*). The initiation theme also figures in a 1983 French article by André Poncet. Laura Ann Hoelscher also takes a Jungian approach in her dissertation "Incommensurate Models: Poe's Fiction and the Inevitability of the Unconscious" (1984). In Poe's sea tales, where the ocean represents the unconscious, and elsewhere, Poe's "models" are "incommensurate" (see the epigraph to "A Descent into the Maelström," M 2:577) "in that none of them depict a successful interrelationship between individual consciousness and the unconscious" (*DAI*).

Strangely, Bettina L. Knapp does not treat *Pym* in her volume *Edgar Allan Poe* (1984), but in her account of the other two sea tales she claims that all the sea tales involve a plunge into Jung's collective and personal unconscious.[18]

Camille Paglia in *Sexual Personae* (1990) treats *Pym* as "an archetypal journey to the heart of creation" or "the womb of matter" and notes that "the mother banished from Protestantism makes her American debut at the climax of . . . *Pym*" (p. 579).

In her dissertation, "America's Gothic Landscape" (1979), Amy Tucker includes an analysis of the topographical imagery in *Pym* as an inward exploration of the dark regions of the American psyche. For Elizabeth Jane Wall Hinds, in her 1989 dissertation "The Hero in Time: The American Gothic Fiction of Charles Brockden Brown, Edgar Allan Poe, and Herman Melville," what distinguishes the American gothic is a refusal of spatialized containment. Combining Gérard Genette's structural categories with Wolfgang Iser's phenomenological procedures, she focuses on *Pym*, along with Poe's short stories and *Eureka,* in her fifth chapter.

(3) *Psychological readings.* With the shift from the text as a reflection of the author's mind to an exclusive New Critical emphasis on the text itself, Bonaparte's psychoanalysis of Poe becomes transformed into a "psychological" interpretation of Pym. Beginning perhaps with Edward H. Davidson's treatment in *Poe: A Critical Study* (1957), *Pym's* inward journey is viewed, according to Robinson, as " 'oneiric,' 'hypnogogic,' a dream-allegory in which all external events are metaphors for internal growth or dissolution" ("Review of *Pym* Criticism," p. 49). The earlier of the two examples relevant to my survey is Paul Rosenzweig's "The Search for Identity: The Enclosure Motif in *The Narrative of Arthur Gordon Pym*" (1980). Building on articles by Robert L. Carringer and Leonard W. Engel,[19] Rosenzweig argues that the womblike enclosures in *Pym* are depicted both positively (in terms of security, connected often with food and drink) and negatively (in images of threatening entombment, phallic penetration, or consumption by the *vagina dentata*). According to Rosenzweig's provocative argument, there is no real growth in the novel because Pym has not resolved the primal birth trauma; he cannot deal with the division between self and other. Pym's fragmentary and inchoate ego, reflected in his doubles (all the other characters in the novel), fails to establish any enduring identity, fails to incorporate the other within himself. Pym merges atavistically into Poe and into the final editor, the editor's "anonymity a fitting comment on the indefinite identity of all earlier personalities" (p. 125).

The first word of Ted Billy's title "Providence and Chaos in *The Narrative of Arthur* 'Goddin' *Pym*" (1989) suggests a link with *visionary readings* of the novel (especially the reading, acknowledged by Billy, of Curtis Fukuchi); the third, "Chaos," suggests *existential readings*. But Billy's main focus is on Pym's psychology, and he relates his article particularly to Rosenzweig's above. Placing what can be seen "as a symbolic religious quest . . . in the context of the patterns of providence and chaos pervading the narrative," Billy argues interestingly that "Poe's references to divine intervention crystallize into an ironic commentary on a narcissistic protagonist who only acknowledges God's omnipotence whenever his foolhardy contact [conduct?] brings him to the end of his tether" (p. 126). At one point pronouncing "Gordon" in dialect as "Goddin" (*P* 1:67), Pym consistently acts "like a God unto himself" (p. 127). "Unworthy of transcendental insight," the white phantom he finally confronts is "his own gargantuan ego" (pp. 131, 132).

(4) *Existential readings.* Regarding the modification of Bonaparte's psychoanalytical study by *existential readings,* Robinson observes that Pym as intellect rather than psyche is "seeking to impose artificial order on existential chaos. The novel's apparent inconclusiveness or incompletion is taken . . . as internal evidence of Poe's absurd world-view; there is no meaning outside the fraudulent order of human creation" ("Review of *Pym* Criticism," p. 49). The existential reading may coexist with the psychological one, and, indeed, Edward H. Davidson pioneers both in *Poe: A Critical Study.* Thus, too, Paul Rosenzweig follows his own psychological reading with an existential analysis, " 'Dust Within the Rock': The Phantasm of Meaning in *The Narrative of Arthur Gordon Pym*" (1982). *Pym* is about "man's frustration with the failure of meaning to emerge" (p. 140); it displays a "pattern of expectation continually frustrated" (p. 142); "nothing can be decided—not even the fact that nothing can be decided" (p. 146). The final italicized warning, quoted in Rosenzweig's title, is "a parody of the Bible" (p. 149).

Half of Judith L. Sutherland's reading in *Problematic Fictions* (1984), a revision of her 1977 University of Iowa dissertation, supports Rosenzweig's view by way of her focus on the reader's relationship to the text. The key to understanding *Pym* is that there is no such key. The text "undermines the structuring activity that it has invited" (p. 14), its language creates "a hermeneutical nightmare" (pp. 16, 36), and its horror partly "derives from the rhythmical construction and collapse of our mental structures" (p. 17). *Pym* presents an absurd world.

Eiichi Fujita treats *Pym* and three other classic American novels in *America Dentoshosetsu to Sogai* [Alienation in the traditional American novel] (1989). Keiko Beppu claims that this "well-prepared reader for college students" presents the "thesis that the pursuit of the modern self to its extremes leads to various forms of alienation in American society." [20] This is a reading that apparently moves from the existential into the next category.

(5) *Social commentary readings.* Dissatisfaction with existential vagueness led to the search in *Pym* for something real, for commentary on society. The social commentary reading of *Pym* began not with Leslie Fiedler (who combines the social with the mythic in *Love and Death in the American Novel*) and Sidney Kaplan's introduction to *Pym* in 1960, as Robinson erroneously states ("Review of *Pym* Criticism," p. 49), but with Harry Levin's *The Power of Blackness* (which combines the existential and the social) in 1958. According to that work, those elements that encourage the reader to interpret Pym's voyage south as a voyage into the southern United States and the black Tsalalians as American slaves are coalesced into a racist Poe's warning of slave insurrection and social disorder. [21] J. R. Hammond (1981) suggests that the Tsalalians should be identified with the mob against which the antidemocratic Poe frequently railed.

Of all the *Pym* criticism covered in this survey, Donald Pease's account in *Visionary Compacts* (1987) is the trickiest to locate in terms of the categories that I am using. I place it here largely because of the book's new historical orientation, signaled by Pease's subtitle, *American Renaissance Writings in Cultural Context*, but the work in fact overlaps with *psychological* cum *psychoanalytical readings* (especially Wuletich-Brinberg's), *existential readings* (Pym's existential absurdity is critiqued), and the literal *strange adventure readings* that I have excluded. It does not, however, overlap with *visionary readings* except to the extent that Pease attacks the deconstructionist view of Poe. The problem is compounded by the fact that I find Pease's interpretation as unconvincing as it is original. For Pease, *Pym* is about "a perverse will for continued adventure" (p. 171), a perversity, analogous to the call for revolution, decried by Poe (who mourned a lost aristocratic connection) as a threat to cultural memory. The final disappearance of the mistakenly self-reliant Pym (who becomes a ghost like that of Rogers which he impersonated) is cautionary. Unlike the hero of the usual adventure story pattern, Pym does not return home to reflect on his experiences. Thus his adventures are "sheer discontinuities unsalvage-able by any reflective consciousness" (p. 195), and the white figure is "unreflective human existence itself"—"the final revenge of the spirit of the past the 'new' world has erased from its memory" (p. 202).

The only other reading hinting at social commentary to appear during the period presently under review occurs in James Louis Berta's dissertation, "Poe and the West" (1987). Berta explores an area of *Pym* previously mapped in Fiedler's *Love and Death in the American Novel* and Edwin Fussell's *Frontier: American Literature and the American West* (1965).

In terms of the chronology that I am following of a reading's first appearance, the visionary reading should figure here as number 6 just before the *Eureka*-inspired reading, but, like Robinson, and for one of the same reasons, reasons that I shall get to, I reserve my treatment of the visionary reading for the end of this survey.

(7) Eureka-*inspired readings.* The *psychoanalytical, psychological, existential,* and *social commentary readings* have in common a refusal to accept at face value those elements in *Pym* that suggest a vision-ary metaphysics. Mythic studies, of course, may or may not be com-fortable with the truly transcendent. In fact, I regard *Eureka*-inspired readings as distinct variants of both mythic and visionary readings. Correspondingly, hoaxical, satiric, ironic, and deconstructive *Eureka*-inspired readings should be distinguished from the noncosmological categories of hoaxical, satiric and ironic, and deconstructive readings. Charles O'Donnell's "From Earth to Ether: Poe's Flight into Space" (1962) might be viewed as the first fully articulated exposition of the *Eureka*-inspired reading, but all such readings derive from Richard Wilbur's notion, first expressed in 1959, that much of Poe's creative work should be interpreted in the light of *Eureka*.[22]

John Limon's "How to Place Poe's *Arthur Gordon Pym* in Science-Dominated Intellectual History and How to Extract It Again" (1983)— derived from his 1981 dissertation and now revised as *The Place of Fic-tion in the Time of Science* (1990)—offers a somewhat impressionistic " 'Eurekan' reading of *Pym*" (p. 36), *Eureka* being "the first intellectual-historical criticism of . . . Poe's greatest work" (p. 33). Since Poe's intellectual context is most apparent in *Eureka*, Limon uses "*Eureka* to describe the ambiguous place of *Pym* in the history of ideas" (p. 36). That context is *Naturphilosophie*, with its belief that all nature is "the fragmentation of a universal man" (p. 34). The universal fluctuation in *Eureka* from spirit to matter and back is reflected in *Pym* in the movement from the *Ariel* (spirit) to the *Grampus* (animal) to the *Jane Guy* (human) to the unnamed canoe. Limon even relates Augustus' statement aboard the *Ariel*, "nothing is the—matter—going home—d-d-don't you see?" (*P* 1:59) and Too-wit's later corresponding line, "*Mattee non we pa pa si*" (*P* 1:180; supposedly, "It matters not when we see our papa"), to the question of matter and nothingness in *Eureka*—an equation that allows for parallels with the concept of entropy in Pynchon's *V.*. Limon's treatment of *V.* and *Pym* in his 1990 book (pp. 169–71, 177–79) should be related to that in Berressem's 1982 article. The polarities whereby Pym approaches the Absolute are all "sub-expressions of the basic antithesis of multiplicity and unity that is overcome in *Eureka*" ("How to Place Poe's *Arthur Gordon Pym*," p. 39). Limon's interpretation of the color symbolism in *Pym* apparently corresponds with O'Donnell's: whiteness represents unity, while the blacks stand for extreme rationality and temporal consciousness. But Limon makes his own contribution with his suggestion that the remnant of the *Jane Guy*—"thirty-two [white] persons in all . . . armed to the teeth" (*P* 1:180)—be related to the teeth in Poe's "Berenice" and the destruction of "individual *identities*" (*The Place of Fiction*, p. 116). Thus, more or less, *Pym* is "an allegory of idealist science" (p. 112).

In *Through the Custom House* (1982), John Carlos Rowe connects *Pym* with *Eureka* in the following terms: "Straining against ordinary temporality and its materiality, poetic writing imitates the cosmic dialectic of 'Attraction and Repulsion,' the consolidation and dispersion which together define the 'throb of the Heart Divine'" (p. 97). Judith Sutherland in *Problematic Fictions* (1984) speaks of a "cosmic aesthetic" (p. 24) in *Pym* whereby the fluctuation between vision and failure of vision, expansion and contraction, corresponds to the perverse principle governing the cosmology of *Eureka*. Thus *Pym* consists of a "long series of collapses and recoveries" and illustrates "the process of creation and destruction" (pp. 25, 26).

O'Donnell's argument that the second half of *Pym* folds back over the first implies that structurally *Pym* reproduces *Eureka*'s universal cycle of irradiation and collapse. Within the context of the view that all of Poe's work should be interpreted in terms of *Eureka*, it may not then be surprising that this doubling pattern can be found in some of Poe's other work, notably the mirror structure of "The Assignation"[23] and the creative/resolvent logic of the Dupin tales. It might then follow, whether explicitly stated or not, that relationships between *Pym* and any other of Poe's tales or poems are ultimately grounded in the common fidelity of such writings to the structure and theme of *Eureka*.

The case for structural symmetry in *Pym*, first explored by O'Donnell and subsequently reinforced by the present writer in *The Rationale of Deception in Poe* (1979),[24] has been further buttressed by Richard Kopley in both "The Secret of *Arthur Gordon Pym*" and "The Hidden Journey of *Arthur Gordon Pym*," and, most recently, in "Poe's *Pym*-esque 'A Tale of the Ragged Mountains'" (1990). In the last article, Kopley demonstrates that *Pym* and "A Tale of the Ragged Mountains" resemble one another in theme and form. Thematically, both works express Poe's desire for reunion with his dead brother and mother (see *psychoanalytical readings* above). In the case of the short story (1844), Kopley presents evidence (albeit somewhat tenuous) that Augustus Bedloe corresponds to Henry Poe, Oldeb to the brothers' mother, and Templeton to Edgar Allan Poe. In terms of form, both works "are symmetrically organized around a richly meaningful midpoint" (pp. 169–70). To Kopley's previous evidence that, like the canoe in *Pym*, that narrative is "modelled with the bow and stern alike" (P 1:200), he adds a list of words and phrases in the first half of *Pym* that are repeated in reverse order in the second half. Similarly, "A Tale of the Ragged Mountains" divides into two halves of seventeen paragraphs each, halves that also contain verbal mirrorings. Finally, Kopley suggests that both works belong in the Providence Tradition and that the symbolic midpoint of "A Tale of the Ragged Mountains," indicative of resurrection, is a particular reflection of that tradition. Works in the Providence Tradition, it seems, are often characterized by symmetrical structural patterning that frames a symbolic midpoint.

Kent Ljungquist in *The Grand and the Fair* suggests that "Mellonta Tauta" (1849), which partly overlaps with *Eureka*, is "a comic version of *Pym*" (p. 80), and he draws dubious parallels between the two works. Following J. O. Bailey, Ljungquist also sees a relationship between *Pym* and the poem "Dream-Land" with its references to "Titan woods" (pp. 59–60; see *influence studies* above).[25]

(8) *Formal and compositional studies.* What unites what might be considered two distinct "readings" is the concern with *Pym*'s narrative coherence or incoherence. Formal studies result from a total overlap with Robinson's fourth focus, "narrative unity." The early thematic and structural readings of *Pym*, such as Patrick F. Quinn's "Poe's Imaginary

Voyage" (1952), silently assumed the work's narrative unity, but beginning in 1966, with J. V. Ridgely and Iola S. Haverstick's pioneering historical study of the stages in the composition of *Pym*, such readings often amounted to conscious arguments for the importance of discontinuities in *Pym* or for its overall disunity and incoherence.[26] Alongside such attacks, however, an increasing number of defenses of *Pym*'s thematic, imagistic, and structural integrity appeared and continue to appear (among which should be included the arguments noted above for the work's symmetrical structure).

Joan Tyler Mead's demonstration in her 1982 dissertation of the "sustained theme of creative activity" in *Pym*, anticipative of "major American prose in the 1950's," counts as a formal reading. As narrators, Poe and Pym simultaneously present two modes of the creative self. Mead further demonstrates that each episode "presents an image which summarizes the surrounding chaotic activity and represents Pym's state of awareness in that episode" (*DAI*). In her 1984 dissertation, Judith Malone Neville reads *Pym* formally as an example of a story within a story (along with "The Fall of the House of Usher," in which the poem tells a story), and she discusses the writer as hero. The fourth and final chapter of Sabiha Kamaluddin's 1986 dissertation, " 'Eureka': Poe's Narrative Strategy and Technique," is devoted to the fragmentary nature of *Pym*. However, in a 1986 article of mixed value and many typos, Andrew Horn defends six of the nine digressions (including two footnotes) in *Pym*, but, surprisingly, not the hoaxical "Preface," as thematically related to a novel unified by its concern with deception. Arnold Goldman's 1987 article also takes an essentially formal approach in placing *Pym* in the context of the premature burial theme in Poe's tales. And Paul Lewis in *Comic Effects* (1989) finds a pattern of humor overcome by fear in *Pym*.

In a 1989 article ("Hurrah for Longinus!") arguing for inductive analysis, for a "return to criticism and related theory rooted in actual literature" (p. 34), and for treating all literary works as poems, M. L. Rosenthal discusses *Pym*, along with other works by Poe, Hawthorne, and Faulkner, in terms of their lyrical structure, "the discernible affective structure that resides in a text in its own right" (p. 51). This lyrical structure, rather than narrative progression, is particularly important to a fantasy like *Pym* where it takes the form of an increasing intensity of external and internal emotional pressures.

While, like many of the works covered in this survey, Burton R.

Pollin's edition of *The Imaginary Voyages* contributes to the formal understanding of *Pym*, it adds more particularly to theories about *Pym*'s composition. Pollin's introduction, essay on sources, and "Notes and Comments" stress the piecemeal construction of *Pym* and its narrative incoherence, but the essay by Joseph V. Ridgely included in Pollin's edition, "The Growth of the Text," retreats from the case for disunity that Ridgely and Haverstick made in their 1966 article. The earlier five stages of composition are reduced to four, and Ridgely notes that the earlier article "neglected to assess the impact on Harper and Brothers of the Panic of 1837 and ascribed the long delay in the publication of *Pym* to Poe's failure to supply copy rather than to business conditions" (P 1:30). Ridgely also now agrees with Alexander Hammond that the title entered for copyright on 10 June 1837 included the long subtitle.[27] Joan Tyler Mead concurs. Further commentary on the composition of *Pym* is offered in Kopley's "The '*Very* Profound Under-current' of *Arthur Gordon Pym*."

(9) *Hoax readings.* It is not always easy to make clear distinctions between the next three categories of readings, the *hoax,* the *satiric and ironic,* and the *deconstructive readings,* but the *hoax reading* is rooted in the idea, supported by Ridgely and Haverstick's 1966 investigation of the curious "Preface" to *Pym*, that Poe originally intended that *Pym* be mistaken for an historical account like "The Balloon Hoax" (1844). The notion that Poe wrote *Pym* for two audiences, the gullible who would take the fiction for fact and the perspicacious who would see through Poe's hoax, is complicated, as noted above (see *source studies*) by the case that Pollin makes for understanding many of the errors and absurdities in *Pym* as deliberate. Those, for example, who do not appreciate that the time scheme in the first chapter is ridiculously concentrated are, in a sense, being hoaxed.[28]

Of dubious assistance here is Annette Goizet's 1988 article. She offers a true/false inventory, according to fictional chronology, classifying events and facts in *Pym* either as real and evident or as meant to deceive, with the intent of demonstrating that Pym's concluding account of a white figure should be judged true. A. Robert Lee's 1987 article, which consists mainly of plot summary, views *Pym*, a "pre-Joycean tour-de-force," as a combination hoax plus "visionary journey" (pp. 115, 116). Describing Poe as a reflexive writer aware of his own procedures, Lee draws attention to Pym's mock documentary technique and mix of literal and mock adventure. The one paragraph on

Pym, in Joseph G. Kronick's 1990 article elaborating on Poe's reiterated claim that truth should be sought on the surface of things and in
the most obvious places, might be regarded as a poststructuralist hoax
reading. As a result of being too profound, Pym misreads the obvious
evidence that the indentures in the chasms were artificially produced.
Poe's critics, Kronick claims, have been similarly fooled.

(10) *Satiric and ironic readings.* The common ground here has to
do with the claim that anyone gullible enough to believe that *Pym*
holds out the possibility of a transcendent reality—whether that person is Pym himself or the reader—is the object of satiric attack (the
case made by Evelyn J. Hinz in 1970) or the dupe of Poe's romantic
irony (the case made by G. R. Thompson in 1973).[29] Obviously there is
a fine line between being the victim of irony and being the victim of a
hoax. The Levines' characterization of Poe as an ironic transcendentalist skeptical of transcendence (see *influence studies* above) is indebted
to Thompson's interpretation. Only two relatively sustained satiric or
ironic readings of *Pym* appeared during the 1980–90 period, perhaps
because such readings rapidly become assimilated to the all-consuming
black hole of deconstruction.

Judith L. Sutherland, whose chapter on *Pym* has already been
briefly noted under the *existential* and Eureka-*inspired* categories,
finally comes around to arguing that Pym's obtuseness is the object
of Poe's irony and satire, and also to identifying Peters with Poe's ironic
voice. Pym fails to grow. Sutherland emphasizes the humor and burlesque in *Pym*, sometimes overingeniously as with her claim that Too-
wit sees the *Jane Guy* as a person upside down. But the humor is in
tension with the text's serious side, and hence the two voices of *Pym*
derive from "the self intoxicated by the illusion and the distanced ironic
self that frees itself from Pym but not from Poe" (p. 36).

G. R. Thompson's essay in this volume offers a condensed version of only portions of his provocative 1989 monograph "Romantic Arabesque, Contemporary Theory, and Postmodernism: The Example of Poe's *Narrative*." My comments here apply particularly to the
monograph. If subsumed under the case that Northrop Frye makes in
Anatomy of Criticism (1957) for the predominance of the ironic mode
in our time, Thompson's claim that "the concept of 'romantic irony'
prefigures much of the avant garde in literature and criticism of the
second half of the twentieth century" (p. 163) is not especially startling. More interesting is the evidence that Thompson amasses for what

he calls the "arabesque romance" as a genre of romantic irony that *Pym* exemplifies. The arabesque romance is characterized by "indeterminacy," or what Wayne C. Booth in *A Rhetoric of Irony* (1965) calls "unstable irony," and, markedly in the case of *Pym*, by a quincuncial patterning derived, it is argued, from the geometric arabesque designs of "Persian" carpets. Thompson's re-elaboration of Poe's conception of the arabesque modifies his argument in *Poe's Fiction* that Poe viewed the terms *grotesque* and *arabesque* as virtual synonyms. It now seems clearer that there are important distinctions as well as similarities between the two terms and, from the point of view of Thompson's now enlarged understanding of the arabesque, that the arabesque can subsume the grotesque. It is also apparent that Thompson has become more willing to accommodate the visionary Poe (within a context of ironic indeterminacy) than he appears to be in *Poe's Fiction*.

Participants at the *Pym* Conference were struck by the coincidence that, like Thompson's, the paper by John T. Irwin in this volume also focuses on the quincunx structure of the albatross and penguin rookery in chapter 14 of *Pym* and argues that Poe might have derived his understanding of the symbolic importance of the quincunx from Sir Thomas Browne's *The Garden of Cyrus* (1658).[30] (Unfortunately for Thompson, Browne does not discuss the quincuncial design of Persian carpets.) Since the version of Irwin's essay that was published in 1988 is essentially the same as that published here, I have not commented on it in the account which follows of *deconstructive readings*. Both Thompson's monograph and Irwin's article are highly speculative, but it may well be that, with the quincunx, they have introduced a new area of controversy in *Pym* criticism. Does it matter that nowhere in *Pym* (or anywhere else on record) does Poe actually use the word "quincunx," nor does the word appear in Poe's accepted rookery source, passages in Benjamin Morrell's *A Narrative of Four Voyages* (P 1:294–98)?

As yet insufficiently observed is the extent to which Poe's irony is not antagonistic to his apparent meaning as is generally assumed but is a defense mechanism protective of that meaning. The biographical evidence of Poe's using self-protective irony or downright lying when under attack is germane here. Thus, in responding to a hostile review following his unsuccessful public reading of "Al Aaraaf" on 16 October 1845, Poe "explained" in the *Broadway Journal* that, in view of the nature of "an audience of Transcendentalists . . . it could scarcely be supposed that we would put ourselves to the trouble of composing for the Bostonians anything in the shape of an *original* poem" but instead read a juvenile production, published "before we had fairly completed our tenth year" (*P* 3:298–99).

(11) *Deconstructive readings.* Jean Ricardou, in 1967, was the first of several French critics to understand *Pym* as being about writing and a journey to the end of the page.[31] John Carlos Rowe's 1977 article, the first American example of this approach, appears with some revisions as "Writing and Truth in Poe's *The Narrative of Arthur Gordon Pym*" in *Through the Custom House* (1982). An "investigation of the problemat- ics of writing" (p. 93), *Pym* "enacts the deconstruction of representation as the illusion of truth and prefigures the contemporary conception of writing as the endless production of differences" (p. 95). Rowe dis- cusses the "intertwined metaphors of textuality" (p. 99), including the note from Augustus, "*the* palimpsest of language itself" (p. 102), which leads to a connection with Freud's "'Mystic Writing-Pad'" (p. 109), "the doubleness of writing" (pp. 99–100), and "the self-annihilation that is the ultimate entropy of any writing that strains towards the undifferentiated unity of spiritual absence" (p. 100). But Pym him- self learns nothing from his experience.[32] Michael J. S. Williams (1985, 1988) seconds Rowe's reading of the note episode.

John T. Irwin's tour de force, his almost 200-page reading of *Pym* in *American Hieroglyphics* (1980), focuses on the relationships between writing, doubling, and an interest in hieroglyphics resulting from Jean- François Champollion's success in the 1820s in deciphering Egyptian hieroglyphic writing thanks to the bilingual text of the Rosetta stone. By way of writing, the creation of a double or dark shadow, an author attempts to cheat death. Pym's attempt in this regard, analogous to the search for the source of the Nile, takes the form of a quest for that origi- nal act of differentiation which binds writing and selfhood. The quest is doomed. For Irwin it ends, as I have already noted, in solipsism, Pym's confrontation with his own white shadow.[33]

In a muddled 1981 article, "Language and the Void: Gothic Land- scapes in the Frontiers of Edgar Allan Poe," presumably derived from his 1982 dissertation, Stephen Mainville focuses on the interior fron- tiers between the conscious and the unconscious, the known and the unknown, subject and object, language and the void in *Pym* and "The Journal of Julius Rodman." He writes, "To step out of language [repre- sented by Tsalal] . . . is to inhabit the inhuman void [represented by the blank page]" (p. 357). But nothing is also everything. As Mainville says in his dissertation, *Pym* "questions the possibility of ever achieving unity in a world of language" (*DAI*).

Takayuki Tatsumi's "Violence as Metaphor: Deconstruction of Authority in *The Narrative of Arthur Gordon Pym*" (1984)—part of his 1987 Cornell University dissertation "Disfiguration of Genres: A Reading in the Rhetoric of Edgar Allan Poe"—seems indebted primarily to John Carlos Rowe. Tatsumi argues that Pym, the Christian romantic narrator, is displaced by Pym the writer as performed by Mr. Poe, the writer, who is in turn displaced by writing itself as performed by Edgar Allan Poe, the postromantic author. As a result of this authority-violating strategy, the inhuman text comes to dominate completely the human point of view. Likewise, absence, the chasm, the GAP (an anagram of A. G. P.) replaces presence. In the Poe section that Tatsumi contributed to *Bungaku sura Wakaki America* (1989), he restates his view of the importance of writing in *Pym*.

Patrizia Lombardo in *Edgar Poe et la Modernité* (1985) comments briefly on writing and hieroglyphics in *Pym*, concentrating on the concluding "Note's" tentative identification of Ethiopian, Arabic, and Egyptian characters.

Klaus Martens' 1986 book on Brockden Brown, Poe, and Melville places *Pym* in a self-reflexive "antinomian" tradition in American literature that is indebted to such German Romanticists as Friedrich Schlegel and Jean Paul. In the chapter devoted to the "discovery of the word" in Poe, *Pym* is discussed in terms of its deconstructive self-conscious fictionality (it is a parodic "montage" of different kinds of fiction) and its concern with writing. In addition, Martens anticipates G. R. Thompson's argument in his 1989 monograph and in the present volume by pointing out that *Pym*, with its contrast between form and content and its "symmetry of contradictions," also fulfills Schlegel's criteria for the "arabesque" romantic novel.

In his 1986 dissertation, "Architects of the Abyss: The Indeterminate Fictions of Poe, Hawthorne and Melville," Dennis Pahl is concerned with the "indeterminate boundaries between fiction and criticism." The narrators of "The Fall of the House of Usher," "The Assignation," and *Pym* "cannot define themselves outside a world of textuality and so must inevitably fail in their romantic quest for truth, presence and origins" (*DAI*). Pahl's third chapter, published first as "Poe/Script: The Death of the Author in *The Narrative of Arthur Gordon Pym*" (1987), demonstrates that "the truth of the self . . . is not discovered but invented. In . . . *Pym* Poe challenges whatever authenticity, or truth value, the narrator might lend to his narrative by putting in question the narrator's self—that is, his ability to stand outside his own system of representation, total and present to himself" (p. 51). Foucault on writing and the death of the author is quoted in support, and later Lacan's theory is applied to the mirror scene aboard the *Jane Guy*. Dominated by the voice of nature, Tsalal exists outside of language; its pure black identity is a fiction as is the pure white identity of the region to the south. In moving toward an originary state, Pym encounters "not a world of self-sameness, but one of self-difference" (p. 59). The book version of Pahl's dissertation appeared in 1989.

In "Unreadable Books, Unspeakable Truths," a powerfully argued chapter from *Poe, Death, and the Life of Writing* (1987), J. Gerald Kennedy builds on his two previous *Pym* articles.[34] At the same time, the overall study constitutes the first sustained attempt with regard to Poe to combine history—albeit essentially of the old sort—with deconstructive theory. Kennedy explores *Pym*'s "implications of illegibility, focusing first on the nature of the hermeneutic dilemma which the reader shares with Pym, and then shifting attention to the metaphysical crux of this impasse. The narrator's abortive quest for meaning seems ultimately related to his progressive immersion in the phenomenology of death" (pp. 145–46). Kennedy pairs the note from Augustus, "a paradigm of unreadability" (p. 153), with an equally unreadable event in the book's narrative world, the death ship episode. This "frame" is comparable in importance to that provided by the "Preface" and the concluding "Note," which Kennedy also stresses. Within the context of analyses of "Pym's several rehearsals for death" (p. 166), Kennedy sees Providence as part of the scheme of deception in *Pym*. As for the hieroglyphics, "the representation of a human form within the abyss of shadow or darkness refers to the universal fate of mortals" (p. 168). The white figure corresponds to the "body of the narrative" about to gather Pym "into the artifice of the text" where he will "become an enduring subject caught in language like a fly in amber" (pp. 172–73).

While Roberto Cagliero does relate *Pym* to *Eureka* in "La questione dell'origine in *Gordon Pym* di Edgar Allan Poe" (1988), his focus is on *Pym*'s enigmatic origin in language. The object of Poe's bifurcated narrative strategy (ambiguous double meanings and double narration) is to instruct the reader in language's undecidability and to demonstrate that a text can work without satisfying the expectation of revelation that underlies the process of reading. In this regard, Poe is a precursor of postmodernism and quantum physics' understanding of reality. Leo Marchetti discusses *Pym* in the context of Poe's poetics of writing in *Edgar Allan Poe: la scrittura eterogenea* (1988).

An approach through language influenced by the deconstructive and Lacanian theory of Shoshana Felman informs Félix Martín's treatment of *Pym* in his comprehensive introduction to a 1988 Spanish edition of Poe's tales. The Viconian narrative structure of *Pym*, it is argued, with its "return . . . to the original written enigmas, has as objective to situate the reader in an indeterminate historic, linguistic, and philosophical region in an original condition in which man's destiny and that of the universe merge."[35]

By applying the five semiotic codes from Barthes' *S/Z* "as programs in a computing system," Herbert F. Smith in a 1988 article reveals *Pym* as a classic of playful metafiction; thus, it is claimed, the dispute between hoaxical and symbolic (for Smith largely Freudian) readings is beside the point. Although *Pym*'s structure "as a cycle of cycles" suggests that the conclusion should be read as another "fortunate fall" (i.e., orgasmic)/rebirth "rescue" into "a new and somehow 'higher' state," for the reader what is involved is simply the creation of another text, another "cycle of meaning" (pp. 91, 89, 92).

The third chapter of Jeffrey George DeShell's 1989 dissertation "The Peculiarity of Literature" is devoted to *Pym*. Using an approach based on Walter Benjamin's theory of allegory (a noncommunicative "pure language" that can be separated from the surrounding material text by way of deconstruction), DeShell "demonstrates how difference . . . works to make the search for any stable origin, especially a psychological origin [like Marie Bonaparte's], impossible" (*DAI*).

In a 1990 article that also belongs in the Eureka-*inspired* category, "End(ing)s and Mean(ing)s in *Pym* and *Eureka*," Cynthia Miecznikowski claims that both texts "illustrate the inadequacy of language to capture" what eludes the imagination (p. 55). But *Pym* as a "novel" and *Eureka* as a "prose-poem" are concerned with something other than "truth," and "in both . . . resistance to the disclosure of full meaning becomes the subject of the writing" (p. 58). However, in conclusion, this deconstructive approach swerves into at least the possibility of a visionary reading.

(6) *Visionary readings.* Like Robinson, I have reserved the visionary reading for last not because it can be proven correct (although it

is the preferred reading of both Robinson and myself) but because it is the most inclusive. Not only, in taking account of Poe's intention, does the visionary reading initiate a return from Robinson's "fifth- and sixth-level interpretation to the first level" (p. 51), but it can potentially employ all eight foci and subordinate to a greater or lesser degree aspects of the ten other distinct readings. But my displacement of the visionary reading is also designed to put it up against the deconstructive reading and thus accentuate the main combatants in *Pym* criticism today. According to Robinson, "The visionary reading was anticipated in negative form by Allen Tate (1953) [actually 1952], Patrick Quinn (1952), Edward Davidson (1957), and Charles O'Donnell (1962), but was first (and, I believe, most persuasively) articulated by John Lynen in his 1969 book *The Design of the Present*" (p. 51).[36]

By definition, treatments of *Pym* as a "fantastic" text assert the possibility of an extramundane (i.e., visionary) reality. Hans Holländer's 1980 article constitutes one such example. While drawing on, or contributing to, *formal, mythic,* and *psychological readings,* Frederick S. Frank's "The Gothic at Absolute Zero" (1980) is essentially a visionary reading. Classifying *Pym* as both "aqua-Gothic" (p. 21) and "early science fiction" (p. 29), Frank combines notions of *Pym*'s "primal return to an amniotic paradise" (p. 22), his "reunion with the white goddess" (p. 21), and his being welcomed by "the deadly madonna . . . to the last of his live burials" (p. 26), all of which amount to a "sublime self-nullification" (p. 23). Like Frank, Donald A. Ringe in *American Gothic* (1982) comments on the release from gothic enclosures in *Pym* while, without much elaboration, J. R. Hammond (1981) claims that *Pym* involves both "an actual and a spiritual journey" (p. 125).

Koji Hayashi's three-part "Pym's Voyage and Poe's Poetics" (1982, 1984, 1985) covers a lot of ground, including connections between Poe, Baudelaire, Mallarmé, and Valéry, in fractured English. But his essential aim is to interpret *Pym* in terms of Poe's visionary poetics.

Kent Ljungquist contributes to the visionary reading in *The Grand and the Fair* (1984) in his characterization of *Pym* as "Poe's most prolonged fictional exercise in sublimity" (p. 48). And Charles Samuel Feigenoff's 1983 dissertation, "The Celestial Scenery: Poe and the Universe of *Eureka*," while linked to *Eureka-inspired readings,* includes some discussion of the cultivation of the sublime in *Pym* (and in other early works such as "MS. Found in a Bottle" and "Hans Phaall"). Curtis Ken Fukuchi in his 1986 dissertation, "Poe's 'Plot of God,'" claims that "Poe's fictional voyages are providential shipwreck narratives." (cf. Kopley's dissertation in *source studies* above) which relate to the "theodicy of landscape" discussed by M. H. Abrams in *Natural Supernaturalism*: sublime and beautiful landscapes are manifestations of God's wrath and mercy. Fukuchi concludes that Poe is concerned with the wholeness of the individual in a context that is not merely aesthetic but also spiritual and moral (*DAI*). Part of this dissertation has been published as "Poe's Providential *Narrative of Arthur Gordon Pym*" (1981). There Fukuchi begins by remarking that reading *Pym* as "a spiritual quest for final knowledge or perfect unity" "is closest to the mark, I believe" (p. 147). He goes on to stress *Pym*'s references to Providence during the *Ariel* episode and the relationship between Providence and the southward pull felt throughout *Pym*, and concludes that *Pym*, influenced by John Lloyd Stephens' *Arabia Petraea*, is "a prophetic text contrasting the aborted materialistic pursuits of the other characters to Pym's completed spiritual quest for knowledge, both human and divine, inner and outer" (p. 155).

John Limon, in his 1983 article on *Pym* and *Eureka*, also points to a number of biblical references in *Pym* that would contribute to a visionary reading. He notes that at the middle of *Pym* are metaphors of the Protestant sacraments (Pym and Parker's immersion, Parker's sacrifice and cannibalism). Pym out of the hold, he suggests, is Jonah out of the whale.

Perhaps the most important boost to the visionary reading of *Pym* in the 1980–90 period is provided by Richard Kopley's 1987 *Pym* article, "The '*Very* Profound Under-current' of *Arthur Gordon Pym*." By way of a new source for the *Ariel* episode (see *source studies* above), understanding the word "*Ariel*" to mean Jerusalem, correspondences with the early scriptural tale attributed to Poe, "A Dream," and the etymology of the word "*Penguin*" from the Welsh for "a white head" (suggesting Revelation 1:14), Kopley mounts a detailed and intricate argument for understanding the first chapter of *Pym* as "the *key* to *all* of Poe's *Pym*" (p. 151): "Poe's fundamental idea . . . was comprised of two allegories— the first involving the *Ariel*, the destruction of which signifies the fulfillment of the prophecy of the destruction of Jerusalem; and the second involving the *Penguin*, the figurehead of which—whether coded or undescribed—signifies Christ in the Vision of the Seven Candlesticks, come to prophecy" (p. 157). Kopley's reading does, it must be admitted, finally come down to the interpretation of two words, and some of his argumentation is a little wiredrawn (e.g., he sees the repetition of the words "stakes" and "cords" in the Tsalal landslide episode as an allusion to the same words in a passage from Isaiah describing Jerusalem [pp. 148–49], and he links the phrase "heavy cross" as in "heavy cross sea" [*P* 1:149] to the crucifixion [p. 152]), but the overall case he makes is provocative. I would only wish that he had allowed for Poe's parodically, satirically, or ironically undercutting—albeit, it would seem to me, protectively—his Christian allegory. After all, there *is* something humorous about Christ's revealing Himself as a penguin.

In *God and Circumstances* (1989), the first book-length study predominantly devoted to *Pym* (but actually more of a pumped-up article in terms of real content), G. K. Watkins explores parallels with Twain's "The Great Dark" and overdogmatically interprets both works positively as "journeys away from man-made chaos [and "the doom of reason"] to spiritual order" (pp. 111, 182) by way of the subconscious and " 'dream transcendence' " (p. 2). Watkins shows no awareness of structuralist, deconstructionist, or generally poststructuralist readings of *Pym*.

Douglas Lee Semark treats *Pym* in his 1987 dissertation "The Visionary Tradition: The Ancients, Dante, and Poe." It is the secular branch of the visionary tradition in Western literature with which Semark is concerned. Within that context, *Pym*'s "immediate message is the perfection of will and desire over the dictates of reason" while its "ultimate message is a personal statement about the arrival/return of the individual and the world to mythic perfection" (*DAI*).

In the fourth chapter of a 1989 dissertation, "Romance within a Romance: The Fiction of Edgar Allan Poe," Lou Ann Norman discusses *Pym* "not as a symbolic voyaging but as a moment of romancing which is about the perils of romancing." The narrator's designs can "only contribute to a higher preestablished design—the eventual return to cosmic oneness through the annihilation of the individual self or through death" (*DAI*).

At the end of his survey of *Pym* criticism, Robinson suggests that in the years to come the attempt should be made "to fuse transcendental vision and romantic irony [which he conflates with deconstruction] in a far more thoroughgoing fashion than the visionary critics offer" and thereby move toward "the establishment of a critical consensus on *Pym*" (p. 52). Four or possibly five such studies have in fact appeared, including A. Robert Lee's 1987 article, which I have described, perhaps a little arbitrarily, under the hoax category; Miecznikowski's 1990 article; and Robinson's own reading, a reading his survey's conclusion anticipates.

The one I am not sure about since I cannot read Japanese is Shoko Itoh's account of *Pym* in *The Road to Arnheim* (1986). An English translation of her contents page lists, under the subsection heading "The Sea of Genres, *Arthur Gordon Pym*," the following: "The process of writing," "Satire and Fantasy?", "On the 'Preface,'" and "On the aspects of narrator, Pym." This synopsis indicates that Itoh certainly takes account of satiric, ironic, and deconstructive readings. And a translation of her following final chapter title as "Gnostic Apocalypse in Edgar Allan Poe" reveals that Itoh sees all of Poe's work in terms of a visionary gnosticism.[37] It seems reasonable to conclude, then, that Itoh's reading of *Pym* fuses deconstructive and visionary approaches.

Evan Carton in *The Rhetoric of American Romance* (1985) walks the slippery tightrope between deconstruction and visionary reality as follows: "Poe's world is one in which the fiction that masquerades as truth may simultaneously comprise a truth masquerading as a fiction"—hence the radical unsettling of "questions of authority and authenticity, as the pair of notes that frame . . . *Pym* exemplifies" (p. 137). Carton adds, "By obscuring the boundaries of the certain and the incredible alike," Poe fills "the consequent void with an expanded sense of the possible" (p. 138).

In his survey, Robinson accurately anticipates his own reading of *Pym* in *American Apocalypses* (1985) as involving "a negation of transcendence that yet preserves the *possibility* of transcendence imagistically . . . through the image of the white figure above the misty polar veil" (p. 52). According to Robinson's book, this figure, whether Christ's shadow or the shadow of Pym's perfected body, functions as "an iconic dream-body that will permit a visionary habitation of the gap" (p. 119), the abyss of difference between presence and absence. The "uncertainty of interpretation," the novel's "rhetorical focus" (p. 121), makes this interpretation as inevitable as any other.[38]

By way of a transition to my "shadowy conclusions" below, here would seem to be the most logical place to locate Curtis Dahl's "Port Wine, Roast Mutton, and Pickled Olives: Gourmet Food in Poe's *The Narrative of Arthur Gordon Pym*," a 1989 article (previously presented at the *Pym* Conference) which contrives to occupy virtually all the above interpretive categories and thus to arrive at its own shadowy conclusions. Dahl distinguishes *Pym* from other "gentleman's son afloat" stories (p. 109) by "its curious, constant, and insistent emphasis on food, especially gourmet food" (p. 110), but also including food calculated to arouse the reader's disgust. Dahl then relates this element to possible sources and to a variety of biographical, social, ironic, mythic, Christian, satiric, existential, and psychological readings. Alexander Hammond's contribution to this volume suggests a further connection with the theme of consumption in Poe's scheme for his "Tales of the Folio Club."

Shadowy Conclusions

What finally have we learned from eleven more years of *Pym* criticism? Much of it, it must be acknowledged, is repetitious. One hundred eighteen items in eleven years is excessive, maybe thirty more than warranted by strict standards of evidence and originality. (In the year 2001, someone else can survey the three hundred or so items of *Pym* criticism that will have appeared in the 1990s if the present rate of increase continues!) In 1990, as in 1980, deconstructive readings face off against visionary readings. This conflict is, of course, a version of F. O. Matthiessen's positive-transcendentalist/negative-romantic dialectic in classic American literature, a dialectic that Poe criticism reflects in miniature. Generally speaking, criticism of American literature has fluctuated between emphasizing the positive or the negative. Until quite recently, the negative appeared to be gaining most ground. Between 1980 and 1990 (counting Miecznikowski's article for both sides), twenty more-or-less deconstructive readings appeared and eighteen more-or-less visionary readings (to which might be added at least a couple of Eureka-*inspired readings*). I noted in my introduction that claims for *Pym*'s importance and talk of shadows account for what is genuinely new in *Pym* criticism of the 1980s; to that should now be added talk of quincunxes. What shaky "fusion" of deconstructive and visionary readings has occurred certainly does not yet constitute a consensus. The examples described above in fact do all that is really possible in this regard; they subsume traces of deconstruction under essentially visionary readings. A genuinely stable fusion of the deconstructive and the visionary would surely constitute a contradiction in terms and hence itself become subject to immediate deconstruction. Perhaps that is why, in his survey, Robinson uses the term "romantic irony" (p. 52) as a cover for deconstruction.

It seems to me that even if a fusion of visionary and deconstructive readings were possible, such a synthesis would not be particularly desirable. Why not suppose, reasonably enough, that, in whatever proportion, Poe, with greater or lesser self-awareness, was simply divided between belief in a supernal realm and a corresponding doubt? This would appear, in fact, to be the reading that our present understanding of *Pym* most strongly supports. It is to be expected, then, that what I take to be the predominantly visionary impetus of *Pym*, but what others might see as a marginal possibility, coexists in unresolved tension with "contradictory" hoaxical, satiric, ironic, and deconstructive elements that collectively express the alternative skeptical position. To understand *Pym*'s mixed signals in this way surely maximizes the text's interest. After all, given the area of inquiry, the response of nihilism, no less than that of faith, is not amenable to rational demonstration or certitude.

Robinson's projection that *Pym* criticism would continue to travel the circle of the six foci he identifies has, thus far, proved correct, although, I believe, these six foci need to be expanded to eight or even nine. The kind of *Pym* metacriticism exemplified by Robinson's survey and the present article involves an additional issue or focus: "The text's relation to the commentary it has generated."

The eleven readings (twelve if the *strange adventure reading* is counted) generated by these six, eight, or nine foci have remained constant, although, like the *adventure* reading, the Eureka-*inspired reading* was not one of Robinson's distinct categories. These readings might be sorted, with some overlapping, into three broad groups: (1) naturalized, indirectly antitranscendental readings (the *psychoanalytical,* some of the *mythic,* the *psychological,* the *existential,* the *social commentary,* and some of the *formal and compositional*); (2) directly antitranscendental readings (the *hoax,* the *satiric and ironic,* some of the Eureka-*inspired,* and all the *deconstructive*); and (3) transcendental readings (the *strange adventure,* the remaining *mythic,* the remaining *formal and compositional,* the remaining Eureka-*inspired,* and the *visionary*).

I would project that most of the *Pym* commentary to come will derive from the increasingly sophisticated cross-fertilization of the twelve readings that Robinson and I have identified. At the moment, there appears to be some interest in mixing the *existential* and the *deconstructive* along with the *visionary/deconstructive* mix described above. New historicist versions of *social commentary* readings are also to be expected.

It is at least possible that the years ahead may produce additional distinct readings. It is likely, in fact, that, as the twelve existent readings are increasingly refined, it will make interpretive sense to subdivide one or more of them. Thus, my Eureka-*inspired* category is broken off from the *visionary* category and, to a lesser extent, from the *satiric and ironic* and *deconstructive* categories. I was tempted, on the basis of Richard Kopley's 1987 article, to split off from the *visionary* category a category of *Christian readings*. Hints at baptism, communion, and the white figure as Christ have been noted, more or less incidentally, by *Pym* critics over the years, but Kopley's article represents the first sustained Christian reading of *Pym*.[39] It remains to be seen whether or not this reading gains ground to the extent that it merits being distinguished from the more general *visionary reading*. It just might, of course, fall prey to deconstruction and/or new historicism. As with the straight reading versus ironic reading of Melville's *Billy Budd*, the *visionary* and *deconstructive readings* seem likely to remain the basic, more-or-less evenly matched antagonists in the successive bouts of shadowboxing that is *Pym* criticism. A knockout blow—even one historically backed—is not anticipated.

One of the present volume's main contributions to *Pym* criticism lies in the area of new sources and their interpretive consequences. Even two of the essays grouped under "Figuration" (those by Irwin and Thompson) offer considerations of possible source material (Browne). At the same time, in what are predominantly source studies and so grouped in this collection, J. Lasley Dameron, and Carol Peirce with Alexander G. Rose III are concerned to emphasize the new readings that are implicated. In fact, all the essayists take pains to anchor even their most speculative flights to some outcropping of factual/"factual" bedrock.

Should the reader be so motivated, he or she may consider how all but one of the essays herein can be placed in one or some combination of the categories that Robinson and I have adduced. The exception is David H. Hirsch's account of *Pym* as prefiguring the worst horrors of contemporary history. Francis Ford Coppola similarly yoked Conrad's *Heart of Darkness* to the Vietnam War in *Apocalypse Now*. What I am suggesting is that some readers may regard Hirsch's essay (like Barth's novel *Sabbatical*) as more akin to a creative adaptation than to a critical reading of Poe's novel, a matter of E. D. Hirsch's sense of "significance" as opposed to intentional "meaning."[40] At issue here in finally deciding whether or not a thirteenth distinct category of reading is required to accommodate David Hirsch's essay is also the contestable distinction between prefiguration or prophecy (involving another sense of the visionary) and coincidence. On 24 or 25 July 1884, long after *Pym's* publication, there was an authenticated case of three out of four castaways surviving at sea in an open boat by drawing lots (with the outcome fixed according to one report) and cannibalizing one of their member so "selected." In this historical case, and in the similar circumstances in *Pym*, the victim was named Richard Parker.[41] Perhaps Poe *was* prescient.

Finally, the strength of this volume is not the fusion of methodologies but their complementarity.[42] And Pym's own conclusion seems the most apposite: "In no affairs of mere prejudice, pro or con, do we deduce inferences with entire certainty even from the most simple data" (*P* 1:65).

Bibliography: *Pym* Criticism, 1980–1990

Al-Madani, Uusur Wajeeh. "Errand to the Center: The Archetypal Journey Image in Thoreau, Poe, and Melville." Ph.D. diss., University of Colorado at Boulder, 1982 (192 pp.). *DAI*, 43 (1983), 3909A.

Berressem, Hanjo. "Godolphin, Goodolphin, Goodol'phin, Goodol'Pyn, Good ol'Pym: A Question of Integration." *Pynchon Notes*, 10 (1982), 3–17.

Berta, James Louis. "Poe and the West." Ph.D. diss., Bowling Green State University, 1986 (195 pp.). *DAI*, 47 (1987), 2583A.

Billy, Ted. "Providence and Chaos in *The Narrative of Arthur* 'Goddin' *Pym*." *Journal of Evolutionary Psychology*, 9 (1989), 126–33.

Black, James Ronald. "The Paradoxical Structure of the Sea Quest in Dana, Poe, Cooper, Melville, London, and Hemingway." Ph.D. diss., Wayne State University, 1979 (300 pp.). *DAI*, 40 (1980), 5862A–5863A.

Black, Lynette C. "Pym's Vision Transcribed by 'Le Bateau Ivre.' " *Mississippi Quarterly*, 41 (1987–88), 3–19.

Brody, Selma B. "Poe's Use of Brewster's *Letters on Natural Magic*." *English Language Notes*, 27 (1989), 50–54.

Cagliero, Roberto. "*Arthur Gordon Pym's* Influence on Italian Literature." *Poe Studies Association Newsletter*, 15 (1987), 8.

————. "La questione dell'origine in *Gordon Pym* di Edgar Allan Poe." *Quaderni di Lingue e Letterature*, 13 (1988), 29–47.

Carton, Evan. *The Rhetoric of American Romance: Dialectic and Identity in Emerson, Dickinson, Poe, and Hawthorne*. Baltimore: Johns Hopkins University Press, 1985 (pp. 137–38).

Dahl, Curtis. "Port Wine, Roast Mutton, and Pickled Olives: Gourmet Food in Poe's *The Narrative of Arthur Gordon Pym*." *The University of Mississippi Studies in English*, n.s. 7 (1989), 109–17.

DeShell, Jeffrey George. "The Peculiarity of Literature: An Allegorical Approach to Edgar Allan Poe." Ph.D. diss., State University of New York at Buffalo, 1989 (340 pp.). *DAI*, 50 (1990), 3950A–3951A.

Di Maio, Mariella. "Jules Verne e il modello Poe." *Rivista di Letterature Moderne e Comparate*, 35 (1982), 335–54.

Engel, Leonard W. "Claustrophobia, the Gothic Enclosure and Poe." *Clues: A Journal of Detection*, 10 (1989), 107–17 (esp. 115–16).

Feigenoff, Charles Samuel. "The Celestial Scenery: Poe and the Universe of *Eureka*." Ph.D. diss., University of Virginia, 1983 (242 pp.). *DAI*, 45 (1985), 2527A.

Frank, Frederick S. "The Gothic at Absolute Zero: Poe's *Narrative of Arthur Gordon Pym*." *Extrapolation*, 21 (1980), 21–30.

———. "Polarized Gothic: An Annotated Bibliography of Poe's *Narrative of Arthur Gordon Pym*." *Bulletin of Bibliography*, 38 (1981), 117–27.

Fujita, Eiichi. *America Dentoshosetsu to Sogai* [Alienation in the traditional American novel]. Kita-ku, Osaka: Sogensha, 1989 (pp. 11–42).

Fukuchi, Curtis Ken. "Poe's 'Plot of God.'" Ph.D. diss., Harvard University, 1986 (164 pp.). *DAI*, 47 (1986), 2156A.

———. "Poe's Providential *Narrative of Arthur Gordon Pym*." *ESQ: A Journal of the American Renaissance*, 27 (1981), 147–56.

Goizet, Annette. "Mensonges et vérités . . . pour une lecture des *Aventures d'Arthur Gordon Pym*." *Métaphores*, nos. 15–16 (1988), 101–10.

Goldman, Arnold. "Poe's Stories of Premature Burial: 'That 'Ere Kind of Style.'" In *Edgar Allan Poe: The Design of Order*, ed. A. Robert Lee, pp. 48–65. London: Vision Press, 1987 (*Pym*: pp. 53–55).

Gouaux, Mireille. "*Les Aventures d'Arthur Gordon Pym* et *Le sphinx des glaces*: Une intertextualite exemplaire." *Métaphores*, nos. 15–16 (1988), 111–16.

Hammond, J. R. *An Edgar Allan Poe Companion: A Guide to the Short Stories, Romances and Essays*. Totowa, N.J.: Barnes and Noble, 1981 (pp. 119–29).

Hanson, Thomas S. "Arno Schmidt's Reception of Edgar Allan Poe; Or, The Domain of Arn(o)heim." *Review of Contemporary Fiction*, 8 (1988), 166–81.

Hayashi, Koji. "Pym's Voyage and Poe's Poetics (1)." *Memoirs of the Faculty of General Education, Ehime University*, 15 (1982), 171–98.

———. "Pym's Voyage and Poe's Poetics (2)—The Arabesque of Mirror." *Memoirs of the Faculty of General Education, Ehime University*, 17 (1984), 273–303.

————. "Pym's Voyage and Poe's Poetics (3)—From Poe to Valéry." *Memoirs of the Faculty of General Education, Ehime University*, 18 (1985), 145–87.

Hernández del Castillo, Ana. *Keats, Poe, and the Shaping of Cortázar's Mythopoesis*. Purdue University Monographs in Romance Languages, vol. 8. Amsterdam: John Benjamins B.V., 1981 (pp. 55–67, 75–91, 110, 112).

Hinds, Elizabeth Jane Wall. "The Hero in Time: The American Gothic Fiction of Charles Brockden Brown, Edgar Allan Poe, and Herman Melville." Ph.D. diss., University of Tulsa, 1989 (306 pp.). *DAI*, 50 (1990), 2053A.

Hoelscher, Ann Laura. "Incommensurate Models: Poe's Fiction and the Inevitability of the Unconscious." Ph.D. diss., Purdue University, 1984 (236 pp.). *DAI* 45 (1985), 2102A.

Holländer, Hans. "Das Bild in der Theorie des Phantastischen." In *Phantastik in Literatur und Kunst*, ed. Christian W. Thomsen and Jens Malte Fischer, pp. 52–78. Darmstadt: Wissenschaftliche Buchgesellschaft, 1980.

Hollister, Michael. "Melville's Gam with Poe in *Moby-Dick*: Bulkington and Pym." *Studies in the Novel*, 21 (1989), 279–91.

Horn, Andrew. " 'But to Return from This Digression . . .': The Functions of Excursus in Edgar Allan Poe's *Narrative of Arthur Gordon Pym*." *Communiqué* (University of the North, South Africa), 11 (1986), 7–22.

Immelmann, Thomas. " 'Kaff' und 'Arthur Gordon Pym,' oder: Der Abgrund des Unbewussten." *Bargfelder Bote*, 119 (1987), 23–27.

Irwin, John T. *American Hieroglyphics: The Symbol of the Egyptian Hieroglyphics in the American Renaissance*. New Haven: Yale University Press, 1980 (pp. 64–235).

————. "The Quincuncial Network in Poe's *Pym*." *Arizona Quarterly*, 44, no. 3 (1988), 1–14.

Itoh, Shoko. " 'Dream-Voyage' and Poe's Sea" [1: "The Continuity of Poe's Seascape Fiction," 2: "Polar-Gulf Fantasy and Poe's Narrative Technique," 3: "The Sea of Genres, *Arthur Gordon Pym*"]. In Shoko Itoh, *The Road to Arnheim: The World of Edgar Allan Poe*. Tokyo: Kirihara Shoten, 1986 (pp. 176–204).

————. "Kyokuchi o Motomeru Narrative [Narrative searching for the pole]: *Arthur Gordon Pym*." *Eigoseinen* (Kenkyusha), 130 (1985), 486–88.

————. "Poe and 'The Rime of the Ancient Mariner.' " *Language and Culture* (The Faculty of Integrated Arts and Sciences, Hiroshima University), 11 (February 1985), 204–19.

Kamaluddin, Sabiha Ahmed. " 'Eureka': Poe's Narrative Strategy and Technique." Ph.D. diss., State University of New York (SUNY) at Buffalo, 1986 (135 pp.). *DAI*, 47 (1987), 3757A.

Kennedy, J. Gerald. "The Invisible Message: The Problem of Truth in *Pym*." In *The Naiad Voice: Essays on Poe's Satiric Hoaxing*, ed. Dennis W. Eddings, pp. 124–35. Port Washington, N.Y.: Associated Faculty Press, 1983. Revision of " 'The Infernal Twoness' in *Arthur Gordon Pym*," *Topic 30*, 16 (1976), 41–53.

———. "Unreadable Books, Unspeakable Truths." In J. Gerald Kennedy, *Poe, Death, and the Life of Writing*. New Haven: Yale University Press, 1987 (pp. 145–76, 221–22).

Kimura, Shinichi. "The Whirl and the Pendulum—On the Suspension-Motif in Poe." *The Annual Report of Cultural Science* (The Faculty of Letters, Hokkaido University), 34 (1985), 87–106.

Kopley, Richard. "Early Illustrations of *Pym*'s 'Shrouded Human Figure.' " In *Scope of the Fantastic—Culture, Biography, Themes, Children's Literature*, ed. Robert A. Collins and Howard D. Pearce, pp. 155–70. Westport, Conn.: Greenwood Press, 1985.

———. "The Hidden Journey of *Arthur Gordon Pym*." In *Studies in the American Renaissance 1982*, ed. Joel Myerson, pp. 29–51. Boston: Twayne Publishers, 1982. Reprinted and slightly abridged in *The Poe Messenger*, 15 (1985), 15–25.

———. "*The Narrative of Arthur Gordon Pym*." In *Survey of Modern Fantasy Literature*, vol. 3, ed. Frank N. McGill, pp. 1092–95. La Canada, Calif.: Salem Press, 1983.

———. " 'No Tie More Strong': Brotherhood and Beyond in *The Narrative of Arthur Gordon Pym*." Ph.D. diss., SUNY at Buffalo, 1982 (146 pp.). *DAI*, 43 (1982), 1545A.

———. "Poe's *Pym*-esque 'A Tale of the Ragged Mountains.' " In *Poe and His Times: The Artist and His Milieu*, ed. Benjamin Franklin Fisher IV, pp. 167–77. Baltimore: The Edgar Allan Poe Society of Baltimore, 1990.

———. "The Secret of *Arthur Gordon Pym*: The Text and the Source." *Studies in American Fiction*, 8 (1980), 203–18.

———. "The '*Very* Profound Under-current' of *Arthur Gordon Pym*." In *Studies in the American Renaissance 1987*, ed. Joel Myerson, pp. 143–75. Charlottesville: University Press of Virginia, 1987.

Kronick, Joseph G. "Edgar Allan Poe: The Error of Reading and the Reading of Error." In *Southern Literature and Literary Theory*, ed. Jefferson Humphries, pp. 206–25 (esp. p. 217). Athens: The University of Georgia Press, 1990.

Lee, A. Robert. " 'Impudent and ingenious fiction': Poe's *The Narrative of Arthur Gordon Pym of Nantucket*." In *Edgar Allan Poe: The Design of Order*, ed. A. Robert Lee, pp. 112–34. London: Vision Press, 1987.

Levine, Susan F. and Stuart. "Poe and Fuentes: The Reader's Prerogatives." *Comparative Literature*, 36 (1984), 34–53.

Lewis, Paul. *Comic Effects: Interdisciplinary Approaches to Humor in Literature*. Albany: State University of New York Press, 1989 (pp. 135–38).

Limon, John. "How to Place Poe's *Arthur Gordon Pym* in Science-Dominated Intellectual History, and How to Extract It Again." *North Dakota Quarterly*, 51 (1983), 31–47.

———. "Imaginary Science: The Influence and Metamorphosis of Science in Charles Brockden Brown, Edgar Allan Poe, and Nathaniel Hawthorne." Ph.D. diss., University of California at Berkeley, 1981 (460 pp.). *DAI*, 42 (1982), 5122A–5123A.

———. *The Place of Fiction in the Time of Science: A Disciplinary History of American Writing*. New York: Cambridge University Press, 1990 (pp. 23, 71, 80, 89, 91, 92, 111–20, 169, 178–79, 185, 203 n. 82).

Ljungquist, Kent. *The Grand and the Fair: Poe's Landscape Aesthetics and Pictorial Techniques*. Potomac, Md.: Scripta Humanistica, 1984 (pp. 48, 56–72, 80–82, 189).

———. "'Speculative Mythology' and the Titan Myth in Poe's *Pym* and Melville's *Pierre*." *The Sphinx* (special issue: Edgar Allan Poe), 4 (1985), 250–57.

Lombardo, Patrizia. *Edgar Poe et la Modernité: Breton, Barthes, Derrida, Blanchot*. Birmingham, Ala.: Summa Publications, 1985 (pp. 28–29).

Mainville, Stephen. "Language and the Void: Gothic Landscapes in the Frontiers of Edgar Allan Poe." *Genre*, 14 (1981), 347–62.

———. "Language and the Void: Poe's Discourse of Horror." Ph.D. diss., University of Oklahoma, 1982 (231 pp.). *DAI*, 43 (1982), 1973A.

Marchetti, Leo. *Edgar Allan Poe: la scrittura eterogenea*. Ravenna: Longo, 1988.

Martens, Klaus. *Die antinomische Imagination—Studien zu einer Amerikanischen literarischen Tradition (Charles Brockden Brown, Edgar Allan Poe, Herman Melville)*. Frankfurt am Main: Lang, 1986 (pp. 107–52).

Martin, Félix. Introduction to *Relatos*, by Edgar Allan Poe. Madrid: Cátedra, 1988 (pp. 9–119).

Mead, Joan Tyler. "'An Impudent and Ingenious Fiction': Creative Process as Theme in Edgar Allan Poe's 'Narrative of Arthur Gordon Pym.'" Ph.D. diss., Ohio University, 1982 (299 pp.). *DAI*, 43 (1983), 2668A.

Miecznikowski, Cynthia. "End(ing)s and Mean(ing)s in *Pym* and *Eureka*." *Studies in Short Fiction*, 27 (1990), 55–64.

Morita, Takeshi. "The True Character of What Goes On Calling—*The Narrative of Arthur Gordon Pym*." *American Literary Review* (Tsukuba University), 5 (1983): 37–46.

Motoyama, Chitoshi. *Poe wa Doracula Daroka* [Is Poe Dracula?]. Tokyo: Keiso-shobo, 1989.

Neville, Judith Malone. "Interpolated Narratives in Selected Works of Hawthorne, Poe, and Melville." Ph.D. diss., Brandeis University, 1984 (120 pp.). *DAI*, 45 (1984), 1753A.

Nishiguchi, Masahiro. "On Poe's Sea Stories." *Journal of Otsuki Junior College*, 16 (1985), 81–101.

Norman, Lou Ann. "Romance within a Romance: The Fiction of Edgar Allan Poe." Ph.D. diss., University of Cincinnati, 1989 (259 pp.). *DAI*, 51 (1990), 853A.

Paglia, Camille. *Sexual Personae: Art and Decadence from Nefertiti to Emily Dickinson*. London and New Haven: Yale University Press, 1990 (pp. 325, 579–80, 585, 590–91).

Pahl, Dennis Alan. "Architects of the Abyss: The Indeterminate Fictions of Poe, Hawthorne and Melville." Ph.D. diss., SUNY at Buffalo, 1986 (224 pp.). *DAI*, 47 (1987), 3429A.

———. "Poe/Script: The Death of the Author in *The Narrative of Arthur Gordon Pym*." *New Orleans Review*, 14 (1987), 51–60. Reprinted in *Architects of the Abyss: The Indeterminate Fictions of Poe, Hawthorne and Melville*. Columbia: University of Missouri Press, 1989 (pp. 41–56).

Pease, Donald. *Visionary Compacts: American Renaissance Writings in Cultural Context*. Madison: University of Wisconsin Press, 1987 (pp. 168–75, 195–202).

Picot, Jean-Pierre. "Shéhérazade et le sphinx, Jules Verne explorateur de la mort sur les pas d'Edgar Poe." *Métaphores*, nos. 15–16 (1988), 289–97.

Pillat, Monica. "Arthur Gordon Pym sau poetica melancoliea." *Steaua*, 34 (1984), 55.

Pollin, Burton R. *Images of Poe's Works: A Comprehensive Descriptive Catalogue of Illustrations*. New York: Greenwood Press, 1989.

———. Introduction to and commentary on *The Imaginary Voyages: The Narrative of Arthur Gordon Pym, The Unparalleled Adventure of One Hans Pfaall, The Journal of Julius Rodman*. Vol. 1 of *Collected Writings of Edgar Allan Poe*. Edited by Burton R. Pollin. Boston: G. K. Hall, 1981 (pp. 4–16, 17–28, 37–50, 51–52, 211–14, 215–363).

———. "Poe 'Viewed and *Reviewed*': An Annotated Checklist of Contemporaneous Notices." *Poe Studies*, 11 (1980), 17–28.

Poncet, André. "Le Voyage initiatique du héros d'Edgar Poe dans les *Aventures d'Arthur Gordon Pym*." *Métaphores*, 7 (1983), 83–101.

Pozzo, Felice. "I figli di Gordon Pym." *LG Argomenti*, 20 (1984), 63–69.

Rainwater, Catherine. "Encounters with the 'White Sphinx': Poe's Influence in Some Early Works of H. G. Wells." *English Literature in Transition (1880–1920)*, 26 (1983), 35–51.

———. "H. G. Wells' Re-Vision of Poe: *The Undying Fire* and *Mr. Blettsworthy on Rampole Island*." *English Literature in Transition (1880–1920)*, 30 (1987), 423–36.

Reynolds, David S. *Beneath the American Renaissance: The Subversive Imagination in the Age of Emerson and Melville*. New York: Knopf, 1988 (pp. 173, 238, 241–3).

Richard, Claude. "L'Ecriture d'Arthur Gordon Pym." In Claude Richard, *Edgar Allan Poe Ecrivain*. Montpellier: Service des Publications—Université Paul Valéry, 1990 (pp. 151–77). (First published as a 1975 article in *Delta*.)

Ridgely, Joseph V. "The Growth of the Text." In *The Imaginary Voyages: The Narrative of Arthur Gordon Pym, The Unparalleled Adventure of One Hans Pfaall, The Journal of Julius Rodman*, pp. 29–36. Vol. 1 of *Collected Writings of Edgar Allan Poe*. Edited by Burton R. Pollin. Boston: G. K. Hall, 1981.

Ringe, Donald A. *American Gothic: Imagination and Reason in Nineteenth-Century Fiction*. Lexington: University Press of Kentucky, 1982 (pp. 148–49).

Robinson, Douglas. *American Apocalypses: The Image of the End of the World in American Literature*. Baltimore: Johns Hopkins University Press, 1985 (pp. 111–22).

———. "American Apocalypses: The Image of the End of the World in American Literature." Ph.D. diss., University of Washington, 1983 (614 pp.). *DAI*, 44 (1983), 1793A.

———. "Reading Poe's Novel: A Speculative Review of *Pym* Criticism, 1950–1980." *Poe Studies*, 15 (1982), 47–54.

Rosenthal, M. L. "Hurrah for Longinus! Lyric Structure and Inductive Analysis." *Southern Review*, 25 (1989), 30–51 (esp. 38–42).

Rosenzweig, Paul. "'Dust Within the Rock': The Phantasm of Meaning in *The Narrative of Arthur Gordon Pym*." *Studies in the Novel*, 14 (1982), 137–51.

———. "The Search for Identity: The Enclosure Motif in *The Narrative of Arthur Gordon Pym*." *ESQ: A Journal of the American Renaissance*, 26 (1980), 111–26.

Rowe, John Carlos. "Writing and Truth in Poe's *The Narrative of Arthur Gordon Pym*." In John Carlos Rowe, *Through the Custom House: Nineteenth-Century American Fiction and Modern Theory*. Baltimore: Johns Hopkins University Press, 1982 (pp. 91–110, 205–207). (Revision of "Writing and Truth in *The Narrative of Arthur Gordon Pym*." *Glyph 2: Johns Hopkins Textual Studies* [1977], 102–21.)

Semark, Douglas Lee. "The Visionary Tradition: The Ancients, Dante, and Poe." Ph.D. diss., Case Western Reserve University, 1987 (142 pp.). *DAI*, 48 (1988), 1764A.

Sharp, Roberta. "Poe's Chapters on 'Natural Magic.'" In *Poe and His Times: The Artist and His Milieu*, ed. Benjamin Franklin Fisher IV, pp. 154–66. Baltimore: The Edgar Allan Poe Society, 1990.

Smith, Herbert F. "P/P . . . Tekelili: *Pym* Decoded." *English Studies in Canada*, 14 (1988), 82–93.

Sutherland, Judith L. "Poe: The Captain Regrets . . ." In Judith L. Sutherland, *The Problematic Fictions of Poe, James, and Hawthorne*. Columbia: University of Missouri Press, 1984 (pp. 12–37).

Swann, Charles. "Poe and Maturin—A Possible Debt." *Notes and Queries* 37 (1990), 424–25.

Tatsumi, Takayuki. "Disfiguration of Genres: A Reading in the Rhetoric of Edgar Allan Poe." Ph.D. diss., Cornell University, 1987 (216 pp.). *DAI*, 48 (1988), 2339A.

——— . "Edgar Allan Poe: American Rhetoric." In *Bungaku sura Wakaki America* [American Renaissance Re-presented]: *Poe, Hawthorne, Melville*, by Tatsumi, Hiroko Wasizu, and Michiko Shimokobe. Tokyo: Nan'undo, 1989 (pp. 33–108).

——— . "Violence as Metaphor: Deconstruction of Authority in *The Narrative of Arthur Gordon Pym*." *Studies in English Literature* (The English Literary Society of Japan), 61 (1984), 253–67.

Thompson, G. R. *Romantic Arabesque, Contemporary Theory, and Postmodernism: The Example of Poe's "Narrative." ESQ: A Journal of the American Renaissance*, 35 (1989), 163–271.

Tucker, Amy. "America's Gothic Landscape." Ph.D. diss., New York University, 1979 (336 pp.). *DAI*, 40 (1980), 5868A.

Udono, Etsuko. "Infinity in the Mirror—On *The Narrative of Arthur Gordon Pym of Nantucket*." *American Literary Review*, 5 (1983), 28–36.

——— . "Studies of *The Narrative of Arthur Gordon Pym* (1)." *The 20th Anniversary of Founding Memorial Number* (Aichi Prefectural University) (1985), 639–56.

——— . "Studies of *The Narrative of Arthur Gordon Pym* (2)." *Mulberry*, 35 (1985), 109–21.

Voloshin, Beverly Rose. "The Lockean Tradition in the Gothic Fiction of Brown, Poe, and Melville." Ph.D. diss., University of California at Berkeley, 1979 (277 pp.). *DAI*, 40 (1980), 4047A.

Walker, I. M. Introduction to *Edgar Allan Poe: The Critical Heritage*, ed. I. M. Walker. London: Routledge, 1986 (pp. 2, 6, 21–24, 49).

Watkins, G. K. *God and Circumstances: A Lineal Study of Intent in Edgar Allan Poe's* The Narrative of Arthur Gordon Pym *and Mark Twain's* The Great Dark. New York: Peter Lang, 1989.

Welsh, Susan Booker. "Edgar Allan Poe and the Rhetoric of Science." Ph.D. diss., Drew University, 1986 (249 pp.). *DAI*, 47 (1987), 3760A.

Williams, Michael John Stuart. "'The Charnel Character to the Figure': Language and Interpretation in the Fiction of Edgar Allan Poe." Ph.D. diss., Washington State University, 1985 (269 pp.). *DAI*, 46 (1986), 3354A.

————. *A World of Words: Language and Displacement in the Fiction of Edgar Allan Poe*. Durham: Duke University Press, 1988 (pp. 54, 55, 125–26, 137).

Wuletich-Brinberg, Sybil. *Poe: The Rationale of the Uncanny*. New York: Peter Lang, 1988 (pp. 188–98).

Zanger, Jules. "Poe's Endless Voyage: *The Narrative of Arthur Gordon Pym*." *Papers on Language & Literature*, 22 (1986), 276–83.

Notes

Kopley: Introduction

1. Edward H. Davidson, *Poe: A Critical Study* (Cambridge, Mass.: Harvard University Press, 1957), p. 157.

2. Frederick S. Frank, "Polarized Gothic: An Annotated Bibliography of Poe's *Narrative of Arthur Gordon Pym*," *Bulletin of Bibliography*, 38 (1981), 117.

3. Ibid., 119–27; Douglas Robinson, "Reading Poe's Novel: A Speculative Review of *Pym* Criticism, 1950–1980," *Poe Studies*, 15 (1982), 52–54.

4. Richard Wilbur, introduction to *The Narrative of Arthur Gordon Pym* (Boston: Godine, 1973), p. x; Malcolm Cowley, "Aidgarpo," *New Republic*, 5 November 1945, 610.

5. For the "shrouded human figure" as death, see Joseph J. Moldenhauer, "Imagination and Perversity in *The Narrative of Arthur Gordon Pym*," *Texas Studies in Literature and Language*, 13 (1971), 267; and William Peden, "Prologue to a Dark Journey: The 'Opening' to Poe's *Pym*," in *Papers on Poe: Essays in Honor of John Ward Ostrom*, ed. Richard P. Veler (Springfield, Ohio: Chantry Music Press, 1972), p. 89. For *Pym*'s apparition as a death-conquering Lazarus figure, see Paul John Eakin, "Poe's Sense of an Ending," *American Literature*, 45 (1973), 15–22. The figure is considered emblematic of knowledge in Charles O'Donnell, "From Earth to Ether: Poe's Flight into Space," *PMLA*, 77 (1962), 87–89, and in Helen Lee, "Possibilities of *Pym*," *English Journal*, 55 (1966), 1153; it is read as signifying the limits of knowledge in Maurice Levy, "*Pym*, Conte Fantastique?" *Études Anglaises*, 27 (1974), 44. For the figure as goodness, see John H. Stroupe, "Poe's Imaginary Voyage: Pym as Hero," *Studies in Short Fiction*, 4 (1967), 320; for its symbolizing perversity, see James M. Cox, "Edgar Poe: Style as Pose," *Virginia Quarterly Review*, 44 (1968), 77. The imagination is suggested by Pym's enigmatic vision according to Todd M. Leiber, "The Apocalyptic Imagination of A. Gordon Pym," in *Endless Experiments—Essays on the Heroic Experience in American Romanticism* (Columbus: Ohio State University Press, 1973), p. 188, and Daniel A. Wells, "Engraved within the Hills: Further Perspectives on the Ending of *Pym*," *Poe Studies*, 10 (1977), 13–14; the narrative itself is intimated by that vision in J. Gerald Kennedy, *Poe, Death, and the Life of Writing* (New Haven: Yale University Press, 1987), pp. 172–73; and the white at the bottom of the page is implied by the

white figure according to Jean Ricardou, "'The Singular Character of the Water,'" *Poe Studies*, 9 (1976), 4–5. Kent P. Ljungquist reads the "shrouded human figure" as a Titan in "Poe and the Sublime: His Sea Tales in an Aesthetic Tradition," in *The Grand and the Fair: Poe's Landscape Aesthetics and Pictorial Techniques* (Potomac, Md.: Scripta Humanistica, 1984), pp. 56–72; see also Ljungquist's "'Speculative Mythology' and the Titan Myth in Poe's *Pym* and Melville's *Pierre*," *The Sphinx*, 4 (1985), 250–57. The figure is treated as a divinity in numerous works: Marie Bonaparte, *The Life and Works of Edgar Allan Poe: A Psycho-analytic Interpretation*, trans. John Rodker (London: Imago, 1949), pp. 350–51; Leslie Fiedler, *Love and Death in the American Novel* (1960; rpt., New York: Stein and Day, 1975), pp. 394–400; Walter E. Bezanson, "The Troubled Sleep of Arthur Gordon Pym," in *Essays in Literary History Presented to J. Milton French*, ed. Rudolph Kirk and C. F. Main (New Brunswick: Rutgers University Press, 1960), pp. 172–73; Richard A. Levine, "The Downward Journey of Purgation—Notes on an Imagistic Leitmotif in *The Narrative of Arthur Gordon Pym*," *Poe Newsletter*, 2 (1969), 31; David M. LaGuardia, "Poe, *Pym*, and Initiation," *ESQ: A Journal of the American Renaissance*, 60 (1970), 83; Haldeen Braddy, *Three Dimensional Poe* (El Paso: Texas Western Press, 1973), p. 38; Robert L. Carringer, "Circumscription of Space and the Form of Poe's *Arthur Gordon Pym*," *PMLA*, 89 (1974), 514; John P. Hussey, "'Mr. Pym' and 'Mr. Poe': The Two Narrators of 'Arthur Gordon Pym,'" *South Atlantic Bulletin*, 39 (1974), 26–30; and Kathleen Sands, "The Mythic Initiation of Arthur Gordon Pym," *Poe Studies*, 7 (1974), 16. The figure is linked specifically to Christ in Sidney Kaplan's introduction to *The Narrative of Arthur Gordon Pym* (New York: Hill and Wang, 1960), pp. xxii–xxiii; Wilbur's introduction, p. xxiv; and Richard Kopley, "The '*Very* Profound Under-current' of *Arthur Gordon Pym*," in *Studies in the American Renaissance 1987*, ed. Joel Myerson (Charlottesville: University Press of Virginia, 1987), pp. 151–57. (Introductory to this last essay are "The Secret of *Arthur Gordon Pym*: The Text and the Source," *Studies in American Fiction*, 8 [Autumn 1980], 203–18, and "The Hidden Journey of *Arthur Gordon Pym*," in *Studies in the American Renaissance 1982*, ed. Joel Myerson [Boston: Twayne Publishers, 1982], pp. 29–51.) That the "shrouded human figure" is Pym's "white shadow" is argued in John T. Irwin, *American Hieroglyphics: The Symbol of the Egyptian Hieroglyphics in the American Renaissance* (New Haven: Yale University Press, 1980), pp. 205–35. The "shadow thesis" is developed by Douglas Robinson in "Dream's Body," in *American Apocalypses: The Image of the End of the World in American Literature* (Baltimore: Johns Hopkins University Press, 1985), pp. 116–21. For an overview of scholarly commentary on the "shrouded human figure" as of 1981, see P 1:356–59.

6. Robinson, "Reading Poe's Novel," 47.

Beegel: "Mutiny and Atrocious Butchery"

I would like to thank the staffs of the Nantucket Atheneum and the Nantucket Historical Association's Research Center for their assistance with this project. Nantucket librarian Louise Hussey and island historian Edouard Stackpole have been especially generous with their advice. Editor Richard Kopley has improved this paper substantially with numerous suggestions, and, as always, I have relied on my husband Wes Tiffney's knowledge of matters nautical.

1. The quotation is from the title page of the first American edition of *Pym*, published by the New York firm of Harper and Brothers in 1838. See *P* 1:53.

2. Alexander Starbuck, *History of the American Whale Fishery* (Secaucus, N.J.: Castle Books, 1989), p. 243.

3. The following brief history of the *Globe* mutiny is derived chiefly from three primary sources, each written by one or more participants in the drama. See William Lay and Cyrus Hussey, *A Narrative of the Mutiny on Board the Whaleship Globe of Nantucket* (New London: William Bolles, 1828); Lieutenant Hiram Paulding, *Journal of a Cruise of the United States Schooner Dolphin . . . In Pursuit of the Mutineers of the Whaleship Globe* (New York: G. & C. & H. Carvill, 1831); and William Comstock, *The Life of Samuel Comstock, The Terrible Whaleman* (Boston: James Fisher, 1840). I have also relied heavily on secondary sources by the *Globe* mutiny's preeminent historian, Edouard A. Stackpole: *The Sea-Hunters: The Great Age of Whaling* (Philadelphia: J. B. Lippincott, 1953), pp. 413–33; *The Mutiny on the Whaleship Globe: A True Story of the Sea* (Nantucket: Edouard A. Stackpole, 1981); and his introduction to William Lay and Cyrus Hussey's narrative, reprinted in New York by Corinth Books, 1963. Stackpole's years of painstaking research on the subject have resulted in the discovery and reprinting of numerous additional primary materials. Where those primary materials are in conflict, I have accepted Stackpole's carefully judged interpretation of events.

4. Unlike most mutinies, the tragedy on board the *Globe* does not seem to have been inspired by the officers' ill-usage of the crew or unusually harsh conditions, but rather by the charismatic insanity of Nantucket boatsteerer Samuel Comstock. Anyone doubting this is invited to compare *The Life of Samuel Comstock, The Terrible Whaleman*, by the mutineer's younger brother William, with any standard profile of criminal psychosis.

5. Stackpole, *Mutiny*, pp. 26–27.

6. Lay and Hussey, *Narrative of the Mutiny*, reprinted in the American Experience Series, ed. Henry Bamford Parkes (New York: Corinth Books,

1963), p. 43. Subsequent page citations of the 1963 edition will be given in parentheses in the text.

7. Stackpole, *Mutiny*, p. 66.

8. Ibid. In 1843, when Herman Melville shipped on board the frigate *United States* to earn his passage home, he met Catesby-Jones, by then a commodore, and one whose Pacific fleet echoed its commander's enthusiasm for flogging the rebellious. See Leon Howard, *Herman Melville: A Biography* (Berkeley: University of California Press, 1951), pp. 74, 84–85.

9. Stackpole, *Mutiny*, p. 66.

10. Comstock, *The Life of Samuel Comstock*, p. 115.

11. See Hervey Allen, *Israfel: The Life and Times of Edgar Allan Poe*, 2nd ed. (New York: Farrar and Rinehart, 1934), pp. 160–61, 163–69; Arthur Hobson Quinn, *Edgar Allan Poe: A Critical Biography* (New York: D. Appleton-Century, 1941; New York: Cooper Square, 1969), pp. 118–19, 129; and Dwight Thomas and David K. Jackson, *The Poe Log: A Documentary Life of Edgar Allan Poe 1809–1849* (Boston: G. K. Hall, 1987), pp. 78–81.

12. See *Boston Patriot and Mercantile Advertiser*, 26 April 1827, p. [2], col. 3; *Boston Daily Advertiser*, 26 April 1827, p. [2], col. 3; *New England Palladium and Commercial Advertiser*, 27 April 1827, p. [1], col. 4; and *Boston Courier*, p. [2], col. 4 (Boston Public Library).

13. See *Boston Patriot* as cited in the Nantucket *Inquirer*, 26 Aug. 1826 (Nantucket Atheneum), and Stackpole, *Mutiny*, p. 37.

14. J. N. Reynolds, *Report to the Secretary of the Navy*, 23rd Congress, 2nd Session, House Document no. 105 (January 1835).

15. Stackpole, *Mutiny*, p. 9.

16. See J. N. Reynolds, *Report to the Secretary*; and Reynolds to Macy, Tuck, Mitchell, Gardner, and West, 19 Aug. 1828, in the Nantucket *Inquirer*, 23 Aug. 1828 (Nantucket Atheneum).

17. Stackpole, *Mutiny*, p. 9.

18. An incomplete survey shows articles on the *Globe* mutiny appearing in issues of the Nantucket *Inquirer* for 15 Nov. 1824, 29 Nov. 1824, 22 May 1825, 26 Aug. 1826, 28 Oct. 1826, 19 May 1827, and 29 May 1829 (Nantucket Atheneum).

19. Stackpole, *The Sea-Hunters*, p. 462.

20. Stackpole, *Mutiny*, pp. 9–11.

21. Stackpole, *The Sea-Hunters*, p. 465.

22. *Boston Patriot*, 26 April 1827, p. [2], col. 3.

23. Stackpole, *The Sea-Hunters*, p. 465. See also J. N. Reynolds, *The Voyage of the United States Frigate Potomac Around the World* (New York: Harper and Brothers, 1835).

24. Stackpole, *Mutiny*, p. 61.

25. Paulding, *Journal of a Cruise*, p. iii. I am indebted to Edouard Stackpole for loaning me his copy of this rare book.

26. For extended discussion of Reynolds' influence on Poe, see Robert Lee Rhea, "Some Observations on Poe's Origins," *University of Texas Studies in English*, 10 (8 July 1930), 135–46; Robert F. Almy, "J. N. Reynolds: A Brief Biography with Particular Reference to Poe and Symmes," *Colophon*, n.s. 2 (Winter 1937), 227–45; Aubrey Starke, "Poe's Friend Reynolds," *American Literature*, 2 (March 1939–Jan. 1940), 152–59; Daniel J. Tynan, "J. N. Reynolds' *Voyage of the Potomac*: Another Source for *The Narrative of Arthur Gordon Pym*," *Poe Studies*, 4 (Dec. 1971), 35–37; Richard Kopley, "The Secret of *Arthur Gordon Pym*: The Text and the Source," *Studies in American Fiction*, 8 (Autumn 1980), 203–18; Kopley, "The Hidden Journey of *Arthur Gordon Pym*," in *Studies in the American Renaissance 1982*, ed. Joel Myerson (Boston: Twayne Publishers, 1982), pp. 29–31; Richard G. Woodbridge III, "J. N. Reynolds: Father of American Exploration," *Princeton University Library Chronicle*, 45 (Winter 1984), pp. 107–21; and W. T. Bandy, "Dr. Moran and the Poe-Reynolds Myth," in *Myths and Reality: The Mysterious Mr. Poe*, ed. Benjamin Franklin Fisher IV (Baltimore: The Edgar Allan Poe Society, 1987), pp. 26–36.

27. Edgar Allan Poe, review of J. N. Reynolds' *Address on the Subject of a Surveying and Exploring Expedition to the Pacific Ocean and the South Seas, Southern Literary Messenger*, 3 (January 1837), p. 70; or H 9:314.

28. In a letter of 19 January 1837, T. W. White wrote, "I formed an acquaintance with him [J. N. Reynolds] in this city [Richmond] about 10 years ago, and absolutely became almost devotedly attached to the fellow. . . . To me he owes the favor he has received in the Messenger. . . ." See David K. Jackson, *Poe and The Southern Literary Messenger* (Richmond: Dietz Printing Co., 1934), p. 111.

29. Stackpole, *Mutiny*, p. 9.

30. Paulding, *Journal of a Cruise*, p. 145.

31. Ibid.

32. Ibid.

33. D. M. McKeithan, "Two Sources of Poe's *Narrative of Arthur Gordon Pym*," *University of Texas Studies in English*, 13 (8 July 1933), 117–18.

34. Ibid., p. 118.

35. Keith Huntress, "Another Source of Poe's *Narrative of Arthur Gordon Pym*," *American Literature*, 16 (March 1944–Jan. 1945), 22.

36. Herman Melville, *Moby-Dick, or The Whale*, ed. Harrison Hayford, Hershel Parker, and G. Thomas Tanselle, vol. 6 of *The Writings of Herman Melville* (Evanston and Chicago: Northwestern University Press and The Newberry Library, 1988), pp. xxvi–xxvii.

37. Howard, *Herman Melville*, pp. 70–71. *The Oxford Companion to*

Ships and the Sea indicates that the frigate *United States* had a remark-ably long life. One of the "six original frigates" of the U.S. Navy, she was completed at Philadelphia in 1798 and survived until burned by the Con-federates at Norfolk in 1862. No other ship bearing the name *United States* has ever been built. My thanks to Wesley N. Tiffney, Jr. for locating this information.

38. Charles Olson, *Call Me Ishmael: A Study of Melville* (San Francisco: City Lights Books, 1947), pp. 77–85.

39. Stackpole, *Mutiny*, p. 7.

Mead: Poe's "Manual of 'Seamanship' "

1. For Poe's borrowings from Benjamin Morrell's 1832 *Narrative of Four Voyages* in the digressions of chapters 12, 14–16, and 20, see D. M. McKeithan, "Two Sources of Poe's 'Narrative of Arthur Gordon Pym,' " *University of Texas Studies in English*, 23 (1933), 127–37. That Morrell's *Narrative* was a ghostwritten mixture of fact, exaggeration, and outright fabrication (a point which Poe may or may not have known) is discussed by Burton R. Pollin, "The *Narrative* of Benjamin Morrell: Out of 'The Bucket' and into Poe's *Pym*," *Studies in American Fiction*, 4 (1976), 157–72. For the close relationship between J. N. Reynolds' 1836 *Address on the Subject of a Surveying and Exploring Expedition to the Pacific Ocean and South Seas* and the digression in chapter 16, see R. L. Rhea, "Some Observations on Poe's Origins," *University of Texas Studies in English*, 10 (1930), 135–44.

2. George Edward Woodberry, Notes to *Narrative of Arthur Gordon Pym*, vol. 5 of *The Works of Edgar Allan Poe*, ed. Edmund Clarence Stedman and George Edward Woodberry (Chicago: Stone and Kimball, 1895), 359.

3. In his notes on both passages in vol. 1 of *Collected Writings of Edgar Allan Poe*, Burton Pollin repeats Woodberry's idea of the source being an unidentified "manual of 'Seamanship.' " See pp. 251, 256.

4. See J. V. Ridgely, "The Growth of the Text" (*P* 1:31–32), for his theory that "Stage II" of *Pym*, encompassing the section from chapter 4, paragraph 4 (the end of the second *Messenger* installment) through chapter 13, was undertaken soon after Poe was settled in New York by February 1837. Be-sides noting several changes made in the *Messenger* installments, Ridgely observes that "Stage II" can be delineated because in it Poe relied heavily on "books of voyage narratives, specifically collections of short pieces which nearly always dealt with marine disasters" (*P* 1:32).

5. Early in 1836, Harper and Brothers decided not to publish Poe's *Tales of the Folio Club*, in part because a large number of the tales had already ap-peared in print. Poe's friend James K. Paulding, himself a successful author with Harper and Brothers, encouraged Poe to write a "series of original Tales" or a "single work" (*P* 1:5).

6. For example, see E. M. Blunt, *Seamanship*, 2nd ed. (New York, 1824); Nathaniel Bowditch, *The New American Practical Navigator*, 7th ed. (New York, 1832); William Falconer, *A New Universal Dictionary of the Marine* (London, 1769; ed. William Burney, 1815); Alexander Dingwall Fordyce, *Outlines of Naval Routine* (London, 1837); W. N. Glascock, *Naval Service or Officers' Manual* (London, 1836); Richard Hall Gower, *A Treatise on the Theory and Practice of Seamanship* (London, 1808); Anselm John Griffiths, *Observations on Some Points of Seamanship* (Cheltenham, 1824); Darcy Lever, *The Young Sea Officer's Sheet Anchor*, (London, 1808; 2nd. ed. 1819 (?); rpt., Charles E. Lauriat Co., 1930); Charles Lorimer, *Letters to a Young Master Mariner* (London, 1835); Sir Henry Manwayring, *The Sea-mans Dictionary* (London, 1644); J. J. Moore, *The Mariner's Dictionary* (Washington City, 1805). Also see the comprehensive bibliography in John Harland, *Seamanship in the Age of Sail* (Naval Institute Press, 1984), pp. 313–15.

7. Pollin comments, "As a view of maritime reality, this entire paragraph must be humorously offered by Poe. The screwing or tight packing with braces of cargo is used only for bale goods, and only when a whole section is being made up. Barrel, box, crate, and other noncompressable containers are never screwed; obviously Poe's specified conditions would entirely break them" (*P* 1:251).

8. Peter Kemp, ed., *The Oxford Companion to Ships and the Sea* (London: Oxford University Press, 1976), p. 780.

9. See *P* 1:252.

10. From the title page of the 1780 edition of Falconer's *Dictionary*, which adds "By William Falconer, author of *The Shipwreck*. A New Edition, Corrected. London: Printed for T. Cadell, in the Strand. MDCCLXXX" (rpt., David and Charpes Reprints, 1970).

11. For a brief, insightful discussion of *The Shipwreck*, see Thomas Philbrick, *James Fenimore Cooper and the Development of American Sea Fiction* (Cambridge, Mass.: Harvard University Press, 1961), pp. 11–12. The tribute to Falconer's poem is from J. S. Clarke's "Biographical Memoir of William Falconer" (London: printed for William Miller, 1811), p. xxix. Within the "Memoir," Clarke states that "Falconer's principal amusement always consisted in literary occupation," adding that the purpose of his memoir is to "induce my Countrymen to honour the watery Grave of the shipwrecked Falconer" (pp. xl, lii).

12. Preface to the 1780 edition of the *Dictionary*.

13. William Burney, preface to the 1815 edition of the *Dictionary*. The title page reads "London: printed for T. Cadell & W. Davies in the Strand; and J. Murray, Bookseller to the Admiralty, 50, Albemarle-Street 1815." See also the entry under "Burney, William" in S. Austin Allibone's *A Critical Dictionary of English Literature, and British and American Authors* (Philadelphia: Childes and Peterson, 1859), 1:301.

14. See n. 6.

15. Phyllis M. Young, head of Public Services, Virginia State Library, Richmond, Va. (letter to author, 10 March 1987), stated that this library's copy of Falconer's *Dictionary* was purchased in 1953. Claire J. Roth, Director of the Mercantile Library of New York, supplied the information about the copy in the Mercantile Library which Poe may have used (letters to author, 5 March and 17 March 1987). Copies of the *Dictionary* in the New York Historical Society and the Library of Columbia University were acquired after the mid-1850s and so were not available to Poe.

16. See Bowditch, *Practical Navigator*, p. 257; Fordyce, "Routine in Laying To," in *Naval Routine*, pp. 139–41; Gower, *Treatise*, pp. 45–50; Griffiths, *Observations*, pp. 199–200, on "Laying-Too"; Lever, *Sheet Anchor*, p. 89; and Manwayring, *Dictionary*, p. 64, an entry titled "Lie under the sea." J. J. Moore's *The Mariner's Dictionary* (Washington City, 1805) copies entries from Falconer. *The Nautical Magazine*, published in London, discusses "Lying to at Sea" in vol. 5 (1836), pp. 211–12.

17. Lever, *Sheet Anchor*, pp. 89–90.

18. All citations within the text are to the 1815 edition of Falconer's *Dictionary* (see n. 6).

19. Harland, *Seamanship*, p. 213.

20. The guides to seamanship which were current in Poe's day treated their discussions of lying to and scudding as separate items. Bowditch has separate entries concerning lying to (in a gale of wind, under various sails), followed by another entry, "On scudding or bearing away in a storm" (*Practical Navigator*, pp. 274–77). Fordyce separates descriptions of the "Routine in Laying to" and "Scudding" by four sections, (*Naval Routine*, pp. 139–44). In Gower's *Treatise*, the section "Of Lying-to in a Gale of Wind" is followed by two sections concerning a floating anchor and then by "Upon Reefing" before the section "Upon Scudding before the Wind in a hard Gale" (pp. 45–50, 54). Lever gives instructions for maneuvering a ship from "Lying To under Different Sails" to "Waring" to "Waring under Bare Poles" to "Scudding" (*Sheet Anchor*, pp. 89–91).

21. Poe's insistence on the foresail and his mention of the jib for lying to appear to be his own ideas. There could be no strict rules for what canvas to use while lying to since that depended upon the immediate conditions of wind and water. Consider the variety of sails recommended by these sources: Bowditch observes that "there are some ships which lie-to better under the foresail than mainsail, others are more easy under the mainsail, some under a mizen, and many vessels lie-to best under a main staysail" (*Practical Navigator*, pp. 273–74). Fordyce names the "Fore Staysail and Fore Trysail, with or without Main Topsail, according to the violence of the wind and other circumstances" (*Naval Routine*, p. 139). Gower states

that "the best sails to lie-to under are, a reefed fore-top-sail, mizen stay-sail, and storm-mizen, with the helm so much a-lee as is found best to answer the purpose" (*Treatise*, p. 49). Lever lists the mizen staysail (with and without the mizen), a close-reefed main topsail, a main staysail, the three lower staysails and the mizen, the foresail, and lying to under bare poles (*Sheet Anchor*, pp. 89–90). Manwayring states that "Trying is to have no more sail forth, but the mainsail, the tack aboard, the bowline set up, the sheet close aft, and the helm tied down close aboard. Some try with their mizzen only, but that is when it blows so much that they cannot maintain the mainsail" (*Dictionary*, p. 250, cited in Harland, *Seamanship*, p. 213). No source mentions using the jib for lying to.

22. See Burton R. Pollin, ed., *Word Index to Poe's Fiction* (New York: Gordian Press, 1982), pp. 311, 378.

23. Gower states that "great care must be taken to have an excellent helmsman, a compass by the tiller, and careful people to attend the re-lieving tackles, as, either through want of experience in the helmsman, or the breaking of a tiller-rope, the ship may be broached-to, and many ill consequences follow" (*Treatise*, p. 55). Pollin states that Poe's idea of an unattended helm is "preposterous" (P 1:256).

24. John McLeod Murphy and W. N. Jeffers, Jr., *Nautical Routine and Stowage, with Short Rules in Navigation* (New York: Henry Spear, 1849). Murphy became a state senator in New York and also wrote another book, *American Ships and Ship-builders*, which was published in New York by C. W. Baker in 1860. Jeffers eventually attained the naval rank of commo-dore, and he wrote five other books, on the subjects of gunnery, armament, and nautical surveying, according to the *Catalogue of Works by American Naval Authors*, compiled by Lieutenant Lucien Young and published by the Bureau of Navigation, Navy Department, Washington, D.C., 1888.

25. Murphy and Jeffers, *Nautical Routine*, pp. 39, 40.

26. "Am Pub." does not stand for the title of any known American book, newspaper, or periodical (citations checked in Sabin, title index to Gregory, and the *Union List of Serials*, respectively). Murphy may well have used this abbreviation to disguise his use of the passages from the American publication *The Narrative of Arthur Gordon Pym*.

Dameron: *Pym's* Polar Episode

1. See Douglas Robinson's "Reading Poe's Novel: A Speculative Review of *Pym* Criticism, 1950–1980," *Poe Studies*, 15 (1982), 47–54, for a brief informative discussion of interpretive readings of *Pym*. Perhaps the most perceptive recent interpretation is John T. Irwin, *American Hieroglyphics: The Symbol of the Egyptian Hieroglyphics in the American Renaissance* (New

Haven: Yale University Press, 1980), pp. 205–35. Irwin proposes that the figure at the pole is Poe's "own shadow," resembling "numerous examples of the trope of the white shadow in Romantic tradition" (p. 205). See also Richard Kopley's "The '*Very* Profound Under-Current' of *Arthur Gordon Pym*," in *Studies in the American Renaissance 1987*, ed. Joel Myerson (Charlottesville: University Press of Virginia, 1987), pp. 143–75.

2. William Scoresby, Jr., *Journal of a Voyage to the Northern Whale-Fishery; Including Researches and Discoveries on the Eastern Coast of West Greenland, Made in the Summer of 1822, in the Ship Baffin of Liverpool* (1823; rpt., Yorkshire, England: Scolar Press, 1980). Subsequent citations of this volume will be given in parentheses in the text.

3. Merton M. Sealts, Jr., *Melville's Reading: A Check-List of Books Owned and Borrowed* (Madison: University of Wisconsin Press, 1966), pp. 91–92.

4. Alfred Kazin, *An American Procession: The Major American Writers from 1830 to 1930, the Crucial Century* (New York: Knopf, 1984), p. 95.

5. Harold Bloom, "Inescapable Poe," review of *Edgar Allan Poe: Poetry and Tales*, ed. Patrick F. Quinn, and *Edgar Allan Poe: Essays and Reviews*, ed. G. R. Thompson, *New York Review of Books*, 11 Oct. 1984, p. 34.

6. Richard Kopley, "The Secret of *Arthur Gordon Pym*: The Text and the Source," *Studies in American Fiction*, 8 (1980), 203–18.

7. David Brewster, review of *Narrative of a Second Voyage in Search of a Northwest Passage . . .* , by Sir John Ross, *Edinburgh Review*, 61 (July 1835), p. 420.

8. Poe, like other Romantics, alludes to cataracts throughout his works. See Poe's "Hans Phaall" (*P* 1:417) and his 1831 lyric "The Valley of Unrest" (*M* 1:192). In *Pym*, Poe likely intended a cataract of mist, rather than one of rushing water. See, also, Captain Adam Seaborn's (pseud.) *Symzonia; Voyage of Discovery*, introduction by J. O. Bailey, ed. Harry W. Warfel (1820; Gainesville: Scholars' Facsimiles & Reprints, 1965) for an account of a hurricane which "gave the whole face of the ocean the appearance of one immense cataract" (p. 230). According to J. O. Bailey, *Symzonia* is a likely source for *Pym* (see p. 3).

9. See *Symzonia*, p. 231, for a description "of a sea of liquid fire, boiling and whirling with ceaseless agitation."

Weiner: Novels, Tales, and Problems of Form in *Arthur Gordon Pym*

1. Duyckinck Family Papers, Literary Correspondence of E. A. Duyckinck, Rare Books and Manuscripts Division, New York Public Library, Astor, Lenox and Tilden Foundations.

2. Duyckinck's and Mathews' roles in New York literary circles are discussed by Perry Miller, *The Raven and the Whale: The War of Words and*

Wits in the Era of Poe and Melville (New York: Harcourt, Brace, 1956); John P. Pritchard, *Literary Wise Men of Gotham* (Baton Rouge: Louisiana State University Press, 1963); and John Stafford, *The Literary Criticism of "Young America": A Study in the Relationship of Politics and Literature, 1837–1850* (Berkeley: University of California Press, 1952). The rise of New York as literary center and Harpers' role in publishing American fiction are discussed by William Charvat, *Literary Publishing in America, 1790–1850* (Philadelphia: University of Pennsylvania Press, 1959) and Eugene Exman, *The Brothers Harper* (New York: Harper and Row, 1965).

3. Poe toasted "The *Monthlies* of Gotham" at the 30 March 1837 Booksellers Dinner; see Dwight Thomas and David K. Jackson, *The Poe Log: A Documentary Life of Edgar Allan Poe, 1809–1849* (Boston: G. K. Hall, 1987), p. 243.

4. Quoted in Thomas and Jackson, *The Poe Log*, p. 212. Another prominent publisher, Henry C. Carey, wrote John Pendleton Kennedy in 1834 about Poe's efforts to publish his tales: "Writing is a very poor business unless a man can find the way of taking the public attention, and *that is not often done by short stories*. People want something larger and longer" (Thomas and Jackson, *Poe Log*, p. 142). Writing Poe after Harpers had rejected his tales, James Kirke Paulding advised him to "undertake a Tale in a couple of volumes, for that is the magical number" (*The Letters of James Kirke Paulding*, ed. Ralph M. Aderman [Madison: University of Wisconsin Press, 1962], p. 178).

5. See Joseph V. Ridgely, "The Growth of the Text" (*P* 1:29–36). This essay revises slightly conclusions drawn by Ridgely and Iola S. Haverstick in "Chartless Voyage: The Many Narratives of Arthur Gordon Pym," *Texas Studies in Literature and Language*, 8 (1966), 63–80.

6. See Joseph V. Ridgely, "Tragical-Mythical-Satirical-Hoaxical: Problems of Genre in *Pym*," *American Transcendental Quarterly*, 24 (Fall 1974), 4–9; and Sidney P. Moss, "*Arthur Gordon Pym*, or The Fallacy of Thematic Interpretation," *University Review*, 23 (1967), 299–306.

7. Modern critical responses to *Pym* are surveyed by Ridgely, "Genre in *Pym*," and Douglas Robinson, "Reading Poe's Novel: A Speculative Review of *Pym* Criticism," *Poe Studies*, 15 (December 1982), 47–54.

8. Poe also wrote briefer, less consequential notices of Longfellow's *Outre-Mer* and Eliza Leslie's *Pencil Sketches* for the June 1835 *Messenger* (1:594–95).

9. A representative sampling of reaction to Poe's contributions to the *Messenger* in 1835 and 1836 can be found in Thomas and Jackson, *Poe Log*, pp. 151–237. For Poe's views of the advantages of periodical publishing, see *O* 1:162 and *P* 2:248.

10. Poe's contempt for the "sustained effort" of the novelist may be a re-

action to criticism of his early tales. The *Baltimore American* describes "The Duc de L'Omelette," which appeared in the February 1836 *Messenger*, as "one of those light, spirited, fantastic inventions . . . betokening a fertility of imagination and power of execution, that with discipline, could, under a sustained effort, produce creations of enduring character" (Thomas and Jackson, *Poe Log*, p. 194). Similar criticism of Poe's first sea tale, "MS. Found in a Bottle," was conveyed by Thomas White to Poe shortly before he began to write *Pym* (Thomas and Jackson, *Poe Log*, p. 182).

11. Nina Baym, *Novels, Readers, and Reviewers: Responses to Fiction in Antebellum America* (Ithaca, N.Y.: Cornell University Press, 1984), pp. 63–81.

12. As in the case of *Pym*, Poe's intentions in his early tales are not clear. See Alexander Hammond, " 'Lionizing' and the Design of Poe's *Tales of the Folio Club*," *Emerson Society Quarterly*, 18 (1972), 154–65 and "Edgar Allan Poe's *Tales of the Folio Club*: The Evolution of a Lost Book," in *Poe At Work: Seven Textual Studies*, ed. Benjamin Franklin Fisher IV (Baltimore: The Edgar Allan Poe Society, 1978), pp. 13–43; G. R. Thompson, *Poe's Fiction: Romantic Irony in the Gothic Tales* (Madison: University of Wisconsin Press, 1973), pp. 39–67; Richard P. Benton, "Is Poe's 'The Assignation' a Hoax?," *Nineteenth Century Fiction*, 18 (1963), 193–97; and Benjamin Franklin Fisher IV, "Poe's 'Metzengerstein': Not a Hoax," *American Literature*, 42 (1971), 487–94.

13. *Letters of James Kirke Paulding*, p. 174.

14. Burton R. Pollin, "Poe's *Narrative of Arthur Gordon Pym* and the Contemporary Reviewers," *Studies in American Fiction*, 2 (1974), 43.

15. Burton R. Pollin, "*Pym* and the Contemporary Reviewers," 44. The terms of novelistic unity were sometimes applied to tales, too. One reviewer found Poe's "The Visionary—A Tale" (later titled "The Assignation"), which appeared in the July 1835 *Messenger*, a "wild, imaginative, romantic tale, full of deep interest, which however is left too much ungratified" (Thomas & Jackson, *Poe Log*, p. 170).

16. On this point I concur with Alexander Hammond in "The Composition of *The Narrative of Arthur Gordon Pym*: Notes toward a Reexamination," *American Transcendental Quarterly*, 37 (Winter 1978), 17. Pollin sees a consistent "practice of parody" in Poe's handling of sources but no unifying theme (*P* 1:9–12).

17. See *O* 1:57–59 for Poe's defense of his early stories. Arguing in his review of Hawthorne that "terror, or passion, or horror" are legitimate subjects for the prose tale, Poe condemns the prejudice of "the usual animadversions against those *tales of effect,* many fine examples of which were found in the earlier numbers of Blackwood" (*H* 11:109).

18. See, for example, in *Blackwood's*, "The Buried Alive," 10 (1821),

262–64; "The Man in the Bell," 10 (1821), 373–75; "Singular Recovery from Death," 10 (1821), 582–87; "Le Revenant," 21 (1827), 409–16; and "The Involuntary Experimentalist," 42 (1837), 487–92. Poe's parody of these tales, I might note, in "Loss of Breath" (1832), "How to Write a Blackwood Article" (1838), and "A Predicament" (1838), mimics similar parody in *Blackwood's* and extends the rationalism of the tales of effect. I discuss their epistemology and influence in "Poe and the *Blackwood's* Tale of Sensation," in *Poe and His Times: The Artist and His Milieu*, ed. Benjamin F. Fisher IV (Baltimore: The Edgar Allan Poe Society, 1990), pp. 45–65. On Poe and *Blackwood's*, see also Margaret Alterton, *Origins of Poe's Critical Theory* (Iowa City: University of Iowa, 1925; New York: Russell & Russell, 1965); Michael Allen, *Poe and the British Magazine Tradition* (New York: Oxford University Press, 1969); and Benjamin F. Fisher IV, "Blackwood Articles à la Poe: How to Make a False Start Pay," *Revue des Langues Vivantes*, 39 (1973), 418–32, and "Poe's 'Tarr and Fether': Hoaxing in the Blackwood Mode," *Topic*, 31 (1977), 29–40.

19. David Ketterer, *The Rationale of Deception in Poe* (Baton Rouge: Louisiana State University Press, 1979), p. 125. Poe recast the serialized text slightly for book publication, adding a sentence just before the first episode ("I will relate one of these adventures by way of introduction to a longer and more momentous narrative" [*P* 1:57–58]) and making some other changes which suggest that he had not planned out a whole novel carefully when he began and that his conception of it changed when he left off serialization and began to think more immediately about book publication. Ketterer is right, however, in recognizing that Poe repeats essentially the pattern of the first episode throughout the narrative.

20. Edward Davidson, *Poe: A Critical Study* (Cambridge, Mass.: Harvard University Press, 1957), p. 169.

21. Patrick F. Quinn, *The French Face of Edgar Poe* (Carbondale: Southern Illinois University Press, 1954), p. 203.

22. Paul John Eakin, "Poe's Sense of an Ending," *American Literature*, 45 (1973), 1–22. According to G. R. Thompson, Poe employs the "explained Gothic" mode ironically in his tales to express a radical skepticism, a sense of the "deceptive illusoriness of the world" and the inability of the mind to penetrate it. Although his discussion of the "explained Gothic" does not extend explicitly to *Pym*, Thompson's conclusions about the novel follow from it. *Pym*, in his view, is a "gigantic hoax . . . played upon rational man" (*Poe's Fiction*, pp. 68–104, 176–83). Thompson enlarges his argument, primarily to establish an affinity between Poe's ironic vision and postmodernism, in "Romantic Arabesque, Contemporary Theory, and Postmodernism: The Example of Poe's *Narrative*," *ESQ: A Journal of the American Renaissance*, 35 (1989), 163–271. In order to make a case for the

significance of *Pym* as "arabesque," Thompson ignores the circumstances of its composition, Poe's sources, the pattern of "explained Gothic," and frames of reference other than German romantic irony which influenced Poe, such as the Scottish philosophy of common sense that permeated *Blackwood's*, and assumes a unity of vision and design in *Pym* that, in my view, is unsupported by the text and the circumstances of its composition. My contention is that Poe was ambivalent rather than skeptical, using the "explained Gothic" to rein in romantic imagination, which reason perceives as delusive and destructive. I agree with Douglas Robinson that Poe's intention in his best tales and *Pym* is "not to move beyond the spatial or temporal boundary [of human life and common sense] but to stand *at* it and thus achieve a dual vision—of earth in terms of God's transcendental universe and the universe in terms of our present life on earth" (*American Apocalypses: The Image of the End of the World in American Literature* [Baltimore: Johns Hopkins University Press, 1985], p. 111). Standing *at* the boundary, I would argue, is consistent with Eakin's idea of approach and return, suggesting ambivalence toward imaginative and rational modes of experience, vision and explanation (or narration). The duality is not always contained, as Thompson would have it, by a romantic irony that playfully and skeptically denies all truths.

23. See, for example, John T. Irwin, *American Hieroglyphics: The Symbol of the Egyptian Hieroglyphics in the American Renaissance* (Baltimore: Johns Hopkins University Press, 1980), pp. 43–235; John Carlos Rowe, *Through the Custom House* (Baltimore: Johns Hopkins University Press, 1983), pp. 91–110; J. Gerald Kennedy, *Poe, Death, and the Life of Writing* (New Haven: Yale University Press, 1987), pp. 145–76; and Michael J. S. Williams, *A World of Words: Language and Displacement in the Fiction of Edgar Allan Poe* (Durham: Duke University Press, 1988), pp. 125–27.

24. Morse Peckham employs the term "negative Romanticism" in "Toward a Theory of Romanticism," *PMLA*, 66 (1951), 5–23, to describe a frame of mind in transition between Enlightenment and Romantic thought, which has abandoned static rationalism but not yet embraced organic imagination. Richard P. Adams attributes this frame of mind to Poe in "Romanticism and the American Renaissance," *American Literature*, 23 (1952), 419–32. Poe is more accurately described, I think, as a "negative Romantic" than as a "Romantic ironist," in that the latter, as Thompson argues, embraces a liberating, organic imagination, even though it envisions, paradoxically, a contradictory, fluid, and indeterminate world. Indeed, I believe Poe was more wedded to rationalism than Peckham's "negative Romantic." See Thompson, "Romantic Arabesque," pp. 184–87, and on Poe's rationalism, see Robert D. Jacobs, *Poe: Journalist & Critic* (Baton Rouge: Louisiana State University Press, 1969), pp. 20–33, 358–64.

25. Quinn, *The French Face of Poe*, pp. 203–4. On Poe's borrowings for these chapters, see Burton R. Pollin, "The *Narrative* of Benjamin Morrell: Out of 'The Bucket' and into Poe's *Pym*," *Studies in American Fiction*, 4 (1976), 157–73.

26. As Douglas Robinson notes, the shrouded figure stands in place of "what *happens* beyond the polar veil," a crucial gap in the narrative which "has acted in *Pym* criticism as a kind of interpretive license," inviting critics to define the transcendental presence or absence beyond the veil that Pym never relates. The gap, Robinson maintains, should steer us "past false ontological interpretations to a pragmatic concern with the mediatory act of interpretation" (*American Apocalypses*, pp. 111–12). Interpretations of what lies beyond the veil in *Pym* are proposed by Davidson, Quinn, Thompson, and Ketterer in studies cited above, and by Richard Kopley in "The '*Very* Profound Under-current' of *Arthur Gordon Pym*," in *Studies in the American Renaissance 1987*, ed. Joel Myerson (Charlottesville: University Press of Virginia, 1987), pp. 143–75. Focusing more on Poe's concern with the "mediatory act of interpretation" are studies cited above by Irwin, Rowe, Kennedy, and Williams.

Peirce and Rose: Poe's Reading of Myth

1. Harry Levin, "Some Meanings of Myth," in *Myth and Mythmaking*, ed. Henry A. Murray (Boston: Beacon Press, 1960), p. 112.

2. John B. Vickery, ed., *Myth and Literature: Contemporary Theory and Practice* (Lincoln: University of Nebraska Press, 1966), p. xi.

3. Richard Wilbur, "Poe and the Art of Suggestion," in *Critical Essays on Edgar Allan Poe*, ed. Eric W. Carlson (Boston: G. K. Hall, 1987), pp. 160, 171. Poe explains his own principles in a review of *Twice-Told Tales*: "Where the suggested meaning runs through the obvious one in a *very* profound under-current so as never to interfere with the upper one without our own volition, so as never to show itself unless *called* to the surface, there only, for the proper uses of fictitious narrative, is it available at all" (*H* 13:148).

Other "suggestive," symbolic, and mythic criticism has been turned toward *Pym* in this century, beginning with Marie Bonaparte's Freudian study in *Edgar Poe: sa vie, son oeuvre—Étude psychanalytique* (Paris: Denoël et Steele, 1933), translated by John Rodker as *The Life and Works of Edgar Allan Poe: A Psycho-Analytic Interpretation* (London: Imago, 1949) (see pp. 290–352). Complementing Bonaparte's work is Gaston Bachelard's introduction to *Les Aventures d'Arthur Gordon Pym*, trans. Charles Baudelaire (Paris, 1944), pp. 7–23. Early attempts to plumb its inner meaning include Harry Levin's portrayal of Pym as the archetypal American boy "initiated into manhood" (*The Power of Blackness: Hawthorne, Poe, Melville* [New York: Knopf, 1958], pp. 108–25) and Wilbur's introduction to his 1973 edition of *Pym* (Boston: Godine), pp. vii–xxv, in which he sees Pym's as a spiritual and gnostic quest.

In more clearly mythic criticism in the 1970s, Grace Farrell Lee explores the story as mythic quest in "The Quest of Arthur Gordon Pym," *Southern Literary Journal*, 4, no. 2 (1972), 22–33. Kathleen Sands sees the journey as exploring rites of passage in "The Mythic Initiation of Arthur Gordon Pym," *Poe Studies*, 7 (1974), 14–16. Barton Levi St. Armand considers its relation to alchemy in "The Dragon and the Uroboros: Themes of Metamorphosis in *Arthur Gordon Pym*," *American Transcendental Quarterly*, 37 (1978), 57–71.

In the 1980s, studies have been undertaken connecting *Pym* with specific mythic heritages. In *American Hieroglyphics* (New Haven: Yale University Press, 1980), pp. 43–235, John Irwin relates *Pym* to the mythic origin and nature of language. Richard Kopley pursues in depth the biblical connection in "The 'Very Profound Under-current' of *Arthur Gordon Pym*," in *Studies in the American Renaissance 1987*, ed. Joel Myerson (Charlottesville: University Press of Virginia, 1987), pp. 143–75. Both Kent Ljungquist, in "Descent of the Titans: The Sublime Riddle of *Arthur Gordon Pym*," *Southern Literary Journal*, 10, no. 2 (1978), 75–92 (a revised version of which appears in *The Grand and the Fair: Poe's Landscape Aesthetics and Pictorial Techniques* [Potomac, Md.: Scripta Humanistica, 1984], pp. 56–72), and Ana Hernández del Castillo, in *Keats, Poe, and the Shaping of Cortázar's Mythopoesis*, Purdue University Monograph in Romance Languages (Amsterdam: John Benjamins B. V., 1981), investigate the novel's relation to the ideas of speculative mythographers whose works Poe was reading.

4. Burton Feldman and Robert D. Richardson, *The Rise of Modern Mythology: 1680–1860* (Bloomington: Indiana University Press, 1972), pp. 511–12.

5. Ibid., p. 298.

6. Ibid., p. 513.

7. Ibid., p. 512.

8. Burton R. Pollin, *Dictionary of Names and Titles in Poe's Collected Works* (New York: Da Capo Press, 1968), pp. 14, 82.

9. Ljungquist, *The Grand and the Fair*, p. 61n.

10. Isaac Preston Cory, *Ancient Fragments of the Phoenician, Chaldaean, Egyptian, Tyrian, Carthaginian, Indian, Persian, and Other Writers* (London, 1832), p. x.

11. Jacob Bryant, *A New System; or, an Analysis of Antient Mythology*, 6 vols. (London, 1807). All further references to Bryant will be cited as *B*, volume, and page number.

12. Charles Anthon, *A Classical Dictionary Containing an Account of the Principal Proper Names Mentioned in Ancient Authors* (New York: Harper and Brothers, 1841; reprinted 1860). Harper also, interestingly, published *Pym*.

13. Hernández del Castillo, *Cortázar's Mythopoesis*, pp. 56–57, 121. See, also, for later correspondence, *O* 1:266–72 and *H* 17:193.

14. George Stanley Faber, *Origin of Pagan Idolatry: Ascertained from Historical Testimony and Circumstantial Evidence*, 3 vols. (London, 1816). All further references to Faber will be cited in the text as *F*, volume, and page number.

15. See, for instance, "The Philosophy of Composition" (*H* 14:193–208) and "The Poetic Principle" (*H* 14:266–92). See also Krishna Rayan, "Edgar Allan Poe and Suggestiveness," *The British Journal of Aesthetics* 9 (1969), 73–79.

16. Anthon, *Classical Dictionary*, p. vii.

17. Abraham Rees, *The Cyclopaedia; or, Universal Dictionary of Arts, Sciences, and Literature*, 1st American ed. 41 vols. (Philadelphia, n.d.), vol. 25, s.v. "mystical."

18. See also *The Early Lectures of Ralph Waldo Emerson*, ed. Stephen E. Whicher and Robert E. Spiller (Cambridge, Mass.: Harvard University Press, 1959), p. 25. Emerson, discussing the influence of "The Age of Fable," writes: "He who constructs a beautiful fable only with the design of making it symmetrical and pleasing, will find that unconsciously he has been writing an allegory. He finds at the end of his task that he has only been holding a pen for a higher hand which has overseen and guided him."

19. Emerson, *Early Lectures*, pp. 239, 241, 257.

20. Thomas Percy, ed., *Reliques of Ancient English Poetry* (London, 1765; reprinted 1767), 3:xvii, 26, 37.

21. Killis Campbell, "Poe's Reading," *University of Texas Studies in English*, no. 5 (1925), 180, 176.

22. Burton R. Pollin, *Discoveries in Poe* (Notre Dame: University of Notre Dame Press, 1970), p. 291.

23. This information may have come from Rees' *Cyclopaedia* (25), which devotes five pages to Stonehenge, but works concerning Stonehenge were among the favorites of the mythographers and were well-known references for Arthurian materials. For instance, it is from William Owen's *Cambrian Biography: or Historical Notices of Celebrated Men among the Ancient Britons* (London, 1803) that Rees derives his abridged discussion of Arthur. Owen's work mentions Nennius and the *Welsh Triads*; and, in fact, Faber refers to *Cambrian Biography* along with Edward Davies' *The Mythology and Rites of the British Druids* (London, 1809) and the "*Morte Arthur*" a number of times. Davies' other major work, *Celtic Researches on*

the Origin, Traditions and Language of the Ancient Britons (London, 1804), is listed in Anthon's *Classical Dictionary*. All the writers mentioned seem well acquainted with early Welsh material such as the *Triads* and the songs and stories to be gathered shortly in *The Mabinogion* (partially trans. by Edward Williams in *The Cambridge Quarterly*, 1833; trans Lady Charlotte Guest, 1838–49).

24. Owen, *Cambrian Biography*, p. 13.

25. Bryant tells us that Isis, also, "is mentioned as the mother of all Beings" (*B* 3:320–21). Quoting Plutarch's *Isis and Osiris* copiously, he sees Osiris and Isis almost as archetypes. And speaking of the Celts, he concludes: "Tacitus takes notice, that this people worshipped Isis: and he mentions that the chief object at their rites, was an Ark or ship."

26. Davies (*Celtic Researches*, p. 555) refers to *Taliesin* and the cauldron. See also Adam McLean, "Alchemical Transmutation in History and Symbol," in *At the Table of the Grail: Magic and the Use of Imaginations*, ed. John Matthews (London: Routledge and Kegan Paul, 1984), p. 60. The Cauldron of Annwfn can be achieved only by a progress through seven "caers" or inner castles. They seem to be related to a series of mazes through which mystery initiates had to find their way. In coincidence or connection, *Pym* contains a series of seven boats that affect Pym's passage.

27. From *Perlesvaus*, quoted in John Matthews, *The Grail: Quest for the Eternal* (London: Thames and Hudson, 1981), p. 4.

28. Harry Levin, *Power of Blackness*, p. 113.

29. Nennius, *Historia Brittonum*, in *Arthur, King of Britain*, ed. Richard L. Brengle (Englewood Cliffs: Prentice Hall, 1964), p. 6.

30. Samuel Johnson, *Samuel Johnson's Dictionary: A Modern Selection*, ed. E. L. McAdam, Jr., and George Milne (New York: Pantheon, 1964), p. 287.

31. Kopley, " 'Very Profound Under-current,' " pp. 155–56.

32. Phrase derived from Byron's life and *Childe Harold's Pilgrimage*.

33. *Sir Gawain and the Green Knight* had become so well known in Poe's time as to be reissued in a collection of its various versions: *Sir Gawayne: A Collection of Ancient Romance-Poems*, ed. Sir Frederic Madden (London, 1839).

34. Robert Graves, *The White Goddess: A Historical Grammar of Poetic Myth* (1948; rpt., New York: Vintage, 1960), pp. 184–85.

35. Sidney Kaplan, "An Introduction to *Pym*," in *Poe: A Collection of Critical Essays*, ed. Robert Regan (Englewood Cliffs: Prentice-Hall, 1967), p. 161.

36. Rachel Bromwych, ed. and trans., *Trioedd Ynys Prydein: The Welsh Triads* (Cardiff: University of Wales Press, 1961), pp. 154–56, 380–85.

37. Roger Sherman Loomis, *Celtic Myth and Arthurian Romance* (New York: Columbia University Press, 1927), pp. 11, 286.

38. Ibid., p. 260.

39. Ibid., p. 285; also *B* 3:356.

40. Loomis, *Celtic Myth*, p. 288.

41. Roger Sherman Loomis, *Arthurian Romance and Chrétien de Troyes* (New York: Columbia University Press, 1949), p. 470.

42. Lucy Allen Paton, *Studies in the Fairy Mythology of Arthurian Romance* (New York: Burt Franklin, 1960), p. 5.

43. Bromwych, *Trioedd*, p. 140.

44. One can speculate that three days might equal three seasons for the Goddess and so nine months. Pym journeys from June 21 to March 22 and thus possibly toward a seeing of the "Mother" after a natal journey through her belly and waters. Leslie Fiedler thinks that it "was . . . his mother whom Poe was pursuing in his disguise as Pym," the journey symbolizing Poe's return to the womb (*Love and Death in the American Novel* [1960; rev. ed. New York: Stein and Day, 1966], p. 400).

45. Among the most famous of the prehistoric British mazes is that of the Tor at Glastonbury, regarded as one of the entrances to Annwfn, just as Glastonbury itself is known to have been Avalon. Avalon (including this maze) was presided over by Morgan le Fay and was known as the Isle of Glass. See Geoffrey Ashe, "The Grail of the Golden Age" in *At the Table of the Grail*, ed. John Matthews, pp. 15–16; also Richard Cavendish, *King Arthur and the Grail: The Arthurian Legends and their Meaning* (New York: Taplinger, 1978), p. 35.

46. Galfredi Monumetensis, *Historia Britonum*, ed. J. A. Giles (London: 1844), p. 130; Graves (*Goddess*, pp. 93, 184) says, translating Geoffrey, that the future is closed to the Goddess's new king: "After this Janus shall never have priests again. His door will be shut and remain concealed in Ariadne's crannies."

47. Serpents were among the Goddess's main symbols, along with the Ark, white doves, and the rainbow or aurora. In Apuleius' *Golden Ass*, she holds a boat-shaped golden cup on the handle of which "an asp lifted up his head with a wide-swelling throat" (trans. William Adlington [London, 1566]; revised by Stephen Gaselee [Cambridge, Mass.: Harvard University Press, 1958], p. 545).

48. Paton, *Arthurian Romance*, p. 5.

49. Bromwych, *Trioedd*, pp. 35–36.

50. Owen, *Cambrian Biography*, p. 14.

51. Graves, *Goddess*, p. 354.

52. Ibid., pp. 62, 185.

53. Apuleius, *Golden Ass*, pp. 543–45, 553–55.

54. Graves, *Goddess*, p. 125.

55. John Starkey, *Celtic Mysteries: The Ancient Religion* (New York: Avon, 1975), p. 18.

56. Loomis, *Celtic Myth*, p. 267.

57. Graves, *Goddess*, p. 125.

58. Robert Graves, *The Greek Myths*, 2 vols. (Baltimore: Penguin, 1955), 1:14.

59. Graves, *Goddess*, p. 125.

60. Numerous in Celtic lore, dwarfs moved on into Arthurian romance. The first Arthurian poem in Percy's *Reliques* (3:26) begins on Pentecost Day when "a doughty dwarfe" to Arthur's dais "right pertlye gan pricke."

61. Vernon J. Harward, Jr., *The Dwarfs of Arthurian Romance and Celtic Tradition* (Leiden: J. Brill, 1958), pp. 9, 19, 120.

62. Ibid., pp. 74–81.

63. Ibid., pp. 121–22: "Guivret, Auberon, and the dwarf in the Dutch *Lancelot* are at first hostile toward the hero, then become his fast friend."

64. Owen, *Cambrian Biography*, p. 13; Rees, *Cyclopaedia*, s.v. "Arthur."

65. *Encyclopaedia, or a Dictionary of Arts, Sciences, and Miscellaneous Literature*, 18 vols. (Philadelphia: 1798), 2:371, s.v. "Arthur"; Giraldis Cambrensis, "De Principis Instructione," in *Arthur*, ed. Richard Brengle, pp. 9–10.

66. Graves, *Goddess*, pp. 170–71.

67. This description is almost a parody of the picture of the Goddess with animal's head or with dragon's tail guarding the tree.

68. Loomis, *Celtic Myth*, p. 268.

69. Wolfram von Eschenbach, *Parzival*, trans. Helen M. Mustard and Charles E. Passage (New York: Vintage, 1961), pp. 251–52; John Matthews, *The Grail: Quest for the Eternal*, pp. 19–20.

70. John Matthews, *The Grail: Quest for the Eternal*, p. 90.

71. Sir James George Frazer, *The "New" Golden Bough*, ed. Theodor H. Gaster (New York: S. G. Phillips, 1959), p. 310.

72. They are careful at first not to hurt the ship and soothe it when it is accidentally struck. They are also astonished to see two large mirrors in the cabin. While an explanation for the mirrors has been offered (Kopley, "'Very Profound Under-current,'" pp. 31–32), it is interesting that Isis wears "a circlet in the fashion of a mirror" on her forehead (Apuleius, *Golden Ass*, p. 543).

73. Sidney Kaplan says that Tsalal is Hell, its water the Styx ("Introduction to *Pym*," in *Poe*, ed. Robert Regan, p. 157). Hernández del Castillo, who also identifies the natives' personification of the *Jane Guy* with the White Goddess, sees the island as the body of the "Mother" and its waters as her blood (*Cortázar's Mythopoesis*, p. 58). But the water also can be seen, in paradox, as water/wine in the process of transmutation into the blood of Christ, as happens in communion, but especially in drinking from the Grail.

74. Hernández del Castillo, *Cortázar's Mythopoesis*, p. 59.

75. Anthon, *Classical Dictionary*, pp. 137–38. See also Hernández del Castillo, *Cortázar's Mythopoesis*, pp. 60, 122. Maureen Gallery Kovacs (*The Epic of Gilgamesh* [Stanford: Stanford University Press, 1985], p. 111) speaks of the goddess Aruru as creating mankind in the "'Myth of Abrahasis,' where she was called Beletili, 'Lady of the Gods.'" Graves adds, "And indeed if one needs a single, simple, inclusive name for the Great Goddess, Anna is the best choice" (*Goddess*, p. 411).

76. Hernández del Castillo, *Cortázar's Mythopoesis*, p. 60. On Ishtar, see N. K. Sanders, trans., *The Epic of Gilgamesh* (Baltimore: Penguin, 1960), pp. 25–26.

77. James M. Whiton, ed., *A Lexicon Abridged from Liddell and Scott's Greek-English Lexicon* (New York, 1871), p. 705.

78. Anthon, *Classical Dictionary*, p. 218; see also Hernández del Castillo, *Cortázar's Mythopoesis*, pp. 122–23.

79. Frazer, *Golden Bough*, p. 311; Anthon, *Classical Dictionary*, pp. 395–96. Sanders (*Epic of Gilgamesh*, p. 46) reiterates that the old Babylonian gods went underground to appear in later religions and that behind Celtic legend and Arthurian romance lie the stories of the Middle East.

80. Whiton, *Liddell and Scott's Lexicon*, p. 406. See also *Greek and English Lexicon* (London, 1831), where *lamia* is seen as "a fabulous monster, a kind of large sea fish" from *lamos,* meaning "a gulf, a large cavity."

81. They enter a grotto like that described under "Magic" (*Encyclopaedia Britannica* [3rd American ed., 1797], 10:417) as the temple of Apollo at Cumae: "This rock was probably of the same kind with that which the temple at Delphi was built, full of fissures." The Delphi grotto belonged to the White Goddess before Apollo wrested it from her; and the Chapel Perilous probably derived from a combination of her ancient cave temple, the underground grottos of mystery rites, and the Christian cell. Bryant writes: "I have shown that Gaia in its original sense signifies a sacred cavern . . . looked upon as an image of the Ark. Hence Gaia, like Hesta, Rhoia, Cybele, is often represented as the mother of mankind" (*B* 5:45). He adds in regard to Cumae, the cave of the Latin sybil, "It was a cave in the rock, abounding with variety of subterranes, cut out into various apartments" (*B* 1:145).

82. Faber describes Lancelot, who also loves Gwenhwyvar, as entering the White Goddess's grotto, the Chapel Perilous. Inside he meets phantom warriors and dead knights, but he miraculously escapes (*F* 3:323). In the high romance of Sir Thomas Malory's *La Mort d'Arthure: The History of King Arthur and the Knights of the Round Table* (2nd ed., ed. Thomas Wright, 3 vols. [London, 1866], 3:112–13), however, he cannot attain the Grail because he has sinfully loved Guinevere. He dreams of a tournament

in which he supports the wrong: "The earthly knights were they the which were clothed all in blacke, and the covering betokneth the sinnes whereof they bee not confessed; and they with the covering of white betokneth virginitie, and they that choose chastitie, and thus was the quest begun in them." Lancelot, however, because of his valor and nobility, attains a vision of the Grail.

83. Graves, *Goddess*, p. 429; Hernández del Castillo, *Cortázar's Mythopoesis*, p. 123. See also, Catullus 63, 1.5.

84. Graves, *Greek Myths*, 1:12.

85. Rees, *Cyclopaedia*, vol. 25, s.v. "Stonehenge."

86. Davies (*Celtic Researches*, pp. 558–61) tells the story of a prince overtaken by a tempest near the seashore. He enters a cavern, "which proves to be inhabited by the *Goddess of Nature*." She lifts him into the air, where he meets souls of the dead, and she then carries him into the vortex of the moon, where he sees millions of souls crossing vast fields of ice. At the end Davies asserts: "This is neither *Gothic* nor *Roman*;—it is *Druidical*."

87. Malory, *La Mort d'Arthure*, 3:147; John Matthews, *The Grail: Quest for the Eternal*, p. 86. Perceval, unlike Galahad, is very human and attains the Grail through growing into understanding. Pym resembles him, next to Arthur, the most of any Arthurian character.

88. Emma Jung and Marie-Louise Franz, *The Grail Legend*, trans. Andrea Dykes (New York: G. P. Putnam, 1970), pp. 95, 98.

89. Barton Levi St. Armand (p. 68) suggests that "the 'gigantic curtain' he [Pym] encounters can be nothing less than 'the veil of Isis'" and the figure "none other than the Great Mother herself." Robert Graves states, "The most . . . inspired account of the Goddess in all ancient literature is contained in Apuleius's *Golden Ass*" (*Goddess*, p. 62). It concludes with a wonderful saving vision of her, a vision Poe may have known. Although Poe mentions Apuleius four times, it is always in regard to the same phrase, *ventum textilem* (M 2:917). He translates it as "woven air" or "woven snow," saying Apuleius refers thus to "fine drapery" (H 8:304). In *Alciphron*, Moore, he says, "has stolen his 'woven snow' from the *ventum textilem* of Apuleius" (H 10:70). Although the phrase comes from Petronius, Poe credited it to Apuleius, and he may well have tied it to Isis as he constructed his "curtain" and "veil" here. A veil is always associated with Isis, a central reference being that of Plutarch, "I am all that has been or that shall be; and no mortal has hitherto taken off my veil" (Anthon, *Classical Dictionary*, p. 688).

90. John Matthews, *The Grail: Quest for the Eternal*, p. 17.

91. Malory, *La Mort d'Arthure*, 3:337.

Moldenhauer: *Pym,* the Dighton Rock, and the Matter of Vinland

1. See, for example, P 1:333, 343, 344–45, 356; J. V. Ridgely and Iola S. Haverstick, "Chartless Voyage: The Many Narratives of Arthur Gordon Pym," *Texas Studies in Literature and Language,* 8 (1966), 63–80, esp. 72–79; Ridgely, "The End of Pym and the Ending of *Pym,*" *Papers on Poe,* ed. Richard P. Veler (Springfield, Ohio: Chantry Music Press, 1972), pp. 104–12; Richard Kopley, "The Secret of *Arthur Gordon Pym*: The Text and the Source," *Studies in American Fiction,* 8 (1980), 203–18.

2. Alexander Hammond, "The Composition of *The Narrative of Arthur Gordon Pym*: Notes toward a Re-examination," *American Transcendental Quarterly,* no. 37 (Winter 1978), 9–20. See also J. V. Ridgely, "The Growth of the Text," in P 1:29–36.

3. A facsimile edition has been published by Otto Zeller, Osnabrück, Germany, 1968.

4. Richard Kopley has called my attention to the probable acquaintance of Poe and Jackson, who both attended the Booksellers' Dinner in New York, 30 March 1837. Jackson toasted "Literary intercourse between different nations—An exchange which enriches both parties"; later, Poe made a toast to "The *Monthlies* of Gotham—Their distinguished Editors, and their vigorous *Collaborateurs*" (*New-York American,* 7 April 1837). Kopley suggests that Poe's bookseller friend William Gowans might have introduced Poe and Jackson at the dinner. (Kopley, letter to Moldenhauer, 18 March 1988; see also Dwight Thomas and David K. Jackson, *The Poe Log: A Documentary Life of Edgar Allan Poe, 1809–1849* [Boston: G. K. Hall, 1987], pp. 243–44.)

5. Edward Everett, unsigned review in the *North American Review,* 46 (1838), 161–203; hereafter cited as "Everett."

6. For Mabbott's comment, see M 2:633. For Poe's references to the *North American Review* in his "Marginalia," see P 2:308, 346, 352, 354, 417.

7. *North American Review,* 43 (1836), 265. I have examined a prospectus dated 19 November 1835 (Library of the American Philosophical Society).

8. *Knickerbocker,* 11 (1838), 193, 288–89.

9. *United States Magazine and Democratic Review,* 2 (1838), 85–96, 143–58.

10. *New-York Review,* 2 (1838), 352–71.

11. Everett, p. 162.

12. *American Monthly Magazine,* n.s. 5 (1838), 103–4 (brief mention), 365–68 (review).

13. *Foreign Quarterly Review,* 21 (1838), 89–118; *Museum of Foreign Literature,* n.s. 5 (1838), 449–63.

14. *New-Yorker*, 5, no. 2 (31 March 1838).

15. Paul Henri Mallet, *Northern Antiquities*, trans. Thomas Percy (London: T. Carnan and Co., 1770); John Reinhold Forster, *History of the Voyages and Discoveries Made in the North* (London: G. G. J. and J. Robinson, 1786).

16. Jeremy Belknap, *American Biography*, 2 vols. (Boston: Thomas and Andrews, 1794, 1798).

17. Washington Irving, *A History of the Life and Voyages of . . . Columbus* (New York: G. and C. Carvill, 1828), 3:292–99, 300–3; *P* 2:265.

18. These citations appear at pp. 163–68 of Everett's review.

19. *North American Review*, 45 (1837), 149–85.

20. Lydia Sigourney, *Scenes in My Native Land* (Boston: James Munroe & Co., 1845), pp. 262–66.

21. *Southern Literary Messenger*, 2 (1836), 166–71, 514–15. See also *H* 9:77–78. William Doyle Hull II, "A Canon of the Critical Works of Edgar Allan Poe with a Study of Poe as Editor and Reviewer," Ph.D. diss., University of Virginia, 1941, pp. 4, 138–44, attributes the July reviews to Poe.

22. *American Monthly Magazine*, n.s. 1 (1836), 67–71.

23. *Knickerbocker*, 10 (1837), 173.

24. *United States Magazine and Democratic Review*, 1 (1837), 38, 46.

25. *Knickerbocker*, 11 (1838), 205.

26. *North American Review*, 44 (1837), 312.

27. *American Monthly Magazine*, n.s. 1 (1836), 71; n.s. 5 (1838), 104.

28. Edmund Burke Delabarre provides a comprehensive study of the pictorial, philological, historical, prophetic, and genealogical interpretations of the carvings, from the seventeenth century through the early twentieth, in his series "Early Interest in Dighton Rock," "Middle Period of Dighton Rock History," and "Recent History of Dighton Rock," *Publications of the Colonial Society of Massachusetts*, 18 (*Transactions, 1915–16*, published 1917), 235–99; 19 (*Transactions, 1916–17*, published 1918), 46–149; and 20 (*Transactions, 1917–19*, published 1920), 286–462. See also Delabarre's book, *Dighton Rock* (New York: Walter Neale, 1928).

29. John T. Irwin, *American Hieroglyphics: The Symbol of the Egyptian Hieroglyphics in the American Renaissance* (New Haven: Yale University Press, 1980), pp. 170–74.

30. Everett, p. 189.

31. Ibid., pp. 189, 197.

32. *New-Yorker*, 31 March 1838, p. 1.

33. *New York Review*, 2 (1838), 362.

34. *Foreign Quarterly Review*, 21 (1838), 111, 112, 109.

35. *Foreign Quarterly Review*, 21 (1838), 96, 105, 108.

36. Everett, p. 197.

37. Everett, pp. 178–82; see also *Foreign Quarterly Review*, 21 (1838), 109–10.

38. Everett, p. 164.

39. Everett, p. 190; see also pp. 162–65, 169–70, 199–202.

Pollin: Poe's Life Reflected through the Sources of *Pym*

1. Poe did not represent merely an emblematic writer of the American Renaissance to Saul Bellow, as here in *Humboldt's Gift* (New York: Viking, 1975), p. 370. In this and many other works, Bellow found in Poe a varied source of imagery, inspired utterances, and acute critical dicta; see Burton Pollin, "Poe and Bellow: A Literary Connection," *Saul Bellow Journal*, 7 (Winter 1988), 15–26.

2. Poe and his wife and aunt occupied quarters in this modest boarding-house, owned by the widow of carpenter Yarrington, from October 1835 to January 1837, a sojourn tacitly implied by all the editors and biographers of Poe (e.g., T. O. Mabbott, Hervey Allen, Mary E. Phillips, Arthur H. Quinn, and Dwight Thomas and David K. Jackson).

3. Roger E. Stoddard, *'Put a Resolute Hart to a Steep Hill': William Gowans, Antiquary and Bookseller* (New York: Book Arts Press, 1990), p. 26.

4. Mary Neal Gove: "A hanging bookshelf completed its furniture [the sitting room's]"—quoted by Arthur H. Quinn, *Edgar Allan Poe* (New York: Appleton Century, 1941), p. 509, from her February 1863 *Six Penny Magazine* article.

5. See, for example, Poe's use of D'Israeli's book as source for 62 of the 604 short notes or essays in the *Brevities* (1844–1849) and his use of Bielfeld's book for 29, indexed in *P*, vol. 2.

6. For these reviews, see his letter of 2 September 1836 to the editor of the Richmond *Courier and Daily Compiler* (*O* 1:100–2).

7. For a detailed study, see W. T. Bandy, "Poe, Duane and Duffee," *University of Mississippi Studies in English*, n.s. 3 (1982), 81–95. See also *The Library of H. Bradley Martin: Highly Important American and Children's Literature* (New York: Sotheby's, 1990), Lot 2194. For relevant letters and commentary, see George E. Woodberry, *The Life of Edgar Allan Poe*, 2 vols. (Boston: Houghton Mifflin, 1909), 2:365–68; Quinn, *Poe*, pp. 406–10; and *O* 1:251–53.

8. These years circumscribe his working for the *Southern Literary Messenger, Burton's Gentleman's Magazine, Graham's Magazine*, and the *Broadway Journal*.

9. For the reinforcement of the name of the boat, earlier used by Cooper in *The Pilot*, through the account of the seamen Wiseman and Mann, see the able presentation by Richard Kopley in "The 'Very Profound Under-

Current' of *Arthur Gordon Pym*," *Studies in the American Renaissance 1987*, ed. Joel Myerson (Charlottesville: University Press of Virginia, 1987), pp. 143–75, specifically, 143–45, 160–62. For the use of Reynolds' "Leaves from an Unpublished Journal" see n. 23, below, second part.

10. See Hervey Allen, *Israfel*, 2nd ed. (New York: Farrar and Rinehart, 1934), pp. 211, 315, 664; and Dwight Thomas and David K. Jackson, *The Poe Log: A Documentary Life of Edgar Allan Poe, 1809–1849* (Boston: G. K. Hall, 1987), p. 104.

11. See Allen, *Israfel*, p. 267, and M 1:502.

12. For Gowans' very warm, detailed view of the Poe family during this period, see Quinn, *Poe*, p. 267, and Mary Phillips, *Edgar Allan Poe—The Man*, 2 vols. (Chicago: John C. Winston, 1926), 1:549–62, although she intersperses some obvious errors about Poe's tale-writing activities then. See also Stoddard, *William Gowans*, p. 26.

13. For the instrumentality of Gowans in arranging for Poe's presence, see Allen, *Israfel*, p. 335; see pp. 330–40 for other observations on Gowans and Poe. For Poe's toast, see Thomas and Jackson, *Poe Log*, p. 243.

14. For the year-long war between Poe, consistently censorious of Theodore Fay, the author of *Norman Leslie*, and Fay's powerful New York coterie who used the pages of the *Mirror* and *Knickerbocker* for their rancorous attacks, see Sidney P. Moss, *Poe's Literary Battles* (Durham: Duke University Press, 1963), pp. 40–62; see also, Burton Pollin, " 'Mystification' by Poe: Its Source in Fay's *Norman Leslie*," *Mississippi Quarterly*, 25 (Spring 1972), 111–30.

15. Thomas and Jackson, *Poe Log*, p. 193.

16. See also, Burton Pollin, "Poe and Daniel Defoe: A Significant Relationship," *Topic 30*, 16 (Fall 1976), 3–22.

17. The long review appeared in the March 1836 *Southern Literary Messenger* and bore results in Hawks' invitation to Poe early in 1837 to contribute to his *New York Review* (see Thomas and Jackson, *Poe Log*, pp. 237, 239). Perhaps disappointment over receiving only the one assignment, to review John L. Stephens' *Arabia Petraea*, led Poe to deprecate Hawks' mere "*fluency*" of style in the November 1841 "Autography" in *Graham's Magazine* (H 15:205) and in a reference in *Godey's* "Literati" of September 1846 (H 15:115).

18. Poe adapted this old word to mean "grotesqueness," that is, "humorous or absurd oddity," and used it six times; see *Poe, Creator of Words*, ed. Burton Pollin, 2nd ed. (Bronxville: N. Smith, 1980), p. 27. It is perhaps relevant, too, to note Poe's own evaluation of his book in a private and presumably sincere letter to William E. Burton, of 1 June 1840: "You once wrote in your magazine [a sharp critique] upon a book of mine—a [very silly book—Pym . . .]. . . . Your criticism was essentially correct . . . although severe" (O 1:130).

19. These are so numerous as to justify ascribing to Poe the intention to parody narrative methods and genres in *Pym*; see *P* 1:9–10.

20. For his use of "a style half plausible, half bantering" as a "hoax" in "Hans Pfaall," see his "Literati" sketch of Richard Adams Locke in the October 1846 *Godey's* (*H* 15:128–29); see also his letter of 11 February 1836 (*O* 1:84).

21. J. V. Ridgely pertinently observes that many of Poe's sources for *Pym* were books published by Harper and Brothers (*P.* 1:32–33). For James Harper's encouragement of J. L. Stephens to borrow from Harper and Brothers books, see Eugene Exman, *The Brothers Harper* (New York: Harper and Row, 1965), pp. 94–95.

22. See the four lettered annotations in *Pym* for these chapter and paragraph loci: 4.5B, 5.6B, 9.6A, 18.3A (*P* 1:246–47, 249, 265–66, 319).

23. Poe reviewed Reynolds' *Report of the Committee on Naval Affairs* in August 1836 (*H* 9:84–90) and his *Address on the Subject of a Survey-ing and Exploring Expedition* in the January 1837 issue of the *Messenger* (*H* 9:306–14; see also *P* 1:18–19, 224–25), and certainly he knew well and used in *Pym* Reynolds' *Voyage of the United States Frigate Potomac.* For the review of this last work in the *Messenger* as possibly by Poe, see *P* 1:18. See also Richard Kopley, "The Secret of Arthur Gordon Pym: The Text and the Source," *Studies in American Fiction*, 8 (Autumn 1980), 203–18. Also in this piece is a consideration of Poe's possible use of Reynolds' "Leaves from an Unpublished Journal" in the *Mirror* of 21 April 1838, which I discuss in *P* 1:334, 356. See the Index to *Pym* for over sixteen separate commentary-notes on Reynolds as author of sources in Poe's novel.

24. Published by the Harpers in October 1836 and read during the ges-tation of *Pym* for Poe's *Messenger* review of January 1837, *Astoria* can be traced as a source of over fifteen passages or paragraphs; see the index to *P*, vol. 1.

25. Benjamin Morrell, *A Narrative of Four Voyages* (New York: J. and J. Harper, 1832).

26. Morrell: "An Account of some new and valuable Discoveries, in-cluding the Massacre Islands, where thirteen of the Author's Crew were massacred and eaten by Cannibals"; Poe: "An account of . . . the massacre of her crew among a group of islands . . . together with the incredible adventures and discoveries still farther south. . . ." (see *P* 1:53).

27. For background details about the book, Woodworth's play, and the unauthentic, melodramatic aspects of both—promoted by the public exhibiting of the Polynesian, "Prince Darco," imported by Morrell—see my study, "The *Narrative* of Benjamin Morrell: Out of 'The Bucket' and into Poe's *Pym*," *Studies in American Fiction*, 4 (1976), 157–72; see also *P* 1:661–62, for over one hundred designated loci about Morrell in the text and notes.

28. Poe's use of the famous *Journal of a Cruise made to the Pacific* . . . (1815, 1822), by David Porter, may have been through the intermediation of the works of others (see *P* 1:278–79); for the lurid book by Riley, see *P* 1:283, 339. Most important was Stephens' *Incidents* for the terrain of Tsalal (see nine discussions, listed in *P* 1:665).

29. Heinrich Wilhelm Gesenius (1786–1842), renowned German orientalist and biblical critic, published numerous grammars and lexicons of Hebrew and related languages. An apparent compilation of several of them appeared in translation as *A Hebrew and English Lexicon of the Old Testament Including the Biblical Chaldee. Translated from the Latin of W. Gesenius by Edward Robinson* (Boston: Crocker and Brewster, 1836; vii + 1090 pages). After Charles Anthon responded to Poe's query about biblical lore with a reference to "Leo's transl." of Gesenius, on 1 June 1837, Poe apparently searched out (probably with help) and used Gesenius' entries in this 1836 volume for names, root meanings, and implications of Tsalal et al.; he made some errors in his applications. (See *P* 1:26, 360–62; for Anthon's letter, see *H* 17:42–43.)

30. For an explanation of Poe's knowledge and use of Anthon's article on Meiran's *Principes de l'étude comparative des langues* . . . , see *P* 1:26, 361.

31. For James Bruce, *Travels to Discover the Source of the Nile* (London, 1790), see *P* 1:361; for the Rev. Keith's defense against surging antitheological skepticism, see the index to *P*, vol. 1 for eight annotations (p. 659).

32. Captain Adam Seaborn, *Symzonia: A Voyage of Discovery* (New York: J. Seymour, 1820). For the important influence of this novel (probably by John Cleves Symmes) in Poe's work, see *P* 1:26 and numerous annotations (under "Symmes" in the index and, particularly, *P* 1:290). For Richard Kopley's very thorough presentation of all possibilities concerning the white figure and its role, see his studies indicated in nn. 9 and 23, above, and see also his "The Hidden Journey of *Arthur Gordon Pym*," *Studies in the American Renaissance 1982* (Boston: Twayne Publishers, 1982), pp. 29–51, and his "Early Illustrations of *Pym's* 'Shrouded Human Figure,'" in *Scope of the Fantastic—Culture, Biography, Themes, Children's Literature*, ed. Robert A. Collins and Howard D. Pearce (Westport: Greenwood Press, 1985), pp. 155–70.

33. Poe seems to be assimilating Hawthorne's tale to his own narrative of "Marie Rogêt," the publication of which began November 1842. It was based on the notorious death of Mary Rogers in 1841 and composed at the time of this review (see *O* 1:199–200). In view of the themes and story lines of the other works in *Twice-Told Tales*, we may ask whether Poe's mind was really peculiarly "congenial" with Hawthorne's.

Farrell: Mourning in Poe's *Pym*

1. Ralph Waldo Emerson, "Experience," in *Selected Writings*, ed. Donald McQuade (New York: Random House, 1981), p. 326. My statement that to lose is to become lost may seem to echo the title of Anna Freud's essay "About Losing and Being Lost," *The Psychoanalytic Study of the Child*, 22 (1967), 9–19. However, her discussion of the dynamic and libido-economic dimensions of losing and retaining is something quite different from the sense of disassociation from everything and everyone to which I refer and which I think Emerson felt and expressed in "Experience." For a comprehensive analysis of "Experience" as an essay on grief, see Susan Cameron, "Representing Grief: Emerson's 'Experience,'" *Representations*, 15 (Summer 1986), 15–41.

2. It is indeed commonplace to note that the brief life of Edgar Poe was a life filled with loss: the abandonment by his father sometime before the end of July 1811 when Edgar was two-and-a-half years old; the death of his mother within the year; the loss of his siblings with the breakup of the family; the death of his foster mother, Frances Allan, in 1829; the repeated rejections by his foster father; the death in 1831 of his brother Henry with whom he lived, in the household of Maria Clemm, between 1829 and 1831; the death of his child wife; and the losses of various homes, jobs, and friends.

3. Neal L. Tolchin, *Mourning, Gender, and Creativity in the Art of Herman Melville* (New Haven: Yale University Press, 1988), p. 3.

4. Hervey Allen, *Israfel: The Life and Times of Edgar Allan Poe*, 2nd ed. (New York: Farrar and Rinehart, 1934), pp. 17–21.

5. Dwight Thomas and David K. Jackson, *The Poe Log: A Documentary Life of Edgar Allan Poe, 1809–1849* (Boston: G. K. Hall, 1987), p. 14.

6. James J. Farrell, *Inventing the American Way of Death* (Philadelphia: Temple University Press, 1980), p. 218.

7. Ibid., pp. 146, 32.

8. Ann Douglas, *The Feminization of American Culture* (New York: Knopf, 1977), p. 200.

9. Farrell, *Death*, p. 33.

10. Ibid., pp. 33–34.

11. See Dorothy Burlingham and Anna Freud, *Young Children in Wartime* (London: Allen and Unwin, 1942).

12. John Bowlby, *Loss: Sadness and Depression* (New York: Basic Books, 1980), pp. 9–19.

13. Allen, *Israfel*, p. 20.

14. See J. Piaget, *The Child's Construction of Reality* (London: Routledge, 1955).

15. Of course, no forgetting is simple nor simply a forgetting. Everything is remembered, although not everything remembered is available to consciousness.

16. Edward H. Davidson, *Poe: A Critical Study* (Cambridge, Mass.: Harvard University Press, 1957).

17. J. Gerald Kennedy, *Poe, Death, and the Life of Writing* (New Haven: Yale University Press, 1987), p. 4.

18. Ibid., p. 4.

19. See Richard Kopley, "The Hidden Journey of *Arthur Gordon Pym*," in *Studies in the American Renaissance 1982*, ed. Joel Myerson (Boston: Twayne Publishers, 1982), pp. 29–51; see also the earlier study, "The Secret of *Arthur Gordon Pym*: The Text and the Source," *Studies in American Fiction*, 8 (1980), 203–18, and the later work, "The 'Very Profound Under-Current' of *Arthur Gordon Pym*," *Studies in the American Renaissance 1987*, ed. Joel Myerson (Charlottesville: University Press of Virginia, 1987), pp. 143–75.

20. Kopley, "The Hidden Journey of *Arthur Gordon Pym*," 44, 46.

21. Marie Bonaparte, *Edgar Poe: Sa vie, son oeuvre—Étude psychanalytique* (Paris: Denoël et Steele, 1933); *The Life and Works of Edgar Allan Poe: A Psycho-Analytic Interpretation*, trans. John Rodker (London: Imago, 1949).

22. Paul Rosenzweig, "The Search for Identity: The Enclosure Motif in *The Narrative of Arthur Gordon Pym*," *ESQ: A Journal of the American Renaissance*, 26 (1980), p. 124.

23. Davidson, *Poe*, p. 160.

24. Ana Maria Hernández, "Poe, Pym and Mythological Symbolism in Cortázar's First Novel," *Gypsy Scholar*, 4 (1977), 8, 12. My own work on archetypes in *Pym* has acknowledged the perils of the mythic descent but has emphasized that the goal of the journey is rebirth of the self. See "*Pym* and *Moby-Dick*: Essential Connections," *American Transcendental Quarterly*, 37 (1978), 73–86; and "The Quest of Arthur Gordon Pym," *Southern Literary Journal*, 4 (1972), 22–33.

25. See Sigmund Freud, "On Narcissism: An Introduction," in *Collected Papers*, vol. 4, ed. Ernest Jones, trans. Joan Riviere (New York: Basic Books, 1959), pp. 30–59.

26. See Bowlby, *Loss*, pp. 30, 84.

27. I am grateful to Albert P. Steiner, Jr., Professor of Classical Languages at Butler University, for his research which supplied me with the text of this second-century Greek version of the myth:

> They say that Narcissus looked into this water, and not understanding that he saw his own reflection, unconsciously fell in love with himself, and died of love at the spring. But it is utter stupidity to imagine that a man old enough to fall in love was incapable of distinguishing a man

from a man's reflection. There is another story about Narcissus, less popular indeed than the other, but not without some support. It is said that Narcissus had a twin sister; they were exactly alike in appearance, their hair was the same, they wore similar clothes, and went hunting together. The story goes on that Narcissus fell in love with his sister, and when the girl died, would go to the spring, knowing that it was his reflection that he saw, but in spite of this knowledge finding some relief for his love in imagining that he saw, not his own reflection, but the likeness of his sister. (Pausanias, *Description of Greece*, trans. W. H. S. Jones [Cambridge, Mass.: Harvard University Press, 1935], p. 311)

28. Herman Melville, *Moby-Dick or The Whale*, ed. Harrison Hayford, Hershel Parker, and G. Thomas Tanselle, vol. 6 of *The Writings of Herman Melville* (Evanston and Chicago: Northwestern University Press and The Newberry Library, 1988), p. 5.

29. Ibid., p. 492.

30. Melville makes it quite clear in *Moby-Dick* that the ontological quest involves a death experience. Ishmael is impelled by a sickness unto death: "Whenever it is a damp, drizzly November in my soul; whenever I find myself involuntarily pausing before coffin warehouses, and bringing up the rear of every funeral I meet . . . then, I account it high time to get to sea as soon as I can. This is my substitute for pistol and ball. With a philosophical flourish Cato throws himself upon his sword; I quietly take to the ship" (p. 3). Death, Ishmael tells us, is "only a launching into the region of the strange Untried . . . the immense Remote, the Wild, the Watery," and thus is the sea a lure for those "who still have left in them some interior compunctions against suicide" (p. 486).

31. See Jacques Lacan, "The Mirror-phase as Formative of the Function of the I," trans. Jean Roussel, *New Left Review*, 51 (1968), 71–77.

32. "Desire and the Interpretation of Desire in *Hamlet*," in *Literature and Psychoanalysis: The Question of Reading Otherwise*, ed. Shoshana Felman (Baltimore: Johns Hopkins University Press, 1982), pp. 37ff.

33. Julia Kristeva, *Black Sun: Depression and Melancholia*, trans. Leon S. Roudiez (New York: Columbia University Press, 1989), pp. 27–28.

34. Ibid., p. 9. For Freud on bereavement see "Mourning and Melancholia," in *Collected Papers*, vol. 4.

35. Of course it is the death of Melville's *father* which is a central issue in his life and work. However, according to Tolchin, Melville associated his grief with that of his mother and therefore conflated the sexes in *Moby-Dick*.

36. Melville, *Moby-Dick*, p. 492.

37. Michael Vannoy Adams, "Ahab's Jonah-and-the-Whale Complex: The Fish Archetype in *Moby-Dick*," *ESQ: A Journal of the American Renaissance*, 28 (1982), 167–82.

38. See Tolchin's study of Ahab as Melville's most dramatic example of male bereavement (*Mourning*, pp. 117–37).

39. Melville, *Moby-Dick*, p. 573.

40. Ibid., p. 482.

41. Ibid., p. 573.

42. The once-perplexing scream of totem birds circling overhead, "*Tekeli-li!*" has been identified as the title of a play in which Poe's mother had a role (David K. Jackson and Burton Pollin, "Poe's 'Tekeli-li,'" *Poe Studies*, 12 [1979], 19). Richard Kopley's discussion of the cry suggests that "the mysterious white 'shrouded human figure' of *Arthur Gordon Pym*, which appeared heralded by birds crying 'Tekeli-li!,' compellingly represents Poe's poignant image of his deeply beloved mother appearing on stage as Christine in *Tekeli*—an incomparable vision, resplendent in bridal white." It is even possible, Kopley suggests, although "impossible to determine," that Poe, aged two years and two months, may have remembered his mother's performance. In any event, he dates the cry of the heralding birds to match that of his mother's first scheduled performance (Kopley, "The Hidden Journey of *Arthur Gordon Pym*," 43–44).

43. Davidson, *Poe*, p. 160.

Rowe: Poe, Antebellum Slavery, and Modern Criticism

1. The historical focus of this essay on Poe's proslavery sympathies does not depend exclusively on new arguments favoring Poe's authorship of the disputed review of James Kirke Paulding's *Slavery in the United States* and [William Drayton's] *The South Vindicated from the Treason and Fanaticism of the Northern Abolitionists*. This unsigned review of two proslavery "histories" appeared in the April 1836 issue of the *Southern Literary Messenger* and was included in the James A. Harrison edition of *The Complete Works of Edgar Allan Poe*. William Doyle Hull II argued in his doctoral dissertation ("A Canon of the Critical Works of Edgar Allan Poe with a Study of Poe as Editor and Reviewer," Ph.D. diss., University of Virginia, 1941) that the surviving evidence did not support Poe's authorship but rather that of Judge Beverly Tucker, a proslavery advocate (p. 124). Both before and after Hull's thesis appeared, however, scholars and critics have argued that Poe's writings and his personal beliefs were compatible with Southern aristocratic values, including the defense of the institution of and laws pertaining to chattel slavery. For the purposes of this essay, this tradition of Poe criticism is best represented by Ernest Marchand's "Poe as Social Critic," *American Literature*, 6 (1934), 28–43; F. O. Matthiessen's "Edgar Allan Poe," in *The Literary History of the United States*, 3 vols. ed. Robert Spiller et al. (New York: Macmillan, 1948), 1:321–42; and Bernard

Rosenthal's "Poe, Slavery, and the *Southern Literary Messenger*: A Reexamination," *Poe Studies*, 7 (1974), 29–38. Sidney Kaplan's introduction to *The Narrative of Arthur Gordon Pym of Nantucket* (New York: Hill and Wang, 1960) discusses Poe's racism and explicitly refers to the disputed review but without apparent knowledge that Poe's authorship had been disputed by Hull. And, of course, Harold Beaver's introduction to *Pym* (Harmondsworth, England: Penguin Books, 1975) is the fullest treatment of *Pym* as an allegory of Southern racism in the antebellum period. This tradition of Poe criticism has been strong enough, albeit marginalized by both literary historians (in part, as a consequence of Hull's thesis) and modern critical theorists, that it deserves renewed attention *as* a tradition that tells us much about Poe. Whether or not such new attention will lead to new scholarly discoveries that will revise Hull's thesis regarding the disputed review is less important, however, than continuing discussion of the ways in which Poe's major literary works are structured around racist, sexist, and aristocratic themes.

2. John C. Miller, "Did Edgar Allan Poe Really Sell a Slave?" *Poe Studies*, 9 (1976), 52–53.

3. Hull, "Canon," p. 124.

4. In "Paul de Man's Past" (*London Review of Books*, 4 February 1988, 6–13), Christopher Norris argues in de Man's defense that "the articles have been mined for passages that show him up in the worst possible light, often by being juxtaposed with other items from *Le Soir* whose content bears no relation to anything that de Man wrote" (p. 6). Yet it is just this latter point I would make about both de Man's wartime writings *and* Poe's work as editor of the *Southern Literary Messenger*. Newspapers and journals are "written" by the authors of their different articles, but they nevertheless have a certain *corporate* authority that is familiar to even the most casual reader. Although this corporate authority sometimes takes the explicit form of an "editorial," it is normally communicated by the *dominant political tone* of the periodical. Periodicals that encourage a wide range of opinions and subjects are not exceptions to this rule; they generally reflect a political attitude of liberal pluralism. For contributors, of course, this means that they must share responsibility with the other contributors for that corporate authority. For an editor of a periodical, that responsibility is even more binding. The political rhetoric of *Le Soir* during the German occupation of Belgium is unmistakable: shrill German nationalism punctuated by the ugliest anti-Semitic and racist rancor. The *Southern Literary Messenger* is just as propagandistic when its anti-Northern, pro-Southern, and proslavery attitudes are added up.

5. In this essay, I criticize postmodern critical theorists—notably, Lacan, Derrida, and Barbara Johnson—for having ignored Poe's antebel-

lum attitudes, proslavery views which in turn raise questions about the emancipatory purposes of deconstruction in particular. Given this argument, it is important for me to distinguish my views from the differing view that de Man's wartime writings reveal the secret proclivities of deconstruction for fascism. Jacques Derrida's "Like the Sound of the Sea Deep within a Shell: Paul de Man's War" (*Critical Inquiry*, 14 [Spring 1988], 590–652) eloquently defends deconstruction against such charges, although I do not agree with Derrida's contrived defense of de Man's wartime writings. The valuable lesson of the de Man scandal has definite applicability to what I consider the critical "forgetting" of Poe's historical circumstances in recent scholarship on Poe. The continuity between de Man's wartime writings and his deconstructive writings in the United States is by no means clear, but it certainly ought to be investigated. In an analogous sense, the fascination with Poe among Symbolists and then deconstructive critics (who also celebrated the Symbolists and High Moderns) needs to be studied in terms of Poe's historicality, rather than simply in terms of his reputation as an avant-garde artist.

6. Bernard Rosenthal, "Poe, Slavery," p. 30.

7. See Walter Bezanson, "The Troubled Sleep of Arthur Gordon Pym," in *Essays in Literary History Presented to J. Milton French*, ed. Rudolf Kirk and C. F. Main (New Brunswick: Rutgers University Press, 1960), pp. 149–75. See especially p. 169 on the curious water of Tsalal: "Even fresh water runs purple, and the use of the word 'veins' to describe its peculiar structure suggests a fantasy on negro blood."

8. G. R. Thompson, "Poe," in *American Literary Scholarship: An Annual/ 1974*, ed. James Woodress (Durham: Duke University Press, 1976), p. 33.

9. G. R. Thompson, "Edgar Allan Poe and the Writers of the Old South," in *Columbia Literary History of the United States*, ed. Emory Elliott (New York: Columbia University Press, 1988), pp. 268–69. Given Poe's well-documented friendship with Tucker, the disassociation of Poe from the proslavery sentiments in the Paulding-Drayton review seems even more improbable. In his edition *Edgar Allan Poe: Essays and Reviews* (New York: The Library of America, 1984), Thompson includes Poe's review of Beverley Tucker's *George Balcombe, A Novel*, which appeared in the January 1837 *Messenger* only nine months after the Paulding-Drayton review. *George Balcombe* is an utterly conventional Southern chivalric romance, rendered thinly contemporary by setting the usual plot of misplaced wills and elusive fortunes primarily in the Missouri frontier. Poe judges it with his typical critical hyperbole as "upon the whole, . . . *the best* American novel. There have been few books of its peculiar kind, we think, written in *any* country, much its superior" (p. 978). One of the few "philosophical" points that Poe challenges in the novel is Balcombe's (and, for Poe, the *author's*)

view that "when truth and honor abound, they are most prized. They depreciate as they become rare." Poe responds in the manner of a Southern aristocrat: "But it is clear that were *all* men true and honest, then truth and honor, *beyond their intrinsic,* would hold no higher value, than would wine in a Paradise where all the rivers were Johannisberger, and all the duck-ponds Vin de Margaux" (p. 978).

10. Thompson, "Poe and the Writers of the Old South," p. 269.

11. Thompson, *Poe: Essays and Reviews,* p. 1483. Although Poe's critical evaluations of Simms' works vary throughout the reviews collected in Thompson's *Essays and Reviews,* Simms is one of the most frequently cited writers and, like Tucker, receives one of Poe's longest reviews (for *The Partisan: A Tale of the Revolution*). In his review of Simms' *The Wigwam and the Cabin,* Poe writes, "The fiction of Mr. Simms gave indication . . . of genius, and that of no common order. Had he been even a Yankee, this genius would have been rendered *immediately* manifest to his countrymen" (p. 904).

12. John T. Irwin's *American Hieroglyphics: The Symbol of the Egyptian Hieroglyphics in the American Renaissance* (New Haven: Yale University Press, 1980) devotes two-thirds of its pages to Poe. Emerson, Thoreau, and Whitman serve as a kind of brief prologue to the Poe section; Hawthorne and Melville are treated in two short chapters in the book's final section. Irwin's rhetorical organization of the book baffled many reviewers, but at least one important purpose was to treat Poe as a *center* for American Romanticism. Irwin's argument is thus implicitly directed at Matthiessen, who barely treats Poe in *American Renaissance: Art and Expression in the Age of Emerson and Whitman* (New York: Oxford University Press, 1941). Irwin's strategy is in its own right a remarkable instance of criticism enacting an aesthetic argument. By the same token, Matthiessen's neglect of Poe in *American Renaissance* may have had more to do with Matthiessen's understanding of Poe's antebellum Southern attitudes than we have previously thought. I address Matthiessen's interpretation of Poe toward the end of this essay.

13. The rapid institutionalization of the post-Freudian psychoanalytical approaches to Poe of Lacan, Derrida, and Barbara Johnson is well represented by the recent publication of *The Purloined Poe: Lacan, Derrida and Psychoanalytic Reading,* edited by John P. Muller and William J. Richardson (Baltimore: Johns Hopkins University Press, 1988). Further references to Lacan, Derrida, and Barbara Johnson on Poe will be to this collection.

14. Of course, the whole of Marie Bonaparte's extraordinary *The Life and Works of Edgar Allan Poe: A Psycho-Analytic Interpretation,* trans. John Rodker (London: Imago Publishing Company, 1949) revolves around psy-

chic costs to Poe of John Allan's brutal treatment of him. For the particular ways Bonaparte understands Poe to have incorporated Allan into the *Narrative of Arthur Gordon Pym*, see pp. 295–97.

15. Derrida, "The Purveyor of Truth," in *The Purloined Poe*, pp. 173–212.

16. Lacan, "Seminar on 'The Purloined Letter,'" *The Purloined Poe*, pp. 28–54.

17. In addition to Sidney Kaplan's and Harold Beaver's interpretations of *Pym* as an allegory of Southern white fears regarding slave insurrections, Kenneth Alan Hovey's "Critical Provincialism: Poe's Poetic Principle in Antebellum Context" (*American Quarterly*, 4 [1987], 341–54) complements my own approach to Poe's writings. Focusing on Poe's criticism of Longfellow and other Northeastern writers, Hovey argues that Poe endorsed an aesthetic formalism as a reaction to Northern artists' "double error of didacticism and progressivism." For Hovey, Poe "formulated a poetic principle which eliminated messages altogether. A 'poem written solely for the poem's "sake"' could have no social implications. It might be morbid, but it could never be incendiary or fanatical" (p. 350). The combination of Kaplan, Beaver, and Hovey's readings presents a convincing case that Poe's antebellum values are integral to his major writings and not just a matter for scholars deciding his authorship of an objectionable review. This is what I mean by recognizing anew the *tradition* of critical interpretation of Poe as Southern writer.

18. David Reynolds, *Beneath the American Renaissance: The Subversive Imagination in the Age of Emerson and Melville* (New York: Knopf, 1988), pp. 241, 242.

19. John Carlos Rowe, *Through the Custom-House: Nineteenth-Century American Fiction and Modern Theory* (Baltimore: Johns Hopkins University Press, 1982), pp. 99–102.

20. Throughout my rereading of *Pym*, I am indebted to the work of Scott Bradfield, whose chapter on Poe in his doctoral dissertation, "Dreaming Revolution: Transgression in Nineteenth-Century American Literature" (Ph.D. diss., University of California, Irvine, 1988), convinced me that the relation of Poe's antebellum Southern attitudes to his literary production should be discussed more widely by Poe scholars and critical theorists.

21. See the statement by members of the court, Jerusalem, Virginia, in the preface to *The Confessions of Nat Turner*, the twenty-page pamphlet published in Richmond in 1832, the year following Nat Turner's Southampton Insurrection. This document is conveniently reproduced in the section, "To the Public," in William Styron's *The Confessions of Nat Turner, A Novel* (New York: Random House, 1966).

22. In Hervey Allen's *Israfel: The Life and Times of Edgar Allan Poe*, 2d ed. (New York: Farrar and Rinehart, 1934), appendix 6, "History of Poe's

Friend, F. W. Thomas," Allen reprints a piece by John Bennett, Esq., of Charleston, South Carolina, "Ebenezer S. Thomas: Book-seller, Stationer, Editor, *City Gazette*, Charleston, S. C." (pp. 706–9). In Bennett's account, Frederick W. Thomas' father, Ebenezer, is presented as a staunch defender of the Union and of the Jeffersonian party, which he joined with Pinckney, Freneau, and Lehre, "they being dubbed the Triumvirs," and Thomas the "'lever of the Triumvirate,' . . . [as] their official spokesman through the *City Gazette*: they were nicknamed Caesar, Pompey, and Lepidus, by the Federal Party" (p. 708).

An "ardent supporter of the Federal Union, and an antagonist of John C. Calhoun from the discovery of the end and aim of Nullification onward," Ebenezer Thomas had earlier supported Langdon Cheves for Congress in a campaign that "sent Calhoun, Lowndes and Cheves from South Carolina" (p. 708). Sometime after that campaign, Thomas published in the *City Gazette* "a political letter from M. M. Noah, attacking Jos. Alston, for alleged participation in Burr's so-called conspiracy, and for alleged misconduct of an election which made Alston governor of S. C." As a consequence,

> Thomas was prosecuted by Jos. Alston for libel, found technically guilty by the jury, was escorted from his prison by a brass band and parade of admirers; and *shot at through a window by some un-identified supporter of Alston's.*
>
> It was at Thomas's suggestion to David Ramsay, the historian, that the latter undertook his *Life of Washington*; . . . and it was at the very moment of the conclusion of Thomas's trial in the Charleston court that a *loud report of a pistol was heard from the street near by . . . when Ramsay was shot by one Lining whom Ramsay, as a consulting physician, had pronounced insane.* This is just incidental. (p. 708; emphasis added)

Poe met Frederick W. Thomas, a minor literatus, in May of 1840, when the latter visited the Poes in Philadelphia "on his way home to St. Louis from the Whig presidential convention held in Baltimore the same month" (Allen, p. 381). Thomas and Poe worked in the campaign for William Henry Harrison—the 1840 Whig campaign noted for its youthful exuberance, progressive hopes, and wild rhetoric—against the Democratic incumbent, Martin Van Buren. As Allen points out, "While in Philadelphia in May, 1840, Thomas made a speech for 'Tippecanoe and Tyler too'—and was pelted by a mob of the Locofocos" (the radical wing of the Democratic party, also known as the "Equal Rights" party) (p. 381).

Let me connect these historical details by way of a certain strategic condensation—that of the "lunatic or drunkard" whom Dupin places in the street to distract the minister's attention from his switch of messages (M 3:992). Frederick Thomas may have told Poe about the shot fired anonymously at his father as he left the Virginia courthouse, and the coincidence of Dr. Ramsay's death by the shot of a lunatic on the day of Ebenezer Thomas' release from jail (and thus its simultaneity with the shot fired against him). Poe knew about the pelting Frederick Thomas endured at the hands of the Locofocos in Philadelphia. The threats to his friend, his friend's father (although the assailant was undoubtedly proslavery), and to his father's acquaintance Dr. Ramsay are all "mastered" by Poe in the "event" staged by Dupin in Paris. That these historical events belong to the "same" time that we have tried to locate vaguely in "The Purloined Letter" (1814–15 to 1845) should not surprise us, because Poe/Dupin's enactment substitutes its own fictive temporality for the "accidents" of the empirical world—"accidents" that increasingly would provoke Poe's own paranoia about the uncontrollable savagery directed against him and his kind.

23. Irwin, *American Hieroglyphics*, pp. 204–5.

24. Barbara Johnson, "The Frame of Reference: Poe, Lacan, Derrida," *The Purloined Poe*, p. 248.

25. Ibid.

26. Matthiessen, "Edgar Allan Poe," in *Literary History of the United States*, ed. Robert Spiller et al., p. 328.

27. Ibid., p. 342.

28. Ibid.

Hirsch: "Postmodern" or Post-Auschwitz

1. Vernon L. Parrington, *The Romantic Revolution in America (1800–1860)*, vol. 2 of *Main Currents in American Thought* (1927; rpt., New York: Harcourt, Brace, 1954), p. 56; Harry Levin, *The Power of Blackness: Hawthorne, Poe, Melville* (New York: Alfred A. Knopf, 1958); G. R. Thompson, ed., *The Gothic Imagination: Essays in Dark Romanticism* (Pullman, Washington: Washington State University Press, 1974); Patrick F. Quinn, *The French Face of Edgar Poe* (Carbondale, Illinois: Southern Illinois University Press, 1957); Charles Feidelson, Jr., *Symbolism and American Literature* (Chicago: University of Chicago Press, 1953); David H. Hirsch, "The Pit and the Apocalypse," *The Sewanee Review*, 76 (1968), 632–52.

2. George Steiner, "New Movements in European Culture," *Times Literary Supplement*, 1–7 January 1988, p. 10.

3. Allen Tate, "The Angelic Imagination," in *Essays of Four Decades* (Chicago: Swallow Press, 1968), pp. 405, 402.

4. D. H. Lawrence, *Studies in Classic American Literature* (1923; rpt., New York: Doubleday, 1953), p. 73.

5. Bruno Bettelheim, *The Informed Heart: Autonomy in a Mass Age* ([Glencoe, Illinois]: Free Press of Glencoe, 1960), p. 238.

6. Quoted from Robert Con Davis, *Contemporary Literary Criticism* (New York: Longman, 1986), p. 38.

7. Harold Bloom, "Inescapable Poe," review of *Edgar Allan Poe: Poetry and Tales*, ed. Patrick F. Quinn, and *Edgar Allan Poe: Essays and Reviews*, ed. G. R. Thompson, *New York Review of Books*, 11 October 1984, pp. 25–26.

8. Ibid., p. 26.

9. Quinn, *The French Face of Edgar Poe*, p. 12.

10. Eric Kahler, *The Tower and the Abyss* (New York: George Braziller, 1957), p. 145.

11. Quinn, *The French Face of Edgar Poe*, p. 175ff.

12. Paul de Man, *Blindness and Insight* (New York: Oxford University Press, 1971), p. 70.

13. Cited in Quinn, *The French Face of Edgar Poe*, p. 191.

14. Lawrence, *Studies in Classic American Literature*, p. 78.

15. Richard Kopley, "The 'Very Profound Under-current' of *Arthur Gordon Pym*," *Studies in the American Renaissance 1987*, ed. Joel Myerson (Charlottesville: University Press of Virginia, 1987), pp. 143–75.

16. Grace Farrell Lee, "The Quest of Arthur Gordon Pym," *Southern Literary Journal*, 4 (1972), 22–33.

17. Farrell Lee, "Quest," p. 28. See also John T. Irwin, *American Hieroglyphics: The Symbol of the Egyptian Hieroglyphics in the American Renaissance* (New Haven: Yale University Press, 1980), pp. 136–40 and passim.

18. For the Lacan and Derrida essays and details of original publication, see John P. Muller and William J. Richardson, eds., *The Purloined Poe: Lacan, Derrida and Psychoanalytic Reading* (Baltimore: Johns Hopkins University Press, 1988).

19. In a note, T. O. Mabbott attributes this idea to Tommaso Campanella (*M* 3:994–95).

20. James W. Gargano, "The Question of Poe's Narrators," *College English*, 25 (1963), 177–81; reprinted in *Poe: A Collection of Critical Essays*, ed. Robert Regan (Englewood Cliffs, N.J.: Prentice-Hall, 1967), pp. 164–71.

21. Stated in Quinn, *The French Face of Edgar Poe*, p. 173.

22. *Shelley's Poetry and Prose*, ed. Donald H. Reiman (New York: Norton, 1977), p. 133.

23. Walter E. Bezanson, "The Troubled Sleep of Arthur Gordon Pym," in *Essays in Literary History Presented to J. Milton French*, ed. Rudolf Kirk and C. F. Main (New Brunswick: Rutgers University Press, 1960), pp. 149–75.

24. Johann Paul Kremer, "Diary of Johann Paul Kremer," in *KL Auschwitz Seen by the SS*, ed. Jadwiga Bezwinska and Danuta Czech ([Auschwitz]: Publications of Panstwowe w Oswiecimiu, 1972), pp. 215–17.

25. Tate, "Angelic Imagination," in *Essays*, p. 404.

Hammond: Consumption, Exchange, and the Literary Marketplace

1. Michael T. Gilmore, *American Romanticism and the Marketplace* (Chicago: University of Chicago Press, 1985), p. 4.

2. Ibid., pp. 1, 12, 13.

3. Michael Allen, *Poe and the British Magazine Tradition* (New York: Oxford University Press, 1969); Bruce Weiner, *The Most Noble of Professions: Poe and the Poverty of Authorship* (Baltimore: The Enoch Pratt Free Library and The Edgar Allan Poe Society, 1987); and Michael J. S. Williams, *A World of Words: Language and Displacement in the Fiction of Edgar Allan Poe* (Durham: Duke University Press, 1988).

4. See John Carlos Rowe, "Writing and Truth in Poe's *The Narrative of Arthur Gordon Pym*," *Glyph*, 2 (1977), 102–21; Paul Rosenzweig, "'Dust Within the Rock': The Phantasm of Meaning in *The Narrative of Arthur Gordon Pym*," *Studies in the Novel*, 14 (1982), 137–51; and J. Gerald Kennedy, *Poe, Death, and the Life of Writing* (New Haven: Yale University Press, 1987), pp. 145–76.

5. Eugene Exman, *The Brothers Harper* (New York: Harper and Row, 1965), p. 94.

6. Quoted in Dwight Thomas and David K. Jackson, *The Poe Log: A Documentary Life of Edgar Allan Poe, 1809–1849* (Boston: G. K. Hall, 1987), p. 193.

7. Quoted in Thomas and Jackson, *Poe Log*, p. 212.

8. Alexander Hammond, "Edgar Allan Poe's *Tales of the Folio Club*: The Evolution of a Lost Book," *Library Chronicle* (University of Pennsylvania), 41 (1976), 34.

9. Nina Baym, *Novels, Readers, and Reviewers: Responses to Fiction in Antebellum America* (Ithaca: Cornell University Press, 1984), pp. 56–58.

10. James W. Brown, *Fictional Meals and Their Function in the French Novel 1789–1848* (Toronto: University of Toronto Press, 1984), pp. 3–8 especially. For discussions relevant to earlier eras, see Robert Forster and Orest Ranum, eds., *Food and Drink in History*, vol. 5 of *Selections from the Annales Economies, Sociètès, Civilisations*, trans. Elborg Forster and Patricia M. Ranum (Baltimore: Johns Hopkins University Press, 1979), and Ronald W. Tobin, *Tarte à la crème: Comedy and Gastronomy in Molière's Theater* (Columbus: Ohio State University Press, 1990).

11. For the correction of the misattribution to Poe of the review from which this passage is drawn, see William Doyle Hull II, "A Canon of the Critical Works of Edgar Allan Poe with a Study of Poe as Editor and Reviewer," Ph.D. diss., University of Virginia, 1941, pp. 80–81; and J. Lasley Dameron, "Thomas Ollive Mabbott on the Canon of Poe's Reviews," *Poe Studies*, 5 (1972), 56–57.

12. Quoted in Thomas and Jackson, *Poe Log*, p. 232; and I. M. Walker,

ed., *Edgar Allan Poe: The Critical Heritage* (London: Routledge, 1986), p. 93.

13. For a fuller discussion, see Hammond, "Poe's *Tales of the Folio Club*," 13–33, and scholarship cited therein.

14. Benjamin Franklin Fisher IV, *The Very Spirit of Cordiality: The Literary Uses of Alcohol and Alcoholism in the Tales of Edgar Allan Poe* (Baltimore: The Enoch Pratt Free Library and The Edgar Allan Poe Society, 1978), pp. 2–10.

15. Williams, *World of Words*, p. 65.

16. Ibid., p. 46.

17. Ibid., p. 63.

18. See J. Gerald Kennedy, "The Invisible Message: The Problem of Truth in *Pym*," in *The Naiad Voice: Essays on Poe's Satiric Hoaxing*, ed. Dennis W. Eddings (Port Washington, New York: Associated Faculty Press, 1983), pp. 126–27, 132; see also the same author's "The Preface as a Key to the Satire in *Pym*," *Studies in the Novel*, 5 (1973), 191–96.

19. See Alexander Hammond, "The Composition of *The Narrative of Arthur Gordon Pym*: Notes Toward a Re-examination," *American Transcendental Quarterly*, 37 (1978), 9–20; cf. Joseph V. Ridgely, "The Growth of the Text" (*P* 1:29–36).

20. Evelyn J. Hinz, " 'Tekeli-li': *The Narrative of Arthur Gordon Pym* as Satire," *Genre*, 3 (1970), 391. Joan Tyler Mead's "Poe's 'Manual of Seamanship,' " which appears in the first part of this volume, observes that sections of the stowage passage, especially those involving tobacco and the *Firefly* disaster, are reproduced in quotes in John McLeod Murphy and W. N. Jeffers, Jr., *Nautical Routine and Stowage, with Short Rules in Navigation* (New York: Henry Spear, 1849). Presumably the source is *Pym* itself, although an unlocated common source is possible. A paper from the Nantucket conference published elsewhere, Curtis Dahl's "Port Wine, Roast Mutton, and Pickled Olives: An Essay in Gastronomical Criticism," discusses the range and pervasiveness of food references in *Pym* (*University of Mississippi Studies in English*, n.s. 7 [1989], 109–17).

21. Fisher, *Very Spirit of Cordiality*, pp. 3–10.

22. See Hammond, "Poe's *Tales of the Folio Club*," 24, and Mabbott's commentary (*M* 2:83–84, 206) on identifying this tale, rather than its 1832 version "The Bargain Lost," as part of the 1833 Folio Club collection. See also James W. Christie, "Poe's 'Diabolical' Humor: Revisions in 'Bon-Bon,' " in *Poe at Work: Seven Textual Studies*, ed. Benjamin Franklin Fisher IV (Baltimore: The Edgar Allan Poe Society, 1978), pp. 44–55, which stresses the role of food and the devil in the tale's revision.

23. Joan Dayan, *Fables of Mind: An Inquiry into Poe's Fiction* (New York: Oxford University Press, 1987), pp. 199–204.

24. Marc Shell, *Money, Language, and Thought: Literary and Philosophi-

cal *Economies from the Medieval to the Modern Era* (Berkeley: University of California Press, 1982), pp. 5–23.

25. See John T. Irwin, *American Hieroglyphics: The Symbol of the Egyptian Hieroglyphics in the American Renaissance* (Baltimore: Johns Hopkins University Press, 1980), p. 162. Irwin's extended discussion of language in *Pym*—and his comments on cannibalism and metaphors of the body (pp. 129–48)—are also relevant to this essay.

26. On the role of the devil in the Folio Club framework, see Christie, "Poe's 'Diabolical' Humor," in *Poe at Work*, ed. Benjamin Fisher, pp. 45–50; Fisher, *Very Spirit of Cordiality*, pp. 7–9; and Alexander Hammond, "A Reconstruction of Poe's 1833 *Tales of the Folio Club*: Preliminary Notes," *Poe Studies*, 5 (1972), 25–32, and scholarship cited therein.

27. See Kennedy, *Poe, Death*, pp. 23–31 and passim, for discussion of Poe's concern with the physicality of texts.

28. Rowe, "Writing and Truth," 110.

29. See ibid., 111–13; Kennedy, *Poe, Death*, pp. 152–54; and G. R. Thompson, "Romantic Arabesque, Contemporary Theory, and Postmodernism: The Example of Poe's *Narrative*," *ESQ: A Journal of the American Renaissance*, 35 (1989), 243–48.

30. Hinz, " 'Tekeli-li,' " 393.

31. Rowe, "Writing and Truth," 112.

32. Irwin, *American Hieroglyphics*, pp. 216–18.

33. For a recent addition to discussions of Poe's attitudes toward audience, see Kenneth Dauber, *The Idea of Authorship in America: Democratic Poetics from Franklin to Melville* (Madison: University of Wisconsin Press, 1990), pp. 118–53.

Kennedy: *Pym* Pourri

1. Georges Bataille, *Erotism: Death and Sensuality*, trans. Mary Dalwood (1957; rpt., San Francisco: City Lights Books, 1986), pp. 46, 56–57.

2. Edgar Morin, *L'homme et la mort* (Paris: Editions du Seuil, 1970), pp. 36, 41, 43. The translation is my own.

3. In his comments on "nausea," Bataille concludes that disgust at decay, like our response to other "shameful" processes—menstruation, urination, and defecation—persists through cultural conditioning. See *Erotism*, pp. 57–58.

4. René Girard, *Violence and the Sacred*, trans. Patrick Gregory (1972; rpt., Baltimore: Johns Hopkins University Press, 1977), p. 254.

5. Ibid., p. 256. Bossuet calls the corpse "this object which has no name in any language."

6. See Philippe Ariès, *The Hour of Our Death*, trans. Helen Weaver (New

York: Knopf, 1981), pp. 409–74. The subversive, contradictory aspects of *Pym* receive more extensive treatment in my *Poe, Death, and the Life of Writing* (New Haven: Yale University Press, 1987), pp. 145–76.

Irwin: The Quincuncial Network in Poe's *Pym*

This chapter previously appeared in *Arizona Quarterly*, vol. 44, no. 3 (1988), 1–14. Copyright © 1988 by Arizona Board of Regents.

    1. Frank Livingstone Huntley, *Sir Thomas Browne: A Biographical and Critical Study* (Ann Arbor: University of Michigan Press, 1968), p. 209. All subsequent quotations from Huntley are taken from this edition.

    2. Sir Thomas Browne, *Selected Writings*, ed. Sir Geoffrey Keynes (Chicago: University of Chicago Press, 1968), pp. 160–61. All subsequent quotations from *The Garden of Cyrus* are taken from this edition.

    3. Benjamin Morrell, *A Narrative of Four Voyages* (New York: J. and J. Harper, 1832), p. 53. This source for the rookery passage in *Pym* was brought to my attention by Professor Richard Kopley. That Morrell's notes were only the basis for a work largely ghostwritten by Samuel Woodworth is revealed by Eugene Exman in *The Brothers Harper* (New York: Harper and Row, 1965), pp. 29–30, and then elaborated by Burton Pollin in "The *Narrative* of Benjamin Morrell: Out of 'The Bucket' and Into Poe's *Pym*," *Studies in American Fiction* 4 (Autumn 1976), 157–72. However, in view of the problematic nature of the precise origins of the penguin passage— and for the sake of convenience—the name of the author initially given, Benjamin Morrell, is retained in this essay.

Thompson: The Arabesque Design of *Arthur Gordon Pym*

The following essay is a version of the text from which was derived the keynote address ("*Arthur Gordon Pym*: An American Arabesque") given at the 1988 conference "*Arthur Gordon Pym* and Contemporary Criticism." At the conference, Professor John T. Irwin simultaneously gave a paper on the quincunx network of *The Narrative of Arthur Gordon Pym* from a somewhat different perspective, an unexpected critical fortuity. The present text, which emphasizes the quincunx symbolism in "Arab" and European traditions and its pervasiveness in *Pym*, is a severe reduction of a monograph, titled *Romantic Arabesque, Contemporary Theory, and Postmodernism*, which appears in vol. 35, nos. 3 and 4 of *ESQ: A Journal of the American Renaissance* (1989), printed here with the permission of the editors of *ESQ* and Washington State University Press. The present version omits large portions of the argument and most of the citations. Readers interested in pursuing the concept of the arabesque are referred especially to chapters 1 and 3 and the notes of the *ESQ* text; references to and quotations from Friedrich Schlegel and others will be found there in full, along with a critical and bibliographical overview of criticism on Poe's text. Further discussion of the icons of indeterminacy mentioned in the second half of the present essay will be found in chapter 4 of the *ESQ* text.

1. The basic *formal* definition of the "arabesque" is "a bifurcated shape extending out from a curving stem." Ernst Kühnel writes: "The arabesque was born from the idea of a leafy stem, but just as branches turn into unreal waves and spirals, so do leaves furcate and split into forms that do not occur in nature" (*The Arabesque: Meaning and Transformation of an Ornament*, trans. Richard Ettinghausen [Graz, Austria: Verlag für Sammler, 1977], p. 5); see also Michael Craig Hillmann, *Persian Carpets* (Austin: University of Texas Press, 1984), p. 21.

2. Two articles emphasize the Oriental context of Poe's use of the arabesque: L. Moffit Cecil, "Poe's Arabesque," *Comparative Literature*, 18 (1966), 55–70; and Patricia C. Smith, "Poe's Arabesque," *Poe Studies*, 7 (1974), 42–45. See notes to chapter 1 of *Romantic Arabesque*.

3. Raymond Immerwahr, "The Practice of Irony in Early German Romanticism," in *Romantic Irony*, ed. Frederick Garber (Budapest: Akadémiai Kiadó, 1988), pp. 82–96 (quotation, p. 82).

4. Ibid., p. 84. See chapter 2 of *Romantic Arabesque* for discussion of Lawrence Buell's skepticism regarding the idea of an American romantic irony in this sense.

5. Ernst Behler, "The Theory of Irony in German Romanticism," in *Romantic Irony*, ed. Garber, pp. 43–81.

6. Translations may be found in *German Romantic Criticism*, ed. A. Leslie Willson (New York: Continuum, 1982), cited hereafter as *GRC*, and *Friedrich Schlegel's "Lucinde" and the "Fragments"*, trans. Peter Firchau (Minneapolis: University of Minnesota, 1971).

7. Raymond Immerwahr, "Romantic Irony and the Romantic Arabesque Prior to Romanticism," *German Quarterly*, 42 (1969), 665–85; see pp. 678, 683.

8. Friedrich Schlegel, "Brief über den Roman," section 3 of the *Gespräch*; see translation in *GRC*, p. 108.

9. The permutations he takes modern fiction through are valuable in themselves in suggesting the struggle of Schlegel and other German Romantics to describe a concept for which they had no satisfactory new term, only a range of old terms that overlapped one another. See discussion in chapter 3 of *Romantic Arabesque*.

10. *Literary Notebooks, 1797–1801*, ed. Hans Eichner (Toronto: University of Toronto Press, 1957), nos. 69, 103.

11. Eric A. Blackall, *The Novels of the German Romantics* (Ithaca: Cornell University Press, 1983), pp. 29–31.

12. For a discussion of Schlegel as a romantic critic adumbrating later twentieth-century criticism (but remaining quintessentially romantic), see chapter 3 of *Romantic Arabesque*. Among the chief differences is that Schlegel is deeply committed to an "expressive poetics": the author is the ultimate subject, and the text is an expression of the author's mind; the subject does not "disappear" into the space created by the "game of writing." Rather than the text orientation of Foucault or Derrida, Schlegel's concept of the artist is more akin to Bakhtin's reconstitution of the "self" (or even like that of the pre-deconstructionist phenomenological structuralists of the "Geneva School"). Another major difference is that Schlegel's theory of genre, incompletely worked out as it is, has at its center a concept of a hierarchy of genres, with the arabesque being at the top—a theory that no poststructuralist would find congenial. But Bakhtin would. The arabesque is the ordered artistic frame that in some way "contains" all indeterminants and contradictories and thereby achieves a "transcendental" unity. It is the most comprehensive strategy of containment, even though its "order" is not necessarily coterminous with any "reality" outside of itself, except insofar as the arabesque mimes chaos and order both.

13. See Sidney Kaplan's insightful introduction to *The Narrative of Arthur Gordon Pym* (New York: Hill and Wang, 1960). At the Nantucket conference, Professor John Carlos Rowe reasserted Poe's authorship of a *Southern Literary Messenger* review of two proslavery books, despite evidence to the contrary, but Rowe presented no new evidence that the review is Poe's (see "Poe, Antebellum Slavery, and Modern Criticism" in this volume).

14. See especially Edward Davidson, *Poe: A Critical Study* (Cambridge, Mass.: Harvard University Press, 1957); Richard Kopley, "The Secret of *Arthur Gordon Pym*: The Text and the Source," *Studies in American Fiction*, 8 (1980), 203–18, and "The Hidden Journey of *Arthur Gordon Pym*," *Studies in the American Renaissance 1982*, ed. Joel Myerson (Boston: Twayne Publishers, 1982), pp. 29–51, and "The 'Very Profound Under-current' of *Arthur Gordon Pym*," *Studies in the American Renaissance 1987*, ed. Joel Myerson (Charlottesville: University Press of Virginia, 1987), pp. 143–75; and John T. Irwin, *American Hieroglyphics: The Symbol of the Egyptian Hieroglyphics in the American Renaissance* (New Haven: Yale University Press, 1980). See also the bibliography of Frederick S. Frank, "Polarized Gothic: An Annotated Bibliography of Poe's *Narrative of Arthur Gordon Pym*," *Bulletin of Bibliography*, 38 (1981), 117–27; the bibliographical survey by Douglas Robinson, "Reading Poe's Novel: A Speculative Review of *Pym* Criticism, 1950–1980," *Poe Studies*, 15 (1982), 47–54; and that by

David Ketterer, "Tracing Shadows: *Pym* Criticism, 1980–1990," printed in the present volume.

15. See especially Evelyn J. Hinz, "'Tekeli-li': *The Narrative of Arthur Gordon Pym* as Satire," *Genre* 3 (1970), 379–99; and J. V. Ridgely, "Tragical-Mythical-Satirical-Hoaxical: Problems of Genre in *Pym*," *American Transcendental Quarterly*, no. 24, pt. 1 (1974), 4–9.

16. In fact, *Pym*'s "latter" portions may begin when Pym and Augustus first drunkenly sail into a nightmare storm and return without apparent ill effects—despite the fact that Pym has been pinned to the hull of a ship by *a bolt through his neck* and has been submerged for well over five minutes. Does he "die" in this opening incident, and is the rest of the *Narrative* the narrative of his "letting go"? Or do the "latter" portions begin after Pym climbs into his coffinlike box in the dark hold of the *Grampus* and begins his "perturbed sleep"? Or does the suspect portion begin at any of several other points of sleep, sleep-waking, half-waking, or life-threatening dangers and burials and seeming deaths throughout the narrative? Generally speaking, questions raised in former portions of a narrative are usually answered in latter portions. Here no questions are resolved. Instead, we are moved irrevocably away from any possibility of resolving them. Throughout the increasingly dreamlike narrative, one ironic reversal succeeds another until all conventional perceptions are inverted, and the narrative acquires the feel and movement of dream. The dream motif merges with explicitly Oriental ("Arabic") materials in descriptions of the limitless deserts in Pym's nightmare vision in his coffinlike box. Such arabesque nightmares occur in other of Poe's works. See chapter 2 of *Romantic Arabesque* for further discussion.

17. Perhaps the best recent treatment of this aspect of the narrative is John Carlos Rowe's in *Through the Custom-House: Nineteenth-Century American Fiction and Modern Theory* (Baltimore: Johns Hopkins University Press, 1982), pp. 91–110.

18. See especially Jean Ricardou, "Le caractère singulier de cette eau," *Critique*, n.s. 14 (1967), 718–33; or the English translation, "The Singular Character of the Water," trans. Frank Towne, *Poe Studies*, 9 (1976), 1–6.

19. See chapter 4 of *Romantic Arabesque* for discussion of the others and the symmetry of their placement.

20. References are to Sir Thomas Browne, *"Urne Buriall" and "The Garden of Cyrus,"* ed. John Carter (Cambridge: Cambridge University Press, 1958); note frontispiece, p. 56.

21. See chapters 1 and 2 of *Romantic Arabesque* for further discussion.

22. *The Power of Blackness: Hawthorne, Poe, Melville* (New York: Knopf, 1958), p. 114; cf. Charles F. O'Donnell, "From Earth to Ether: Poe's Flight into Space," *PMLA* 77 (1962), 85–91; see also Richard A. Levine, "The

Downward Journey of Purgation: Notes on an Imagistic Leitmotif in *The Narrative of Arthur Gordon Pym*," *Poe Newsletter* 2 (1969), 29–31; and Richard Kopley, "Poe's *Pym*-esque 'A Tale of the Ragged Mountains,'" in *Poe and His Times: The Artist and His Milieu*, ed. Benjamin Franklin Fisher IV (Baltimore: The Edgar Allan Poe Society, 1990), pp. 167–77.

    23. Harold Beaver, introduction to Poe, *The Narrative of Arthur Gordon Pym* (Harmondsworth, England: Penguin Books, 1975), p. 29.

    24. Originally, the chapters were probably numbered 1 to 24, but with Poe's late insertion of a chapter, the Harpers in the 1838 edition and Griswold in the 1856 ("second") edition (*The Works of Edgar Allan Poe*, vol. 4, *Arthur Gordon Pym, & c.* [New York: Redfield]) numbered two contiguous chapters as chapter 23. So there are in fact twenty-five chapters plus an opening and closing frame, making chapter 13 the arithmetic center. Many commentators have observed that a "new" narrative seems to begin after the rescue and boarding of the *Jane Guy* and the journey farther south.

    25. John P. Hussey, "'Mr. Pym' and 'Mr. Poe': The Two Narrators of 'Arthur Gordon Pym,'" *South Atlantic Bulletin*, 39 (1974), 29. Sequentially, by pages (in the A. H. Quinn and E. H. O'Neill *Complete Poems and Stories of Edgar Allan Poe* [New York: Knopf, 1970]): [1½, 3½, 29, 16, {27}, 16, 29, 3½, 1½].

    26. "Nothingness" in *Eureka* is discussed in the last chapter of my *Poe's Fiction: Romantic Irony in the Gothic Tales* (Madison: University of Wisconsin Press, 1973).

    27. Ketterer criticizes my attribution of wordplay on "nothingness" in Poe's sentence in *Eureka*: "A perfect consistency can be nothing but the absolute truth." He truncates a quotation from *Poe's Fiction* (p. 191), in effect reversing his charge that I put words in Poe's mouth. What he leaves out is my point that the "perfect consistency of the design of the universe which Poe sets up in *Eureka* is its cycle of nothing: the absolute truth." See Ketterer, "Protective Irony and 'The Full Design' of *Eureka*," in *Poe as Literary Cosmologer: Studies in "Eureka"*, ed. Richard P. Benton (Hartford: Transcendental Books, 1975), pp. 49, 55. In basic agreement with the argument that *Eureka* is an arabesque on the extended conceit of nothingness is Harriet R. Holman; see her "Hog, Bacon, Ram, and Other 'Savans' in *Eureka*: Notes Toward Decoding Poe's Encyclopedic Satire," *Poe Newsletter* 2 (1969), 49–55; and "Splitting Poe's 'Epicurean Atoms': Further Speculation on the Literary Satire of *Eureka*," *Poe Studies*, 5 (1972), 33–37.

    28. John Barth, *The Friday Book: Essays and Other Nonfiction* (New York: G. P. Putnam's Sons, 1984), p. 221.

Barth: "Still Farther South"

1. John Barth, *Sabbatical: A Romance* (New York: G. P. Putnam's Sons, 1982), pp. 213–15.
2. Ibid., p. 321.
3. Ibid., pp. 361–65.
4. A contemporary astronomer, Edward Harrison, in his recent book *Darkness at Night: A Riddle of the Universe* (Cambridge, Mass.: Harvard University Press, 1988), reviews Poe's explanation of why the night sky is in fact dark and judges it essentially correct. Harrison accounts for *Eureka*'s being all but ignored by scientists and literary scholars alike by saying that "its science was too metaphysical and its metaphysics too scientific for contemporary tastes."

Ketterer: *Pym* Criticism, 1980–1990

1. Shoko Itoh, "A Bibliographical Survey of the Studies of *The Narrative of Arthur Gordon Pym*," *Bulletin of Notre Dame Seishin Junior College*, 8 (1978), 13–26. Also from Japan is Etsuko Udono's two-part "Studies of *The Narrative of Arthur Gordon Pym*" (1985). (See the Bibliography at the end of this chapter.)
2. Full citations for all 1980–90 *Pym* scholarship can be located in the bibliography that follows the text of this essay. All other citations appear in the notes.
3. David R. Saliba, *A Psychology of Fear: The Nightmare Formula of Edgar Allan Poe* (Lanham, Md.: University Press of America, 1980).
4. All parenthetical page references are to items listed in the bibliography.
5. Paul J. Eakin, "Poe's Sense of an Ending," *American Literature*, 45 (March 1973), 1–22. See also Judith M. Osowski, "Structure and Metastructure in the Universe of Edgar Allan Poe: An Approach to *Eureka*, Selected Tales, and *The Narrative of Arthur Gordon Pym*," Ph.D. diss., Washington State University, 1972 (124 pp.); *Dissertation Abstracts International* (hereafter cited as *DAI*), 33 (1973), 3598A.
6. Kent P. Ljungquist, "Poe," in *American Literary Scholarship: An Annual/1984*, ed. J. Albert Robbins (Durham: Duke University Press, 1986), p. 49.
7. Kent P. Ljungquist, "Poe," in *American Literary Scholarship: An Annual/1985*, ed. J. Albert Robbins (Durham: Duke University Press, 1987), p. 43.

8. In the notes to *The Works of Edgar Allan Poe*, ed. Edmund Clarence Stedman and George Edward Woodberry (London: Lawrence and Bullen, 1895), 5:356–58, passages from *Pym* are printed in parallel with corresponding extracts from Captain Benjamin Morrell's *Narrative of Four Voyages to the South Seas and Pacific, 1822–1831* (1832). The first source study article appears to be Robert Lee Rhea, "Some Observations on Poe's Origins," *University of Texas Studies in English*, 10 (1930), 134–46.

9. Patrick F. Quinn, "The Poe Edition: Annotating *Pym*," *Poe Studies*, 16 (1983), 14–16. For other reviews of Pollin's *Pym*, see Harold Beaver, *Modern Language Review*, 79 (1984), 912–14; William Goldhurst, *South Atlantic Quarterly*, 80 (1983), 346; David B. Kesterson, "New Resources for Poe Studies" (Pollin's *Word Index to Poe's Fiction* is the other resource), *Southern Literary Journal*, 15 (1983), 102–6; and Kent Ljungquist, "The Growth of Poe Texts" (which also covers Thomas Ollive Mabbott's three-volume *Collected Works of Edgar Allan Poe*), in *Review*, vol. 5, ed. James O. Hoge and James L. W. West III (Charlottesville: University Press of Virginia, 1983), pp. 49–57.

10. Joan Dayan, *Fables of Mind: An Inquiry into Poe's Fiction* (New York: Oxford University Press, 1987).

11. Kent Ljungquist, "Descent of the Titans: The Sublime Riddle of *Arthur Gordon Pym*," *Southern Literary Journal*, 10 (1978), 75–92; Susan and Stuart Levine, "History, Myth, Fable and Satire: Poe's Use of Jacob Bryant," *ESQ: A Journal of the American Renaissance*, 21 (1975), 197–214. *The Grand and the Fair* is a revision of Ljungquist's "Poe's Landscape Aesthetics and Pictorial Techniques," Ph.D. diss., Duke University, 1975.

12. For the first or early influence studies involving *Pym* and these writers, see Henri Potez, "Edgar Poe et Jules Verne," *La Rev* (Paris), 15 May 1909, 191–97; August W. Derleth, *H. P. L.: A Memoir* (New York: B. Abramson, 1945), passim; and Luther S. Mansfield and Howard P. Vincent, "Explanatory Notes," in Herman Melville, *Moby-Dick*, ed. Mansfield and Vincent (New York: Hendricks House, 1952), pp. 602, 607, 705, 710, 807, 828; and Patrick F. Quinn, "Poe's Imaginary Voyage," *Hudson Review*, 4 (1952), 562–85, reprinted in Quinn, *The French Face of Edgar Poe* (Carbondale: Southern Illinois University Press, 1957), pp. 169–215.

13. David Ketterer, "The Time-Break Structure of *Moby-Dick*," *The Canadian Review of American Studies*, 19 (1988), 313.

14. I take this opportunity to cite a 1970s item relevant to the *influence studies* category overlooked in the bibliographies of Frederick S. Frank and Douglas Robinson: Walter Pache, "Symbolism vs. Allegory: Whiteness in Poe's *Narrative of Arthur Gordon Pym*, Melville's *Moby-Dick*, and Thomas Mann's *Der Zauberberg*," in *Actes du VIIᵉ congrès de l'Association Internationale de Littérature Comparée/Proceedings of the 7th Congress of*

the International Comparative Literature Association, 1: *Littératures améri-caines: Dépendance, indépendance, interdépendance/Literature of America: Dependence, Independence, Interdependence*, ed. Milan V. Dimić and Juan Ferraté (Stuttgart: Bieber, 1979), pp. 493–99.

15. Irwin has been preceded here by Patricia Fulton Teague, "Borges, Hawthorne and Poe: A Study of Significant Parallels in their Theories and Methods of Short Story Writing," Ph.D. diss., Auburn University, 1979; *DAI*, 40 (1980), 5461A. See also Susan Antoinette Garfield, "The Appear-ance of Reality/The Reality of Appearance: Art, Science, and Mathematics in the Works of Borges and Poe," Ph.D. diss., Johns Hopkins University, 1983; *DAI*, 44 (1983), 1080A. Two articles by Maurice J. Bennett have concerned Poe and Borges: "The Detective Fiction of Poe and Borges," *Com-parative Literature*, 35 (1983), 262–75; and "The Infamy and the Ecstasy: Crime, Art, and Metaphysics in Edgar Allan Poe's 'William Wilson' and Jorge Luis Borges' 'Deutsches Requiem,' " in *Poe and Our Times: Influences and Affinities*, ed. Benjamin Franklin Fisher IV (Baltimore: The Edgar Allan Poe Society, 1986), pp. 107–23. See also Reinhard H. Friederich, "Nec-essary Inadequacies: Poe's 'A Tale of the Ragged Mountains' and Borges' 'South,' " *Journal of Narrative Technique*, 12 (1982), 155–66.

16. It should be added that in 1981 Pollin published a two-part survey of Poe illustrations which mentions *Pym* illustrations; see "Edgar Allan Poe and His Illustrators," *American Book Collector*, pt. 1, vol. 2, no. 2, n.s. (March/April 1981), 3–17; pt. 2, vol. 2, no. 3, n.s. (May/June 1981), 33–40.

17. Gaston Bachelard, introduction to *Les Aventures d'Arthur Gordon Pym*, trans. Charles Baudelaire (Paris: Stock, Delamain, et Boutelleau, 1944); Leslie Fiedler, *Love and Death in the American Novel* (1960; rev. ed., New York: Stein and Day, 1966), pp. 391–400.

18. Bettina L. Knapp, *Edgar Allan Poe* (New York: Ungar, 1984), pp. 108–19.

19. Robert L. Carringer, "Circumscription of Space and the Form of Poe's *Arthur Gordon Pym*," *PMLA*, 89 (1974), 506–16; Leonard W. Engel, "Edgar Allan Poe's Use of the Enclosure Device in *The Narrative of Arthur Gordon Pym*," *American Transcendental Quarterly*, no. 37 (1978), 35–44. Engel returns to the topic, treating "The Premature Burial," "MS. Found in a Bottle," "A Descent into the Maelström," and *Pym*, in "Claustrophobia, the Gothic Enclosure and Poe" (1989). He relates enclosures to the death of an old psychological identity and the birth of a new.

20. See Keiko Beppu, "Japanese Contributions," in *American Literary Scholarship: An Annual/1989*, ed. David J. Nordloh (Durham: Duke Uni-versity Press, 1991), p. 441.

21. Harry Levin, *The Power of Blackness: Hawthorne, Poe, Melville* (New York: Knopf, 1958), pp. 120–23.

22. Charles O'Donnell, "From Earth to Ether: Poe's Flight into Space," *PMLA*, 77 (1962), 85–91; Richard Wilbur, introduction and notes to the Laurel Poetry Series *Poe*, ed. Wilbur (New York: Dell, 1959), pp. 7–39.

23. David Ketterer, *The Rationale of Deception in Poe* (Baton Rouge: Louisiana State University Press, 1979), pp. 184–85.

24. O'Donnell, "From Earth to Ether," 89–90; Ketterer, *The Rationale of Deception in Poe*, pp. 139–41.

25. J. O. Bailey, "Sources of Poe's *Arthur Gordon Pym*, 'Hans Pfaal,' and Other Pieces," *PMLA*, 57 (1942), 531–35; Bailey, "The Geography of Poe's 'Dream-Land' and 'Ulalume,'" *Studies in Philology*, 45 (1948), 512–23.

26. Patrick F. Quinn, "Poe's Imaginary Voyage" (1952; reprinted in Quinn, *The French Face of Edgar Poe*); J. V. Ridgely and Iola S. Haverstick, "Chartless Voyage: The Many Narratives of Arthur Gordon Pym," *Texas Studies in Literature and Language*, 7 (1966), 63–80.

27. Alexander Hammond, "The Composition of *The Narrative of Arthur Gordon Pym*: Notes Toward a Re-Examination," *American Transcendental Quarterly*, no. 37 (1978), 9–20.

28. This time scheme was first spelled out in Walter E. Bezanson, "The Troubled Sleep of Arthur Gordon Pym," in *Essays in Literary History Presented to J. Milton French*, ed. Rudolf Kirk and C. F. Main (New Brunswick: Rutgers University Press, 1960), pp. 153–54.

29. Evelyn J. Hinz, "'Tekeli-li': *The Narrative of Arthur Gordon Pym* as Satire," *Genre*, 3 (1970), 379–99; G. R. Thompson, *Poe's Fiction: Romantic Irony in the Gothic Tales* (Madison: University of Wisconsin Press, 1973), pp. 176–83. Hinz sees the compositional inconsistencies of *Pym* as reflecting her generic placement of the work as Menippean satire.

30. While the quincunx had not arisen in *Pym* criticism prior to the work of Irwin and Thompson, it had been mentioned in one earlier Poe article: Robert Giddings, "Was the Chevalier Left-Handed? Poe's Dupin Stories," in *Edgar Allan Poe: The Design of Order*, ed. A. Robert Lee (London: Vision Press, 1987), p. 89. (I am grateful to Richard Kopley for relaying to me this information.) The Giddings article would no doubt have caught the attention of Irwin, in particular; he is the author of "Handedness and the Self: Poe's Chess Player," *Arizona Quarterly*, 45 (1989), 1–28.

31. Jean Ricardou, "Le Caractère singulier de cette eau," *Critique*, n.s. 14 (1967), 718–33; "The Singular Character of the Water," trans. Frank Towne, *Poe Studies*, 9 (1976), 1–6.

32. See also Louis A. Renza on *Through the Custom House*, "Poe and the Marginalia of American Criticism: A Review Essay," *Poe Studies*, 17 (1984), 24–27.

33. See also David Halliburton's review-essay on Irwin's book, "Inscriptions of the Self," *Poe Studies*, 14 (1981), 9–11.

34. J. Gerald Kennedy, "The Preface as a Key to the Satire in *Pym*," *Studies in the Novel*, 5 (1973), 191–96; and "'The Infernal Twoness' in *Arthur Gordon Pym*," *Topic 30*, 16 (1976), 41–53, reprinted with revisions as "The Invisible Message: The Problem of Truth in *Pym*," in *The Naiad Voice: Essays on Poe's Satiric Hoaxing*, ed. Dennis W. Eddings (Port Washington, N.Y.: Associated Faculty Press, 1983), pp. 124–35.

35. Translation and information provided by José Antonio Gurpegui, "Spanish Contributions," in *American Literary Scholarship: An Annual' 1988*, ed. J. Albert Robbins (Durham: Duke University Press, 1990), p. 552.

36. Allen Tate, "The Angelic Imagination," *Kenyon Review*, 14 (1952), 455–75, reprinted in *The Recognition of Edgar Allan Poe: Selected Criticism Since 1829*, ed. Eric W. Carlson (Ann Arbor: University of Michigan Press, 1966), pp. 236–54; Patrick Quinn, "Poe's Imaginary Voyage"; Edward H. Davidson, *Poe: A Critical Study* (Cambridge, Mass.: Harvard University Press, 1957), pp. 156–80; Charles O'Donnell, "From Earth to Ether"; Lynen, *The Design of the Present: Essays on Time and Form in American Literature* (New Haven: Yale University Press, 1969), pp. 205–71, esp. 222, 227, 266–67. For the record, my own visionary reading of *Pym*, which appeared in my 1969 University of Sussex dissertation, "The Rationale of Deception in Poe," was first drafted in 1967. However, more than a decade passed before it appeared, in revised form, as "Devious Voyage: The Singular *Narrative of A. Gordon Pym*," *American Transcendental Quarterly*, no. 37 (1978), 21–33, reprinted (with further revisions and without the title) in Ketterer, *The Rationale of Deception in Poe*, pp. 125–41.

37. Shoko Itoh, "Gnostic Apocalypse in Edgar Allan Poe," *Studies in American Literature* (American Literature Society of Japan), 22 (1985), 1–17.

38. See also the following review-essays on Robinson's book: David Ketterer, "The *American* Face of Edgar *Allan* Poe," *Poe Studies/Dark Romanticism*, 20 (1987), 16–19; and Michael Williams, "Exhumations as a Fine Art: Two Recent Studies of Poe" (the other study is Carton's *The Rhetoric of American Romance*), *ESQ: A Journal of the American Renaissance*, 32 (1986), 135–50.

39. For the early linking of *Pym* with the New Testament, see William Mentzel Forrest, *Biblical Allusions in Poe* (New York: Macmillan, 1928), p. 157. Harry Levin suggests the possibility of a Christian reading with his identification of the white figure as the angel at Christ's sepulchre (Mark 16:5); see *The Power of Blackness*, p. 117.

40. E. D. Hirsch, *Validity in Interpretation* (1967; rpt., New Haven: Yale University Press, 1976.

41. See Donald McCormick, *Blood on the Sea: The Terrible Story of the Yawl "Mignonette"* (London: F. Muller, 1962); and A. W. Brian Simpson,

Cannibalism and the Common Law: The Story of the Tragic Last Voyage of the "Mignonette" and the Strange Legal Proceedings to Which It Gave Rise (Chicago: University of Chicago Press, 1984). Simpson points out that "A Reader" first drew attention to this "bizarre coincidence" in the *Times* of 9 December 1884 (p. 144).

42. The same might, of course, have been concluded of the 1988 conference from which the essays in this volume derive. For reports on that conference, see Shoko Itoh, "*Pym* Conference and Poe Studies Now," *The Rising Generation*, 1 September 1988, 16; Angus Paul, "Fantastic Portions of Poe's *Pym* Found Based on Fact," *Chronicle of Higher Education*, 15 June 1988, A5; and Ichigoro Uchida, "Books on Books: Edgar Allan Poe, 'Gordon Pym,'" *Nikon Koshotsushin*, July 1988, 7–8.

Contributors

JOHN BARTH is the author of eight novels (*The Floating Opera, The End of the Road, The Sot-Weed Factor, Giles Goat-Boy, LETTERS, Sabbatical: A Romance, The Tidewater Tales: A Novel*, and *The Last Voyage of Somebody the Sailor*), as well as a series of short fictions for print, tape, and live voice (*Lost in the Funhouse*); a volume of novellas (*Chimera*), which won the National Book Award for Fiction in 1973; and a collection of essays and other nonfiction (*The Friday Book*). He is Professor Emeritus in The Writing Seminars at The Johns Hopkins University, and a member of the National Institute of Arts and Letters and the American Academy of Arts and Sciences.

SUSAN F. BEEGEL, Visiting Scholar at the University of West Florida, is the author of *Hemingway's Craft of Omission: Four Manuscript Examples* and the editor of both *Hemingway's Neglected Short Fiction: New Perspectives* and the *Hemingway Review*.

J. LASLEY DAMERON, Professor Emeritus of English at Memphis State University, is the compiler of *Edgar Allan Poe: A Checklist of Criticism 1942–1960*, co-compiler of *Edgar Allan Poe: A Bibliography of Criticism, 1827–1967* and *An Index to Poe's Critical Vocabulary*, and coeditor of *Selections from the Critical Writings of Edgar Allan Poe* and *No Fairer Land: Studies in Southern Literature Before 1900*. He has published scholarly articles on nineteenth-century American literature, including studies of Poe, Hawthorne, and Emerson, and has served as chief compiler of "Current Poe Bibliography" for *Poe Studies* and managing editor of the *Poe Studies Association Newsletter*.

GRACE FARRELL is Rebecca Clifton Reade Professor of English at Butler University. Author of *From Exile to Redemption: The Fiction of Isaac Bashevis Singer* and a forthcoming collection of interviews, she has published essays on nineteenth- and twentieth-century American literature. She is presently recovering the periodical work of nineteenth-century fiction writer, essayist, and suffragist, Lillie Blake, and writing

Spiritual Rememberings: Reconsiderations of the Secular, a study of affirmative voices in the American secular tradition.

ALEXANDER HAMMOND, Associate Professor of English at Washington State University, is editor of *Poe Studies* and author of scholarly articles on Poe, with a focus on Poe's Folio Club tales. He is currently working on a book-length study of Poe and marketing.

DAVID H. HIRSCH, Professor of English Literature and Judaic Studies at Brown University, is the editor of *Modern Language Studies*, and the author of *The Deconstruction of Literature: Criticism after Auschwitz* and numerous articles on American literature. With his wife Roslyn Hirsch, he has translated *Auschwitz: True Tales from a Grotesque Land*, by Sara Przytyk, as well as other works in Polish and in Yiddish.

JOHN T. IRWIN is Decker Professor in the Humanities and Chairman of The Writing Seminars at The Johns Hopkins University. He is the author of two scholarly books—*Doubling and Incest/Repetition and Revenge: A Speculative Reading of Faulkner* and *American Hieroglyphics: The Symbol of the Egyptian Hieroglyphics in the American Renaissance*—and a variety of scholarly articles. Forthcoming is his book *The Mystery to a Solution: Poe, Borges, and the Analytic Detective Story*.

J. GERALD KENNEDY, Professor of English at Louisiana State University, is the author of *Poe, Death, and the Life of Writing* and has just finished a new book, *The Paris of Writing: Place, Exile, and American Identity*. He has also published many articles and reviews concerning nineteenth-century American literature. His work-in-progress is a volume titled *"The Narrative of Arthur Gordon Pym": The Abyss of Interpretation*.

DAVID KETTERER is Professor of English at Concordia University in Montreal. He is the author of *New Worlds for Old: The Apocalyptic Imagination, Science Fiction, and American Literature*; *The Rationale of Deception in Poe*; *Frankenstein's Creation: The Book, the Monster, and Human Reality*; *Imprisoned in a Tesseract: The Life and Work of James Blish*; *Edgar Allan Poe: Life, Work, and Criticism*; and the forthcoming *Canadian Science Fiction and Fantasy*. He is also the editor of *The Science Fiction of Mark Twain*. He is currently working on an edition of Charles Heber Clark's ("Max Adeler's") unpublished autobiography, *A Family Memoir*.

RICHARD KOPLEY, Associate Professor of English at The Pennsylvania State University, DuBois Campus, is the author of the study *Edgar Allan Poe and "The Philadelphia Saturday News"* and of scholarly articles on Poe and Melville. He served as chief compiler of "International Poe Bibliography" for *Poe Studies*, editor of the *Poe Studies Association Newsletter*, and organizer of the *Pym* Conference. His work-in-progress is a volume in *Collected Writings of Edgar Allan Poe* featuring Poe's critical contributions to the *New York Evening Mirror* and *Godey's Lady's Book*.

JOAN TYLER MEAD, Associate Professor of English at Marshall University in West Virginia, has published articles on Poe, Melville, and sea shanties. She has written the libretto for an opera by composer Paul W. Whear and coauthored a composition text that will be published shortly. Her work-in-progress concerns the prose of Royall Tyler.

JOSEPH J. MOLDENHAUER, Mody C. Boatright Professor in American and English Literature at The University of Texas at Austin, is the editor of three volumes of *The Writings of Henry D. Thoreau: The Maine Woods, Early Essays and Miscellanies,* and *Cape Cod*. He is also the compiler of *A Descriptive Catalog of Poe Manuscripts in the Humanities Research Center Library, the University of Texas at Austin*. He has written critical, bibliographical, and textual essays and monographs, primarily on Poe and Thoreau but also on Melville, Faulkner, and other writers. His work-in-progress is an edition of "A Yankee in Canada" for the *Excursions* volume of the Thoreau edition.

CAROL PEIRCE, Professor of English at the University of Baltimore, is cofounder, with Ian S. MacNiven, of the Lawrence Durrell Society. She is coeditor, with Professor MacNiven, of two Durrell issues of *Twentieth Century Literature* and, with Lawrence W. Markert, of *On Miracle Ground II: Second International Lawrence Durrell Conference Proceedings*. She also publishes on Poe and Pynchon. Her work-in-progress is *Lawrence Durrell's City of the Imagination: The Alexandria Quartet*.

BURTON R. POLLIN, Professor Emeritus at City University of New York, is the supervisory editor of *Collected Writings of Edgar Allan Poe*, the scholarly edition which continues Thomas Ollive Mabbott's *Collected Works of Edgar Allan Poe*. He edited the first four volumes of *Collected Writings: The Imaginary Voyages, The Brevities,* and *Writings in The Broadway Journal: Nonfictional Prose,* Parts 1 and 2. He is also the author of more than one hundred essays on Poe, and the author or editor of

Dictionary of Names and Titles in Poe's Collected Works; *Discoveries in Poe*; *Poe, Creator of Words*; *Word Index to Poe's Fiction*; *Insights and Outlooks*; and *Images of Poe's Works*. He has also written numerous works on Shelley and his broad circle.

ALEXANDER G. ROSE III, Professor Emeritus at the University of Baltimore, is the author of *A History of The Edgar Allan Poe Society of Baltimore, 1923–1982* and coeditor, with Jeffrey Alan Savoye, of *Such Friends as These: Edgar Allan Poe's List of Subscribers and Contributors to His Dream Magazine.*

JOHN CARLOS ROWE teaches the literature and culture of the United States at the University of California, Irvine. He has recently coedited, with Rick Berg, *The Vietnam War and American Culture* and written *Literary Modernism in the United States*. Previous books of his are *Henry Adams and Henry James: The Emergence of a Modern Consciousness*, *Through the Custom-House: Nineteenth-Century American Fiction and Modern Theory*, and *The Theoretical Dimensions of Henry James.*

G. R. THOMPSON, Professor of English and Comparative Literature at Purdue University, is the author of *Poe's Fiction: Romantic Irony in the Gothic Tales*, of numerous essays on Poe, and of review-essays on Poe scholarship in *American Literary Scholarship*. Former editor of the journals *Poe Studies* and *ESQ: A Journal of the American Renaissance*, he has also edited *Essays and Reviews of Edgar Allan Poe* and coedited *Ruined Eden of the Present: Hawthorne, Melville, Poe*. He is presently working on a book-length study of authorial presence in Hawthorne.

BRUCE I. WEINER, Associate Professor of English at St. Lawrence University, is the author of *The Most Noble of Professions: Poe and the Poverty of Authorship* and several other scholarly studies of Poe; he is currently completing a study of the aesthetics of nineteenth-century American periodicals.

Index

Note: This index lists all titles of works under the author's name only. Entries under *Narrative of Arthur Gordon Pym of Nantucket, The,* are grouped in a general section followed by separate headings for "characters in," "critical readings of," "places in," and "possible sources for." Entries under Poe, Edgar Allan, are grouped in a general section followed by "fictional characters of," "reviews of," and "works by."

The name *Pym* in italics refers to the book, *Narrative of Arthur Gordon Pym of Nantucket, The;* the name Pym in Roman type refers to the character, Arthur Gordon Pym.